Solaris 9 Administration:
A Beginner's Guide

Solaris 9
Administration:
A Beginner's Guide

Dr. Paul A. Watters

McGraw-Hill/Osborne

New York   Chicago   San Francisco
Lisbon   London   Madrid   Mexico City
Milan   New Delhi   San Juan
Seoul   Singapore   Sydney   Toronto

McGraw-Hill/Osborne
2600 Tenth Street
Berkeley, California 94710
U.S.A.

To arrange bulk purchase discounts for sales promotions, premiums, or fund-raisers, please contact **McGraw-Hill**/Osborne at the above address. For information on translations or book distributors outside the U.S.A., please see the International Contact Information page immediately following the index of this book.

Solaris 9 Administration: A Beginner's Guide

1234567890 FGR FGR 0198765432

ISBN 0-07-222317-0

Publisher   Brandon A. Nordin
Vice President & Associate Publisher   Scott Rogers
Acquisitions Editor   Jane Brownlow
Project Editor   Mark Karmendy
Acquisitions Coordinator   Emma Acker
Technical Editor   Nalneesh Gaur
Copy Editors   Dennis Weaver, Lisa Theobald
Proofreader   Pam Vevea
Indexer   Karin Arrigoni
Computer Designers   Carie Abrew, George Toma Charbak
Illustrators   Michael Mueller, Lyssa Wald
Series Design   Gary Corrigan
Cover Series Design   Sarah F. Hinks

This book was composed with Corel VENTURA™ Publisher.

This book is dedicated to Honey Abangan who graduated as a computer engineer this year.

About the Author

Paul A. Watters, PhD, (paul@paulwatters.com) is an e-commerce architect, building systems with Solaris, Java 2 Enterprise Edition, and Web Services. He received his PhD from Macquarie University (Sydney, Australia) and has degrees from the University of Cambridge, University of Tasmania, and University of Newcastle. He is the author of *Solaris 9: The Complete Reference*, *Solaris Administration: A Beginner's Guide*, and *All-In-One Sun Certified Solaris 8 System Administrator*, all published by McGraw-Hill/Osborne.

About the Tech Reviewer

Nalneesh Gaur is a sales engineer with Exodus, a cable and wireless service. He works with several Fortune 500 companies to create solutions matched to their business needs. His expertise includes IT security and designing e-business solutions for the enterprise to provide scalability, availability, reliability, performance, and interoperability. Nalneesh is Sun Enterprise certified and works on Sun Sparc 5 and Sun Ultra 2 machines as part of his home network.

Contents at a Glance

PART 4

Managing Internet Services

PART 5

Managing Intranet Services

Contents

PART 1
Installation

PART 3
Single Host Administration

Acknowledgments

I would like to acknowledge the hard work and dedication of the team at McGraw-Hill/Osborne—Jane Brownlow, Emma Acker, and Mark Karmendy have ensured that this book has developed from a good idea to a great learning tool. Many thanks to Nalneesh Gaur for his insightful technical editing. Dennis Weaver and Lisa Theobald have improved the quality of the manuscript by careful copyediting. Thanks to Bill Moffitt and Ravindra Iyer from Sun Microsystems for some very useful comments and suggestions.

The team at Studio B—Neil Salkind, Kristen Pickens, Stacey Barone, Jessica Richards, and Sherry and David Rogelberg—deserves absolute praise for their excellent work in representing me.

I would like to thank my wife Maya and my parents Wal and Judy for all their support over the years.

Introduction

This book is for administrators who are learning to use the SunOS 5.9 operating system, which is the core of the Solaris 9 operating environment. The face of enterprise computing is changing—we are moving into a time of tighter coupling within heterogeneous environments in terms of authentication, file sharing, and service provision. Since Solaris is the most popular UNIX system available, it's likely that Linux and Microsoft Windows administrators will need to learn Solaris skills to develop and support the future range of Web Services. While there is a lot of marketing hype floating around about the future of the Internet, Java, SOAP, UDDI, and a wide range of new technologies, it's clear that system administrators will still need solid skills in the traditional areas of user and group management, disk configuration, network information and naming services, and security. This book will help you to learn these skills by using a number of teaching elements, including 1-minute drills, practical hands-on projects, and a set of mastery checks for each module. If you can answer all of the questions, then you've mastered the material contained in the module. Also, you will have an opportunity to "Ask the Expert" for his opinion on operational issues. Of course, you will have your own valuable opinions and experiences—please share them with me at opinions@paulwatters.com.

Note

You'll find an answer key to all the Mastery Check questions in the appendix of the book.

Part 1 of the book begins with an overview of Solaris and where it fits in the enterprise, and then walks through common installation scenarios, including a review of hardware platforms. In the next part, you will learn how to use standard GUIs, such as the Common Desktop Environment (CDE), and work with the command-line—issuing commands and writing scripts. Part 3 deals with single host administration issues—user and group administration, working with devices and processes, installing patches and new software packages, and storage management. The final sections deal with managing Internet and Intranet services; e-mail, the Domain Name Service (DNS), the Internet daemon, remote access, Web servers, and file sharing are core technologies that every administrator must learn. The most important module, Module 18, covers security; read this if you read nothing else.

If you have mastered all of the material in this book, I suggest reading the sister publication, *Solaris 9: The Complete Reference*, also published by McGraw-Hill/Osborne, which covers similar material in greater depth.

I wrote this book to be accessible to new Solaris administrators, that is, new administrators who use Solaris, and Linux and Microsoft Windows administrators who are learning new skills. Please send any suggestions you have that would have made your reading and learning more enjoyable, to improvements@paulwatters.com.

Part 1

Installation

Module 1

Introduction to Solaris 9

Critical Skills

This book is about the Solaris 9 operating system, developed and distributed by Sun Microsystems. In Part 1, we will give the reader all the information required to install and configure a Solaris system. Beginning with this module, we will briefly cover the history of the Solaris operating system and the distinguishing features of Sun SPARC hardware, and highlight the improvements introduced with the latest release (Solaris 9). In addition, we will introduce the common features that Solaris shares with other network operating systems, such as TCP/IP networking, and highlight key advantages over its competitors, such as multi-user logins, multiprocessing, and lightweight processes. We also provide a comprehensive review of resources on the Internet (WWW, FTP, and USENET), which can be a very useful complement to professional support services.

1.1 Review the Solaris 9 Operating Environment

Solaris 9 is an enterprise-level operating environment which encompasses the multiprocess, multi-user Sun Operating System (SunOS). It is a network operating system that runs primarily on systems built around the SPARC CPU architecture. These systems can have up to 106 CPUs operating concurrently in the Sun Fire 15K server system, with 512G RAM and 8M L2 cache, and can be logically divided into 18 highly available domains. Thus, when administrators speak of "Sun," they could be referring to SPARC-based computer systems or the Solaris operating environment.

As an experienced administrator of Linux and/or Microsoft Windows, you might be wondering what Solaris can do, where it came from, and why you should (or shouldn't) use it. Some administrators may be concerned about the use of proprietary hardware, or the often-reported statistic that 80 percent of the world's computers run a Microsoft operating system. Because the average Solaris system can support GUI logins for hundreds of users, making comparisons with single-user operating systems like some versions of Microsoft Windows is quite meaningless. Different scenarios may well justify the expense of purchasing an E10000 in some organizations—but if you just need domain support and/or centralized file system management, Microsoft Windows might be more appropriate.

Solaris is the dominant UNIX-like operating system on the market today. Sun systems are the hardware of choice for high-availability applications, such as database systems, Web servers, and for computationally intensive tasks such as modeling and simulation. They are widely deployed in commercial and R&D organizations. They also integrate well into heterogeneous networks, composed of Linux and Microsoft Windows systems, particularly as reliable file servers. For example, Linux clients are supported by the Network File System (NFS) and the Network Information System (NIS), while Microsoft Windows clients are supported with SMB networking and samba-based primary domain control. Because Solaris operates largely on a client/server model, clients from multiple operating systems are usually supported.

Sun recently released Solaris 9, which is the latest in a long line of releases that have delivered increased functionality and reliability at each stage. Recent innovations in Solaris include support for 64-bit kernels, high-availability "full moon" clustering, and the adoption of the Common Desktop Environment (CDE), which is the standard X11-based desktop deployed by most UNIX vendors in recent years. Alternatively, Linux users can now choose to use the GNOME desktop environment, which is commonly deployed on the Linux desktop (**http://www.gnome.org/**).

1-Minute Drill

- What is the dominant UNIX system on the market today?
- What is the current release of Solaris?
- What is the maximum number of CPUs that a Solaris server can have?

1.2 Review the SunOS 5.9 Operating System

You may be wondering at this point exactly how different Solaris is from your existing operating system. If you're from a Microsoft Windows background, you're probably used to a GUI desktop like the one shown in Figure 1-1.

- Solaris
- Solaris 9
- 106

Figure 1-1 Microsoft Windows desktop

You'll be pleased to know that the CDE desktop, the toolbar of which is shown next, has many similar features, including icons, workspaces, menus, and tool tips. Just like Microsoft Windows, all of these features can be customized to an individual user's preferences, or they can be mandated site wide if there is an organization policy governing the appearance of desktops.

Alternatively, if you're a Microsoft Windows administrator, you no doubt write batch files that can be executed at various intervals using the `at` command. A sample batch file and command prompt interface is shown next.

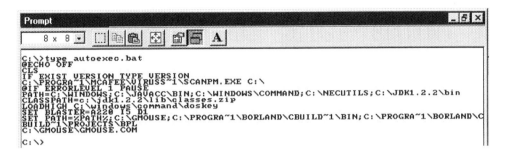

Here, commands may be issued interactively, such as the command for a directory listing, `dir`. Similarly, when a user shell is spawned by the initialization of a CDE terminal window, various commands can be issued on the command line, which are then interpreted by a command interpreter, as shown here:

Although these examples may seem trivial, they illustrate a very important point: a lot of operating systems share a set of core features that are differentiated by presentation, but not necessarily in functionality. For example, Microsoft Windows, Linux, and Solaris are all process-based operating systems; that is, independent activities can be carried out in discrete processes, which can be managed by process tools. Processes can be prioritized, stopped, or started by using a GUI interface or command-line tools.

Some of the major differences between UNIX and UNIX-like platforms on the one hand and the Microsoft platforms on the other, can be traced back to the early days of multi-user, multiprocess systems. For example, Solaris kernels can trace their origins to both the System V and BSD variants of UNIX, while Microsoft NT was based on the VMS kernel originally developed for the high-end VAX systems. There are many similarities that have arisen from need; however, in Windows 2000, Microsoft introduced a new service called Active Directory that is reminiscent of Sun's hierarchical Network Information Service (NIS/NIS+), which is used to manage user, system, and domain data on large networks. Some common services are also implemented across platforms: Windows 2000 has an authentication model based on Kerberos, and Solaris 9 also provides client and server applications that use Kerberos 5.

1.3 Compare and Contrast Solaris 9 with Other Network Operating Systems

The benefits of using Solaris over other operating systems typically become apparent in a symmetric multiprocessing (SMP) and/or multi-user environment. Although Microsoft Windows does support multiple-CPUs, Solaris supports up to 106 CPUs operating concurrently, with almost linear scaling of performance. Some other operating systems appear to devote most of the processing capacity of a second, third, or fourth CPU to scheduling rather than operations. In addition, Solaris is particularly suited to supporting hundreds of interactive users on a single system; that is, every user can be "logged in," using a desktop that is being executed on a central server. Although Microsoft Windows features great products like pcAnywhere that allow users to run a desktop remotely, these products typically only allow a single user to run a session at any one time. Windows 2000 features a "Telnet server," but this does not support X11 graphics and remote desktops along the lines of Solaris and the X Display Manager (xdm). There are few hard constraints placed on Solaris systems in terms of support for concurrently logged-in users. This is one major reason why Solaris systems are favored at the enterprise level.

Project 1-1: Log into a Solaris System from Windows 2000

This project shows you how to log in to a Solaris system using a Windows 2000 Telnet client.

Step-by-Step

1. Obtain the name or IP address of the server that you want to connect to.

2. Start the Windows 2000 Telnet client:

```
C:\> telnet
```

3. Type the `open` command followed by the name or IP address of the server (such as walrus.cassowary.net):

```
Microsoft Telnet> open walrus.cassowary.net
```

4. When prompted with "login:", type in your username and press ENTER:

```
login: tarquin
```

5. When prompted with "password:", type in your password and press ENTER:

```
password: barnaby
```

Summary

Windows 2000 supports remote access to Solaris systems by using the `telnet` command. Users who do not have console access to a Solaris system will most likely use this form of access.

The number of clients that a Sun system can serve concurrently, and the wide variety of services available under Solaris, make it a natural choice for high-end SMP environments as well as for supporting workgroups.

Often, I hear administrators saying that Linux does all of this and more. It's true that Linux has SMP support, and it's also true that Linux is a multi-user system. However, you have to consider the investment that a company makes in both hardware and software to really understand the main benefits of Solaris as a platform. Solaris is 100-percent owned and managed by Sun Microsystems: the Linux kernel was developed by Linus Torvalds, while commercial support and "Linux distributions" are provided by a number of different vendors, including Red Hat (**http://www.redhat.com/**) and SuSE (**http://www.suse.com/**). Although you can pay support fees to these organizations, just like you can pay them to Sun, they do not "own" the source code to the operating system they support, while Sun does. In this sense, Solaris has more in common with Microsoft Windows: it is a proprietary platform that is 100-percent owned and supported by its managing organization. Changes to copyright legislation in some countries have brought to light the issue of "moral rights" of software coders with respect to their work, even when copyright has been assigned through the types of licenses popular among developers of freeware products. It may be difficult to determine who owns the moral rights to a large piece of software that has been developed by a large number of independent developers, rather than being the product of a single corporate entity. This uncertainty is causing concern among organizations that have based their commercial efforts around the extended development of "free" software.

1-Minute Drill

- What is the difference between Solaris and Linux source code?
- Name three process-based operating systems.
- What common authentication is used in Windows and Solaris?

Sun provides Solaris support for educational purposes and for developers: source code and binary licenses can be obtained from Sun at low cost, and developers can purchase several CDs full of Solaris software for around US $45. This is not an evaluation version: this is the same version of the software that an enterprise system user will be installing and using on their Sun Fire 15K. Taking advantage of the "free" Solaris program has lured many administrators away from the uncertainties of Linux to the advantages of a Sun supported and developed product.

Sun has also begun attracting Linux administrators because of its support of the Intel platform for Solaris. There have been several releases of Solaris for Intel now, and in the past Sun has concurrently released Solaris for Intel and Solaris for SPARC. However, Solaris 9 for Intel has not been released by Sun, and Sun has not stated when it will be releasing it. At the same time, Sun has begun releasing low-end server systems based on Linux and Intel, leading to industry speculation that Solaris for Intel will be dropped altogether. This is bad news for organizations that have committed resources to building both SPARC and Intel software releases. Sun has announced that it intends to release its own Linux distribution, which may feature some of the enterprise-level services that administrators have come to expect from Solaris systems.

Another feather in Sun's cap has been the specification and development of the Java programming language, which has rapidly grown to capture around 25 percent of the world market in enterprise software engineering. This is a phenomenal rise, because Java has only been released in full production for around six years. The basic idea behind Java is that the choice of operating systems should be a separate issue from software design and implementation. That is, good object-oriented development principles should not be sacrificed because a particular language is

---

- Sun Microsystems owns the Solaris source code; Linus Torvalds owns the Linux source code.
- Microsoft Windows, Linux and Solaris
- Kerberos

1

not available in a standard format on a particular platform. Thus, Java aims to compile and execute on any platform. Binaries generated on a Microsoft Windows development system, for example, can be shipped across to a Solaris deployment server without having to be recompiled—thanks to the cross-platform bytecode developed by Sun. Java also incorporates cross-platform networking and GUI development methods, meaning that a network monitoring tool written on Solaris should execute exactly the same on a Microsoft Windows or Linux system. This means that the choice of deployment platform can be governed by performance studies and objective testing, rather than irrational and subjective arguments about which operating system is "the best."

In summary, Solaris shares some key features with other operating systems, but excels in the support of SMP systems, cross-platform operating systems, and developer support—Sun has the ability to control its operating system but make it available free of charge to educational users and developers. The adoption of the Intel hardware platform is one key attraction for existing Microsoft Windows and Linux administrators. Another recent advantage is the acquisition of Star Division's StarOffice suite. This product is competitive with Microsoft's Office suite, but it is relatively inexpensive for both commercial and noncommercial use. It provides an integrated environment for word processing, spreadsheets, presentations, and database applications. It is available in several different European languages. This means that SPARC system users can share data seamlessly with users on the Microsoft Windows and Linux platforms, as StarOffice is available on all three.

Learning Solaris is just like learning any new operating environment: there is a fairly steep learning curve to begin with, which will eventually flatten out as you develop Solaris-specific skills. For example, Microsoft Windows administrators will have to learn about managing users and groups, and the differences between Active Directory and NIS+ domains. Linux administrators will have to learn to refer to Solaris device names for disks, which are much more complicated than what they are used to. For example, a Linux hard disk

Ask the Expert

Question: Why are there so many Solaris systems, and which one should I buy?

Answer: Because SPARC systems tend to have long operational lifetimes, it's easy to become confused about which model to purchase. To run Solaris 9, only systems that have the sun4u architecture should be purchased, such as Ultra 5, Ultra 10, and so forth.

partition might be called /dev/hda1, which refers to the first partition on the first IDE hard disk. A similar partition on a Solaris system might be called /dev/dsk/c0t0d0s1. If you're ever confused about the devices that have been detected on a system, you can use the `prtconf` command to display their configuration details:

```
# prtconf
System Configuration:  Sun Microsystems  sun4u
Memory size: 256 Megabytes
System Peripherals (Software Nodes):

SUNW,Ultra-5_10
    packages (driver not attached)
        terminal-emulator (driver not attached)
        deblocker (driver not attached)
        obp-tftp (driver not attached)
        disk-label (driver not attached)
        SUNW,builtin-drivers (driver not attached)
        sun-keyboard (driver not attached)
        ufs-file-system (driver not attached)
    chosen (driver not attached)
    openprom (driver not attached)
        client-services (driver not attached)
    options, instance #0
    aliases (driver not attached)
    memory (driver not attached)
    virtual-memory (driver not attached)
    pci, instance #0
        pci, instance #0
            ebus, instance #0
                auxio (driver not attached)
                power, instance #0
                SUNW,pll (driver not attached)
                se, instance #0
                su, instance #0
                su, instance #1
                ecpp (driver not attached)
                fdthree, instance #0
                eeprom (driver not attached)
                flashprom (driver not attached)
                SUNW,CS4231 (driver not attached)
            network, instance #0
            SUNW,m64B (driver not attached)
            ide, instance #0
                disk (driver not attached)
                cdrom (driver not attached)
```

```
                  dad, instance #0
                  sd, instance #30
        pci, instance #1
            scsi, instance #0
                disk (driver not attached)
                tape (driver not attached)
                sd, instance #0 (driver not attached)
                sd, instance #1 (driver not attached)
                sd, instance #2 (driver not attached)
            scsi, instance #1
                disk (driver not attached)
                tape (driver not attached)
                sd, instance #15 (driver not attached)
                sd, instance #16 (driver not attached)
                sd, instance #17 (driver not attached)
                sd, instance #18 (driver not attached)
                sd, instance #19 (driver not attached)
    SUNW,UltraSPARC-IIi (driver not attached)
    SUNW,ffb, instance #0
    pseudo, instance #0
```

Project 1-2: Printing a List of CD-Specific Devices

This project shows you how to obtain a list of the CD-ROM drives and CPUs attached to a Solaris system. This is an important step in many system administration operations, including troubleshooting systems and adding new hardware devices.

Step-by-Step

1. Log in to the system:

```
$ ssh walrus
```

2. Execute the prtconf command, and filter the output by using the grep command for CD-ROMs:

```
$ prtconf | grep cdrom
cdrom (driver not attached)
```

Summary

A list of CD-ROM devices on a system can be displayed by using the prtconf command and filtering the results using the grep command.

This book aims to introduce administrators who have experience with either Windows NT/2000 and/or Linux to Solaris system administration. The book strives to cover the administration of both the Intel and SPARC versions of Solaris, based on the current Solaris release (version 9). However, many of the skills that are developed for Solaris are equally applicable to earlier (and future) versions of the operating system. By building on the reader's experience with Intel hardware, we introduce the major features of the Sun product line. Since the introduction of the "free" Solaris program for the Intel platform, many readers will be evaluating Solaris as a server system for mail, news, and Web services, as well as managing printers and shared file systems. They may well have discovered that their Microsoft Windows or Linux system can no longer cope with the volume of data being transferred, or that uptimes are not to their satisfaction. By the way, you can tell how long a Solaris system has been "up" by using the following command (as I have done on one of my systems):

```
# w | grep "up"
  9:25am  up 288 day(s), 13:50,  39 users,  load average: 1.32, 1.45, 1.48
```

In this case, the last time the system was rebooted was during a system upgrade. Reliability is one the great attractions of Solaris. This book focuses on providing practical solutions rather than an academic discussion of operating systems—we won't discuss process scheduling models, but we will examine how to manage processes, for example. We don't just provide a list of commands, but present the expected output from different commands under several different conditions. The book provides many working examples of configuration files and the installation of third-party software packages, without the assumption that the reader is a "Solaris guru." This book aims to help you transfer the lessons of both practical experience and skill development required to understand the impact of new services and new software products on existing server systems. We do not cover so-called "historical" services, like UUCP, which can easily fill chapters, but focus on applications that are not commonly found in today's production environments. If it's not relevant, or not widely used, you won't find it covered in this book.

The target audience for this book is administrators who already use Linux or Microsoft Windows NT/2000. These readers may be evaluating Solaris as a network server, or need a technical basis upon which to set up Solaris as a replacement for other operating systems, and so we cover key issues in terminology with which they are familiar. Readers will be expected to have knowledge and experience of a networked environment—for an existing network administrator, perhaps trained on legacy network systems like Novell(or having completed NT certification), the book will provide the technical detail they require to install and configure basic Solaris network services.

Solaris (and related products like Java) is rapidly becoming known as the most reliable and scalable platform on which to build reliable systems and networks. One of the problems potential users face is finding out more information about what Solaris offers—in a sense, they want to know how much technical work is involved in migrating to Solaris, and what kind of philosophy Solaris is based around. Unfortunately, there are very few books available on Solaris, other than those published by Sun. While Sun's own system manuals are very good, users will be looking for third-party independent titles that not only praise Solaris, but are critical and realistic in their appraisal. For an independent reference book, administrators can also read *Solaris 9: The Complete Reference*, also published by Osborne/McGraw-Hill. That volume aims to be a reference for Solaris 9, but does not specifically aim to introduce Solaris concepts to administrators trained in other operating systems. Alternatively, those readers interested in certification may benefit from reading the *Solaris 8 All-In-One Certification Guide*, also published by Osborne/McGraw Hill. Reading this book will help you determine when and why to deploy Solaris, and how to provide networked services to the enterprise in a secure and scalable environment.

The SunOS operating system is a variant of the UNIX operating system, which was originally produced at Bell Laboratories in 1969 by Ken Thompson, an era when mainframes were dominant and smaller, leaner systems (such as the DEC PDP-7) were a novelty. Most kernels during the 1960s were written using assembly language or machine (binary) code, so the development of a high-level language for writing kernels (the C language) was one of the founding ideas of UNIX. This level of abstraction from hardware meant that kernels could be ported to other hardware platforms without having to be completely rewritten. The tradition of writing kernels in C continues today, with the Linux kernel (for example) being written in C. Obviously, a kernel alone is not a complete operating environment, so many additional applications, such as the visual editor (vi), were later added to what UNIX users would recognize as the suite of standard UNIX tools. In later years, tools such as the Practical Extraction and Reporting Language (Perl) and the GNU GCC compiler would be added to this toolkit.

There are two main variants of UNIX systems: the commercial version (System V, produced by AT&T), and the Berkeley (BSD) distribution. The split occurred after universities (such as the University of California) were granted source licenses for the UNIX operating system, which they then used as the basis for further development and innovation. After realizing that UNIX may well have some valuable intellectual property, AT&T restricted the terms of the license and began charging fees. The Berkeley group responded by completely rewriting the operating system so that it contained no proprietary code, and contained key innovations such as virtual memory and fast file systems.

However, as the two code bases further diverged, some differences in coding style and command options led to many shell scripts being unportable from one system to the next without major revisions. While the BSD products are still available in the forms of NetBSD and FreeBSD, most commercial UNIX systems are based on AT&T UNIX.

The one exception to this rule is Solaris, which began life as a BSD-style UNIX, but has slowly migrated to the System V standard. This is because some of the "founding fathers" at Sun, including Bill Joy, were instrumental in the development of the BSD distribution. It is also one of the reasons that Sun garnered more support in the early years—because they were perceived to be more in touch with their developers, and their platform growth was essentially developer driven. In later years, Sun has attempted to make Solaris more compatible with other UNIX systems, adopting the Common Desktop Environment (CDE) over its OpenWindows product, and working towards a COSE (Common Open Software Environment) with IBM, HP, and other enterprise market players.

Sun Microsystems distinguished itself early on as providing a complete end-to-end service for their Solaris systems, based on the high-end SPARC CPU architecture that was specifically designed to work with Solaris. Other hardware innovations included the development of the OpenBoot monitor and integrated power management, which far exceeds the capabilities of a PC BIOS. In addition, early versions of Solaris introduced SMP support and implemented the Network File System (NFS) and the OpenWindows graphical user environment, which was based on the X11 graphics system. More recently, Solaris has led the way for the UNIX industry by complying with relevant standards (such as UNIX 95 and UNIX 98), as well improving NFS, developing high-availability and clustering solutions, and providing enhanced volume management. In addition, the introduction of 64-bit kernels, Java, and JumpStart installations, and integration of Kerberos authentication into its security architecture, have greatly benefited Solaris users and administrators. Solaris now features a number of standard tools, such as package, patch, and storage management, which are supported by a POSIX-compliant development environment.

We've looked in broad terms at the key features of Solaris, as well as some of the similarities and differences between Solaris and other network operating systems. In this section, we will focus on one aspect of Solaris in depth so that you can get a feel for what could be termed the "Solaris way." The way that Solaris boots from disk is quite different from other operating systems, and the differences are at the software and hardware levels. SPARC systems have a boot monitor application, known as the OpenBoot monitor, which can be used to boot the system with the boot command, but actually has a Forth language interpreter built in, as well as a number of diagnostic tools. Thus, it is possible to build small programs to perform a wide variety of standard tests using firmware, which are independent of the operating system. Thus, even if you decide to install Linux on your SPARC system, you will still need to understand the OpenBoot monitor and how it operates. In a PC's BIOS, you can typically auto-detect disks and perform several system configuration tasks. You can do all this and more using the OpenBoot monitor, in addition to being able to boot using a local hard disk, tape, or CD-ROM, or through the network. Traffic from any of the Ethernet interfaces can also be captured and examined by using the watch-net command.

In terms of software, Solaris has some similarities to Microsoft Windows and Linux. Although it doesn't have an *AUTOEXEC.BAT* or *CONFIG.SYS* file, Solaris does have a number of script files that are executed in a specific order to start services. These scripts are typically created in the */etc/init.d* directory as Bourne shell scripts, and are then symbolically linked into the "run-level" directories. Just like Microsoft Windows has "safe modes," Solaris supports a number of different modes of operation, from restricted single-user modes to full multi-user run levels. The complete set of run levels, with their respective run-control script directories, is displayed in Table 1-1.

When a Solaris system starts, the init process is spawned, which is responsible for managing processes and the transitions between run levels. You can actually switch manually between run levels yourself by using the init

Run Level	Description	User Status	Run Control Script Directory
0	Hardware maintenance mode	Console access	*/etc/rc0.d*
1	Administrative state; only root file system is available	Single user	*/etc/rc1.d*
2	First multi-user state; NFS resources unavailable	Multi-user	*/etc/rc2.d*
3	NFS resources available	Multi-user	*/etc/rc3.d*
4	User-defined state	Not specified	*N/A*
5	Power-down firmware state	Console access	*/etc/rc5.d*
6	Operating system halted	Single User	*/etc/rc6.d*
S	Administrative tasks and repair of corrupted file systems	Console access	*/etc/rcS.d*

Table 1-1   Solaris Run Levels and Their Functions

command—to halt the operating system (run-level 6), you can simply type the following command:

```
# init 6
```

Every Solaris init state (such as init state 6) has its own run-level script directory (for example, /etc/rc6.d). This contains a set of symbolic links (like shortcuts in Microsoft Windows) that are associated with the service startup files in the /etc/init.d directory. Each linked script starts with a letter S ("start") or the letter K ("kill") and is used to start or kill processes, respectively. When a system is booted, processes are started. When a system is shut down, processes are killed. The start and kill links are typically made to the same script file, which interprets two parameters: start and stop. The scripts are executed in numerical order, so a script like /etc/rc3.d/ S20dhcp is executed before /etc/rc3.d/ S21sshd. If you're curious about what kind of scripts are started or killed in Solaris during startup and shutdown, Table 1-2 shows the startup scripts in /etc/rc2.d, whilst Table 1-3 shows the kill scripts found in /etc/rc0.d. It's important to realize that these will change from system to system.

Script	Description
S05RMTMPFILES	Removes temporary files in the /tmp directory.
S20sysetup	Establishes system setup requirements, and checks /var/crash to determine whether the system is recovering from a crash.
S21perf	Enables system accounting using /usr/lib/sa/sadc and /var/adm/sa/sa.
S30sysid.net	Executes /usr/sbin/sysidnet, /usr/sbin/sysidconfig and /sbin/ifconfig, which are responsible for configuring network services.
S69inet	Initiates second phase of TCP/IP configuration, following the basic services established during single-user mode (rcS). Setting up IP routing (if /etc/defaultrouter exists), performing TCP/IP parameter tuning (using ndd), and setting the NIS domain name (if required) are all performed here.
S70uucp	Initializes the UNIX-to-UNIX copy program (UUCP) by removing locks and other unnecessary files.
S71sysid.sys	Executes /usr/sbin/sysidsys and /usr/sbin/sysidroot.
S72autoinstall	Script to execute JumpStart installation if appropriate.
S72inetsvc	Final network configuration using /usr/sbin/ifconfig after NIS/NIS+ has been initialized. Also initializes Internet Domain Name Service (DNS), if appropriate.

Table 1-2 Typical Multi-User Startup Scripts Under Solaris 9

Script	Description
S80PRESERVE	Preserves editing files by executing `/usr/lib/expreserve`.
S91leoconfig	Configuration for ZX graphics cards (if installed).
S92rtvc-config	Configuration for SunVideo cards (if installed).
S92volmgt	Starts volume management for removable media using `/usr/sbin/vold`.

Table 1-2 Typical Multi-User Startup Scripts Under Solaris 9 (*continued*)

1.4 Explore Solaris Resources

The first place to learn more about Solaris 9 is from the Sun Microsystems home page for Solaris (**http://www.sun.com/solaris**). Some key documents within the Sun site for Solaris include the following:

- Solaris overview (**http://www.sun.com/software/solaris/ds/ds-sol9oe/**)

- Solaris downloads (**http://www.sun.com/software/solaris/downloads.html**)

Script	Description
K00ANNOUNCE	Announces that "System services are now being stopped."
K10dtlogin	Initializes tasks for the CDE (Common Desktop Environment), including killing the dtlogin process.
K20lp	Stops printing services using `/usr/lib/lpshut`.
K22acct	Terminates process accounting using `/usr/lib/acct/shutacct`.
K42audit	Kills the auditing daemon (`/usr/sbin/audit`).
K47asppp	Stops the asynchronous PPP daemon (`/usr/sbin/aspppd`).
K50utmpd	Kills the utmp daemon (`/usr/lib/utmpd`).
K55syslog	Terminates the system logging service (`/usr/sbin/syslogd`).
K57sendmail	Halts the Sendmail mail service (`/usr/lib/sendmail`).
K66nfs.server	Kills all processes required for the NFS server (`/usr/lib/nfs/nfsd`).
K69autofs	Stops the automounter (`/usr/sbin/automount`).
K70cron	Terminates the cron daemon (`/usr/bin/cron`).
K75nfs.client	Disable client NFS.
K76nscd	Kill the name service cache daemon (`/usr/sbin/nscd`).
K85rpc	Disable remote procedure call (`rpc`) services (`/usr/sbin/rpcbind`).

Table 1-3 Typical Single-User Kill Scripts Under Solaris 9

- Solaris support (**http://www.sun.com/software/solaris/support.html**)

- Solaris education (**http://www.sun.com/software/solaris/education.html**)

- Solaris clustering (**http://www.sun.com/software/fullmoon/**)

- Solaris Intel platform (**http://www.sun.com/software/intel**)

Possibly the most important link on the Sun site is the documentation (**http://docs.sun.com/**). Here, you can interactively search or browse all of the Sun documentation and/or download entire manuals in PDF format.

If you're interested in buying Sun hardware, the Sun Solutions Catalog is available online at **http://store.sun.com/**. This page allows you to "build" a SPARC system and obtain a quote in real time. For example, an entry-level Sun Blade system with a 400 MHz CPU, 128M RAM, 9G hard drive, and CD-ROM now costs well under $2,000.

The most important site for Solaris administrators who need software is Steve Christiansen's Sun Freeware site (**http://www.sunfreeware.com/**). This site contains many prebuilt packages for Solaris (SPARC and Intel) that can be downloaded and installed using the Solaris package tools. Packages are available for Solaris 2.5 and above. USENET can also be a great source of information about Solaris. The comp.unix.solaris and alt.solaris.x86 newsgroups are inhabited by many talented and experienced administrators who share information and experiences with each other. There are two FAQs for Solaris available at **http://www.wins.uva.nl/pub/solaris/solaris2/** and **http://sun.pmbc.com/faq/**, respectively, for Solaris SPARC and Solaris Intel. If you prefer a mailing list format to USENET, you should definitely join the Sun Manager's List at **ftp://ftp.cs.toronto.edu/pub/jdd/sun-managers/faq**.

Ask the Expert

Question: Why are there so many shutdown commands?

Answer: Because you never know whether you will have enough time to cleanly shut down a system.

Question: What's the best command to use for shutdowns?

Answer: Probably the init command—it does everything you need, and when used in conjunction with sync, it updates the superblock. You probably won't use the other commands unless it's an emergency.

☑ *Mastery Check*

1. What is the maximum number of CPUs supported in the Star Fire 15K configuration?

   A. 44

   B. 58

   C. 64

   D. 106

2. What *new* desktop will Solaris 9 support in a future maintenance release?

   A. CDE

   B. Open Windows

   C. X11

   D. GNOME

3. Which of the following is *not* an advantage of SPARC systems over Intel-based systems?

   A. Mature 64 bit CPU architecture

   B. High-bandwidth buses

   C. SPARC CPUs are cheap compared to Intel CPUs

   D. Support for PCI, SCSI, and SBUS

4. What is the purpose of the Network Information Service?

   A. To manage user, system, and domain data on large networks

   B. To replace LDAP

   C. To perform DNS operations

   D. To reduce router traffic

☑ *Mastery Check*

5. What is the key advantage of Java technology?

    A. Cross-platform bytecode

    B. High cost of application server software

    C. Increased reliance on C programs

    D. Requires Solaris to run

6. What command is used to display a system's configuration?

    A. `displayconf`

    B. `printconf`

    C. `prtconf`

    D. `confprt`

7. How can you tell how long a system has been "up"?

    A. `w | grep "up"`

    B. `showtime`

    C. `uptime`

    D. `since`

8. What is the purpose of run-level 0?

    A. Hardware maintenance mode

    B. Administrative state; only root file system is available

    C. First multi-user state; NFS resources unavailable

    D. NFS resources available

☑ *Mastery Check*

9. What is the purpose of run-level 1?

   A. Hardware maintenance mode

   B. Administrative state; only root file system is available

   C. First multi-user state; NFS resources unavailable

   D. NFS resources available

10. What is the purpose of run-level 2?

   A. Hardware maintenance mode

   B. Administrative state; only root file system is available

   C. First multi-user state; NFS resources unavailable

   D. NFS resources available

11. What is the purpose of run-level 3?

   A. Hardware maintenance mode

   B. Administrative state; only root file system is available

   C. First multi-user state; NFS resources unavailable

   D. NFS resources available

12. Where are Solaris startup files stored?

   A. */etc/init.d*

   B. */etc/startup*

   C. */var/init.d*

   D. */var/startup*

☑ *Mastery Check*

13. What is the purpose of the *K00ANNOUNCE* script?

    A. Announces that "System services are now being stopped."

    B. Initializes tasks for the CDE (Common Desktop Environment), including killing the dtlogin process.

    C. Stops printing services using `/usr/lib/lpshut`.

    D. Terminates process accounting using `/usr/lib/acct/shutacct`.

14. What is the purpose of the *K10dtlogin* script?

    A. Announces that "System services are now being stopped."

    B. Initializes tasks for the CDE (Common Desktop Environment), including killing the dtlogin process.

    C. Stops printing services using `/usr/lib/lpshut`.

    D. Terminates process accounting using `/usr/lib/acct/shutacct`.

15. What is the purpose of the *K20lp* script?

    A. Announces that "System services are now being stopped."

    B. Initializes tasks for the CDE (Common Desktop Environment), including killing the dtlogin process.

    C. Stops printing services using `/usr/lib/lpshut`.

    D. Terminates process accounting using `/usr/lib/acct/shutacct`.

16. What is the purpose of the *K22acct* script?

    A. Announces that "System services are now being stopped."

    B. Initializes tasks for the CDE (Common Desktop Environment), including killing the dtlogin process.

    C. Stops printing services using `/usr/lib/lpshut`.

    D. Terminates process accounting using `/usr/lib/acct/shutacct`.

Module 2

Installing Solaris SPARC

Critical Skills

In Solaris networks, hosts are either clients or servers (or in some cases, both). A client is simply a host that uses another host (the server) to perform some operation that is greater than its own ability to accomplish. For example, a Sun Fire 15K system with 106 CPUs can obviously compute more floating-point operations per second than a single UltraSPARC 10. If a Mathematical user on the UltraSPARC 10 uses a GUI to display graphics, but uses MathLink to connect through to the 15K to perform the majority of computations, the SPARC 10 is said to be a *client* of the 15K *server*.

2.1 Design Client and Server Systems

Why are client/server relationships so critical to Solaris networks, when the average desktop PC is now hundreds of times faster than its predecessors? There are several good reasons to prefer a client/server arrangement to a peer-to-peer arrangement:

- Management of mission-critical services can be centrally administered on a single host, rather than having to administer multiple systems. This saves time and protects data.

- Fast CPUs and memory can be centralized to provide a large pool of processing capacity for all users of the server, rather than allowing each use to have a single fast CPU on their desktop. Many PCs spend their days displaying screensavers, while centralized server systems operate at peak loads constantly. The client/server approach is cost effective.

- Administration of software can be centralized, while software installation and updates on client systems can be minimized. This reduces the number of administrators required to manage entire networks.

Notice in each of these points that we've used the term "centralize" quite often: centralization is the key characteristic of client/server networks that promotes cost- and time-effective utilization of host resources in the long term. Take the suggested client/server scenario suggested by Sun, which is based around departments and organizational units putting so-called "thin clients" in the form of Sun Rays on desktops, which connect to E450 servers over high-speed Ethernet switches. This removes bulky PCs from desktops, replacing them with a small footprint client that's about the size of this book. In addition, no local software installation is required, apart from firmware updates: the systems boot across the network using the RARP daemon and the Network File System (NFS). Sun Rays provide a full CDE interface, and all clients share the CPU capacity of their centralized servers.

Client/server architectures do have their drawbacks: if a centralized system fails, all of the clients will be unable to work. However, with appropriate high-availability strategies in place, this issue should not affect most systems.

1-Minute Drill

● What is a key benefit of client/server architectures?

2.2 Investigate the New Features of Solaris 9 Servers

Sun has released a new batch of server-side products to improve upon the existing functionality of SunOS with Solaris 9. Of interest to those in the data center will be the new release of Sun's "Cluster" product, which offers high system availability through management of hardware redundancy. This offering caters largely to the corporate world. However, developers who are more interested in championing open source technologies will also be pleased with the inclusion of several different libraries that enhance Linux/Solaris SPARC interoperability, allowing applications designed for Linux to compiled, built, and run on the SPARC platform. These libraries include glib, GTK+, JPEG, libpng, libtif, libxml12, and Tcl/Tk.

● Centralization of system administration

1-Minute Drill

● What is the main advantage of clustering?

Clustering Technology

Confidence in server reliability is often gained by the use of hardware redundancy, which can be achieved on a file system by file system basis by using a software solution, like DiskSuite, or a hardware based solution, like an A1000 RAID drive. This allows partitions to be actively mirrored, so that in the event of a hardware failure, service can be rapidly resumed and missing data can be rapidly restored.

This approach is fine for single-server systems that do not require close to 100-percent uptime. However, for mission-critical applications, where the integrity of the whole server is at stake, it makes sense to invest in clustering technology. Quite simply, clusters are what the name suggests: groups of similar servers (or "nodes") that have similar functions, and that share responsibility for providing system and application services. Clustering is commonly found in the financial world, where downtime is measured in hundreds of thousands of dollars and not in minutes. Large organizations need to undertake a cost-benefit analysis to determine whether clustering is an effective technology for their needs. However, Sun has made the transition to clustering easier by integrating the Cluster 3.0 product with Solaris 9. This version offers even more functionality, with a clustered virtual file system, and cluster-wide load balancing. For more information on introducing clustering technology using Sun Cluster, see Paul Korzeniowski's technical article at **http://www.sun.com/clusters/article/**.

lxrun

One of the advantages of Solaris for Intel over its SPARC companion is the greater interoperability between computers based on Intel architectures. This means that there is greater potential for cooperation between Linux, operating on Intel, and Solaris, also operating on Intel. This potential has been realized recently with the efforts of Steve Ginzburg and Solaris engineers, who developed lxrun, which remaps system calls embedded in Linux software binaries to those appropriate for the Solaris environment. This means that Linux binaries can

---

● Load balancing

2

run without recompilation or modification on Solaris. In some ways, lxrun is like the Java virtual machine in that Linux applications execute through a layer that separates the application from the operating system. This means that your favorite Linux applications are now directly available through Solaris, including

- KDE
- GNOME
- WordPerfect 7 and 8
- Applix
- Quake 2
- GIMP

For more information on lxrun, see its home page at **http://www.ugcs.caltech .edu/~steven/lxrun/**.

Solaris 9 Security Innovations

Security is a major concern for Solaris administrators. The Internet is rapidly expanding with the new IPv6 protocol set to completely supersede IPv4 sometime in the next few years. This will allow very many more addresses to be available for Internet hosts than are currently available. It also means that the number of crackers, thieves, and rogue users will also increase exponentially. Solaris 9 prepares your network for this "virtual onslaught" by embracing IPv6, not only for its autoconfiguration and network numbering features but because of the built-in security measures that form part of the protocol. In particular, authentication is a key issue, after many highly publicized IP-spoofing breaches reported in the popular press over the past few years. A second layer of authentication for internal networks and intranets is provided in Solaris 9 by the inclusion of Kerberos version 5 clients and daemons. Previous releases, such as Solaris 7, only included support for Kerberos version 4.

Kerberos Version 5

Kerberos is the primary means of network authentication employed by many organizations to centralize authentication services. As a protocol, it is designed to provide strong authentication for client/server applications by using secret-key cryptography. Recall that Kerberos is designed to provide authentication to hosts inside and outside a firewall, as long as the appropriate realms have been created. The protocol requires a certificate granting and validation system based around "tickets," which are distributed between clients and the server. A connection request from a client to a server takes a convoluted but secure route from a centralized authentication server before being forwarded to the target server. This ticket authorizes the client to request a specific service from a specific host, generally for a specific time period. A common analogy is a parking ticket machine that grants the drivers of motor vehicles permission to park in a specific street for one or two hours only.

Kerberos version 5 contains many enhancements over Kerberos version 4, including ticket renewal—removing some of the overhead involved in repetitive network requests. In addition, there is a pluggable authentication module, featuring support for RPC. The new version of Kerberos also provides both server- and user-level authentication, featuring a role-based access control feature that assigns access rights and permissions more stringently, ensuring system integrity. In addition to advances on the software front, Solaris 9 also provides integrated support for Kerberos and smart card technology using the Open Card Framework (OCF) 1.1. More information concerning Kerberos is available from MIT at **http://web.mit.edu/network/kerberos-form.html**. A key benefit of Solaris 9 is the provision of Kerberized clients.

IPv6

IPv6, described in RFC 2471, is the replacement IP protocol for IPv4, which is currently deployed worldwide. Although IPv6 support was introduced in Solaris 8, its implementation is only now being widely deployed. The Internet relies on IP for negotiating many transport-related transactions on the Internet, including routing and the Domain Name Service. This means that host information is often stored locally (and inefficiently) at each network node. It is clearly important to establish a protocol that is more general in function, but more centralized for administration, and that can deal with the expanding requirements of the Internet. One of the growing areas of the Internet is obviously the number of hosts that need to be addressed: many subnets are already exhausted, and the situation is likely to get worse. In addition, every IP address needs to be manually allocated to each individual machine on the Internet, which makes the use of addresses within a subnet sparse and less than optimal. Clearly, there is a need for a degree of centralization when organizing IP addresses that can be handled through local administration, and through protocols like DHCP (Dynamic Host Configuration Protocol). However, one of the key improvements of IPv6 over IPv4 is its autoconfiguration capabilities, which make it easier to configure entire subnets and renumber existing hosts. In addition, security is now included at the IP level, making host-to-host authentication more efficient and reliable—even allowing for data encryption. One way that this is achieved is by authentication header extensions: this allows a target host to determine whether or not a packet actually originates from a source host. This prevents common attacks, like IP spoofing and denial of service, and reduces reliance on a third-party firewall by locking in security at the packet level. Although IPv6 is included with the Solaris 9 distribution, it is also now available separately for Solaris at **http://playground.sun.com/pub/solaris2-ipv6/html/solaris2-ipv6.html**.

Tools are also included with Solaris 9 to assist with IPv4 to IPv6 migration.

IPSec

Virtual private network (VPN) technology is also provided with Solaris 9, as it was with Solaris 8, by using IPSec. IPSec is compatible with both IPv4 and IPv6, making it easier to connect hosts using both new and existing networking protocols. IPSec consists of a combination of IP tunneling and encryption technologies, to create sessions across the Internet that are as secure as possible. IP tunneling makes it difficult for unauthorized users (such as intruders) to access data that is being transmitted between two hosts on different sites. This is supported by encryption technologies and an improved method for exchanging keys, using the Internet key exchange (IKE) method. IKE facilitates interprotocol negotiation and selection during host-to-host transactions, ensuring data integrity. By implementing encryption at the IP layer, it will be even more difficult for rogue users to "pretend" to be a target host, intercepting data with authorization. For commercial development and applications, a third-party toolkit like IPSec Express Toolkit (**http://www.ssh.com/products/ipsec/**) will generally be necessary.

2.3 Investigate the Solaris 9 Distribution

The Solaris server operating environment is typically not available in your local computer store—it must be obtained directly from Sun or through an authorized reseller. The good news is that if your SPARC system has 8 CPUs or less, you may now obtain a Solaris license free of charge by applying directly to Sun: the catch is that you must pay for postage and handling, which Sun calculates to be US $75 per package. This is an increase over the previous shipping and handling charges associated with earlier editions of the "free" Solaris program. However, the new package has a number of value-added extras, including the Oracle database server. It is also possible to obtain the source code to Solaris (**http://www.sun.com/software/solaris/source/**).

The free Solaris license program is targeted at home users who wish to take advantage of the stability of the Solaris platform for using StarOffice and other productivity applications, as well as Solaris developers who wish to deploy on the Solaris platform. More information is available from **http://www.sun.com/software/solaris/binaries/**.

The Solaris 9 media pack comes with several CDs, including the following:

- Web Start Installation CD, which is used to install the Solaris operating environment

- Two Solaris Software CDs, which contain all of the standard Solaris packages

- Solaris documentation CDs, which contain all of the Solaris documentation in answer book format

- Languages CD, which contains local customizations for nine different languages

- StarOffice 5.2 productivity suite

- Forte, for Java integrated development environment

- GNU software CD

- iPlanet software suite, which provides a Web server, directory server, certificate manager, Sun Screen firewall, and an application server

- Oracle database server

- Supplemental software CD, including support for OpenGL, Java 3D, and advanced networking support including SunATM, SunFDDI, and Sun GigabitEthernet

The server configuration for Solaris SPARC is approximately 2.4GB in size (Entire Distribution plus OEM Support).

2

1-Minute Drill

● Which Solaris 9 installation types are required for servers?

2.4 Configure Hardware Supported by Solaris 9 SPARC Systems

Sun has developed a wide range of hardware systems over the past few years, much of which is still supported by Solaris 9. These systems are based on the Scalable Processor Architecture (SPARC), which is managed by a SPARC member organization (**http://www.sparc.org/**). In addition to Sun Microsystems, Fujitsu (**http://www.fujitsu.com/**) and T.Sqware (**http://www.tsqware.com/**) also build SPARC-compliant CPU systems. System vendors who sell systems based on SPARC CPUs include Amdahl Corporation (**http://www.amdahl.com/**), Tatung (**http://www.tatung.com/**), Tadpole (**http://www.tadpole.com/**), and Toshiba (**http://www.toshiba.com/**). Vendors of system boards and peripherals for SPARC CPU–based systems include Hitachi (**http://www.hitachi.com/**), Seagate (**http://www.seagate.com/**), and Kingston Technology (**http://www .kingston.com/**). Although media critics and competitors often paint SPARC systems from Sun as standalone, vendor-specific traps for the unwary, the reality is that a large number of hardware vendors also support the SPARC platform. It should also be noted that software vendors, such as Red Hat, also support SPARC versions of Linux, meaning that Solaris is not the only type of operating system that powers the SPARC platform. The SPARC standards can be downloaded free of charge from **http://www.sparc.org/standards.html**.

Often, administrators of Linux and Microsoft Windows systems, who are used to "PC" hardware, are incredulous to discover that some supported systems (such as the SPARCclassic) have CPUs that run at sub-100 MHz. This must seem a very slow CPU speed in the age of Intel CPUs and their clones reaching the 1-GHz mark. However, CPU speed is only one component that contributes to the overall performance of a system—SPARC systems are renowned for their high-speed buses and very fast I/O performance. In addition, many SPARC systems were designed for continuous operation—it is not unheard of for systems to have several years of uptime, compared to several days for other

---

● Entire Distribution without OEM Support

operating systems. The many impressive features of the Solaris operating systems were developed with the SPARC hardware platform as a target, and these systems naturally have the best performance.

However, Sun has not ignored hardware developments and emerging standards—in recent years, they have created the Ultra series of workstations and servers, which feature a PCI bus and compatibility with SVGA multisync monitors commonly sold with PC systems. Of course, SPARC systems have always supported the SCSI standard, and all SCSI devices will work with Solaris. At the same time, Sun has proceeded with innovations, such as the 64-CPU Enterprise 10000 system, which can operate as a single system with massively parallel computational abilities, or it can be logically partitioned to act as up to 64 different systems. Imagine being able to control an entire ASP, with no apparent "shared hosting" to the client, which was actually being serviced by a single physical system. Although the upfront cost of an E10000 far exceeds that required for 64 systems running Linux or Microsoft Windows, only one administrator is required to manage an E10000, while 64 different systems might require more than one administrator.

Supported SPARC Platforms

The following SPARC systems are supported under Solaris 9:

SPARCclassic	SPARCstation LX	SPARCstation 4	SPARCstation 5
SPARCstation 10	SPARCstation 20	Ultra 1 (including Creator and Creator 3D models)	Enterprise 1
Ultra 2 (including Creator and Creator 3D models)	Ultra 5	Ultra 10	Ultra 30
Ultra 60	Ultra 450	Blade 100	Blade 1000
Enterprise 2	Enterprise 150	Enterprise 250	Enterprise 450
Enterprise 3000	Enterprise 3500	Enterprise 4000	Enterprise 4500
Enterprise 5000	Enterprise 5500	Enterprise 6000	Enterprise 10000
SPARCserver 1000	SPARCcenter 2000		

Some popular systems are no longer supported, such as the SPARCstation 1 and SPARCstation 2. Often, these can be upgraded with a firmware or CPU change to be compatible with Solaris 9. In addition, a minimum of 64MB RAM is required to install Solaris 9—the installer will not let you proceed unless it can detect this amount of physical RAM, so be sure to check that your system meets the basic requirements before attempting to install Solaris 9.

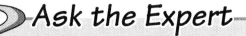

Ask the Expert

Question: Realistically, how much RAM is required to run Solaris 9?

Answer: You will need 64MB of RAM to run SunOS 5.9 without any third-party applications and without resorting to virtual memory. To run a Web server, such as Apache, with a servlet runner or other high-volume module such as Tomcat, you will need at least 128MB of RAM.

Device Nomenclature

Among the most challenging aspects of understanding Solaris hardware are the device names and references used by Solaris to manage devices. Solaris uses a very specific set of naming conventions to associate physical devices with instance names on the operating system. In addition, devices can also be referred to by their device name, which is associated with a device file created in the */dev* directory after configuration. For example, a hard disk may have the physical device *name/pci@1f,0/pci@1,1/ide@3/dad@0,0*, which is associated with the device file */dev/dsk/c0t0d0*. The benefit of the more complex Solaris device names and physical device references is that it is easy to interpret the characteristics of each device by looking at its name. For the disk example given above, we can see that the IDE hard drive is located on a PCI bus at target 0. When we view the amount of free disk space on the system, for example, it is easy to identify slices on the same disk by looking at the device name:

```
$ df -k
Filesystem          kbytes    used    avail capacity  Mounted on
/proc                    0       0        0      0%    /proc
/dev/dsk/c0t0d0s0  1982988  615991  1307508     33%    /
fd                       0       0        0      0%    /dev/fd
/dev/dsk/c0t0d0s3  1487119  357511  1070124     26%    /usr
swap                182040     416   181624      1%    /tmp
```

Here, we can see that */dev/dsk/c0t0d0s0* and */dev/dsk/c0t0d0s3* are slice 0 and slice 3 of the disk */dev/dsk/c0t0d0*. If you're ever unsure which physical disk is associated with a specific disk device name, the `format` command will tell you:

```
# format
Searching for disks...done
```

```
AVAILABLE DISK SELECTIONS:
0. c1t3d0 <SUN2.1G cyl 2733 alt 2 hd 19 sec 80>
         /pci@1f,0/pci@1/scsi@1/sd@3,0
```

Here, we can see that physical device */pci@1f,0/pci@1/scsi@1/sd@3,0* is matched with the disk device */dev/dsk/c1t3d0*. In addition, a list of mappings between physical devices to instance names is always kept in the */etc/path_to_inst* file:

```
"/sbus@1f,0" 0 "sbus"
"/sbus@1f,0/sbusmem@2,0" 2 "sbusmem"
"/sbus@1f,0/sbusmem@3,0" 3 "sbusmem"
"/sbus@1f,0/sbusmem@0,0" 0 "sbusmem"
"/sbus@1f,0/sbusmem@1,0" 1 "sbusmem"
"/sbus@1f,0/SUNW,fas@2,8800000" 1 "fas"
"/sbus@1f,0/SUNW,fas@2,8800000/ses@f,0" 1 "ses"
"/sbus@1f,0/SUNW,fas@2,8800000/sd@1,0" 16 "sd"
"/sbus@1f,0/SUNW,fas@2,8800000/sd@0,0" 15 "sd"
"/sbus@1f,0/SUNW,fas@2,8800000/sd@3,0" 18 "sd"
"/sbus@1f,0/SUNW,fas@2,8800000/sd@2,0" 17 "sd"
"/sbus@1f,0/SUNW,fas@2,8800000/sd@5,0" 20 "sd"
"/sbus@1f,0/SUNW,fas@2,8800000/sd@4,0" 19 "sd"
"/sbus@1f,0/SUNW,fas@2,8800000/sd@6,0" 21 "sd"
"/sbus@1f,0/SUNW,fas@2,8800000/sd@9,0" 23 "sd"
"/sbus@1f,0/SUNW,fas@2,8800000/sd@8,0" 22 "sd"
"/sbus@1f,0/SUNW,fas@2,8800000/sd@a,0" 24 "sd"
"/sbus@1f,0/SUNW,fas@2,8800000/st@1,0" 8 "st"
"/sbus@1f,0/SUNW,fas@2,8800000/st@0,0" 7 "st"
"/sbus@1f,0/SUNW,fas@2,8800000/sd@c,0" 26 "sd"
"/sbus@1f,0/SUNW,fas@2,8800000/st@3,0" 10 "st"
"/sbus@1f,0/SUNW,fas@2,8800000/sd@b,0" 25 "sd"
"/sbus@1f,0/SUNW,fas@2,8800000/st@2,0" 9 "st"
"/sbus@1f,0/SUNW,fas@2,8800000/sd@e,0" 28 "sd"
"/sbus@1f,0/SUNW,fas@2,8800000/st@5,0" 12 "st"
"/sbus@1f,0/SUNW,fas@2,8800000/sd@d,0" 27 "sd"
"/sbus@1f,0/SUNW,fas@2,8800000/st@4,0" 11 "st"
"/sbus@1f,0/SUNW,fas@2,8800000/sd@f,0" 29 "sd"
"/sbus@1f,0/SUNW,fas@2,8800000/st@6,0" 13 "st"
"/sbus@1f,0/SUNW,CS4231@d,c000000" 0 "audiocs"
"/sbus@1f,0/dma@0,81000" 0 "dma"
"/sbus@1f,0/dma@0,81000/esp@0,80000" 0 "esp"
"/sbus@1f,0/dma@0,81000/esp@0,80000/sd@0,0" 30 "sd"
"/sbus@1f,0/dma@0,81000/esp@0,80000/sd@1,0" 31 "sd"
"/sbus@1f,0/dma@0,81000/esp@0,80000/sd@2,0" 32 "sd"
```

2

```
"/sbus@1f,0/dma@0,81000/esp@0,80000/sd@3,0"  33 "sd"
"/sbus@1f,0/dma@0,81000/esp@0,80000/sd@4,0"  34 "sd"
"/sbus@1f,0/dma@0,81000/esp@0,80000/sd@5,0"  35 "sd"
"/sbus@1f,0/dma@0,81000/esp@0,80000/sd@6,0"  36 "sd"
"/sbus@1f,0/dma@0,81000/esp@0,80000/st@0,0"  14 "st"
"/sbus@1f,0/dma@0,81000/esp@0,80000/st@1,0"  15 "st"
"/sbus@1f,0/dma@0,81000/esp@0,80000/st@2,0"  16 "st"
"/sbus@1f,0/dma@0,81000/esp@0,80000/st@3,0"  17 "st"
"/sbus@1f,0/dma@0,81000/esp@0,80000/st@4,0"  18 "st"
"/sbus@1f,0/dma@0,81000/esp@0,80000/st@5,0"  19 "st"
"/sbus@1f,0/dma@0,81000/esp@0,80000/st@6,0"  20 "st"
"/sbus@1f,0/sbusmem@f,0"  15 "sbusmem"
"/sbus@1f,0/sbusmem@d,0"  13 "sbusmem"
"/sbus@1f,0/sbusmem@e,0"  14 "sbusmem"
"/sbus@1f,0/cgthree@1,0"  0 "cgthree"
"/sbus@1f,0/SUNW,hme@e,8c00000"  0 "hme"
"/sbus@1f,0/zs@f,1000000"  1 "zs"
"/sbus@1f,0/zs@f,1100000"  0 "zs"
"/sbus@1f,0/SUNW,bpp@e,c800000"  0 "bpp"
"/sbus@1f,0/lebuffer@0,40000"  0 "lebuffer"
"/sbus@1f,0/lebuffer@0,40000/le@0,60000"  0 "le"
"/sbus@1f,0/SUNW,hme@2,8c00000"  1 "hme"
"/sbus@1f,0/SUNW,fdtwo@f,1400000"  0 "fd"
"/options"  0 "options"
"/pseudo"  0 "pseudo"
```

Here, we see entries for the network interface */sbus@1f,0/SUNW,hme@2,8c00000*, as well as the floppy disk */sbus@1f,0/SUNW,fdtwo@f,1400000* and the *SBUS sbus@1f,0*.

2.5 Administer System Preinstallation Tasks

Before installing your system, you will require the following information from your network administrator:

● **Hostname (for example, www)**   This is the name that you wish to give your host to identify it uniquely on the local area network.

- **IP address (e.g., 204.58.32.46)** The IP address is used by the transport layer to locate a specific host on the worldwide Internet.

- **Domain name (for example, paulwatters.com)** The domain name is the organization to which your host belongs. All hosts on the Internet must belong to a domain.

- **DNS server (for example, ns)** The DNS server maps IP addresses to domain names, and domain names to IP addresses.

- **Subnet mask (for example, 255.255.255.0)** The mask that is used to locate hosts that form part of the same subnet on the local area network.

You will also need to decide which language you wish to use when installing Solaris. The following languages are supported for performing the installation process:

English	French	German	Italian	Japanese
Korean	Simplified Chinese	Spanish	Swedish	Traditional Chinese

If the system has never had Solaris installed, you can simply insert the CD-ROM into its caddy and/or CD-ROM drive, and the Web Start installer will start. Alternatively, once the system has started booting, you can press the STOP-A keys, and when you get the OK prompt, you can simply type the following:

```
ok boot cdrom
```

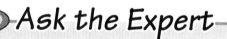

Ask the Expert

Question: What is a hostname?

Answer: A hostname is a unique name on the local area network that identifies a system. A system can have a canonical hostname (such as "patrick") but have several aliases, such as "mail", "www", and "ns", depending on its purpose. By convention, most corporate Web servers will have an alias for "www", for example, so that external users can easily guess its name without having to use a directory service.

You will then see output similar to the following:

```
Boot device: /sbus/espdma@e,8400000/esp@e,8800000/sd@6,0:f File and args:
SunOS Release 5.9 Version Generic 32-bit
Copyright 1983-2002 Sun Microsystems, Inc. All rights reserved.
Configuring /dev and /devices
Using RPC Bootparams for network configuration information.
Solaris Web Start 3.0 installer
English has been selected as the language in which to perform the install.
Starting the Web Start 3.0 Solaris installer
Solaris installer is searching the system's hard disks for a
location to place the Solaris installer software.
Your system appears to be upgradeable.
Do you want to do a Initial Install or Upgrade?
1) Initial Install
2) Upgrade
Please Enter 1 or 2 >
```

Note

Some Ultra systems will require a firmware upgrade if the 64-bit Solaris 9 kernel is to be installed.

If the "upgradeable" message appeared in the boot messages, you may elect to perform an upgrade of the existing Solaris installation. However, most administrators would back up their existing software, perform a fresh install, and then restore their data and applications once their system is operational. In this case, we will choose to perform an Initial Install, which will overwrite the existing operating system.

After you enter **1**, and hit ENTER, you will see a message like this:

```
The default root disk is /dev/dsk/c0t0d0.
The Solaris installer needs to format
/dev/dsk/c0t0d0 to install Solaris.
WARNING: ALL INFORMATION ON THE DISK WILL BE ERASED!
Do you want to format /dev/dsk/c0t0d0? [y,n,?,q]
```

Formatting the hard drive will overwrite all existing data on the drive—you must ensure that if you had previously installed an operating system on the target drive (c0t0d0), that you have backed up all data that you will need in the future. This includes both user directories and application installations.

After answering "y", the following screen will appear:

```
NOTE: The swap size cannot be changed during filesystem layout.
Enter a swap slice size between 384MB and 2027MB, default = 512MB [?]
```

Just hit the ENTER key to accept the default on 512M, if your system has 256M physical RAM, as the sample system has. However, as a general rule, you should only allocate twice the amount of physical RAM as swap space; otherwise, system performance will be impaired. The swap partition should be placed at the beginning of the drive, as the following message indicates, so that other slices are not dependent on its physical location:

```
The Installer prefers that the swap slice is at the beginning of
the disk. This will allow the most flexible filesystem
partitioning later in the installation.
Can the swap slice start at the beginning of the disk [y,n,?,q]
```

After answering "y" to this question, you will be asked to confirm the formatting settings:

```
You have selected the following to be used by the Solaris installer:
Disk Slice : /dev/dsk/c0t0d0
Size : 1024 MB
Start Cyl. : 0
WARNING: ALL INFORMATION ON THE DISK WILL BE ERASED!
Is this OK [y,n,?,q]
```

If you answer "y", the disk will be formatted, and a mini root file system will be copied to the disk, after which the system will be rebooted and the Web Start Wizard installation process can begin:

```
The Solaris installer will use disk slice, /dev/dsk/c0t0d0s1.
After files are copied, the system will automatically reboot, and
installation will continue.
Please Wait...
Copying mini-root to local disk....done.
Copying platform specific files....done.
Preparing to reboot and continue installation.
Rebooting to continue the installation.
Syncing file systems... 41 done
rebooting...
Resetting ...
SPARCstation 20 (1 X 390Z50), Keyboard Present
```

```
ROM Rev. 2.4, 256 MB memory installed, Serial #456543
Ethernet address 5:2:12:c:ee:5a HostID 456543
Rebooting with command: boot /sbus@1f,0/espdma@e,8400000/esp@e,
8800000/sd@0,0:b Boot device: /sbus@1f,0/espdma@e,8400000/esp@e,8800000/sd@
0,0:b File and args:
SunOS Release 5.9 Version Generic 32-bit
Copyright 1983-2000 Sun Microsystems, Inc. All rights reserved.
Configuring /dev and /devices
Using RPC Bootparams for network configuration information.
```

2.6 Install Solaris 9 SPARC Using the Web Start Wizard

Using the Web Start Wizard is the easiest way to install and configure Solaris. Although it is possible to use the Solaris Interactive installer supplied with previous Solaris versions, the Web Start Wizard allows users to install entire distributions or groups of packages, and automatically size, lay out, and create slices on the file system. It also configures the boot disk and other disks that are installed locally. However, if you wish to install individual packages, or change the size of the swap file, you will not be able to use the Web Start Wizard.

Network

The first section of the wizard involves setting up the network. The Network Connectivity screen gives users the option to select a networked or non-networked system. If you don't need to install network support, you will still need a unique hostname, and this must then be entered. Network users will have to enter a hostname, but must first identify how their system obtains IP support. One possibility is that the system will use Dynamic Host Configuration Protocol (DHCP), which is useful when IP addresses are becoming scarce on a Class C network. DHCP allows individual systems to be allocated only for the period during which they are "up." Thus, if a client machine is only operated between 9 A.M. and 5 P.M. every day, it is only "leased" an IP address for that period of time. When an IP address is not leased to a specific host, it can be reused by another host. Solaris DHCP servers can service Solaris clients, as well as Microsoft Windows and Linux clients.

Next, you need to indicate whether IPv6 needs to be supported by this system. The decision to use or not to use DHCP will depend on whether your network is part of the Mbone, the IPv6-enabled version of the Internet. As proposed in RFC 2471, IPv6 will replace IPv4 in the years to come, as it provides for many more IP addresses than IPv4. Once IPv6 is adopted worldwide, there will be less reliance on stopgap measures like DHCP. However, IPv6 also incorporates a number of innovations above and beyond the addition of more IP addresses for the Internet: enhanced security provided by authenticating header information, for example, will reduce the risk of IP spoofing and denial of service attacks succeeding. Because IPv6 support does not interfere with existing IPv4 support, most administrators will want to support it.

Finally, you need to enter the IP address assigned to this system by the network administrator. It is important not to use an IP address that is currently being used by another host, because packets may be misrouted. You will also need to enter the netmask for the system, which will be 255.0.0.0 (Class A), 255.255.0.0 (Class B), or 255.255.255.0 (Class C). If you're not sure, ask your network administrator.

Name Service

A name service allows your system to find other hosts on the Internet or on the local-area network. Solaris supports several different naming servers, including the Network Information Service (NIS/NIS+), the Domain Name Service (DNS), or file-based name resolution. NIS/NIS+ is used to manage large domains by creating maps of hosts, services, and resources that are shared between hosts and can be centrally managed. The domain name service, on the other hand, only stores maps of IP addresses and hostnames. Solaris supports the concurrent operation of different naming services, so it's possible to select NIS/NIS+ at this point and set up DNS manually later. However, since most hosts are now connected to the Internet, it may be more appropriate to install DNS first, and install NIS/NIS+ after installation.

If you select DNS or NIS/NIS+, you will be asked to enter a domain name for the local system. This should be the fully qualified domain name (for example, *paulwatters.com*). If you selected DNS, you will either need to search the local subnet for a DNS server or enter the IP address of the primary DNS server that is authoritative for your domain. You may also enter up to two secondary DNS servers that have records of your domain. This can be a useful backup if your primary DNS server goes down. It is also possible that, when searching for hosts with a hostname rather than a fully qualified domain name, you would want to search multiple local domains. For example, the host

2

www.finance.paulwatters.com belongs to the *finance.paulwatters.com* domain. However, your users may wish to locate other hosts within the broader *paulwatters.com* domain by using the simple hostname, in which case you can add the *paulwatters.com* domain to a list of domains to be searched for hosts.

Date and Time
The next section requires that you enter your time zone, as specified by geographic region, by the number of hours beyond or before Greenwich Mean Time (GMT), or by time zone file. Using the geographic region is the easiest method, although if you already know the GMT offset and/or the name of the time zone file, you may enter that instead. Next, you are required to enter the current time and date, with a four-digit year, a month, day, hour, and minute.

Root Password
The most important stage of the installation procedure occurs next—the selection of the root password. The root user has the same powers as the root user on Linux, or the Administrator account on Windows NT. If an intruder gains root access, he or she is free to roam the system, deleting or stealing data, removing or adding user accounts, or installing Trojan horses that transparently modify the way that your system operates.

One way to protect against an authorized user gaining root access is to use a difficult to guess root password. This makes it difficult for a cracker to successfully use a password-cracking program to guess your password. The optimal password is a completely random string of alphanumeric and punctuation characters. There are some applications that can be used to generate passwords that are easy to remember but that contain almost random combinations of characters.

In addition, the root password should never be written down (unless it is locked in the company safe) or told to anyone who doesn't need to know it. If users require levels of access that are typically privileged (such as mounting CD-ROMs), it is better to use the *sudo* utility to limit the access of each user to specific applications for execution as the super-user, rather than giving out the root password to everyone who asks for it.

The root password must be entered twice—just in case you should happen to make a typographical error, as the characters that you type are masked on the screen.

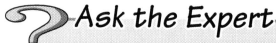

Ask the Expert

Question: What is a root password and what is it used for?

Answer: The root password is the primary authentication token for the super-user. Knowing the root password allows an individual to gain super-user privileges. The root account can be used to gain indirect access to the nobody account, and the root user may assume the identity of any user on the system by using the su command. This makes the root password a very valuable key that must be protected from external interception.

Power Management

Do you want your system to switch off automatically after 30 minutes of inactivity? If you can honestly answer yes to this question (for example, because you have a workstation that does not run services), you should enable power management, as it can save costly power bills. However, if you're administering a server, you'll definitely want to turn power management off. To enable power management after installation is also possible, by editing the */etc/power.conf* file.

Proxy Server

A proxy server acts as a buffer between hosts on a local network and the rest of the Internet. A proxy server passes connections back and forth between local hosts and any other host on the Internet. It usually acts in conjunction with a firewall to block access to internal systems, thereby protecting sensitive data. One of the most popular firewalls is squid, which also acts as a caching server.

To enable access to the Internet through a proxy server, you need to enter the hostname of the proxy server, and the port on which the proxy operates.

Kiosk

After all of the configuration settings have been entered, the following message will be seen on the screen:

```
Please wait while the system is configured with your settings...
```

The installation Kiosk will then appear on the screen. The Kiosk is primarily used to select the type of installation that you wish to perform. To begin the software selection process, you need to eject the Web Start CD-ROM, and insert the Software (1) CD-ROM. Next, you have the option of installing all Solaris software using the default options or customizing your selection before copying the files from the CD-ROM. Obviously, if you have a lot of disk space and a fast system, you may prefer to install the entire distribution, and delete packages after installation that you no longer require. This is definitely the fastest method. Alternatively, you can elect to perform a customized installation.

You are then presented with a screen of all the available software groups. Here, you may select or deselect individual package groups, or package clusters, depending on your requirements. For example, you may decide to install the Netscape Navigator software, but not install the NIS/NIS+ server for Solaris. After choosing the packages that you wish to install, you are then required to enter your locale based on geographic region (the US entry is selected by default). You may also elect to install third-party software during the Solaris installation process—this is particularly useful if you have a standard operating environment that consists of using the Oracle database server in conjunction with the Solaris operating environment, for example. You would need to insert the product CD-ROM at this point so that it could be identified.

After selecting your software, you will need to lay out the disks. This involves defining disk slices that will store the different kinds of data on your system. The fastest configuration option involves selecting the boot disk, and allowing the installer to automatically lay out the partitions according to the software selection that you have chosen. For example, you may wish to expand the size of the /var partition to allow for large print jobs to be spooled, or Web server logs to be recorded.

2.7 Manage Postinstallation Booting

Finally, you will be asked to confirm your software selections and proceed with installation. All of the packages will then be installed to your system. A progress bar displayed on the screen indicates which packages have been installed at any particular point, and how many remain to be installed. After you have installed all of the software, you will have to reboot the system. After restarting, your system should boot directly into Solaris unless you have a dual-booting system, in which case you will need to select the Solaris boot partition from the Solaris boot manager.

Project 2-1: Checking Installed Users

This project shows you how to check the user accounts that have been added to the system during installation. For security reasons, you may need to delete some users by using the `admintool` or the `userdel` command.

Step-by-Step

1. Log in to the system by using the username "root" and root password, as entered during installation.

2. Change directory to the /etc directory, which is where the password file is stored:

   ```
   # cd /etc
   ```

3. Use the `cat` command to display the contents of the /passwd file:

   ```
   # cat passwd
   ```

Summary

The `cat` command can be used to display a list of users in the password file (/etc/passwd) after installation. Surplus accounts can be removed by using the `admintool` or `userdel` command.

After installation, the system will reboot and display a status message when starting up, which is printed on the console. A console display during booting will look something like

```
ok boot
Resetting ...
SPARCstation 20 (1 X 390Z50), Keyboard Present
ROM Rev. 2.4, 256 MB memory installed, Serial #456543
Ethernet address 5:2:12:c:ee:5a HostID 456543
Boot device: /iommu/sbus/espdma@f,400000/esp@f,800000/sd@1,0
File and args:
SunOS Release 5.9 Version generic [UNIX(R) System V Release 4.0]
Copyright (c) 1983-2000, Sun Microsystems, Inc.
configuring network interfaces: le0.
Hostname: server
The system is coming up. Please wait.
add net default: gateway 204.58.62.33
NIS domainname is paulwatters.net
starting rpc services: rpcbind keyserv ypbind done.
Setting netmask of le0 to 255.255.255.0
```

```
Setting default interface for multicast: add net 224.0.0.0: gateway emu
syslog service starting.
Print services started.
volume management starting.
The system is ready.
emu console login:
```

By default, the CDE login screen is then displayed, assuming that you have a high-resolution monitor attached to the system acting as a console.

☑ *Mastery Check*

1. Which is a valid physical device for */pci@1f,0/pci@1,1/ide@3/dad@0,0*?

   A. */dev/dsk/c0t0d0*

   B. */dev/dsk/c0t0d1*

   C. */dev/dsk/c1t0d0*

   D. */dev/dsk/c0t1d0*

2. What is an IP address?

   A. A network address that identifies a group of hosts

   B. A number that is used to locate hosts on the same local subnet

   C. A unique name that is associated with a system

   D. A network number that identifies a single host

3. What is a domain name?

   A. An IP address that identifies a group of hosts

   B. A number that is used to locate hosts on the same local subnet

   C. A unique name that is associated with a system

   D. A network name that identifies a group of hosts

☑ Mastery Check

4. What is a subnet mask?

    A. An IP address that identifies a group of hosts

    B. A number that is used to locate hosts on the same local subnet

    C. A unique name that is associated with a system

    D. A network name that identifies a group of hosts

5. What is DHCP?

    A. A protocol for permanently assigning IP addresses to hosts

    B. A protocol for leasing IP addresses to hosts

    C. A method for invoking super-user privileges

    D. A protocol for identifying a group of hosts

6. Which of the following Solaris 9 installation types requires the greatest amount of disk space?

    A. Entire Distribution without OEM Support

    B. Entire Distribution plus OEM Support

    C. Developer System

    D. End User System

7. The acronym SPARC stands for which of the following names?

    A. Super Processor ARChitecture

    B. Super Processor Adaptable Recurrent Computation

    C. Scalable Processor ARChitecture

    D. Special ARChitecture

8. What are the main advantages of the SPARC architecture?

    A. High speed/bandwidth bus

    B. Fastest available CPU speeds

☑ Mastery Check

    C. Slow I/O performance

    D. Compatibility with Intel CPUs

9. What is the minimum amount of RAM required to run Solaris 9?

    A. 16M

    B. 32M

    C. 64M

    D. 128M

10. What is a root password?

    A. An authentication token for the super-user

    B. A hacking tool used to crack low-level accounts

    C. A password that cannot be used to gain indirect access to the nobody account

    D. A network name that identifies a group of hosts

11. What is the name of Sun's thin client device?

    A. Sun Beam

    B. Sun Ray

    C. Star Fire

    D. Ultra 10

12. Which of the following is a valid installation type?

    A. Initial install

    B. Cross-grade

    C. Uplink

    D. Postinstall

☑ *Mastery Check*

13. What is the rule for allocating swap space?

    A. Half the amount of physical RAM as swap space

    B. The same amount of physical RAM as swap space

    C. One and half times the amount of physical RAM as swap space

    D. Twice the amount of physical RAM as swap space

14. Should you enable power management on a server?

    A. Always

    B. Never

    C. Only when using solar power

    D. Only when connected to a UPS

15. What optional product provides high availability and load balancing?

    A. Sun Cluster

    B. Sun Share

    C. Sun Load Balancer

    D. Sun Kiosk

Module 3

Running Solaris

Critical Skills

Solaris provides a very flexible framework for starting, running, and shutting down a system. Solaris systems can be run at different run levels, or init states, that determine whether multiple users can log in, whether hardware maintenance can be performed, or whether the system is fully operational. In this module we will examine how to work with Solaris to ensure reliable operation, and troubleshoot known problems when they occur.

3.1 Administer OpenBoot PROM

The OpenBoot PROM monitor provides a low-level software interface to SPARC system hardware. It has some similarities to the BIOS system of a PC, since key settings like the boot device can be set. However, the functionality of the PROM extends far beyond setting boot parameters: an entire suite of diagnostic and troubleshooting applications are available from a shell-like interface. For example, a list of all devices attached to the SCSI can be displayed to ensure that they have been detected prior to booting. Alternatively, the network interface can be "watched" to ensure that packets are being seen on the network. In fact, OpenBoot allows complete programs to be written and executed in the Forth programming language. Although many administrators will just use the PROM monitor to boot their system by using the boot command, in times of trouble, the PROM monitor can be invaluable.

There are two prompts for the PROM monitor that administrators should be familiar with: "ok" and ">". To change from the ">" prompt to the command-issuing prompt "ok", the following command may be used:

```
> n
ok
```

A number of different commands may be issued from the ok prompt. For example, to review the hardware configuration and firmware release level for your system, the following command may be used:

```
ok banner
SPARCstation 20, Type 5 Keyboard
ROM Rev. 3.1, 128 MB memory installed, Serial #556443
Ethernet address 6:3:1d:a:ff:6c HostID 556443
```

This output shows that the local system is a SPARCstation 20, with a Type 5 keyboard, ROM revision 3.1, with 128M RAM installed, and with a serial number of 556443. The Ethernet address of the primary network interface is also displayed (6:3:1d:a:ff:6c). In the following sections, we will examine some of the other important commands that can be issued from the ok prompt.

System Hardware Testing

Many hardware devices can be tested directly from the ok prompt by using the test command. For example, the loopback device can be tested as follows:

```
ok test net
Internal Loopback test - (OK)
External Loopback test - (OK)
```

If the test failed, the system may need to be serviced by Sun. Alternatively, all of the SCSI devices attached to a system can be checked by using the following command:

```
ok probe-scsi
Target 1
Unit 0 Disk SUN0104 Copyright (C) 1995 Sun Microsystems
Target 2
Unit 0 Disk SUN0207 Copyright (C) 1996 Sun Microsystems
Target 3
Unit 0 Disk SUN0308 Copyright (C) 1998 Sun Microsystems
```

This displays shows three SCSI disks connected to the bus at targets 1, 2, and 3. Generally, if CD-ROM devices are attached to the system, they will be located at target 6. If one or more devices do not appear, it's possible that the device has not been correctly terminated, or that there is a conflict between the target IDs of one or more devices. Most SCSI devices allow you to set the target ID by a switch at the rear of the device. On each bus, these target IDs must be unique, so the IDs for all devices should be checked to ensure that they don't overlap.

Other devices that can be checked include the internal clock:

```
ok watch-clock
Watching the 'seconds' register of the real time clock chip.
 It should be ticking once a second.
 Type any key to stop.
1
2
3
```

Since the clock chip is widely used within the system, it's important to establish its accuracy and/or identify if it needs to be replaced.

The network can also be checked by using the *watch-net* program. Here, the network is scanned for Ethernet packets—if the localhost can't "see" the network, then a network fault or interface card fault may be the problem. Alternatively, a high number of bad packets may indicate a network design fault:

```
ok watch-net
Internal Loopback test - succeeded
External Loopback test - succeeded
Looking for Ethernet packets.
'.' is a good packet. 'X' is a bad packet.
Type any key to stop
................X................
```

This output indicates that a number of packets can be read successfully from the network.

1-Minute Drill

● What is the OpenBoot PROM monitor?

● What command is used to check the status of SCSI devices?

● What command is used to check the status of the network?

3.2 Manage System Startup and Shutdown

The most commonly used command issued from the ok prompt, when the system is at run-level 0, is the `boot` command. By default, this command brings the system into full multi-user mode. As the system passes through each run level

---

● The OpenBoot PROM monitor provides a low-level software interface to SPARC system hardware.
● `probe-scsi`
● `watch-net`

during booting, status is continually printed to the console, as shown in the
following example:

```
ok boot
SPARCstation 20, Type 5 Keyboard
ROM Rev. 3.1, 128 MB memory installed, Serial #556443
Ethernet address 6:3:1d:a:ff:6c HostID 556443
Rebooting with command:
Boot device: /iommu@f,e0000000/sbus@f,e0001000/espdma@f,400000/esp@f,8...
SunOS Release 5.9 Version Generic 32-bit
Copyright (c) 1983-2002 by Sun Microsystems, Inc.
configuring IPv4 interfaces: hme0.
Hostname: pembroke
The system is coming up. Please wait.
checking ufs filesystems
/dev/rdsk/c0t0d0s1: is clean.
NIS domainname is Paulwatters.Com.
starting rpc services: rpcbind keyserv ypbind done.
Setting netmask of hme0 to 255.255.255.0
Setting default IPv4 interface for multicast: add net 224.0/4:
  gateway pembroke
syslog service starting.
Print services started.
volume management starting.
The system is ready.
pembroke console login:
```

After the login: prompt is displayed, the system may start the Common
Desktop Environment (CDE), if the X Display Manager (xdm) is running.
Alternatively, it is possible to log in directly on the console and issue commands,
if necessary.

If new hardware has been added to the system since the previous boot, a
reconfiguration boot should be performed. This rebuilds all of the device files
in the /dev and /devices directory. To perform a reconfiguration boot, the following
command can be used:

```
ok boot -r
```

Alternatively, a reconfiguration boot will be performed if the /reconfigure
file exists on the file system. If this is created prior to rebooting, by using the
touch command, then only boot needs to be entered at the ok prompt, and
not boot -r:

```
# touch /reconfigure; sync; init 6
```

Alternatively, you may configure a reboot by using the following command sequence:

```
# sync;sync; reboot --r
```

You may also reconfigure reboot by doing a

```
# sync;sync; reboot -r
```

Project 3-1: Reconfiguration Boot from the PROM Monitor

This project shows you how to perform a reconfiguration boot from the PROM monitor. This must be performed when installing new hardware that is not hot-swappable.

Step-by-Step

1. Bring the system down to init state 0, if the system is already running:

```
# sync; init 0
```

2. Boot the system in reconfiguration mode:

```
ok boot -r
```

3. Verify that the device directories are reconstructed by examining the boot output:

```
…
Configuring devices…
Configuring /dev and /devices
```

4. Use the prtconf command to verify that the new device files have been created:

```
# prtconf
```

Summary

The boot command, with the correct options, can be used to perform a reconfiguration boot.

3.3 Use Common OpenBoot PROM Commands

Although a default kernel is chosen by using the `boot` command, it is possible to select a different kernel to boot if required. This may be necessary when using an experimental or patched kernel that you don't want to set as default. It is possible to set the full pathname to the kernel you wish to boot, the full pathname to the modules directory for the new kernel, the path to the kernel's system file, the root file system type, and the root device name. These parameters can be set on the command line during a manual boot. The following example shows a patched kernel being booted manually:

```
Rebooting with command: boot -a
Boot device: /pci@1f,0/pci@1,2/ide@1/disk@0,1:a File and args: -a
Enter filename [kernel/sparcv9/unix]: kernel/patched/unix
Enter default directory for modules [/platform/SUNW,Sparc-20/kernel
/platform/sun4m/kernel /kernel /usr/kernel]:
Name of system file [etc/system]:
SunOS Release 5.9 Version Generic 64-bit
Copyright (c) 1983-2000 by Sun Microsystems, Inc.
root filesystem type [ufs]:
Enter physical name of root device
[/pci@1f,0/pci@1,2/ide@1/disk@0,1:a]:
```

Setting the Boot Device

By default, the system is booted from a kernel located on the device specified by the environment variable boot device. The following are legal values for boot device:

disk	Boots from a disk.
cdrom	Boots from a CD-ROM or DVD-ROM.
net	Boots from the network.
floppy	Boots from a floppy disk.
tape	Boots from a tape drive (this was the default installation method prior to the introduction of bootable CD-ROMs).

The default boot device is set by using the `setenv` command. For example, to set the boot device to disk, the following command would be used:

```
ok setenv boot-device disk
```

Alternatively, to set the boot device to tape, the following command would be used:

```
ok setenv boot-device tape
```

If you want to boot from a nondefault device on a single occasion, you don't need to set the boot device variable. Instead, you can simply pass the name of boot device on the command line. For example, to boot from the CD-ROM device once only, the following command would be used:

```
ok boot cdrom
```

Although the system would boot from the CD-ROM on this occasion, the next boot would use the default device specified by the boot device variable, as long as an alternative device was not once again specified on the command line.

The device aliases like *disk*, *net*, and *cdrom* can be set to point to individual devices by using the `nvalias` command. For example, to set the alias for the network boot device to the device */pci@1f,4000/network@1,1*, the following command would be used:

```
ok nvalias net /pci@1f,4000/network@1,1
```

Other properties can also be set for aliases. For example, to set the network device to use the Dynamic Host Configuration Protocol (DHCP) to retrieve its IP address, the following command would be used:

```
ok nvalias net /pci@1f,4000/network@1,1:dhcp
```

To unset an alias, the `nvunalias` command can be used. For example, to unset the definition for the net device, the following command would be used:

```
ok nvunalias net
```

Diagnosing Booting Faults

Sometimes a system will fail to boot correctly because an error is detected. Typical errors include file system inconsistencies caused by the system not being cleanly shut down, or faulty hardware devices. If the booting procedure appears to hang at a specific point, the system can be halted and rebooted into single-user mode. To halt a SPARC system, use the STOP-A key combination. Typing **go** will resume the system's activity, while typing **boot -s** will reboot the system into single-user mode.

This is a useful (but risky) strategy if a service that is launched during multi-user mode or multi-user with network mode is preventing the system from coming up. In this case, the /etc/init.d file causing the problem can be temporarily removed to ensure that the system can boot. In order to boot into single-user mode, the following command is used:

```
ok boot -s
...
INIT: SINGLE USER MODE
Type Ctrl-d to proceed with normal startup,
(or give root password for system maintenance):
```

At this point, the super-user password should be entered to spawn a shell that is executed on the console.

Another possible scenario for a system involves the loss of the root password or the corruption of the password databases (/etc/passwd or /etc/shadow). Without the root password, the system will continue to operate, but important functions such as managing devices, users, and resources will not be available. In this case, it is necessary to boot the system from the CD-ROM drive, using the installation disk. A temporary mount point needs to be created to mount the normal boot disk on. The disk then needs to be mounted, and the /etc/shadow file edited directly. Leaving the password field blank, or copying the field of a known user's password in the same file will make it possible to log in as root using no password or the user's password, respectively. This procedure is walked through here:

```
ok boot cdrom
...
INIT: SINGLE USER MODE
Type Ctrl-d to proceed with normal startup,
(or give root password for system maintenance):
# mkdir /mnt/rootdisk
# mount /dev/dsk/c0t0d0s1 /mnt/rootdisk
# vi /mnt/rootdisk/etc/shadow
# sync; init 6
```

3

3.4 Write Startup Scripts

At any point in time, a Solaris system exists in a specific init state, or run level. The run level is controlled by the init program—the super-user can execute the init program to change the run level, or it can be invoked during the boot process. When the system changes run level, scripts stored in a directory corresponding to the run level are invoked. These scripts are typically symbolic links back to other scripts stored in the /etc/init.d directory. Table 3-1 contains a list and description of the various run levels that are supported under Solaris.

Each init state is linked to a script that controls the order of execution of scripts for each run level, as described in Table 3-2.

Once a system has reached a specific run level, that run level can be changed by using the *init* command, followed by the desired run level. As the system enters a run level, startup scripts in the corresponding "rc" directory are executed in ascending order, where the script name is prefixed by S*nn*, where *nn* is the sequence number. Thus, a startup script *S60firewall* would be executed before script *S61dblistener*. Conversely, when a run-level change is requested, such as when the system is being rebooted, then kill scripts are executed in ascending order from the corresponding "rc" directory. Kill scripts are prefixed by K*nn*, where *nn* is the sequence number. Both startup scripts and kill scripts are symbolically linked to a single script, with a "start" and "stop" parameter, which are passed correspondingly. A set of typical startup scripts for /etc/rc2.d

Init State/ Run Level	Details	Access Type	Script Directory
0	Firmware mode	Console access	/etc/rc0.d
1	Administration mode	Single user	/etc/rc1.d
2	Multi-user mode	Multi-user	/etc/rc2.d
3	Multi-user mode with network services	Multi-user	/etc/rc3.d
4	User-defined state	Not specified	N/A
5	Powerdown state	Console access	/etc/rc5.d
6	Reboot state	Single user	/etc/rc6.d
S	Administration mode	Console access	/etc/rcS.d

Table 3-1   Solaris 9 init States

3

Init State/ Run Level	Script Name
0	*/etc/rc0*
1	*/etc/rc1*
2	*/etc/rc2*
3	*/etc/rc3*
4	N/A
5	*/etc/rc5*
6	*/etc/rc6*
S	*/etc/rcS*

Table 3-2   Solaris 9 init State Scripts

is shown in Table 3-3, while Table 3-4 shows a typical set of startup scripts for */etc/rc0.d*

Name	Details
S05RMTMPFILES	Deletes temporary files in */tmp*.
S20sysetup	Sets up the system and checks whether the run-level change resulted from a system crash by examining */var/crash*.
S21perf	Starts the accounting system by executing */usr/lib/sa/sadc* and */var/adm/sa/sa*.
S30sysid.net	Sets up the network interfaces and network parameters.
S69inet	Initializes network configuration by setting TCP/IP parameters using *ndd*, and identifies the local domain name and default router.
S70uucp	Starts the UNIX-to-UNIX copy (UUCP) daemon.
S71sysid.sys	Sets up system parameters.
S72autoinstall	Starts a JumpStart installation.
S72inetsvc	Initializes network services like the Domain Name Service (DNS).
S92volmgt	Loads the removable media volume manager (*/usr/sbin/vold*) .

Table 3-3   Typical Multi-User Startup Scripts Under Solaris 9

Name	Details
K00ANNOUNCE	Prints a shutdown message to the console.
K10dtlogin	Shuts down the CDE and prevents new logins.
K20lp	Cancels printing services.
K22acct	Switches off accounting.
K42audit	Switches off auditing.
K47asppp	Kills the Point-to-Point Protocol (PPP) daemon and disables modem access.
K50utmpd	Switches off the utmp service.
K55syslog	Cancels the logging service.
K57sendmail	Turns off the sendmail mail service.
K66nfs.server	Stops sharing Network File System (NFS) volumes.
K69autofs	Stops sharing home directories and other volumes using the automounter.
K70cron	Switches off the scheduling daemon (cron).
K75nfs.client	Unmounts any remotely mounted NFS volumes.
K76nscd	Turns off the name service daemon cache.
K85rpc	Kills Remote Procedure Call (RPC) services.

Table 3-4 Typical Single-User Kill Scripts Under Solaris 9

Project 3-2: Creating a Customized Startup Script

This project shows you how to create your own startup script. Whenever a new service is installed that must be started at boot time, a new startup script must be created.

Step-by-Step

1. Determine the name of a service that needs to be started at boot that is not already started (for example, the Oracle database listener, *lsnrctl*).

2. Insert the contents of the startup script template shown below into the file */etc/init.d/lsnrctl*.

3. Modify the path to the *lsnrctl* binary file as specified by the ORA_HOME environment variable.

4. Insert the command `lsnrctl start` in place of `name` for the start section, and `lsnrctl stop` in place of `name` for the stop section.

Summary

A startup script is a special script file that can be created by using an editor such as vi.

Since you can directly examine the text contents of each startup and kill script by using the `cat` command with the corresponding *etc/init.d* script, it's easy to learn the process of writing your own—it's necessary to do this whenever you introduce a new service that must be started up at boot time and/or turned off during shutdown. The following script is a template for creating your own startup or shutdown scripts:

```sh
#!/bin/sh

#
# Generic start/stop procedure
#

case "$1" in
'start')
        if [ -x /path/to/daemon/name ]
        then
                /path/to/daemon/name
        ;;
'stop')

        if [ -x /path/to/daemon/name ]
        then
                pkill -9 name
        fi
        ;;
*)
        echo "Usage: /etc/init.d/mydaemon{ start | stop }"
        ;;
esac
```

To customize this script, simply replace `/path/to/daemon` with the path to the daemon and insert the name of your own instead of `name`. You can test the script in its startup state by issuing the following command:

```
# /etc/init.d/mydaemon start
```

Conversely, you can test the script in its kill state by issuing the following command:

```
# /etc/init.d/mydaemon stop
```

1-Minute Drill

- What file contains all of the parameters for */sbin/init*?
- What is the purpose of the *S72autoinstall* script?
- What is the purpose of changing to init state 6?

3.5 Manage the init Process and Run Levels

When a kernel is booted, a set of values stored in an EPROM can be accessed. These are often the same values that can be set using the OpenBoot PROM monitor. However, if you want to modify these values during run time without going to the PROM monitor, the eeprom command can be used. The following example shows the variables typically used by the system:

```
# /usr/sbin/eeprom
tpe-link-test?=true
scsi-initiator-id=7
keyboard-click?=false
keymap: data not available.
ttyb-rts-dtr-off=false
ttyb-ignore-cd=true
ttya-rts-dtr-off=false
```

- */etc/inittab*
- Perform JumpStart installations.
- Perform a reboot.

```
ttya-ignore-cd=true
ttyb-mode=9600,8,n,1,-
ttya-mode=9600,8,n,1,-
pcia-probe-list=1,2,3,4
pcib-probe-list=1,2,3
mfg-mode=off
diag-level=max
#power-cycles=50
system-board-serial#: data not available.
system-board-date: data not available.
fcode-debug?=false
output-device=screen
input-device=keyboard
load-base=16384
boot-command=boot
auto-boot?=true
watchdog-reboot?=false
diag-file: data not available.
diag-device=net
boot-file: data not available.
boot-device=disk net
local-mac-address?=false
ansi-terminal?=true
screen-#columns=80
screen-#rows=34
silent-mode?=false
use-nvramrc?=false
nvramrc: data not available.
security-mode=none
security-password: data not available.
security-#badlogins=0
oem-logo: data not available.
oem-logo?=false
oem-banner: data not available.
oem-banner?=false
hardware-revision: data not available.
last-hardware-update: data not available.
diag-switch?=false
```

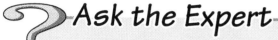

Ask the Expert

Question: How can I change the variable values displayed by
eeprom?

Answer: You can use the eeprom command, or set these variables
using the OpenBoot PROM monitor.

The /sbin/init Process

Since init plays such a vital role in the operation of a Solaris system, we will
now examine its configuration. The */etc/inittab* file contains a number of entries
that define how init handles the following standard process actions:

boot	bootwait	initdefault	off
once	ondemand	Powerfail	powerwait
respawn	sysinit	Wait	

The entries in */etc/inittab* consist of an identifier, run level, action, and
command to execute, delimited by colons. If the process can be executed in all
run levels, then no run level should be specified; otherwise, legal values include
1, 2, 3, 4, 5, 6, s, a, b, and c. The following examples show the standard actions
defined within the */etc/inittab* file:

```
ap::sysinit:/sbin/autopush -f /etc/iu.ap
ap::sysinit:/sbin/soconfig -f /etc/sock2path
fs::sysinit:/sbin/rcS sysinit  >/dev/msglog 2<>/dev/msglog </dev/console
is:3:initdefault:
p3:s1234:powerfail:/usr/sbin/shutdown -y -i5 -g0 >/dev/msglog 2<>
  /dev/msglog
sS:s:wait:/sbin/rcS  >/dev/msglog 2<>/dev/msglog </dev/console
s0:0:wait:/sbin/rc0  >/dev/msglog 2<>/dev/msglog </dev/console
s1:1:respawn:/sbin/rc1  >/dev/msglog 2<>/dev/msglog </dev/console
s2:23:wait:/sbin/rc2  >/dev/msglog 2<>/dev/msglog </dev/console
s3:3:wait:/sbin/rc3  >/dev/msglog 2<>/dev/msglog </dev/console
s5:5:wait:/sbin/rc5  >/dev/msglog 2<>/dev/msglog </dev/console
s6:6:wait:/sbin/rc6  >/dev/msglog 2<>/dev/msglog </dev/console
fw:0:wait:/sbin/uadmin 2 0 >/dev/msglog 2<>/dev/msglog </dev/console
of:5:wait:/sbin/uadmin 2 6 >/dev/msglog 2<>/dev/msglog </dev/console
rb:6:wait:/sbin/uadmin 2 1 >/dev/msglog 2<>/dev/msglog </dev/console
```

```
sc:234:respawn:/usr/lib/saf/sac -t 300
co:234:respawn:/usr/lib/saf/ttymon -g -h -p "`uname -n`
  console login: " -T sun -d /dev/console -l console -m ldterm,ttcompat
```

3.6 Administer System Shutdowns

3

Unlike PCs, Solaris systems are not often shut down, except where maintenance is required. This is because users generally expect to have service 24x7. For example, a Solaris server that hosts an Internet banking application may service customers living in different time zones who need to access their account at any time. The local time zone of the server is irrelevant. A number of features of Solaris systems make them "highly available": many servers feature dual power supplies and other redundant hardware like disk controllers and buses, ensuring that if one fails, the other can take over. In addition, RAID 5 technology ensures that disk volumes can be mirrored and data integrity assured. Faulty disks can also be hot swapped, meaning that service is not disrupted and the system does not need to be halted to replace the disk. Finally, enterprise servers like the E10000 feature configurable domains that allow virtual hosts to be created by grouping CPUs into domains. If one domain fails because of a faulty CPU, another domain can be configured to take over. However, if the system needs to be relocated or moved, the system should be shut down first. In addition, if a reconfiguration boot is required to re-create device files in */dev* and */devices*, then obviously the system will also need to be shut down.

In the following sections, we will examine several common methods for shutting down a Solaris system, including init, shutdown, poweroff, halt, and reboot.

/sbin/init

Although the */sbin/init* program is responsible for spawning processes, it is also used to manage the run level of the system. To shut down the system using init, the following commands would be used:

```
# sync
# init 0
```

This should bring the system to the OpenBoot prompt. At this point, the system can be powered down:

```
ok power-off
```

Alternatively, you can shut down and power down directly by using the following command:

```
# sync; init 5
```

Alternatively, to shut down the system and boot (that is, a reboot) the following commands would be used:

```
# sync
# init 6
```

Note that in both cases, a `sync` command has been issued. This command forces the superblock on the disk to be rewritten, ensuring data integrity. Whenever a run level is changed, it should be preceded by `sync`.

/usr/sbin/shutdown

The `shutdown` command has several advantages over the raw `init` command. For a start, a grace period can be specified whereby users are allowed to continue working in advance of a scheduled downtime. In addition, a security feature is built in to ensure that accidental init state changes don't occur—the difference between init 0 and init 3 is great, and mistyping the run level could have severe consequences. The `shutdown` command requires an administrator to confirm the shutdown procedure before proceeding, and can be used to bring the system to the 0, 1, 5, 6, and S run levels, by passing the run level with the –i parameter on the command line.

Let's look at an example. To reboot the computer with 120 seconds of grace, the following command would be used:

```
# /usr/sbin/shutdown -i 6 -g 120 "System will be rebooted in 120
seconds. Please logout now."
```

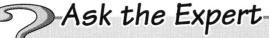

? **Ask the Expert**

Question: Why are there so many shutdown commands?

Answer: Because you never know whether you will have enough time to cleanly shut down a system.

Question: What's the best command to use for shutdowns?

Answer: Probably the `init` command—it does everything you need, and when used in conjunction with `sync`, it updates the superblock. The other commands you probably won't use unless it's an emergency.

At 30-second intervals, the following message will be displayed:

```
Shutdown started.   Tue Feb   19  18:00:00 EST  2002
Broadcast Message from root (pts/1) on mango Tue Feb    19
18:00:00 EST  2002
          The system will be shut down in 2 minutes
System will be powered off for maintenance. LOGOUT NOW.
```

When the 120 seconds has expired, the administrator will be prompted to confirm the shutdown:

```
Do you want to continue? (y or n):
```

Typing y will ensure that the shutdown proceeds and that the desired run level is reached.

3.7 Manage Powerdowns and Reboots

The `halt` command shuts down the system to run-level 0 without executing kill scripts as would normally occur when using the init or shutdown programs. This can be very useful where the system is in danger and it seems discretion rather than valor is required. For example, if a hacker is executing a distributed denial of service attack against hosts in a network, the firewall may be shut down completely until the administrators of the systems from which the attack is being launched can be contacted. By default, the superblock is updated before the init state is changed; however, this can be prevented by passing the -*n* option. In addition, the -*q* option ensures the fastest shutdown possible.

/usr/sbin/poweroff

During extreme conditions, such as an electrical storm, it may be necessary to power down the system rapidly without proceeding through the usual procedures involved in cleanly shutting down the system. Although the `halt` command brings the system to run-level 0, it does not power down the system automatically as `poweroff` does. The `poweroff` command has the advantage that it can be issued from a remote terminal, ensuring that the system is powered down, rather than having to physically sit at the console. Of course, you will need to power the system on again from the console. The superblock is updated by default before the init state is changed; however, this can be prevented by passing the -*n* option. In addition, the -*q* option ensures the fastest power off possible.

/usr/sbin/reboot

As an alternative to init 6, the `reboot` command can be used to reboot the system. It updates the superblock before changing run levels. Passing the -*q* option ensures that the fastest reboot possible occurs.

☑ *Mastery Check*

1. What command is used to set an alias for a device in the OpenBoot PROM monitor?

A. `alias`

B. `nvalias`

C. `eeprom`

D. `promalias`

☑ *Mastery Check*

2. What command is used to test network connectivity in the PROM monitor?

   A. netstat

   B. ifconfig

   C. test net

   D. arp

3. What command is used to perform a reconfiguration reboot?

   A. boot -r

   B. reboot

   C. touch /reconfigure

   D. reconfig

4. What access type is supported by run-level 0?

   A. Console only

   B. Multi-user

   C. Remote users

   D. None

5. What command is used to change from the ">" prompt to the command-issuing prompt "ok"?

   A. go

   B. n

   C. y

   D. start

3

☑ *Mastery Check*

6. What command is used to test the network from the ok prompt?

    A. `test network`

    B. `show network`

    C. `net test`

    D. `test net`

7. What command is used to show the SCSI devices from the ok prompt?

    A. `show scsi`

    B. `test scsi`

    C. `probe-scsi`

    D. `show-scsi`

8. What command is used to set the boot device to the CD-ROM?

    A. `setenv boot-device cdrom`

    B. `set boot-device cd`

    C. `setenv boot-device cd`

    D. `set boot-device cdrom`

9. What command is used to set the boot device to the tape?

    A. `setenv boot-device tape`

    B. `set boot-device rmt`

    C. `setenv boot-device rmt`

    D. `set boot-device tape`

✓ Mastery Check

10. What command is used to set the boot device to the network?

    A. `setenv boot-device net`

    B. `set boot-device eth0`

    C. `setenv boot-device eth0`

    D. `set boot-device net`

11. Which of the following is not a valid keyword for the */etc/inittab* file?

    A. `boot`

    B. `bootwait`

    C. `initdefault`

    D. `create`

12. What is the purpose of the *S21perf* script?

    A. Starts the accounting system by executing `/usr/lib/sa/sadc` and `/var/adm/sa/sa`.

    B. Sets up the network interfaces and network parameters.

    C. Initializes network configuration by setting TCP/IP parameters using *ndd*, and identifies the local domain name and default router.

    D. Starts the UNIX-to-UNIX copy (UUCP) daemon.

13. What is the purpose of the *S30sysid.net* script?

    A. Starts the accounting system by executing `/usr/lib/sa/sadc` and `/var/adm/sa/sa`.

    B. Sets up the network interfaces and network parameters.

    C. Initializes network configuration by setting TCP/IP parameters using *ndd*, and identifies the local domain name and default router.

    D. Starts the UNIX-to-UNIX copy (UUCP) daemon.

☑ *Mastery Check*

14. What is the purpose of the *S69inet* script?

A. Starts the accounting system by executing `/usr/lib/sa/sadc` and `/var/adm/sa/sa`.

B. Sets up the network interfaces and network parameters.

C. Initializes network configuration by setting TCP/IP parameters using *ndd*, and identifies the local domain name and default router.

D. Starts the UNIX-to-UNIX copy (UUCP) daemon.

15. What is the purpose of the *S70uucp* script?

A. Starts the accounting system by executing `/usr/lib/sa/sadc` and `/var/adm/sa/sa`.

B. Sets up the network interfaces and network parameters.

C. Initializes network configuration by setting TCP/IP parameters using *ndd*, and identifies the local domain name and default router.

D. Starts the UNIX-to-UNIX copy (UUCP) daemon.

Part 2

Using Solaris

Module 4

Using X11 and the Common Desktop Environment

Critical Skills

Solaris does not require a graphical user interface (GUI) to operate, because its kernel and shells can be executed through a simple command-line interface (CLI). However, many users will make use of the X Window System, which supports a number of different GUI environments, such as OpenWindows, the Common Desktop Environment (CDE) and GNOME. The current release of the X Window System is X11. Since X11 is based on a client/server model, it supports a number of advanced features, such as thin/diskless client processing and the ability to execute applications on a central server, while displaying the graphical output on a remote system. These features make X11 more complex to configure and manage than the GUI environments for other operating systems, because multiple layers of functionality must be supported. In addition, users must choose to use either CDE or GNOME as their preferred desktop environment (OpenWindows is being deprecated, and is not recommended for general use). In this module, we examine how to configure X11 and use CDE.

4.1 Manage the X11 Graphics System

The X Window System has been in development at MIT since 1984, making it one of the most mature GUI platforms available. Although the last major revision was X version 11 (X11), released in 1987, minor version changes have been taking place at regular intervals, with the latest being X11R6. "Minor revision" is somewhat misleading here, because the functional changes between minor releases can be significant. Current development efforts are overseen by the X Consortium, comprising key industry players like Sun. In addition, a number of toolkits (such as the Motif toolkit) allow sophisticated applications to be written by using standard APIs.

A typical setup for an X11 network is to host a number of diskless X terminals that boot directly from a server, and that have the responsibility of carrying out local graphics rendering, while other processes execute on the server. In previous years, X terminal vendors like Labtam have provided fairly basic diskless clients that can be supported by Solaris. During the PC age, many users eschewed their humble X terminal in place of fatter clients that could perform more local processing. However, Sun's introduction of the Sun Ray appliance, with built-in smart-card authentication and high-resolution graphics based on X11, has resurrected interest in thin client computing. Bear in mind that while X11 is commonly associated with UNIX and Linux, a number of software vendors supply X11 server and client software that runs on Microsoft Windows.

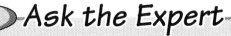

Ask the Expert

Question: Do people really run X11 on Microsoft Windows?

Answer: Yes. Many people run an X11 emulator client system to allow them connect to a Solaris system running the X11 Display Manager (xdm). This configuration allows users to copy and paste data between X11 and Windows applications.

4

The layering of a typical X11 environment is shown in Figure 4-1. Starting at the bottom, the X11 display server, which runs on every system that has a monitor (including both server and client systems), is responsible for managing

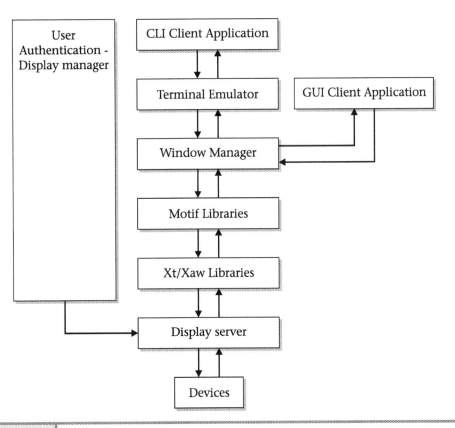

Figure 4-1 X11 architecture

calls to the X Toolkit (Xt) and the Athena Widget Set (Xaw). It acts as the go-between for input/output devices such as the mouse, keyboard, and monitor, and the requirements of individual applications. As an object-oriented system, events are dispatched every time an action is performed, such as clicking a button or typing a key on the keyboard. Specific handlers listen for these events and applications are notified where appropriate. In addition to Xaw, other component libraries such as Motif can greatly enhance the capabilities of individual client applications.

1-Minute Drill

● What is Xaw?

● What is Xt?

The Window Manager is responsible for managing the "look and feel" of the X11 interface. A number of different Window Managers are supplied with the X11 distribution, such as the Tab Window Manager (twm) and the Motif Window Manager (mwm). These are simple interfaces that require little memory or CPU power to operate. However, the resource-hungry CDE Window Manager provides access to more sophisticated libraries for development and display than twm and mwm. The Open Look Window Manager (olwm), which formed the basis of Sun's previous Window Manager (Open Windows), was favored among users and developers alike because of its Motif-inspired layout. However, Open Windows was deprecated in favor of the Common Desktop Environment (CDE), since it is an initiative of the Common Open Software Environment (COSE) that aims to standardize UNIX operations across platforms. In addition to running on Solaris, CDE is also supported on HP-UX, Linux, and other UNIX systems. Before learning about Solaris, it's important to master the CDE, particularly if Microsoft Windows administrators wish to avoid using the command line as much as possible. In this module, the reader will learn how to use the CDE and its clients effectively, by launching applications, editing text files, sending e-mail, and using the Application Manager.

● Athena Widget Set
● X Toolkit

The terminal emulator allows a shell to be executed and run within the Window Manager. While X11 is supplied with its own "xterm" terminal program, CDE is supplied with dtterm, which contains more features. However, before users can access xterm or other clients, they must log in to the system by using the CDE display manager. This display manager performs standard Solaris authentication within a GUI environment. If a user is authenticated, a desktop appears and a number of standard clients are launched. If the user is not authenticated, they can repeatedly attempt to log in after a short delay. By default, the display manager is launched at boot time during run-level 3. However, if the X display manager is not running, it can be started by using the xdm command. Alternatively, the X display server can be started manually by using the `xinit` command. The latter is useful when trying to configure a display card for the first time, and where different settings, such as display resolution and color depth, need to be evaluated visually.

Running X clients on a remote server is one of the key benefits of X11. However, as with all remote access technology, a number of risks exist in common, such as disabling authentication for remote servers executing clients locally using xhost. While this is convenient, it can allow rogue users to execute clients on your system without your knowledge. Let's look at an example. Imagine you are sitting at your client system wolfram and you wish to run a X11 application like matlab from the remote server lorenz. Typically, you will need to perform the following tasks, in order, to enable the graphical output generated on lorenz to be displayed on wolfram:

1. Log in to the wolfram console.

2. On wolfram, run the `xhost` command to enable lorenz to send graphical output to wolfram.

3. Log in to lorenz from wolfram by using Remote Shell (rsh) or Secure Shell (ssh).

4. Set the DISPLAY variable to the wolfram console.

5. Run the matlab application.

6. Graphical output should be displayed on wolfram.

Project 4-1: Running a Remote X11 Client

This project shows you how to run an X11 client remotely from lorenz (server) to wolfram (client). This procedure is important when using a client/server architecture for running X11 applications.

Step-by-Step

1. From wolfram, grant X11 access to lorenz:

```
wolfram$ xhost + lorenz
```

2. From wolfram, ssh to lorenz:

```
wolfram$ ssh lorenz
```

3. From lorenz, set the remote display to wolfram:

```
lorenz$ DISPLAY=wolfram:0.0; export DISPLAY
```

4. From lorenz, execute the X11 application:

```
lorenz$ matlab
```

Summary

The Secure Shell (SSH) can be used to create a transport link between client and server that X11 clients and servers can use.

You may be wondering whether, having granted access to the server lorenz to display client output on the wolfram display, any user on lorenz can do this. The answer is yes, but only if they have a copy of the "magic cookie" that is exported by the local client display server. This allows user-level authentication to occur. It is generally unsafe to allow access from all servers by using the following command:

```
wolfram$ xhost +
```

Once you finished working on lorenz, the following command would explicitly revoke the authorization:

```
wolfram$ xhost - lorenz
```

1-Minute Drill

- How do you allow X11 access from all servers?
- How do you allow X11 access from the server gibson?

4.2 Explore the CDE

Now that we've examined how to set up local servers and remote clients, we'll walk through how to use some of the more common CDE clients. The CDE is best learned by experience: you will quickly become competent at logging in, running applications, configuring your own workspace, and customizing applications. In the following sections, we examine how to run the most popular applications, as well as navigating around the workspace, and running the CDE terminal application (dtterm), to spawn a user's default shell.

dtlogin

After your system has been installed, you will be presented with the graphical login screen shown here:

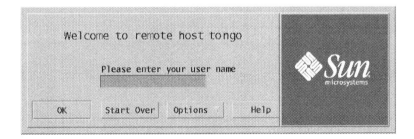

You must enter your username and click OK. A new screen then appears, asking for the correct password for the login that you entered on the previous

---

- `xhost +`
- `xhost + gibson`

screen. If the username and password are authenticated, by using the password database (*/etc/passwd*), the CDE workspace will be launched, as shown here:

Typically, the Front Panel will appear, which consists of a toolbar that contains a set of hierarchical menus, from which various CDE applications may be launched.

One of the nice features of the CDE login screen, which is provided by the dtscreen application and managed by the dtlogin application, is that you can elect to use either the CDE workspace or the old Open Windows desktop if you prefer. This selection can be made by selecting CDE or Open Windows from the Session menu. Prior to the adoption of CDE by Sun, Open Windows was the standard desktop for all Solaris systems, and some users may prefer Open Windows to CDE.

In addition, it is possible to configure a language to be used from the CDE login screen, by selecting a language from one of the menus. Users may choose from all of the languages that are currently supported by Solaris, or use the standard POSIX environment. There are two more menus that are available on

Ask the Expert

Question: Why use CDE when Solaris now supports GNOME?

Answer: While GNOME is popular among Linux users, CDE is the standard UNIX desktop agreed to by major vendors. Thus, while it doesn't have as many bells and whistles as GNOME, it has enough features to make it worthwhile as a standard desktop in a heterogeneous UNIX environment. However, with the slated release of GNOME 2 in a Solaris 9 maintenance release, users may decide to explore how well a Linux desktop can be integrated into the Solaris environment.

the login screen: the remote login menu, where it is possible to log in directly to another host on the local area network using CDE, or to log in using the command line. In a local area network, it is very useful to be able to launch a CDE session on any host using the same terminal, rather than having to physically sit at another console. Alternatively, when performing system maintenance, it is often preferable to log in to a single user session from the CDE login screen, and boot into single-user mode. The dtlogin screen should disappear, and you should see the following message:

```
*************************************************************
* Suspending Desktop Login
* If currently logged out, press [ENTER] for a console prompt.
* Desktop Login will resume shortly after you exit console session
*************************************************************
```

If you press ENTER, you should see a login prompt:

```
cassowary console login:
```

You may then proceed with performing system maintenance or rebooting the system.

4.3 Configure the CDE

The CDE workspace looks very similar to GNOME (for Linux users) and the Windows desktop (for Microsoft users). The main difference for Windows users is that CDE supports a middle mouse button, whereas only left- and right-hand buttons are generally supported under Windows.

When an application is launched from either a menu on the Front Panel or from the Workspace menu (accessed by right-clicking anywhere in the workspace), it appears in its own separate window. For example, the terminal application (dtterm) may be launched by right-clicking on the workspace, selecting the Programs menu, and selecting the Terminal option. A new CDE terminal window will then appear in the workspace, and will be active (that is, it will have the focus). The terminal window activated is shown next. The user's default login shell will be spawned, and commands will be entered interactively on the command line.

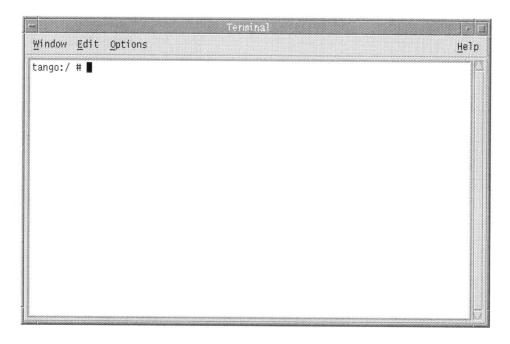

The CDE terminal window has three menus:

- The Window menu has two options: New window, which spawns another CDE terminal window, and Close, which closes the current CDE terminal window. The Close window option also has a keyboard shortcut equivalent (ALT-F4).

- The Edit menu allows the user to copy and paste data to and from any CDE application, including other terminal windows, text editors, and so forth.

- The Options menu is used to set the many different options supported by the CDE terminal window, including whether or not to display the menu and scroll bar, and the width of the terminal window (80 or 132 characters). In addition, a number of dialog boxes can be used to set global options, such as the cursor style, the cursor blink rate, and colors and sounds, as well as the font size and display.

The dtterm can be started with a number of command line parameters that can set some of these properties automatically. The benefit of this approach is that these parameters can be embedded in a script or startup file, so that your favorite settings will automatically be used every time dtterm is started. Table 4-1 shows the most commonly used dtterm command-line parameters.

CDE Windows may be layered, one on top of the other, and activated by left-clicking onto any part of an inactive window. All CDE windows have a drop-down menu at their top left-hand corner. This menu has similar functions in both GNOME and Microsoft Windows. It has items that allow the user to restore the window size, change the window size, lower the window, expand the window to occupy the entire workspace, toggle the display of the window menus, and close the window. In addition, windows may be minimized from the window drop-down menu, or maximized again by double-clicking their icon on the desktop. Figure 4-2 shows a series of minimized CDE windows in the workspace, including the style manager, terminal, process viewer, Application Manager, and mail.

In addition to a point-and-click interface, the CDE workspace supports a number of different keystroke options. This is particularly useful for users who have traditionally used the command line. Table 4-2 summarizes the main keystroke shortcuts used to shift the focus within a window, if that window is active, or within a dialog box that has popped up. These keystrokes can also be used to navigate the different menus on the Front Panel.

Parameter	Purpose
-background	Sets the default background color of the terminal.
-foreground	Sets the default text color of the terminal.
-font	Sets the font size for the terminal.
-geometry	Sets the width and height of the terminal window.
-title	Sets the title of the window to the specified string.

Table 4-1   Commonly Used dtterm Options

Keyboard navigation is slightly different within a workspace, because there are more possible actions than within a single window. Table 4-3 summarizes the main keystroke shortcuts used to shift the focus within a CDE workspace.

Within a menu, the arrow keys may be used to navigate between items, rather than the TAB key.

Keystroke	Action
TAB	Moves to the next tab group.
SHIFT-TAB	Moves to the previous tab group.
DOWN ARROW	Moves to the next control in the tab group.
UP ARROW	Moves to the previous control in a tab group.

Table 4-2 | Keystrokes and Actions Within Windows, Dialog Boxes, and the Front Panel

Keystroke	Action
ALT-TAB	Moves to the next window or icon.
SHIFT-ALT-TAB	Moves to the previous window or icon.
ALT-UP ARROW	Moves to the bottom window in a stack of windows (bringing it forward).
ALT-DOWN ARROW	Moves to the bottom of the window stack.
ALT-F6	Moves to the next window belonging to an application, or between the Front Panel and a subpanel.
SHIFT-ALT-F6	Moves to the previous window belonging to an application, or between the Front Panel and a subpanel.

4

Table 4-3   Keystrokes and Actions Within the Workspace

4.4 Launch CDE Applications

There are two ways to launch applications within CDE: either a command is issued through a shell, from within a CDE terminal window, or it is selected from the Workspace menu or the Front Panel. For example, if we wanted to execute the clock application, we could run the following command from a shell:

```
$ clock&
[1] 8836
$
```

By sending the clock process into the background, it is possible to continue to issue commands using the same shell. Alternatively, to run the clock from the Workspace menu, simply right-click anywhere on the workspace, select the Programs menu, and select the Clock item. Finally, you could select Application Manager from the Applications menu, and open the OpenWindows collection of applications. After double-clicking on the OW Clock icon, the clock will be executed, as shown in Figure 4-3.

The Workspace menu is the fastest way to get an application running, and to perform CDE administrative tasks, such as adding new items to a menu. From the Workspace menu, it is possible to launch applications, manage workspace windows, customize the menu options displayed, lock the system display, and log out of the CDE desktop.

The Front Panel is more comprehensive than the Workspace menu, as there are ten menus instead of one. In addition, the CDE desktop allows for four different workspaces to be maintained: by simply clicking on the One, Two, Three, or Four panels in the center of the Front Panel, users can maintain

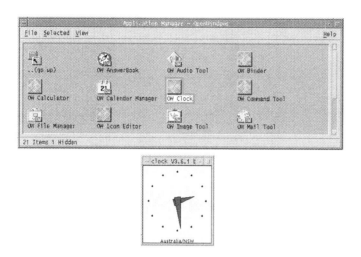

Figure 4-3 Executing the OW Clock application from the Application Manager

completely separate workspaces (one for development, one for system administration, one for playing games, and so forth). Although Linux users will be familiar with multiple workspaces, Microsoft Windows users will find this a refreshing innovation. The nine menus included on the Front Panel are as follows:

- Links, including Clock, Web Browser, Personal Bookmarks, and Find Web Page.

- Cards, including today's card and Find Card.

- Files, including Home Folder, Open Floppy, Open CD-ROM, Properties, Encryption, Compress File, Archive, and Find File.

- Applications, including Text Note, Text Editor, Voice Note, and Application Manager.

- Mail, including the mailer and the Suggestion Box.

- Personal Printers, including the default printer and the Print Manager.

- Tools, including Desktop Style, CDE Error Log, Customize Workspace Menu, Add Item to Menu, and Find Process.

- Hosts, including Performance Meter, This Host, System Info, Console, and Find Host.

- Help, including Help Manager, SunSolve Online, Solaris Support, Information, Desktop Introduction, Front Panel Help, On Item Help and AnswerBook 2.

4

The Application Manager is the encyclopedic directory of most CDE applications on a Solaris system, as shown here:

The applications are divided into six categories:

- Desktop applications, including Address Manager, Application Builder, Audio, Calculator, Calendar, Create Action, File Manager, and the Help Viewer.

- Desktop controls, including AccessX, Add Item to Menu, Customize Workspace Menu, Edit Dtwmrc, Reload Actions, Reload Applications, Reload Resources, and Restore the Front Panel.

- Desktop tools, including Archive, Archive List Contents, Archive Unpack, Check Spelling, Clipboard Contents, Compare Files, Compress File, and Count Words.

- Information, including documentation for Solaris 8, the AnswerBook, and sample bookmarks.

- Open Windows applications, including the old Open Windows AnswerBook, the Audio Tool, OW Binder, OW Calculator, OW Calendar Manager, OW Clock, OW Command Tool, and the OW File Manager.

- System Admin, including Admintool, AnswerBook Admin, Disk Usage, Eject CD-ROM, Eject Floppy, Format Floppy, Open CD-ROM, and Open Floppy.

The main CDE applications that are available from the Workspace Menu are discussed next.

4.5 Execute CDE File Applications

The main panel for the File Manager is shown in Figure 4-4, with a view of the devices directory (*/dev*). The Application Manager shares many of the same features with those found in Microsoft Windows and Linux (for example, in KDE and GNOME). The contents of folders on different file systems may be viewed by double-clicking the appropriate icon. For example, if we clicked on the *pcmcia* directory, we would see all of the PCMCIA card entries for the system. In addition, new files and folders may be created at any time by selecting the appropriate item from the File menu. Files can be located by using the Find facility, and individual file properties may be viewed by selecting the target file's icon and selecting the Properties item from the Selected menu.

Ask the Expert

Question: Should I run the Application Manager as root?

Answer: Probably not—it's easy to make a mistake and drag and drop the right file into the wrong place. For normal user files, this is recoverable, but dragging and dropping the *passwd* file accidentally is likely to cripple the system.

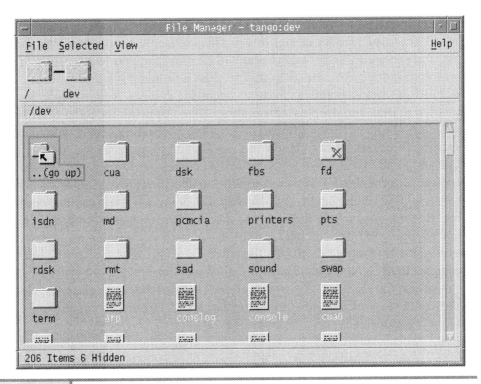

Figure 4-4 The CDE File Manager

Text Editor

In order to write shell scripts, you must come to terms with using a Solaris editor, such as the vi "visual editor" program, which can be executed within a CDE terminal window. The visual editor is not as easy to use as some other editors available for Solaris, such as the pico editor bundled with the pine mail reading program. vi requires users to master separate control, editing, and data entry modes, and requires the user to remember key commands for navigation, data insertion, and text deletion. In contrast, pico allows users to use WordStar-style control commands for copying and pasting text, saving files, and highlighting text. However, pico does not allow users to perform the complex search and replace functions available to vi users. In this section, we examine how to use the vi editor to create shell scripts and any other text files that need to be created or modified (for example, application configuration files).

An easier alternative to vi is the text editor program that operates directly under CDE (dtpad), shown in Figure 4-5. This looks much more like Notepad, Write, and other editing programs that will be more familiar to users of Microsoft Windows. The dtpad application has a number of features that distinguish it from GUI editors in other operating systems. For example, it is possible to drag and drop data from other CDE applications. In addition, dtpad offers standard file and formatting options, including saving data to an existing file, saving data to a new file, opening an existing file for editing, and a handy undo facility that reverses the last change performed on the text. Users can perform global search and replace on specific text strings, and there is even a spell-checking facility, which is almost unique in a text editing facility. Formatting options include the ability to insert text with overstriking, as well as line wrapping to 60 characters. A status bar, which is continuously updated, displays the total number of lines in the current document, as well as the line in which the cursor is currently located.

In the example shown in Figure 4-5, we have opened the */etc/format.dat* system configuration file, which defines formatting data for all supported hard disks.

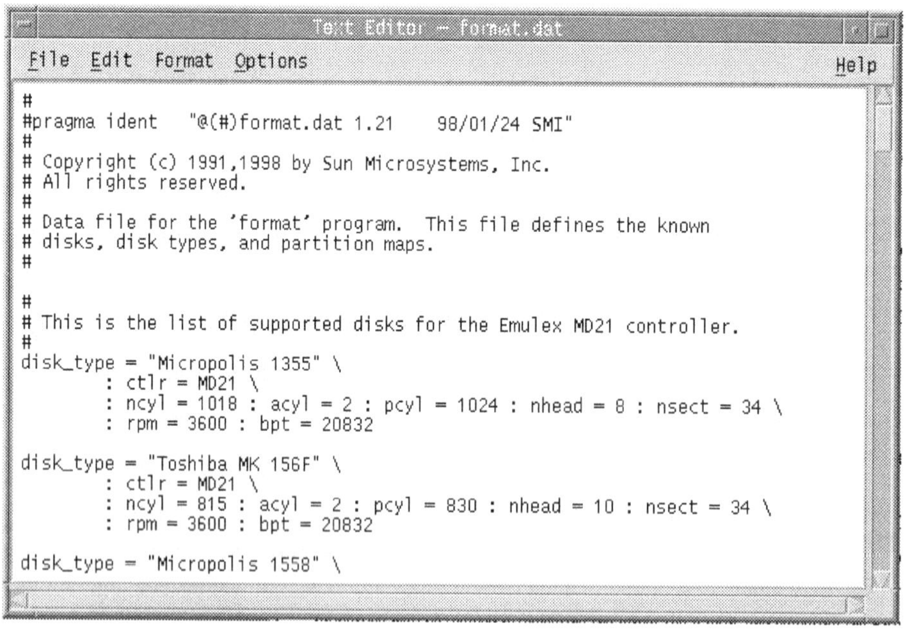

Figure 4-5 The dtpad editor

4.6 Execute CDE Mail and Calendaring Applications

Electronic mail (e-mail) has long been supported on Solaris for both local and remote users. CDE provides an easy-to-use e-mail client known as dtmail. The interface for the dtmail program is shown in Figure 4-6. The inbox for the root user is shown in the top panel—the user has 19 messages, the first of which is being displayed in the bottom window (the message shows an error generated by the cron scheduling facility).

The dtmail program can either be controlled through a menu system or by clicking one of the icons found on the middle panel between the list of inbox

4

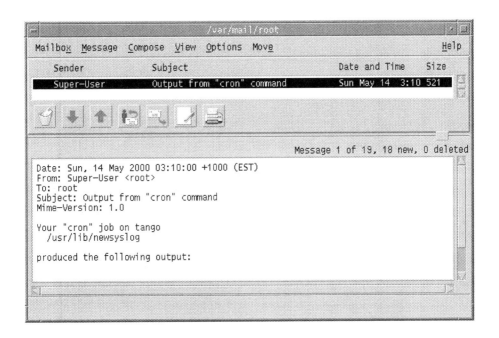

Figure 4-6 Using the dtmail e-mail client

messages and the text of the current message. The icons perform several different functions:

- Send the currently selected message to the trash.

- Read the next message down the list.

- Read the previous message in the list.

- Forward the current message to another user.

- Reply to the current message.

- Create a new message.

- Print the current message.

Using a mail client is only one side of the e-mail equation—it's also necessary to set up a mail server, which is covered in Module 13.

Calendar

The calendar tool is a daily organizer that allows users to view past and current calendars month by month, but also to enter events to be remembered for particular days. The calendar is shown in Figure 4-7, and is operated by either icons on a control panel at the top of the screen or by using one of the menus, which contain options for file management, editing, viewing entries, and browsing entries.

Web Browser

Most Solaris systems will be connected to the Internet, and will require a method of browsing the World Wide Web (WWW) using an HTTP-compliant client. Solaris includes the HotJava client, which is a 100-percent Java implementation. While HotJava has few features compared with other Web

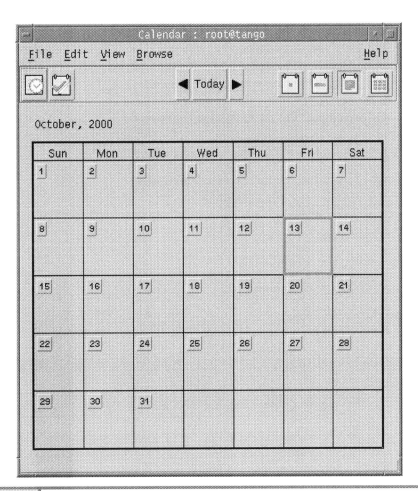

Figure 4-7 The calendar tool

browsers (such as Netscape Navigator), it is part of the Solaris environment and doesn't require any software or licenses from third parties to operate. It can be used in conjunction with the AnswerBook, and any documentation set that is created using the Hypertext Markup Language (HTML). Figure 4-8 shows the HotJava client displaying the default page for the Apache Web server, which is now included in the Solaris operating environment.

HotJava is operated by using the icon bar located at the top of the screen. The icons displayed perform the following functions:

- Navigate backwards to the last accessed document.

- Navigate forward to the last accessed document.

- Go to the home page.

- Refresh the page contents.

- Stop loading the current page.

- Search for a page on the Internet.

- Print the current page.

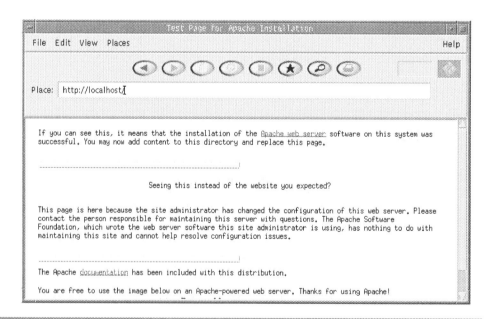

Figure 4-8   HotJava Web browser

4

Console

The console is similar to the dtterm—when executed, the user's default shell is spawned and commands can be executed interactively. The difference between dtterm and the console is that the latter displays informative messages about system status, which are normally sent to the screen of the physical console of a Solaris system. However, if the physical console is actually running CDE, then such messages would be lost. The console provides a facility to view these messages as they are generated. A sample CDE console is shown here:

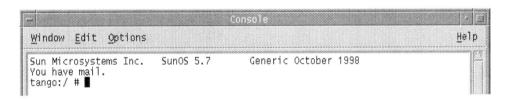

The kinds of messages displayed on the console are controlled by the 007facility. Thus, the file */etc/syslog.conf* would need to be edited to either increase or decrease the number of messages piped to the console, and to change the content of these messages. For example, a typical console message might warn the super-user that someone attempted to log in to an account but typed the wrong password. You probably don't need to see the same message every time someone fumbles their login. However, another kind of message might warn that the root file system is full, and that applications can no longer write to the disk. This is a critical message, and further action should be taken immediately.

Calculator

The CDE calculator is a full-featured scientific calculator, which is capable of computing all trigonometric functions and the most commonly used exponential and factorial functions. Supported functions include the sine, cosine, and tangent, as well as computing e^x, where x is the desired exponent. There are memory facilities available for storing the results of computations, as well as creating expressions by enclosing individual operations within brackets. A number of different base numbering systems are available, in addition to the decimal system, and results of trigonometric functions can be displayed in either degrees or radians. Figure 4-9 shows the interface for the CDE calculator.

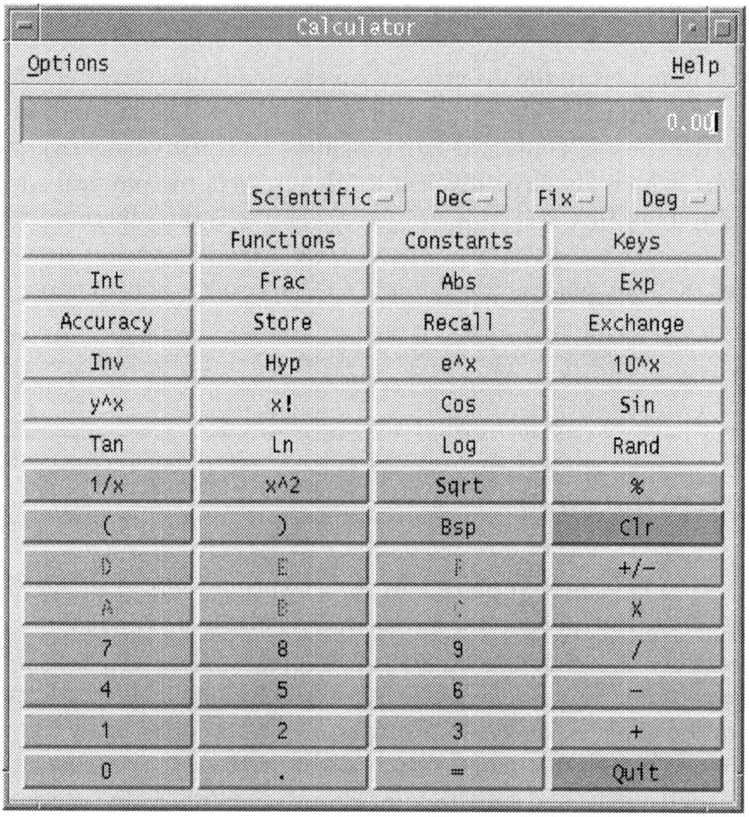

Figure 4-9 CDE calculator

Performance Meter

One of the most common questions a Solaris administrator is asked is "Why is the system slow"? Usually, a Solaris system becomes slow for one of the following reasons:

- Too many processes are being spawned for the CPU to maintain concurrent execution of the applications being run by all users.

- Too many lightweight processes are being created.

- Disk I/O is being challenged by the needs of applications, such as databases, which are disk-intensive.

- The amount of disk space allocated to supporting virtual memory operations is insufficient to support all current applications.

If your system appears to be running more slowly than usual, the first place to look for trouble is the performance meter, which continuously prints the current system load, as shown here:

4

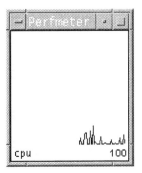

The performance meter often looks like a stock market chart—there are peaks and troughs, as more or fewer processes are executed. This activity is quite normal. However, if you begin to notice a sustained increase in the system load, well above the normal level of 1.0 for a system operating at capacity, it may be time to begin examining which processes are hogging all of the system resources. The system load will be reduced if these processes have their nice value set to a lower priority.

Print Manager

Solaris supports a wide variety of printers, whether attached to a local parallel port, or whether accessed through a local area network by using NFS or samba. One way to examine jobs that have been issued to various printers from a Solaris system is to use the Print Manager, which is similar to the print management facilities found in Linux and Microsoft Windows. The Find Print Jobs window from the Print Manager is shown here:

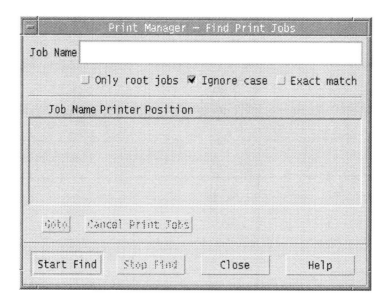

To locate a print job, in order to view its status or cancel it, the job name may be entered into the Job Name field and searching initiated by clicking the Start Find button.

Image Viewer

Solaris has multimedia support, including sound, movies, and images. Although many seasoned Linux users will be familiar with the xv program, which is available under both Solaris and Linux, CDE actually has its own image viewing and manipulation program. The image viewer has the ability to load and save images in a wide variety of popular formats—including GIF, JPEG, and TIF—and output from the snapshot program is reviewed in the next section. It has cropping, cutting, copying, and pasting functions, as well as supporting image rotation, image mirroring, image reduction, and enlargement. These functions are supported by the palette shown here:

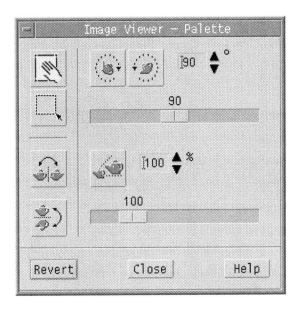

Snapshot

The snapshot program is a screen capture utility that can be used to capture the entire CDE workspace, or the contents of individual windows. The screenshot utility has its own special file format (.*rs* files), which may be easily converted to PC-friendly file formats using the Image Converter program. Fortunately, the snapshot interface actually has a button that allows the current snapshot to be launched with the Image Converter program, making it easy to take a screenshot, edit its contents, and save it in your favorite file format. Many of the images contained in this book were captured using snapshot.

Icon Editor

As you will have realized after reading this module, the CDE uses icons extensively to represent files, applications, folders, and many other display objects within the workspace. However, you are not limited to using the icons supplied with Solaris to represent your own applications: CDE is supplied with an icon editor that allows you to create your own bitmapped images, as shown in Figure 4-10. These images may be used as icons that represent applications or actions within the CDE workspace. The images are 32 × 32 pixels (1,024 pixels), with a choice of eight different colors, or shades of gray. In addition, it is possible to specify dynamic colors for the foreground and background. Standard image editing tools are also included, with cropping, filling, and several geometric shapes (circles, lines, and rectangles) available from the Tools palette.

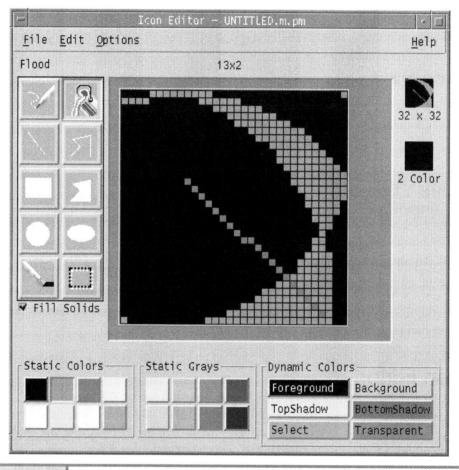

Figure 4-10 CDE icon editor

Style Manager

The Style Manager is similar to the Desktop Themes or Display Settings options available under Microsoft Windows. The Style Manager is responsible for all aspects of presentation for the CDE workspace. It is possible to use different styles for the different workspaces available under the CDE desktop. The Style Manager has several different control panels, which are available by clicking on one of the icons displayed here:

These panels are used to set the following options:

- Available color schemes for the workspace

- Default fonts for all text in CDE applications

- Backdrop patterns for the workspace

- Keyboard options, including key repeat rate

- Mouse configuration, including speed

- Beep settings for warnings

- Screen settings, including the screen saver

- Window options, including whether focus is set by clicking a mouse key or hovering over a window

- Startup configuration, including session saving and loading

4.7 Access CDE Help

On most of the CDE screens we have seen, there has been a menu on the top right-hand corner, which is the most important menu—the Help menu. The Help facility provides information and assistance on using and managing most of the applications that are supplied with the Solaris operating environment, including the File Manager, Style Manager, and Print Manager. Users can browse available Help topics or search by keyword for topics relevant to the current application. For CDE applications that are developed in-house, it is possible to provide customized help in the CDE Help format.

AnswerBook 2

Help is usually only applicable for the standard CDE applications. However, since the vast majority of the applications supplied with Solaris do not require CDE to operate, Solaris provides the AnswerBook facility. The AnswerBook has two components: the HotJava browser, which acts as the AnswerBook client, and the AnswerBook server, which is a Web server that only provides access to HTML versions of the man pages and the various reference manuals that accompany Solaris.

However, one of the best features of the AnswerBook is that it is available over the Internet, from **http://docs.sun.com/**. This means that any Solaris user without local access to an AnswerBook, may freely download PDF versions of the reference manuals, or search interactively across books in all AnswerBook collections.

☑ *Mastery Check*

1. Which of the following is *not* a standard X11 Window Manager?

A. Tab Window Manager (twm)

B. Motif Window Manager (mwm)

C. Open Look Window Manager (olwm)

D. Digital window manager (dwm)

2. What is the name of the standard X11 terminal program?

A. eterm

B. dterm

C. xterm

D. zterm

3. Which of the following operating systems does not support CDE?

A. Solaris

B. MS-DOS

C. HP-UX

D. Linux

4. What authentication token is required to connect to a remote display?

A. Username

B. Password

C. Iris scan

D. Magic cookie

4

☑ Mastery Check

5. How would you add server authorization for "binmore"?

   A. `X11 + binmore`

   B. `x11 + binmore`

   C. `xhost + binmore`

   D. `xterm + binmore`

6. How would you remove server authorization for "binmore"?

   A. `X11 - binmore`

   B. `x11 - binmore`

   C. `xhost - binmore`

   D. `xterm - binmore`

7. What is the name of the X11 display variable?

   A. display

   B. DISPLAY

   C. Xdisplay

   D. XDISPLAY

8. How many mouse buttons does CDE support?

   A. 1

   B. 2

   C. 3

   D. None

☑ Mastery Check

9. Which of the following is *not* a standard CDE application?

   A. dvdplayer

   B. Address Manager

   C. Application Builder

   D. Audio

10. Which of the following is *not* a feature of dtpad?

    A. Undo

    B. Global search and replace

    C. Spell checking

    D. Grammar checking

11. Which dtterm option sets the width and height of the terminal?

    A. –geometry

    B. –width

    C. –height

    D. –windowsize

12. Which of the following is *not* a reason for the performance meter to show an abnormally high reading?

    A. Too many processes are being spawned for the CPU to maintain concurrent execution of the applications being run by all users.

    B. Too many lightweight processes are being created.

    C. Disk I/O is being challenged by the needs of applications, such as databases, which are disk-intensive.

    D. The time zone has been changed.

4

☑ *Mastery Check*

13. Which of the following is *not* a valid panel for the Style Manager?

    A. Available color schemes for the workspace

    B. Default fonts for all text in CDE applications

    C. Backdrop patterns for the workspace

    D. User command history

14. What is the purpose of the snapshot utility?

    A. Record system activity

    B. Monitor thread processing time

    C. Take a copy of the screen

    D. Record accounting data

15. Which of the following actions is *not* supported by the HotJava buttons?

    A. Navigate backward to the last accessed document

    B. Set up a cache

    C. Navigate forward to the last accessed document

    D. Go to the home page

Module 5

Connecting to
the Internet

Critical Skills

Although most servers are connected to the Internet through a router, there are often good reasons to install a modem, which connects the system using an alternative route. This enforces a clean separation of control from data connections. For example, if you're rolling out a new transnational network, you won't want to have an administrator physically located with each server. However, in the case that the network is down, an administrator would need to be physically present to investigate and resolve the problem. However, if the administrator could simply dial into the system using a conventional phone line and modem, an administrator would not need to physically attend the system. While there are security risks in allowing incoming calls from a remote system, there are safeguards that can be put in place to prevent abuse.

Several components are required to allow an Internet connection to be supported over a modem link: a modem (obviously), a protocol that allows point-to-point connections that support TCP/IP, a serial port, a port monitor, and a software facility for connecting the port to the system. In this module, we'll examine how each of these components work together to facilitate modem connectivity. The Service Access Facility (SAF) is a mechanism that processes requests and generates responses with respect to the connection between ports and the system. Although "port" has several meanings in the UNIX world, here it means the physical connection between the system and peripheral devices. Solaris supports serial, parallel, and USB ports for connecting peripheral devices. The SAF allows system requests to be processed from peripheral devices, linking these with the appropriate port monitor, which monitors the serial ports continuously for login requests.

A modem is required to modulate and demodulate acoustic signals transmitted over a phone line. This signal is then transmitted from the modem through a serial cable to an external serial port on the system, completing the hardware linkage. Although setting up a modem-based hardware connection may seem complicated, it is a useful backup to Ethernet-based Internet. While it would not be feasible to provide Internet services ("data") over a slow modem, it is especially suited for remote access ("control") purposes.

To implement TCP/IP across a modem, the Point-to-Point Protocol (PPP) has been developed. PPP allows the modem link to be treated, for the purposes of the transport layer and higher, in the same way as an Ethernet connection. PPP provides authentication through the Challenge Handshake Authentication Protocol (CHAP), allowing the connection to be secured from intruders and unauthorized users. The PPP daemon on Solaris uses the chat program to manage

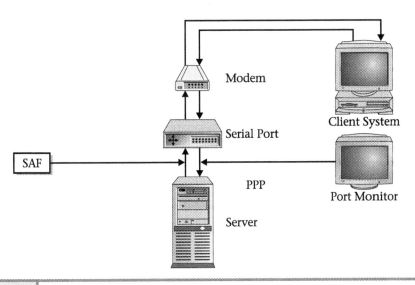

Figure 5-1   Schema for the hardware and software required to set up
modem-based access

connections and perform dial-up services. Figure 5-1 shows the schema for the
hardware and software required to setup modem-based access on Solaris 9.

5.1 Manage Port Monitors

Solaris 9 features a port monitor that supervises a system's serial ports waiting
for requests, which is known as ttymon. While the port monitor is not responsible for
processing the data being communicated directly, it does pass the data along to
the operating system in an appropriate way. In addition, multiple requests can
be handled simultaneously by the same port monitor on Solaris, making it
possible to service multiple devices and requests.

Ports can be configured for use with a terminal by using the admintool, in
either the Basic, More, or Expert mode. Many different parameters can be set
for the port using admintool, including the default terminal type, baud rate for
communications, carrier detection, and flow control. In order to configure
terminal access through the port, the admintool should be started in the Basic
user mode, because this permits the configuration of key port parameters. The
entered values should correspond to those on the related VT-100 terminal.

When the settings have been saved to disk using the admintool, the validity of the settings can be checked by using the pmadm command for each port on the system. The following commands check the settings for the first serial port (*/dev/term/a*) and the second serial port (*/dev/term/b*), respectively:

```
# pmadm -l -s ttya
PMTAG       PMTYPE      SVCTAG      FLGS ID    <PMSPECIFIC>
zsmon       ttymon      ttya        u    root /dev/term/a I -
    /usr/bin/login - 9600 ldterm,ttcompat ttya
    login:  - tvi925 y  #
# pmadm -l -s ttyb
PMTAG       PMTYPE      SVCTAG      FLGS ID    <PMSPECIFIC>
zsmon       ttymon      ttyb        u    root /dev/term/b I -
    /usr/bin/login - 9600 ldterm,ttcompat ttyb
    login:  - tvi925 y  #
```

A key component in the listening process is the listen port monitor, which is managed by the commands nlslisten and nlsadmin. The listen port monitor is different than ttymon, because it listens for access requests for daemons and services directly on network ports. These requests are serviced according to the OSI network layering specification, and of course its TCP/IP implementation. Both the Transport Layer Interface (TLI) and STREAMS are supported by the listen port monitor. The monitor manages specific network ports, with child processes spawned where required. The key benefit in this multiprocess architecture is that network interfaces can be treated quite separately—thus, traffic from a primary network interface is handled separately from modem-based traffic. This is critical to maintaining the data/control distinction implemented by Ethernet and modem traffic, respectively.

5.2 Manage Listeners

The nlsadmin command has the responsibility of managing transports for network services that are STREAMS-compatible. In contrast, the port monitor's ttymon process is managed by the command ttyadm. The ttymon continuously monitors requests for remote access through the serial port. Child processes are spawned in response to valid requests. These serviced requests are numbered sequentially as they are spawned, starting with ttymon1, ttymon2, and so on. Typically, the /usr/bin/login command is requested for interactive logins, although it is possible to implement a customized login procedure.

In order to display the status of all active ttymon processes, the `sacadm` command can be used:

```
# sacadm -l
PMTAG     PMTYPE   FLGS   RCNT   STATUS    COMMAND
ttymon1   ttymon   -      2      ENABLED   /usr/lib/saf/ttymon #ttymon1
ttymon2   ttymon   -      2      ENABLED   /usr/lib/saf/ttymon #ttymon2
ttymon3   ttymon   -      2      ENABLED   /usr/lib/saf/ttymon #ttymon3
```

Here, we can see that there are three ttymon processes active. The pmadm command can be used to investigate the services provided through each of these processes. The following example shows the services provided through ttymon1:

```
# pmadm -l -p ttymon1
PMTAG     PMTYPE    SVCTAG    FLGS    ID        <PMSPECIFIC>
ttymon1   ttymon    11        u       root      /dev/term/17
   -    -   /usr/bin/login - 9600 - login:    -tvi925
ttymon1   ttymon    12        u       root      /dev/term/18
   -    -   /usr/bin/login - 9600 - login:    -tvi925
ttymon1   ttymon    13        u       root      /dev/term/19
   -    -   /usr/bin/login - 9600 - login:    -tvi925
ttymon1   ttymon    14        u       root      /dev/term/20
   -    -   /usr/bin/login - 9600 - login:    -tvi925
```

5

The output shows that ports /dev/term/17 through /dev/term/20 are allowing remote access using the `/usr/bin/login` service. In addition to simply listing the port monitor status, the pmadm command can also be used to manage port monitor services, as described in the following table:

pmadm -a	Adds a port monitor service.
pmadm -d	Disarms a port monitor service.
pmadm -e	Enables a port monitor service.
pmadm -r	Removes a port monitor service.

The `sacadm` command is used to manage ttymon processes. The following functions are supported:

sacadm -a	Attaches a new ttymon.
sacadm -e	Arms a ttymon.
sacadm -d	Disarms a ttymon.
sacadm -s	Initializes a ttymon.

`sacadm -k`	Kills a ttymon.
`sacadm -l`	Lists ttymon details.
`sacadm -r`	Deletes a ttymon.

5.3 Administer the Service Access Facility (SAF)

The process that initiates the service access facility is known as the service access controller (*/usr/lib/saf/sac*). It is started when the system enters run-level 2, 3, or 4, as shown in this */etc/inittab* entry:

```
sc:234:respawn:/usr/lib/saf/sac -t 300
```

Here, the respawn entry indicates that if a process is not running when it should be, it should be respawned. For example, if a system changes from run-level 2 to run-level 3, sac should be running. If it is not present, it will be restarted.

When sac is started, it reads the script */etc/saf/_safconfig*, which contains any local configurations tailored for the system. Next, the standard configuration file */etc/saf/_sactab* is read and sac spawns a separate child process for each of the port monitors it supports (ttymon and listen). A sample *_sactab* is shown here:

```
# VERSION=1
zsmon:ttymon::0:/usr/lib/saf/ttymon #
```

Each of these monitors also reads its own configuration file: the files */etc/saf/ttymon/_config* and */etc/saf/listen/_config* are used to configure the ttymon and listen port monitors, respectively. A sample *_config* file is shown here:

```
# VERSION=1
ttya:u:root:reserved:reserved:reserved:/dev/term/a:I::
     /usr/bin/login::9600:ldterm, ttcompat:ttya login\: ::tvi925:y:#
```

The point of this hierarchical configuration file structure is that values read from */etc/saf/_safconfig* and */etc/saf/_sactab* by sac are inherited by the spawned port monitor processes, which then have the ability to configure their own operations. The SAF has two types of port monitors: the terminal port monitor (ttymon) and the network port monitor (listen). For example, the ttymon port monitor for the console is started in run-levels 2, 3, and 4, through an */etc/inittab* entry like the following:

```
co:234:respawn:/usr/lib/saf/ttymon -g -h -p
  "`uname -n` console login: " -T vt100 -d
  /dev/console -l console -m ldterm,ttcompat
```

The ttymon process is active when a monitor is connected to a server, such as a dumb terminal, rather than a graphics monitor.

1-Minute Drill

- What is the Service Access Facility?
- What is a port monitor?
- What is the listen port monitor?

5.4 Implement Internet Connections

In order to establish an Internet connection through PPP or a similar protocol, hardware devices such as modems and serial ports must be configured first. In this section, we'll examine how to configure these devices under Solaris 9.

Adding a Serial Port

Like any modern server system, Solaris 9 supports the connection of simple external devices through both a serial (RS-232-C or RS-423) and a parallel port. The two most common uses for serial devices on a SPARC system are connecting

---

- A mechanism that processes requests and generates responses with respect to the connection between ports and the system.
- A program that supervises a system's serial ports, waiting for requests.
- A program that listens for access requests to daemons and services directly on network ports.

a VT-100 terminal or equivalent, to operate as the system console if no graphics device is installed, and as a modem, enabling dial-up Internet access using the Point-to-Point Protocol (PPP). The former is a common practice in many server rooms, where the expense of a monitor and video card can be eliminated by using a VT-100 terminal as the console, because many SPARC machines require a display device to boot at all. On x86 systems, there are many more devices available that often only have drivers available for other operating systems. Sun and other third-party hardware vendors are slowly making releases available for these devices through the Solaris Developer Connection. If you need to obtain an updated copy of the Solaris Device Configuration Assistant, and any updated device drivers for supported external devices, these are currently available for download at **http://soldc.sun.com/support/drivers/boot.html**.

Solaris 9 has a graphical user interface (GUI) for serial device configuration, provided through the admintool program. admintool is generally used for system administration tasks, like adding users and groups, but it also has facilities for configuring parallel devices (like printers) and serial devices (like modems). It contains templates for configuring standard modem and terminal devices, and supports multiple ports.

5.5 Use Modems

Solaris 9 works best with external Hayes-compatible modems, which are also supported by other operating systems such as Microsoft Windows. However, modems that require specific operating system support (such as so-called "WinModems"), will not work with Solaris 9. In addition, internal modem cards are generally not supported by Solaris 9. While older modems tend to use external (but sometimes internal!) DIP switches, modern modems can be configured using software to set most of their key operational parameters.

Modem access can be configured to allow inbound-only, outbound-only, and bidirectional access (which allows traffic in both directions) using a similar scheme. In the following example, we'll consider the scenario of dial-out-only access. The modem should be connected to one of the system's serial ports (A or B) and switched on. The A and B serial ports map to the devices /dev/cua/a and /dev/cua/b, respectively.

To test the modem, use the `tip` command:

```
# tip hardwire
```

where hardwire should be defined in */etc/remote*. The hardwire entry should be similar to this entry:

```
hardwire:\
      :dv=/dev/cua/a:br#19200:el=^C^S^Q^U^D:ie=%$:oe=^D:
```

where 19,200 bps is the connection speed between the modem and the serial port. In addition, */etc/remote* should have a connection string associated with each modem that's connected to the system. For example, the string

```
cua1:dv=/dev/cua/a:p8:br#19200
```

specifies that 19,200 bps is the connection speed between the modem and the serial port, with 8-bit transmission and with no parity enabled. To use this entry specifically, you would use the command

```
# tip cua1
```

If the message

```
connected
```

appears on your terminal, the system is able to communicate successfully with the modem. For Hayes-compatible modems, command strings can be entered directly like this:

```
ATE1V1
```

If you see "ok", the modem is communicating as expected and can be configured to run PPP.

5.6 Administer the Point to Point Protocol (PPP)

PPP is the most commonly used protocol for connecting modems over a phone line (or uncommonly over a normal serial line) to support TCP/IP. It replaces the earlier Serial Line Interface Protocol (SLIP), which did not provide any level of security or authentication for serial line services. The Solaris 9 implementation of PPP is based on the ANU version (**ftp://cs.anu.edu.au/pub/software/ppp**). PPP provides reliable access to the Internet because it includes error correction and the ability to autodetect some network parameters automatically. All of the parameters for the PPP daemon (pppd) are stored in *etc/ppp/options*. Alternatively, for options that are specific to each serial port, a new configuration file can be created (such as *etc/ppp/options.cua.a* for the serial port /dev/cua/a). This is useful where two modems are connected to the two standard serial interfaces on a SPARC system that are connected to two separate modems, which in turn dial completely different ISPs—the lesson for high availability is to "be prepared" for the worst-case scenario. Supporting network operations through a 56K modem is going to be challenging, but not impossible, in an emergency.

The first step in configuring PPP is to insert appropriate configuration information in *etc/ppp/options*. The following options are the most commonly used:

- **<tty_name>** The name of the terminal device to use for communication.

- **<speed>** The speed at which to transmit data.

- **auth** Specifies that authentication is required (noauth specifies that no authentication is required).

- **callback** Requests a callback from the remote server. Useful for saving on long-distance charges!

- **connect** or **init** Specifies the chat script to configure line communications.

- **mru** Sets a Maximum Receive Unit (MRU) value, which specifies a limit on the packet size transmitted by the server.

- **mtu** Sets a Maximum Transmit Unit (MTU) value, which specifies a limit on the packet size transmitted by the client.

Other options may be required, especially for authentication, but using these options is generally sufficient to make a connection.

Once the *etc/ppp/options* file has been set up, a connection can then be made from the command line. For example, to connect using a 56K modem using the chat script *emergency1.chat*, the following command will establish a connection without authentication:

```
# pppd connect 'chat -f emergency1.chat' /dev/cua/a 57600 noauth
```

Project 5-1: Configuring a Listen Port Monitor

This project shows you how to configure a listen port monitor using the `nlsadmin` command. The `nlsadmin` command has the responsibility of managing transports for network services that are STREAMS-compatible.

Step-by-Step

1. Create a TCP/IP database:

```
# nlsadmin -i tcp
```

2. Associate a local hex address with the listener, allowing supported services to be executed with respect to the TLI listener database:

```
# nlsadmin -l \x11331223a11a58310000000000000000 tcp
```

Summary

The `nlsadmin` command can be used to configure port listeners.

5.7 Configure an Internet Connection

`tip` is a command that acts like a terminal. It can be used, for example, to access remote systems directly through a serial port, where one system acts as the console for the other. Below, we'll use the `tip` command to connect a Solaris 9 system to a modem. Before proceeding, however, we'll examine some of the key features of `tip` in its own right.

5

`tip` uses the */etc/remote* file to enable it to make connections through the serial port. For example, if you have a profile set up in */etc/remote*, it's possible to fire up a terminal session immediately by using the command

```
# tip -profile
```

where profile is the name of the profile that you've set up with all the settings that the port requires to operate. `tip` also uses initialization settings in the *.tiprc* file to specify its operational parameters.

The following table shows the most commonly used `tip` commands.

Command	Description
~.	Exits the session.
~c	Changes directory.
~!	Spawns a shell.
~>	Sends a local file.
~<	Receives a remote file.
~p	Sends a local file.
~t	Receives a remote file.
~C	Allows a local application to connect to a remote system.
~#	Issues a `break` command.
~s	Defines a variable.
~^z	Suspends tip.

Ask the Expert

Question: Should I buy a modem if I have a network interface?

Answer: You will need a modem to connect to the Internet via your ISP if you don't have a router that connects directly to your ISP, although your configuration may be different if you have a cable modem or DSL connection.

Question: Couldn't I just log in to the console and fix a network problem without buying a modem?

Answer: Yes, as long as you have convenient physical access to the console. Many servers are rack-mounted in secure facilities, where physical access is not always possible. Alternatively, a server may be located in a remote region that is difficult to physically access. In these situations, a modem is very useful.

Question: `tip` sounds like a pretty useless command—what can I use it for?

Answer: If you have two servers (A and B) that both have a spare serial port, a serial cable can be used to allow console access from A to B, or vice versa. This is very useful if you're running short on terminals and/or monitors, and you need to administer multiple systems.

5

Mastery Check

1. What is the purpose of the command `pmadm -a`?

   A. Adds a port monitor service.

   B. Disarms a port monitor service.

   C. Enables a port monitor service.

   D. Removes a port monitor service.

2. What is the purpose of the command `pmadm -d`?

   A. Adds a port monitor service.

   B. Disarms a port monitor service.

   C. Enables a port monitor service.

   D. Removes a port monitor service.

3. What is the purpose of the command `pmadm -e`?

   A. Adds a port monitor service.

   B. Disarms a port monitor service.

   C. Enables a port monitor service.

   D. Removes a port monitor service.

☑ *Mastery Check*

4. What is the purpose of the command `pmadm -r`?

    A. Adds a port monitor service.

    B. Disarms a port monitor service.

    C. Enables a port monitor service.

    D. Removes a port monitor service.

5. What is the purpose of the command `sacadm -a`?

    A. Attaches a new ttymon.

    B. Arms a ttymon.

    C. Disarms a ttymon.

    D. Initializes a ttymon.

6. What is the purpose of the command `sacadm -e`?

    A. Attaches a new ttymon.

    B. Arms a ttymon.

    C. Disarms a ttymon.

    D. Initializes a ttymon.

7. What is the purpose of the command `sacadm -d`?

    A. Attaches a new ttymon.

    B. Arms a ttymon.

    C. Disarms a ttymon.

    D. Initializes a ttymon.

✓ Mastery Check

8. What is the purpose of the command `sacadm -s`?

   A. Attaches a new ttymon.

   B. Arms a ttymon.

   C. Disarms a ttymon.

   D. Initializes a ttymon.

9. What is the purpose of the command `sacadm -k`?

   A. Attaches a new ttymon.

   B. Kills a ttymon.

   C. Lists ttymon details.

   D. Deletes a ttymon.

10. What is the purpose of the command `sacadm -l`?

   A. Attaches a new ttymon.

   B. Kills a ttymon.

   C. Lists ttymon details.

   D. Deletes a ttymon.

11. What is the purpose of the command `sacadm -r`?

   A. Attaches a new ttymon.

   B. Kills a ttymon.

   C. Lists ttymon details.

   D. Deletes a ttymon.

✓ Mastery Check

12. What command is used to test a modem?

    A. `tip hardwire`

    B. `tip -r`

    C. `checkmodem`

    D. `modemcheck`

13. What command establishes a connection to the modem?

    A. `tip modem`

    B. `tip cua1`

    C. `tip -modem`

    D. `tip -cua1`

14. What options can be set in */etc/ppp/options*?

    A. tty_name

    B. speed

    C. auth

    D. All of the above

15. What options can be set in */etc/ppp/options*?

    A. callback

    B. myu

    C. mxu

    D. All of the above

Module 6

Shell Usage

Critical Skills

The UNIX shell provides users with an interface to the kernel, which provides a number of tools for loading and executing applications, developing programs, and performing repetitive tasks that can be scheduled to occur immediately or at a later time. Linux administrators will be familiar with this from the shell they currently use (usually the Bourne Again Shell, or bash), while Windows administrators may be familiar with the command prompt or WindowScript.

In this module we will examine how to use the shell to run applications, edit files, and make use of customizable settings through environment variables.

6.1 Execute the Shell

A shell is simply a program that is executed for each user who logs into a Solaris system. The shell is the core of multi-user functionality as implemented in UNIX and UNIX-like environments: every user who is concurrently logged into a Solaris system has their own shell spawned, and the activities that they perform in that shell (such as developing applications) are protected from other users. For example, a user can create files in their home directory that no one else has the permission to read, modify, or delete. However, one difference between Solaris and other operating systems is that the list of processes that is spawned from within a shell whenever a command is executed is available for every other user on the system to observe—although with the application of role-based access control or sudo, this observation can be prevented.

Tip

While this feature was useful in early academic environments, the openness of the Solaris process model does pose a security risk when untrusted users share a system with each other. For this reason, authentication tokens like passwords are rarely passed on the command line unmasked.

The login shell for a user is specified in the */etc/passwd* file. The following entry for the user austin shows his shell to be */bin/sh*:

```
$ cat /etc/passwd | grep austin
austin:x:1024:100:Austin Smithers:/home/austin:/bin/sh
```

If the shell is executed when a user logs into a Solaris system, you may be wondering how a user actually "logs in" in the first place!

Tip

There are several ways for a user to log in and spawn a shell in Solaris, including console access or remote access.

1-Minute Drill

● What is a shell?

Console Access

In order to obtain console access, the user must physically be able to access the console of a Solaris system. The console usually consists of a pizza box case connected to a low-resolution terminal and keyboard, or to a high-resolution monitor, mouse, and keyboard. The user will either be presented with an OpenBoot PROM monitor prompt (ok), a login: prompt on a white screen, a CDE login screen, or a GNOME login screen. If the ok prompt is present, then the boot command will need to be issued to bring the system up to a multi-user state, so that access for all users can be granted. Alternatively, if single user access from the console only is required, then the command boot -s may be used.

Whether or not you are greeted with a white login screen, CDE login screen, or GNOME login screen depends on the configuration of your startup files in /etc/init.d. However, in all three cases, you will need to enter a valid username and password in order to spawn a shell as a user on the system. The difference is that if you enter your username and password at the white login screen, you will be presented with a shell prompt on the screen, while the GUI environments will spawn a shell that in turn spawns a terminal process that spawns a user shell for you to enter commands into.

6

● A program that is executed for each user who logs into a Solaris system.

Tip

As you may appreciate, there is a large difference between the amount of work required to display a text screen versus a complete, high-resolution GUI environment, so many other processes are spawned when you log in to CDE or GNOME.

Remote Access

If you are not sitting at the console, you must use some kind of remote access tool to communicate with the system. The most commonly used tools are telnet or rsh, which allow a shell to be spawned and an interactive session created, just like the white login screen. Again, you will need to enter a username and password to log in. From a UNIX or Windows system, the `telnet` command can usually be executed from another shell or through the command prompt, respectively. However, since Solaris has now deprecated telnet in favor of the Secure Shell (SSH), it's possible that telnet may have been disabled on the server that you're trying to log in to. In this case, you'll need to use the ssh client on Linux or UNIX to connect to the server, or install an ssh client on Windows, like PuTTY. Once you have connected to the remote server, if your local system is capable of displaying X11 graphics, on which both the CDE and GNOME are based, it may be possible to start up server applications that use your terminal as a remote display. For example, a server might contain an instance of the Matlab mathematical simulation package (**http://www.mathworks.com/**) that runs simulations on stock market data. A client who connects using rsh or ssh is able to execute CPU-intensive tasks on the server while displaying the generated graphics directly on the client system. Thus, the only CPU overhead for the client involves displaying the graphics sent from the server.

1-Minute Drill

● How can you access a system when not logged into the console?

This flexibility is one reason why Solaris is particularly suited to thin client computing, where a central server conducts operations on behalf of remote clients, which devote their local resources to displaying graphics and handling

---

● By using a remote access program like telnet, rsh, or ssh.

multiple-user processes. It also emphasizes the importance of separating core data processing technology from the user interface—while a centralized server in Solaris does not need to display any graphics or GUI environments at all, other operating systems do not have this flexibility. In addition, Solaris users can choose their own desktop environment—while one user might prefer the cross-platform support of CDE, other users (particularly from a Linux background) will want to use GNOME. The separation of kernel, shell, and user applications from the user interface is similarly available to Linux users. However, one key difference between Linux and Solaris here is that Solaris supports thin hardware clients, in the form of Sun Rays, which are not supported by Linux. These inexpensive desktop clients have no hard drive. Instead, they are supported as diskless clients by a central server, which makes better use of shared resources, such as mirrored disks, and makes software administration much easier because individual clients can be administered from a single server.

If you've just installed Solaris, the super-user "root" account will already be created with the password that you specified. You should be able to log in as the root user, and create other user accounts as required, by using `admintool` or the `useradd` command.

Shell Features

Shells are a key component of the Solaris architecture, so it's important to understand what advantages shells have over purely GUI environments. The following shell features should convince hard-core GUI enthusiasts of the advantages of shells.

Programmable

The shell is designed to be programmable, in order to carry out repetitive tasks easily. Thus, while operations like resetting file permissions in a GUI environment might involve clicking on an icon for every file, a single command usually suffices in the shell. For example, the command

```
$ setfacl -m user:giddens:r-- *.txt
```

grants read access to all text files in the current working directory, but only for the user giddens. The wildcard * here indicates that all files will the extension *.txt* will be processed. However, it's important to note that file extensions like *.txt* are conventional and in no way mandatory. This is a key difference between

Solaris and some other operating systems, since executable files are defined as any file that has an executable bit set for the current user rather than being associated with a file extension. For example, the application *cdplayer.exe* must have the executable attribute set in order to be run by a user. However, an executable file in Solaris is just as likely to have no extension at all—thus, *cdplayer* might be a more common executable name.

1-Minute Drill

● How does Solaris identify executable programs?

Tip

Directory listings give information about file permissions such as the executable attribute.

System Configuration

While GUI tools such as the admintool can be used to configure Solaris systems, most system configuration data is stored in text files, which admintool simply reads and writes to as necessary. Traditionally, Solaris configuration files are stored in a flat file database format—often colon-delimited, such as password and group files. Given the large number of text processing tools supplied with Solaris, configuration becomes much easier. For example, consider a system whose domain name is being modified. Rather than individually editing each file, and changing each instance of the old domain name to the new domain name manually, a simple sed filter can achieve the same task by using its powerful regular expression handling:

```
$ cat configuration.txt | sed 's/olddomain.com/newdomain.com/g' \
  > configuration.new; mv configuration.txt configuration.orig; \
  mv configuration.new configuration.txt
```

In a script, the "configuration" name could be replaced by the variable $1, allowing different filenames to be specified from a list. Such a list could be

---

● By checking the executable file permission.

generated by the `find` command, which prints a list of full pathnames to files that match a logical condition. For example, to print a list of all files that have the extension *.txt* in the */usr* file system, the following command could be used:

```
$ find /usr -name '*.txt' -print
```

The `find` command also allows a command to be executed each time a match to the file specification is made, allowing our sed script to be executed individually on each file. It is the powerful combination of tools on the command line that makes the shell attractive.

Command Set

In addition to being able to execute applications from the command line, the shell has built-in keywords and commands that form a complete programming language. This means it is possible to evaluate logical conditions, assign values to variables, operate on variables, and iterate through loops.

Tip

While the data structures available are generally limited to simple variables (that is, no arrays), the C-like syntax of most shells makes it easy for C programmers to write shell scripts that perform useful tasks.

For example, the `for` command can be used to iterate around a loop a number of times. The following script prints out a set of strings defined within the loop itself:

```
for herb in parsley sage rosemary thyme
do
   echo $herb
done
```

The output from the script is shown here:

```
parsley
sage
rosemary
thyme
```

Paths

Commands can be executed by using a relative or absolute path to the file containing the program to be run. For example, if the program */bin/ls* is to be run, it can simply be entered on the command line:

```
$ ls
```

This is a relative reference, because no absolute path is defined. However, if the directory */bin* is not in the user's PATH, then the application will not run because it cannot be located. More insidiously, if the */bin* directory is in the PATH, but it is preceded by another directory that also has a file called *ls*, then that application rather than */bin/ls* will be executed, leading to unexpected results. It's often safer to use an absolute reference to a command to ensure that the intended program is run:

```
$ /bin/ls
```

Alternatively, the . directory name can be used to specify that an application found in the current directory be executed:

```
$ cd /bin
$ ./ls
```

1-Minute Drill

● What environment variable defines the user's path?

6.2 Manage Jobs

The shell features advanced job management and scheduling capabilities. Multiple applications can be started from the shell as individual processes, which can be sent into the background while other command processing occurs in the foreground. For example, if three applications needed to be started in the

---

● The PATH variable.

background to launch a database server, and also run Netscape Navigator and a web server, the following command sequence could be used:

```
# startdb&
[1] startdb &
# netscape&
[2] netscape &
# httpd&
[3] httpd &
#
```

Notice that in each case a sequential job ID is issued to each background process, which allows it to be bought into the foreground at any time by using the fg command. In addition, each process has a unique process ID (PID) that allows signals to be sent to the process to modify its behavior. In all cases, control returns to the foreground after each application is sent to the background by using the ampersand "&" symbol.

If a command has already been executed in the foreground, it can be sent into the background by using the CTRL-Z key combination, at which point the command is simply suspended.

```
$ matlab
^Z[4] + Stopped (SIGTSTP)    matlab
```

To send the job into the background, the bg command must be used:

```
$ bg
[4] matlab&
```

Once the application must be brought back into the foreground, the fg command can be used:

```
$ fg
matlab
```

However, since there are already three other jobs running in the background, how does the shell know which application to bring into the foreground? Since the jobs are pushed into a last in first out (LIFO) stack, the fg command simply pops the job number off the top of the stack, which is the most recent job sent into the background. However, it is possible to bring another job into the foreground by specifying its job number. For example, to bring job 3 into the foreground, the following command can be used:

```
$ fg 3
httpd
```

To generate a list of all jobs running in the background, the jobs command can be used:

```
$ jobs
[4]  +  Running        matlab&
[3]  +  Running        httpd&
[2]  +  Running        netscape&
[1]  +  Running        startdb&
```

Any jobs that are suspended will also be flagged by the jobs command. Note that if jobs have been sent to the background and the parent shell exits, a new shell will not be able to manage those jobs directly. Instead, the kill command must be used to send a signal. For example, to stop the httpd process sent into the background from a shell that has exited, the ps command should be used to obtain a process ID (PID) for the httpd process so that a signal can be sent:

```
$ ps -a | grep httpd
1434 pts/2     0:34 httpd
```

Ask the Expert

Question: Realistically, who ever runs more than one process per terminal?

Answer: Typically, this is done by system administrators and developers who are adept at job management and who can be productive by using a dumb terminal to spawn a shell. This approach may seem alien to administrators who are used to a GUI environment, but using a single shell for running multiple jobs is one of the key advantages of UNIX over its competitors.

Here, the PID for httpd is 1434. To terminate the process, the SIGKILL signal needs to be sent by using the `kill` command:

```
$ kill -9 1434
```

More information on processes and signals is provided in Module 10.

Project 6-1: Running Background Jobs

This project shows you how run multiple applications in the background from a single shell, whether spawned from the console or run on a remote terminal.

Step-by-Step

1. Change directory to */bin*:

```
$ cd /bin
```

2. Run the Bourne shell in the background:

```
$ sh&
[1] sh&
$
```

3. Run csh in the background:

```
$ csh &
[2] csh&
$
```

4. Run the Cornell shell in the background:

```
$ tcsh &
[3] tcsh&
$
```

5. Check the running jobs:

```
$ jobs
[3] +  Running        tcsh&
```

6

```
[2] + Running     csh&
[1] + Running     sh&
```

Summary

Jobs can be managed in the shell effectively by using the ampersand operator and the `jobs` command.

6.3 Use the Shell

Environment variables store data that is used by applications and the shell for common operations. For example, to match a token supplied on the command line that is a program name, the shell reads entries stored in the PATH environment variable. PATH consists of a colon-delimited list of fields that correspond to directory names: thus, the first directory is searched for a match to the token, and if located, the program is executed. If a match is not found, the second directory is checked, and so on. To display the current value of the PATH variable, or any other environment variable, the `echo` command can be used:

```
$ echo $PATH
/:/usr/bin:/usr/sbin:/usr/local/bin:/.
```

Table 6-1 displays the most commonly used environment variables. Of course, your applications may define their own environment variables that must be set in order for an application to operate correctly. For example, Oracle requires the ORA_HOME environment variable to be set to the base directory of installation, while the Java Virtual Machine looks for the JAVA_HOME variable to set its base directory.

Variable	Description
CDPATH	Set of directories searchable by the `cd` command
COLUMNS	Number of columns to display on the screen
DISPLAY	Terminal name for remote X11 display
EDITOR	Path to the default editor
HOME	Current user's home directory
HOSTNAME	Name of the local host
LD_LIBRARY_PATH	Path containing a list of all directories where libraries are stored
LOGNAME	Username of the current user
MAIL	Directory where mail is stored locally

Table 6-1   A Few Commonly Used Environment Variables

Variable	Description
MANPATH	Path to system manual (man) pages
NNTPSERVER	Hostname of the local news (NNTP) server
PS1	Default shell prompt
PS2	Alternative shell prompt
SHELL	Full path to the current shell
TERM	Terminal emulation type
TZ	Time zone setting

Table 6-1 A Few Commonly Used Environment Variables (*continued*)

In order to set an environment variable, the `set` command is used in conjunction with the `export` command. The following example set the TERM variable to the vt100 type, and exports the variable so that applications can access it:

```
$ TERM=vt100; export TERM
```

In order to display the currently set variables and their values, the `set` command can be used:

```
$ set
SHELL=/bin/sh
COLUMNS=132
DISPLAY=felicity:0.0
EDITOR=/usr/bin/vi
HOME=/home/austin
HOSTNAME=felicity
LD_LIBRARY_PATH=/usr/local/lib:/usr/dt/lib:/home/austin/lib
LINES=24
LOGNAME=austin
MAIL=/var/mail/austin
MANPATH=/usr/dt/man:/usr/man:/usr/openwin/share/man:/home/austin/man
PATH=/usr/bin:/bin:/usr/local/bin:/usr/ccs/bin
PS1='\$ '
PS2='> '
TERM=vt220
TZ=Australia/NSW
```

The `env` command also displays the values of environmental variables.

Ask the Expert

Question: How many environment variables do I really need?

Answer: As many as your installed applications require, and as many as you wish to define in your shell.

Customization

Many aspects of the shell are user and site customizable. For example, default *.profile* files can be installed so that all users have access to the correct paths and environment variables to operate effectively on the system. One aspect of customization is the ability to set shell prompts for different levels. The default shell prompt, $ by default and specified by PS1, is used for all operations. The alternative shell prompt is used for prompting input which extends over more than one line. However, since many CDE and GNOME users have multiple terminals operating on different systems, it can be useful to display a string like user@host > as the prompt, because it's easy to become confused between shells with the same $ prompt. To set the default prompt to this format, the following command can be used:

```
$ PS1='\u\@\h>'; export PS1
```

Alternatively, to display the privilege level as well as the username and host, the following command could be used:

```
$ PS1='\u\@\h\$'; export PS1
```

Table 6-2 shows the most commonly used shell prompt settings that can be combined for a customized prompt.

Setting	Description	Output
\a	Beep (not displayed)	audio
\d	Today's date	Tue Feb 5
\h	Unqualified hostname	felicity

Table 6-2 Shell Prompt Options

Setting	Description	Output
\H	Qualified hostname	felicity.cassowary.net
\s	Shell name	sh
\t	Today's time (12 hour form)	11:52:33
\T	Today's time (24 hour form)	15:12:21
\@	Today's time (AM/PM form)	09:32pm
\u	Current username	austin
\$	Privilege level	$ or #

Table 6-2   Shell Prompt Options (*continued*)

Input/Output

6

The shell has two means of allowing data to be passed: standard input allows data to be passed to applications for input, while standard output is passed back to the shell. Whether or not the shell prints the output to the screen depends on whether a pipe or redirection operator is used to pass the standard output of one application as standard input to another. For example, the cat command prints the contents of a file to standard output. The following command prints the group database:

```
$ cat /etc/group
root::0:root
other::1:
bin::2:root,bin,daemon
sys::3:root,bin,sys,adm
adm::4:root,adm,daemon
uucp::5:root,uucp
mail::6:root
tty::7:root,tty,adm
lp::8:root,lp,adm
nuucp::9:root,nuucp
dev::10:
```

A pipe can be used to redirect the standard output to the standard input of a filter, which then prints the result to the screen. The grep command, for example, matches strings for a specific pattern. The following command filters the group database for the string `root`, and thus prints the lines of the group database that contain an entry for root:

```
$ cat /etc/group | grep root
root::0:root
bin::2:root,bin,daemon
sys::3:root,bin,sys,adm
adm::4:root,adm,daemon
uucp::5:root,uucp
mail::6:root
tty::7:root,tty,adm
lp::8:root,lp,adm
nuucp::9:root,nuucp
```

This process can be repeated infinitely—a further filter, such as sort, can be used to order the results of the grep operation in descending alphabetical order based on the first character of each line:

```
$ cat /etc/group | grep root | sort -r
adm::4:root,adm,daemon
bin::2:root,bin,daemon
lp::8:root,lp,adm
mail::6:root
nuucp::9:root,nuucp
root::0:root
sys::3:root,bin,sys,adm
tty::7:root,tty,adm
uucp::5:root,uucp
```

The following are the most commonly used redirection operators in the shell:

a < b	Redirects the contents of file b to the program a.
a > b	Executes program a and sends the output to file b, overwriting the existing contents of b.
a | b	Executes program a and pipes the output to program b.
a >> b	Executes program a and sends the output to file b, appending to the existing contents of b.

Substitution

Closely related to the notion of redirection is substitution—a command being executed whose output is then passed as input to another program. For example, if you have a set of reports that are updated and printed often, they can be printed by using the following command:

```
$ lp `cat reports.txt`
```

If the file report.txt contains the following entries:

```
sales.txt
hr.txt
engineer.txt
forecast.txt
```

Then the command is expanded to form the following command:

```
$ lp sales.txt hr.txt engineer.txt forecast.txt
```

6.4 Manage Different Shells

One of the great features of Solaris is the ability to choose your own shell from the database of system-recognized shells stored in *etc/shells*. Different shells can have quite different features, so you need to match your requirements to the best shell for your day-to-day needs. In the following section, we review the key features of the most commonly used shells. Keep in mind that shell selection is a personal choice, and that your favorite shell may not always suit your users.

6.5 Run the Bourne Shell

The Bourne Shell (/bin/sh) is the original UNIX shell developed by Steve Bourne. By convention, it is always used to write system startup scripts, found in */etc/init.d*, and many other configuration files. It has poor terminal handling and lacks many user-oriented features like command histories. However, it is important to understand the Bourne shell as an administrator so that you can create new scripts and maintain existing ones. The key features of Bourne shell are

●   Support for piping on the command line with the "|" operator: standard output from one application can be piped to the standard input of another application.

- Redirection of input and output using the "<" and ">"operators, respectively, to overwrite data, or redirection of input and output using the "<<" and ">>"operators, respectively, to append data.

- Commands can be executed with a number of arguments that are processed internally by the application.

- Execution of multiple commands when separated by a semicolon ";".

- Setting and reading environment variables.

- Logical evaluation of variable values using "if/then/else".

- Creation of functions that can be called from within the main body of the script and from other functions.

- Iteration of a loop for a specific number of iterations using "for".

- Repeatedly executing a code block until a logical condition is met using "while".

In addition, the following commands are built in to the Bourne shell:

.	Reads in a file containing a script and executes it.
bg	Sends a process into the background.
break	Quits execution of a loop.
cd	Changes working directory.
continue	Continues execution of a loop.
echo	Prints a string and/or variable values to standard output.
eval	Evaluates an expression.
exec	Runs a command.
exit	Quits the shell.
export	Allows variable values to be set for the execution of subsequent commands.
fg	Brings a job into the foreground.
jobs	Displays a summary of jobs sent into the background.
kill	Sends a signal to a job.
newgrp	Assumes a new effective group ID (GID).
pwd	Prints working directory.
read	Reads from standard input.

`return`	Sets a return value for a function.
`set`	Sets the value of a variable.
`stop`	Stops a process from running.
`times`	Displays user and system CPU time used for the shell.
`ulimit`	Sets a resource limit on a command.
`umask`	Sets a default permission string used when creating new files.
`unset`	Removes a variable from memory.

We will examine how some of these commands are used in the scripts developed in Chapter 7.

When the Bourne shell is spawned as part of the login process, it reads the */etc/default/login* and *.profile* files, and executes the statements contained therein. This allows various commands to be initialized every time a user logs into a shell.

6

Tip

When a user wants to log out of a shell, the `exit` command (or CTRL-D key combination) can be entered.

One key command that is often run is the `ls` command, which displays the contents of the current working directory. It has the form `ls dir`, where `dir` is the directory name whose contents are to be printed to standard output. For example, to display the names of files stored in the */home* directory, the following command could be used:

```
$ ls /home
macbeth    campbell    lam    yip    yeung    jang
```

Ask the Expert

Question: Do people really write applications using shell scripting?

Answer: Yes. Since shells support variables, looping, logical decisions, and functions, they are a complete programming language. Many UNIX applications use shell scripts for configuring and building applications.

This command is often used when navigating the file system.

The Bourne shell man page contains a list of commands and options that are specific to Bourne shell (man sh). For Linux users, there is an enhanced version of the Bourne shell called the Bourne Again Shell, which they will know as "bash".

Tip

The bash shell has many advanced features, including terminal handling and arrow key support for command history and line editing.

6.6 Run the Korn Shell

The Korn shell, developed by David Korn, extends the functionality of the Bourne shell in some important ways. For example, case and select commands are included in the basic shell syntax. In addition, command aliasing is also supported, making it easy to invoke commands with many commonly used options by invoking a single command name. An example is an alias called `dir` for the `ls` command, which lists the names of files in a directory. To set this alias, the following command is used:

```
alias dir="/bin/ls "
```

One of the useful features of the Korn shell is that it reads in a file called *.profile* every time a user logs in. The *.profile* can contain any valid shell command, such as alias definitions. In addition, environment variables can be set, along with a number of built-in options such as noclobber and ignoreeof. The noclobber option prevents existing files from being accidentally deleted when their contents are overwritten by output piped to a file. For example, if a file called *report.txt* exists in the current working directory and the following command is executed, the contents of *report.txt* will normally be overwritten:

```
$ cat report.txt
This is the report.
$ cat "This is a fake report." > report.txt
$ cat report.txt
This is a fake report.
```

However, if the noclobber option is set, the following error message will result from an attempt to overwrite the contents of *report.txt*:

```
$ cat "This is a fake report." > report.txt
report.txt: file exists
```

To set the noclobber option, the following option can be set in the *.profile* or issued on the command line:

```
set +o noclobber
```

To remove the noclobber option, the following option can be set:

```
set -o noclobber
```

6

The tilde prefix allows users to refer to home directories based on the tilde character. For example, to change the working directory to your home directory, the following command could be used:

```
$ cd ~
```

Alternatively, another user's home directory can be set as the working directory by appending their username to the tilde. The following command would therefore change the working directory to the user frances' home directory:

```
$ cd ~frances
```

The ignoreeof option prevents a user from accidentally logging out by using the EOF character (CTRL-D), rather than using the `exit` command. To set the ignoreeof option, the following command can be used in the *.profile* or on the command line:

```
$ set -o ignoreeof
```

The Korn shell man page contains a list of commands and options that are specific to Korn shell (man ksh).

6.7 Run the C Shell

The C Shell (/bin/csh) has a command syntax that is based on the C programming language. This makes it easy for experienced C programmers to use the C shell and to write scripts using the same syntax. The Cornell shell (/bin/tcsh) is enhanced version of the C shell that has good terminal handling and support for arrow keys in command history and line editing. Some differences exist between C shell and Bourne shell—for example, environment variables are set using the `setenv` command, rather than `export`, while normal variables are set by using the `set` command. In addition, the initialization file for the shell is *.cshrc*, and not *.profile*.

Tip

C shell has some similarities to the Korn shell in that options like noclobber are supported, and command aliases can be defined on the command line or in the *.cshrc* file.

One of the nice features of C shell is the ability to declare and operate on array-like data structures. For example, the names of a set of users could be defined by the variable users with the following command:

```
% set users = ( joe bill jane bobbi )
```

Members of the array users can be referred to by subscript. Thus, to print the name of the third member, we would use the command

```
% echo $users[3]
```

Command history is advanced in C shell, since previous commands can be repeated by simply using the history number they are associated with. To print a command history, just use the `history` command:

```
% history
512 ls
511 mv new.data old.data
510 netscape
509 file new.data
```

In order to repeat a command (like netscape), the following command can be used:

```
% !510
```

The number of commands kept in the command history can be set by using the history variable. Thus, to set the number of commands to 10, the following command would be used:

```
% set history=10
```

☑ *Mastery Check*

1. What is the purpose of the . command?

    A. Reads in a file containing a script and executes it.

    B. Sends a process into the background.

    C. Quits execution of a loop.

    D. Changes working directory.

2. What is the purpose of the bg command?

    A. Reads in a file containing a script and executes it.

    B. Sends a process into the background.

    C. Quits execution of a loop.

    D. Changes working directory.

3. What is the purpose of the break command?

    A. Reads in a file containing a script and executes it.

    B. Sends a process into the background.

    C. Quits execution of a loop.

    D. Changes working directory.

☑ Mastery Check

4. What is the purpose of the cd command?

  A. Reads in a file containing a script and executes it.

  B. Sends a process into the background.

  C. Quits execution of a loop.

  D. Changes working directory.

5. What is the purpose of the continue command?

  A. Continues execution of a loop.

  B. Prints a string and/or variable values to standard output.

  C. Evaluates an expression.

  D. Runs a command.

6. What is the purpose of the echo command?

  A. Continues execution of a loop.

  B. Prints a string and/or variable values to standard output.

  C. Evaluates an expression.

  D. Runs a command.

7. What is the purpose of the eval command?

  A. Continues execution of a loop.

  B. Prints a string and/or variable values to standard output.

  C. Evaluates an expression.

  D. Runs a command.

☑ Mastery Check

8. What is the purpose of the `exec` command?

   A. Continues execution of a loop.

   B. Prints a string and/or variable values to standard output.

   C. Evaluates an expression.

   D. Runs a command.

9. What is the purpose of the `exit` command?

   A. Quits the shell.

   B. Allows variable values to be set for the execution of subsequent commands.

   C. Brings a job into the foreground.

   D. Displays a summary of jobs sent into the background.

10. What is the purpose of the `export` command?

   A. Quits the shell.

   B. Allows variable values to be set for the execution of subsequent commands.

   C. Brings a job into the foreground.

   D. Displays a summary of jobs sent into the background.

11. What is the purpose of the `fg` command?

   A. Quits the shell.

   B. Allows variable values to be set for the execution of subsequent commands.

   C. Brings a job into the foreground.

   D. Displays a summary of jobs sent into the background.

6

☑ *Mastery Check*

12. What is the purpose of the `jobs` command?

A. Quits the shell.

B. Allows variable values to be set for the execution of subsequent commands.

C. Brings a job into the foreground.

D. Displays a summary of jobs sent into the background.

13. What is the purpose of the `kill` command?

A. Sends a signal to a job.

B. Assumes a new effective group ID (GID).

C. Prints working directory.

D. Reads from standard input.

14. What is the purpose of the `newgrp` command?

A. Sends a signal to a job.

B. Assumes a new effective group ID (GID).

C. Prints working directory.

D. Reads from standard input.

15. What is the purpose of the `pwd` command?

A. Sends a signal to a job.

B. Assumes a new effective group ID (GID).

C. Prints working directory.

D. Reads from standard input.

Module 7

Shell Scripts and File Permissions

Critical Skills

7.1   Administer file permissions

7.2   Set symbolic and octal permission codes

7.3   Manage default permissions

7.4   Set the sticky bit

7.5   Execute common shell script commands

7.6   Write scripts

7.7   Test file properties

One of the great benefits of using shells is the ability to combine shell commands and operators together to form scripts that can be executed by individual users to perform complex operations. The most important skill a Solaris administrator can learn is to write shell scripts that automate many of the mundane tasks that must be performed on a system. Many scripts start as small, single-purpose applications that eventually become more general purpose as iterations of development result in lean, useful code. However, spaghetti code can easily result from a failure to implement good testing and design techniques when writing scripts.

In this module, we will examine how to write scripts to perform a number of key tasks. In addition, we will look closely at the role of file permissions, including executable file permissions, and a set of commands that are commonly used within Solaris scripts.

7.1 Administer File Permissions

Every Solaris file must be owned by a user and have a group associated with it. The file owner is usually, but not always, the user who created the file. In addition, the group associated with the file is usually the primary group of the user who created the file. Super-users can change the owner of any file, and the group associated with any file.

Note

Unprivileged users can only change the group of files that they own—they cannot change the group associated with other files, nor can they change the ownership of any files.

Every Solaris file has a permission set associated with it. This permission can be expressed as an octal code or a string, and defines the type of operations that can be performed on a file, and the users who can perform them. The three basic permission types are

read, r	Allows a file to be opened and its contents read.
write, w	Allows a file to be opened and its contents overwritten.
execute, x	Allows a file to run as an executable program.

Each of these permission types is associated with a user flag. In combination, the permission type and user flag specify what each user can do with a file. The user flags are

user, u	Sets a permission for the file owner.
group, g	Sets a permission for members of the group associated with the file.
other, o	Sets a permission for all users.

When setting a permission, there are two operators that can be used:

+	Sets a permission in the affirmative.
-	Sets a permission in the negative.

For example, to allow members of a group to write to a file, the string g+w would be used. However, to prevent members of a group writing to a file, the string g-w would be used. These strings are used in conjunction with the chmod command.

7.2 Set Symbolic and Octal Permission Codes

7

Note

Users who own files can use chmod on them; however, the super-user can chmod any file on the system.

The ls command, in its long form, reports on the permissions on files contained within a specific directory by displaying the permissions string associated with each file. Let's examine some examples to see how chmod and ls work together.

1-Minute Drill

- What permission allows a file to be opened and read?
- What permission allows a file to be opened for writing?
- What permission allows a file to be opened and executed?

- read, r
- write, w
- execute, x

Say the user jasmine creates a file called */home/jasmine/secrets.txt*. Depending on her umask, or the default permission assigned to a user's files when created, her file listing looks like this:

```
$ cd ~; ls -l secrets.txt
-rw-r--r--   1 jasmine   staff        1024 Feb  1 11:33 secrets.txt
```

Let's read the entry from the left to right:

- The file is a plain file, determined by the leading "-".

- The file has read-write permissions for the file owner indicated by the rw- string (that is, no execute permissions).

- The file has read-only permissions for members of the staff group, indicated by the r-- string (that is, no write or execute permissions).

- The file has read-only permissions for everyone on the system as indicated by the r-- string (that is, no write or execute permissions).

- The owner of the file is jasmine.

- The file is associated with the staff group.

- The size of the file is 1,024 bytes.

- The file creation date and time was Feb 1, at 11:33 A.M.

- The filename is *secrets.txt*.

If jasmine wanted to remove write permissions for herself, she would use the following command:

```
$ chmod u-w secret.txt
$ ls -l secret.txt
-r--r--r--   1 jasmine   staff        1024 Feb  1 11:33 secrets.txt
```

Alternatively, if Jasmine wanted to add execute permissions for herself and for the staff group, the following command could be used:

```
$ chmod ug+x secret.txt
$ ls -l secret.txt
-r-xr-xr--   1 jasmine   staff        1024 Feb  1 11:33 secrets.txt
```

To remove read access for all users, jasmine would type the following:

```
$ chmod -r secret.txt
$ ls -l secret.txt
---x-x---   1 jasmine   staff        1024 Feb  1 11:33 secrets.txt
```

If Jasmine was a member of another group and she wanted that group to have access to the file ahead of her primary group, she could use the chgrp command. For example, to change the group from staff to admin, the following command would be used:

```
$ chgrp admin secrets.txt
```

If the root user decided to change the ownership of the file *secret.txt* to nobody, the following command would be used:

```
# chown nobody secret.txt
```

The file would now be owned by the user nobody, and the user jasmine would not be able to chmod it any longer.

Creating a directory follows a similar path, although the permissions string is a little different. The file is flagged with the permission "d", and users who are allowed to access the directory must have the executable permission set. For example, if the user jade creates a directory called */home/jade/neural.*, depending on her umask, her directory listing would look like this:

```
$ cd ~
$ mkdir neural
$ ls -l
total 8
drwxr-xr-x   2 jade   sales        512 Feb  6 10:02 neural
```

Let's read the entry from the left to right:

- The file is a directory, determined by the leading "d".

- The file has read-write-execute permissions for the file owner, indicated by the rwx string.

- The file has read-execute permissions for members of the sales group, indicated by the r-x string (that is, no write permissions).

- The file has read-execute permissions for everyone on the system, as indicated by the r-x string (that is, no write permissions).

- The owner of the file is jade.

- The file is associated with the sales group.

- The size of the file is 512 bytes.

- The file creation date and time was Feb 6, at 10:02 A.M.

- The filename is *neural*.

Octal Codes

Since directory entries are actually files, Solaris doesn't treat them any differently than normal files in terms of ownership operations such as chgrp and chown. If you find the symbolic permission codes difficult to remember, it may be easier for you to use their octal equivalents, where the appropriate code can be easily calculated. The main difference between symbolic and octal permissions is that the former specifies relative changes in permissions, while the latter specifies absolute changes in permissions. This can be very important when writing scripts, where the existing permissions on a file are not known.

Note

Although it is possible to construct to set of chmod commands using symbolic permission code to remove all permissions, and then explicitly the permissions that are required, it's generally easier just to use the octal.

The octal code consists of three numbers, which are read left to right: the first number represents user permissions, the second number represents group permissions, and the third number represents permissions for all users. The number for each category is composed by adding 4 for read, 2 for write and 1 for execute. Thus, to set read-only permissions for all users on a file, the following command would be used:

```
$ chmod 444 file
```

To set read-write permissions for the owner, but read-only permissions for the group and all other users, the following command would be used:

```
$ chmod 644 file
```

To set read-write-execute permissions for the owner, but read-only permissions for the group and all other users, the following command would be used:

```
$ chmod 744 file
```

To set read-write-execute permissions for the owner, but no permissions for the group and all other users, the following command would be used:

```
$ chmod 700 file
```

File permission octal values can be summarized in the following way:

	U	G	O
R	4	4	0
W	2	0	0
X	1	0	0
	7	4	0

7

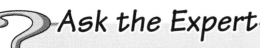

Ask the Expert

Question: Should I use octal or symbolic codes?

Answer: This depends on whether you are a "symbolic" thinker or an "arithmetic" thinker. Some administrators find it easier to apply symbolic file permissions, while others find octal much faster since all permissions can be bundled into a single code. The only trap with octal codes is that they set permissions absolutely—symbolic permissions are always relative.

7.3 Manage Default Permissions

Each system has a default specification for setting file permissions whenever a file is created. This value is known as the user mask (umask) and is specified as an octal code, just like normal permissions can be. The selection of an appropriate system umask will depend on organizational requirements—while some university departments prefer to allow group read access, by default, to a user's files, commercial organizations may decide to restrict all nonuser access to a user's files. The system-wide setting can be overridden by individual users, who can set their own umask on the command line in the file that is read in by their login shell (for example, *.profile* for the Bourne shell).

The trick with setting a umask is to subtract the permissions that you want to remove by default from the umask. Assuming that the default file permission is 777 (that is, all permissions), then to remove write permissions from all files for the group and other users, the umask would be 022. This umask also sets read-write-execute access by default on a user's files.

Tip

To remove all access permissions from groups and other users, the umask should be set to 700.

Special Permissions (setuid and setgid)

The file permissions for user, group, and all users that we've covered in the previous sections suffice for the normal file operations of most users. There are a number of special file permissions, however, which can be set by the super-user to allow commands to be executed by an unprivileged user as a privileged user or as a member of a privileged group. If this sounds like it defeats the Solaris security model—it does. However, with appropriate restrictions and sandboxing, setting these permissions can allow useful access to certain services without users having to annoy the sysadmin. For example, some previous versions of Solaris (in the SunOS 4.x range) did not allow anyone but the root user to eject a mounted CD-ROM volume. While this obviously prevents file corruption from occurring, or a malicious user from ejecting a disk while others are using it, the restriction means that when a console user needed to change disks, he or she had to call the sysadmin. Fortunately, the volume daemon (vold) is now provided as a setuid program that allows users on the console to eject floppy disks and CD-ROMs as required. The risk is that many applications allow users to spawn a shell, in which case the shell would be spawned with the effective user ID of root, and not of the unprivileged user. This would give the unprivileged user super-user access to the system. It's therefore necessary to closely examine any such features in an application that you are allowing to run as setuid root.

The setuid bit can be set by using a different permission code to form a permissions string for use with chmod. For example, to set a permission on an application called vold, owned by root, the following command would be used:

```
# chmod u+s vold
```

To set the file as setgid for root's default group, the following command would be used:

```
# chmod g+s vold
```

7.4 Set the Sticky Bit

The sticky bit can be set on shared directories to prevent users from overwriting each other's files, even though the directory allows multiple users to write files in a directory. This allows a public file area to be maintained, for print or e-mail spooling (or file sharing), while maintaining the integrity of each file as created by each user. While the super-user can delete any file in a directory protected by a sticky bit, other users cannot do so unless given explicit group write permissions. This allows users to write files in a common area without fearing that their data will be tampered with.

The sticky bit can be set by using a specific permission code to form a permissions string for use with chmod. To set the sticky bit on a directory called /scratch, owned by root, the following command would be used:

```
# chmod +t /scratch
```

7.5 Execute Common Shell Script Commands

When writing scripts, many shell and system commands are used. However, a subset of these commands is used often enough that it's worth knowing them before starting to write scripts. In this section, we'll examine how to use these commands individually before combining them in scripts.

basename

The basename command is used to remove a matched expression from a text string. It is often used in scripts to manually change a file's extension after some file operation has been performed. For example, to remove the extension *.txt* from a file called *datafile.txt* and assign it the extension *.bak*, the following commands could be used:

```
$ base=`basename datafile.txt .txt`.bak
$ mv datafile.txt $base
```

cat

The cat command is used to send the contents of a file to standard output. It is one of the most commonly used commands. For example, to print the contents of the file */home/paul/dna.txt*, the following command could be used:

```
$ cat /home/paul/dna.txt
cggatgctagcggtaatgcttaggat
```

cd

The cd command changes the current working directory for the user. Since pathnames can be specified as relative or absolute, changing the working directory can have a profound effect on a command's execution. For example, if the user jade has a directory called *bin* located in her home directory (that is, */home/jade/bin*), then typing the following command where the current working directory is her home directory will take her to */home/jade/bin*:

```
$ cd bin
```

However, when the same command is executed from the root directory (/), then jade would be taken to the /bin directory.

date

The date command is used to print the current date and time. The default display looks like this:

```
$ date
Thu Feb  7 08:49:25  2002
```

The format of the date command can be customized for a specific script's requirements. For example, to display the date in MMDDYYYY format, the following command could be used:

```
$ date '+%m/%d/%Y'
02/07/2002
```

echo

The echo command is used to print character strings to standard output. These strings can be composed of plaintext or mixed with environment variables. For example, to display the current working directory, echo can be used to print the PWD environment variable:

```
$ echo $PWD
/home/jade
```

In this case, $PWD is expanded by the shell to produce the string /home/jade. Alternatively, it is possible to combine normal strings with expansions of environment variables to produce more useful text:

```
$ echo Dir: $PWD
Dir: /home/jade
```

Strings to be echoed can either be enclosed in single or double quotes. When enclosed in single quotes, the string is treated as literal—that is, expansion is performed:

```
$ echo 'Dir: $PWD'
Dir: $PWD
```

However, if double quotes are used, then $PWD will be expanded as expected:

```
$ echo "Dir: $PWD"
Dir: /home/jade
```

The output from `echo` can be redirected to a file for create or append operations. For example, the following redirects the output of echoing `date` to a file /tmp/date.txt:

```
$ echo "Date: `date`" > /tmp/date.txt
$ cat /tmp/date.txt
Date: Thu Feb  7 10:26:21  2002
```

If we repeat the command one hour later, the contents of /tmp/date.txt will be overwritten:

```
$ echo "Date: `date`" > /tmp/date.txt
$ cat /tmp/date.txt
Date: Thu Feb  7 11:26:21  2002
```

However, if we wish to append new date entries to existing date entries, we would need to use the appropriate redirection operator:

```
$ echo "Date: `date`" >> /tmp/date.txt
$ cat /tmp/date.txt
Date: Thu Feb  7 10:26:21  2002
Date: Thu Feb  7 11:26:21  2002
```

grep

The `grep` command searches for regular expressions in a file according to a pattern specification. If a match is found in a file, the line of the file where the match is made is printed to standard output. It is very useful for searching text databases. For example, if we had a database of country names stored in *names.txt*, searching for a string like `denmark` should produce the following result:

```
$ grep denmark names.txt
denmark
```

If "denmark" wasn't found in *names.txt*, no output would be produced. Alternatively, `grep` has a number of options that can be used to modify its output. For example, to print the lines that did not have a match for the string `denmark`, the following command would be used:

```
$ grep -v denmark names.txt
iceland
finland
sweden
norway
```

head

The `head` command is used to print the first few lines or page of a file to standard output. The number of lines to be printed can be specified by passing the "-" argument with the number of lines to be printed. For example, to print the first five lines of the file */etc/syslog.conf*, the following command would be used:

```
$ head -5 /etc/syslog.conf
#ident  "@(#)syslog.conf        1.4     96/10/11 SMI"   /* SunOS 5.0 */
# Copyright (c) 1991-1993, by Sun Microsystems, Inc.
# syslog configuration file.
# This file is processed by m4 so be careful to quote (`') names
# that match m4 reserved words.  Also, within ifdef's, arguments
```

7

mkdir

The `mkdir` command creates new directory entries whose names can be specified by using absolute or relative pathnames. For example, the following command creates a directory called *data* in the */home/jasmine* directory:

```
$ mkdir /home/jasmine/data
```

Alternatively, the following relative directory name reference has the same effect:

```
$ cd /home/jasmine
$ mkdir data
```

To create a directory several levels deep where the immediate parents do not exist, the −p option must be passed. For example, to create the directory */opt/SUNWabcd/adm/log* where only the directory */opt* exists, the following command could be used:

```
# mkdir -p /opt/SUNWabcd/adm/log
```

This would create the directories *SUNWabcd*, *adm*, and *log* in that order.

mv

The mv command moves a directory or file from one location to another. For example, to move the file */home/paul/security.txt* to the directory */home/paul/clients/security.txt*, the following command could be used:

```
$ mv /home/paul/security.txt /home/paul/clients/security.txt
```

Alternatively, relative paths could be used:

```
$ cd /home/paul
$ security.txt clients
```

pwd

The pwd command prints the current working directory of the user like this:

```
$ cd /home/paul
$ pwd
/home/paul
```

rmdir

The rmdir command removes a directory entry that is empty. Relative or absolute paths can be used. For example, to remove the directory *etc* from the current working directory, the following command could be used:

```
$ rmdir etc
```

Alternatively, if the directory is non-empty, the following command could be used:

```
$ rm -fr etc
```

Note that `rm -fr` should be avoided by root since a mistyped command can remove significant branches of the directory tree (the command `rm -rf /` removes all files on every mounted file system when executed as root).

sort

The `sort` command sorts files in alphabetical, reverse alphabetical, and a number of different orders. It is very useful for processing text files that are lists or databases. For example, if we have a list of country names stored in *names.txt*, we can sort them alphabetically by using the following command:

```
$ sort names.txt
denmark
finland
iceland
norway
sweden
```

Alternatively, to sort the list in reverse alphabetical order, the following command could be used:

```
$ sort -r names.txt
sweden
norway
iceland
finland
denmark
```

source "."

The source command " . " reads in the contents of an external script file and then executes the commands contained therein as if they were part of the calling script. For example, if a script called *ora_env.sh* contained a set of environment variable definitions that were to be used for setting Oracle environments, the following command would read them in:

```
$ . ora_env.sh
```

If the script had been executed in another shell, like this,

```
$ sh ora_env.sh
```

the environment variable settings would not be preserved in the current shell.

tail

The `tail` command is used to print the last few lines or page of a file to standard output. The number of lines to be printed can be specified by passing the "-" argument with the number of lines to be printed. For example, to print the last five lines of the file */etc/group*, the following command would be used:

```
mail::6:root
tty::7:root,tty,adm
lp::8:root,lp,adm
nuucp::9:root,nuucp
workers::10:
```

Alternatively, the `tail -f` command will print any new lines appended to the file in real time.

touch

The `touch` command can be used to create a new empty file, or to modify the properties of an existing file. For example, to create a new file called *data.txt* in the current working directory, the following command could be used:

```
$ touch data.txt
```

Alternatively, if you need to reset the creation date of a file to the current time, the following command could be used:

```
$ touch -m names.txt
$ ls -l names.txt
-rw-r--r--   1 jade        staff         41 Feb  7 09:48 names.txt
```

It's also possible to reset the creation date to a past (or future) time by passing a time string. The following string touches the file's creation date to the February 3, 2002:

```
$ touch -m -t 02032002 names.txt
$ ls -l names.txt
-rw-r--r--   1 jade        staff         41 Feb  2 20:02 names.txt
```

7.6 Write Scripts

So far, we've looked at individual commands—what they do, and how they work with other commands. Once you've worked out a useful combination of commands for solving a specific problem, it's useful to create a script that can perform those actions repetitively—without having to retype all of the commands. Scripts are used on the system to start services from the */etc/init.d* directory, rather than having to be started manually each time the system is rebooted. As a Solaris administrator, you should develop a set of scripts that can be used to monitor system behavior and carry out repetitive actions wherever possible. Automation of important but repetitive tasks is a key advantage of using shell scripts.

When executing a script, a new shell process is spawned. This allows a separate command interpreter to process the statements and commands contained within a script separately from the login shell. This is very important, because executing shell scripts should not interfere with the current operational environment. A good example is creating scripts to start a database server, such as Oracle, with different versions—the values for environment variables like ORA_HOME and SID are different between versions, and when upgrading it's common to have two separate systems running. They should have their own startup scripts so that there's no interference between the two.

There are three differences between running shell commands and executing them as part of a script. Firstly, the file that the script is stored in must have the executable permission set for the executing user. For example, to set the executable permission for the currently logged in user on the file *print_env.sh*, the following command would be used:

```
$ chmod u+x print_env.sh
```

Secondly, the first line of the script must invoke the shell that is to execute the commands contained in the script. For example, to execute the script using the Bourne shell, the following line must appear as the first line in the file:

```
#!/bin/sh
```

Thirdly, parameters passed to the script are labeled as $1 for the first parameter, $2 for the second parameter, and so on, and can be referred to by using $1, $2, and so forth within the script.

Note

The script name is always referred to as $0.

Let's see how these concepts work in practice by creating a script that generates an MD5 checksum for a file that is passed on the command line. The MD5 algorithm computes a digital signature for a file, which changes every time the content of the file changes. After a system has been installed, it is useful to keep a copy of the MD5 signatures for system files to protect against Trojan horse attacks, where a new version of the binary is installed without your knowledge by a rogue user or program. The following script computes the MD5 signature for the file specified by parameter $1, and writes it to the database file specified by parameter $2:

```
#!/bin/sh
# checksum.sh
# Computes MD5 checksum for file $1 and creates entry in file $2
echo "Computing checksum for $1"
md5sum $1 >> $2
echo "Entry written to $2"
```

The first line of the script specifies the shell to be executed. The next two lines are comments explaining what the program does and what parameters it requires. The next line displays a status message to the screen before performing the operation on $1 and redirecting the output to $2 as an append operation. Finally, a second status message confirms that the operation has been completed. Let's run the script with the parameter "/bin/pr", and verify that the checksum has been written correctly:

```
$ checksum.sh /bin/pr md5.db
Computing checksum for /bin/pr
Entry written to md5.db
$ cat md5.db
MD5 (/bin/pr) = 2e3d1f57bc8556dbbec48c82928a257d
```

After running this script against your key system files, you may decide to check the current MD5 signature against the signature stored in the database, and to be alerted if the signatures do not match. Let's create a second script that performs this operation:

```
#!/bin/sh
# checkchecksum.sh
# Checks MD5 checksum for file $1 and verifies against entry in
# file $2
echo "Computing checksum for $1"
CKSUM=`md5sum $1`
echo "Checking for entry in $2"
FOUND=`grep $CKSUM $2`
CKSUM=$2:$CKSUM
if test "$CKSUM" = "$FOUND"
  then
    echo "Signatures match"
  else
    echo "Signatures DO NOT match"
    echo "MD5 signature change detected on $1" | \
    mailx -s "URGENT MD5 ISSUE" root
fi
```

In this example, we've used variables extensively to store values and make comparisons. The script begins by calculating the current checksum of the target file $1, and assigning this value to the variable $CKSUM. Next, the database file $2 is grepped for an occurrence of this checksum string, with the resulting value being assigned to the variable $FOUND. After prepending the name of the database file to $CKSUM, $FOUND and $CKSUM are compared.

If the values match, the contents of the file have not changed since the file was created. Otherwise, a message is displayed indicating that the signature has changed, and an e-mail is sent to the administrator of the local host. Let's examine how this script is executed, and what output is generated:

```
$ checkchecksum.sh /bin/pr md5.db
Computing checksum for /bin/pr
Checking for entry in md5.db
Signatures match
```

However, if the target file has been tampered with, the following message would be displayed:

```
$ checkchecksum.sh /bin/pr md5.db
Computing checksum for /bin/pr
Checking for entry in md5.db
Signatures DO NOT match
```

In addition to generating the message "Signatures DO NOT match", the local super-user would also receive an e-mail message stating "MD5 signature change detected on /bin/pr".

Project 7-1: Checking File Checksums

This project shows you how to search for a file checksum from a database that contains a list of valid checksums. This procedure is useful in situations where a file must be checked to see if it has been registered with an application or security provider.

Step-by-Step

1. Create a checksum for the file /bin/ls:

```
$ md5 /bin/ls
MD5 (/bin/pr) = 2e3d1f57bc8556dbbec48c82928a257d
```

2. Search the database file to see if the checksum is contained therein:

```
$ cat md5.db | grep 2e3d1f57bc8556dbbec48c82928a257d
```

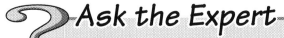

Ask the Expert

Question: Is there any limit to how big a shell script can be?

Answer: No, apart from the normal limits imposed on the size of files. Since I've never seen a script more than a few hundred kilobytes, you should be safe creating fairly sophisticated scripts.

3. If no result is returned, the entry is not contained in the file. If the entry is found, it is displayed:

```
MD5 (/bin/pr) = 2e3d1f57bc8556dbbec48c82928a257d
```

Summary
The md5 command can be used to compute checksums from files to ensure they are valid.

7

7.7 Test File Properties

The test command, as shown in the previous script, is used to evaluate logical conditions. There are three types of tests: string, integer, and file. The string test that we used to determine whether the digital signatures were different is only one of a number of string tests that the shell provides. The other tests available include the following:

-n str	True if and only if the string str has nonzero length.
str	True if and only if the string str is non-null.
str1 != str2	True if and only if the characters comprising the string str1 are not identical and in the same order as the characters comprising the string str2.
-z str	True if and only if the string str has zero length.

Integer tests allow comparisons to be made between two numbers. Note that floating-point arithmetic is not supported. The tests for integers include the following:

a −eq b	True if and only if *a* is equal to *b*.
a −ge b	True if and only if *a* is greater than or equal to *b*.

a −gt b	True if and only if *a* is greater than *b*.
a −le b	True if and only if *a* is less than or equal to *b*.
a −ne b	True if and only if *a* is not equal to *b*.

File tests allow checks to be made on the status of files. These checks include the following:

-b file	True if and only if file is a special block file.
-c file	True if and only if file is a special character file.
-d file	True if and only if file is a directory.
-f file	True if and only if file is a normal file.
-h file	True if and only if file is a symbolic link.
-p file	True if and only if file is a named piped.
-s file	True if and only if file has nonzero size.
-w file	True if and only if file is writeable by the current user.
-x file	True if and only if file is executable by the current user.

Let's review an example that uses a `for` loop to iterate a section of code several times, each time with a different argument. The purpose of the script is to test whether or not a set of countries each have their own databases located in the current directory. If a database is missing, an error message is displayed and the file is created:

```
#!/bin/sh
for COUNTRY in iceland sweden denmark norway
do
   if test -f $COUNTRY.db
     then
     echo "$COUNTRY.db exists"
   else
      echo "$COUNTRY.db does not exist"
      touch $COUNTRY.db
   fi
done
```

☑ *Mastery Check*

1. What is the logical result of the test -n `str`?

  A. Is true if and only if the string `str` has zero length.

  B. Is true if and only if the characters comprising the string `str1` are not identical and in the same order as the characters comprising the string `str2`.

  C. Is true if and only if the string `str` is non-null.

  D. Is true if and only if the string `str` has non-zero length.

2. What is the logical result of the test `str`?

  A. Is true if and only if the string `str` has zero length.

  B. Is true if and only if the characters comprising the string `str1` are not identical and in the same order as the characters comprising the string `str2`.

  C. Is true if and only if the string `str` is non-null.

  D. Is true if and only if the string `str` has nonzero length.

3. What is the logical result of the test `str1` != `str2`?

  A. Is true if and only if the string `str` has zero length.

  B. Is true if and only if the characters comprising the string `str1` are not identical and in the same order as the characters comprising the string `str2`.

  C. Is true if and only if the string `str` is non-null.

  D. Is true if and only if the string `str` has nonzero length.

4. What is the logical result of the test - z `str`?

  A. Is true if and only if the string `str` has zero length.

  B. Is true if and only if the characters comprising the string `str1` are not identical and in the same order as the characters comprising the string `str2`.

7

☑ Mastery Check

    C. Is true if and only if the string `str` is non-null.

    D. Is true if and only if the string `str` has nonzero length.

5. What is the logical result of the test `a -eq b`?

    A. Is true if and only if *a* is less than or equal to *b*.

    B. Is true if and only if *a* is greater than *b*.

    C. Is true if and only if *a* is greater than or equal to *b*.

    D. Is true if and only if *a* is equal to *b*.

6. What is the logical result of the test `a -ge b`?

    A. Is true if and only if *a* is less than or equal to *b*.

    B. Is true if and only if *a* is greater than *b*.

    C. Is true if and only if *a* is greater than or equal to *b*.

    D. Is true if and only if *a* is equal to *b*.

7. What is the logical result of the test `a -gt b`?

    A. Is true if and only if *a* is less than or equal to *b*.

    B. Is true if and only if *a* is greater than *b*.

    C. Is true if and only if *a* is greater than or equal to *b*.

    D. Is true if and only if *a* is equal to *b*.

8. What is the logical result of the test `a -le b`?

    A. Is true if and only if *a* is less than or equal to *b*.

    B. Is true if and only if *a* is greater than *b*.

    C. Is true if and only if *a* is greater than or equal to *b*.

    D. Is true if and only if *a* is equal to *b*.

☑ Mastery Check

9. What is the logical result of the test -b file?

    A. Is true if and only if file is a special block file.

    B. Is true if and only if file is a special character file.

    C. Is true if and only if file is a directory.

    D. Is true if and only if file is a normal file.

10. What is the logical result of the test -c file?

    A. Is true if and only if file is a special block file.

    B. Is true if and only if file is a special character file.

    C. Is true if and only if file is a directory.

    D. Is true if and only if file is a normal file.

11. What is the logical result of the test -d file?

    A. Is true if and only if file is a special block file.

    B. Is true if and only if file is a special character file.

    C. Is true if and only if file is a directory.

    D. Is true if and only if file is a normal file.

12. What is the logical result of the test -f file?

    A. Is true if and only if file is a special block file.

    B. Is true if and only if file is a special character file.

    C. Is true if and only if file is a directory.

    D. Is true if and only if file is a normal file.

13. What is the logical result of the test -p file?

    A. Is true if and only if file is a named piped.

    B. Is true if and only if file has nonzero size.

7

☑ *Mastery Check*

    C. Is true if and only if `file` is writeable by the current user.

    D. Is true if and only if `file` is executable by the current user.

14. What is the logical result of the test `-s file`?

    A. Is true if and only if `file` is a named piped.

    B. Is true if and only if `file` has nonzero size.

    C. Is true if and only if `file` is writeable by the current user.

    D. Is true if and only if `file` is executable by the current user.

15. What is the logical result of the test `-w file`?

    A. Is true if and only if `file` is a named piped.

    B. Is true if and only if `file` has nonzero size.

    C. Is true if and only if `file` is writeable by the current user.

    D. Is true if and only if `file` is executable by the current user.

Part 3

Single Host Administration

Module 8

Devices and File Systems

Critical Skills

S olaris represents all hardware devices attached to a system by means of special device files that are found in the /dev and /devices directories. The /dev directory is used to store logical device files, including block and raw devices for disks, while the /devices directory contains physical device files. For example, the /sbus@1f,0/SUNW,fas@2,8800000/sd@1,0 physical device file would be stored in the /devices directory, while the raw and block devices for a disk (/dev/rdsk/c0t0d0s7 and /dev/dsk/c0t0d0s7) would be stored in /dev. Because device representations are often much simpler on other operating systems, you may be wondering why SunOS requires a greater level of abstraction than Windows or Linux. The answer is the wide variety of bus types and hardware that a SPARC system might support.

8.1 Manage Physical Hardware Devices

Devices may be referred to by their physical device names and/or files (/devices), and by their logical device names and/or files (/dev). The /devices directory uses a treelike structure that represents device objects hierarchically. The following output shows the /devices directory structure for the SBUS identified as /sbus@2,0:

```
$ du /devices | grep "sbus@2,0"
2        ./sbus@2,0/SUNW,socal@d,10000/sf@0,0
3        ./sbus@2,0/SUNW,socal@d,10000
2        ./sbus@2,0/dma@2,81000/esp@2,80000
3        ./sbus@2,0/dma@2,81000
1        ./sbus@2,0/QLGC,isp@1,10000
1        ./sbus@2,0/lebuffer@2,40000
9        ./sbus@2,0
```

Note that the devices attached to the SBUS are stored under the /devices/sbus@2,0 directory. The physical hardware layout of the system is completely described by the entries in the /devices directory. Physical device names always take this form

   driver@address:arguments

where *driver* represents the driver names, *address* represents the device address, and *arguments* corresponds to the device arguments.

Applications generally refer to devices by their logical names—thus, you will not ordinarily need to deal with physical device names. However, if you need to change default boot devices, or diagnose hardware faults, you'll need to use physical device names. During the boot process, physical device names are used by the OpenBoot programmable read-only memory (PROM) monitor, because the operating system defines logical devices rather than the PROM. The drvconfig command is used to construct entries in the /devices directory when required, such as after a reconfiguration boot. The drvconfig command interprets information for new nodes relating to file permissions in the tree from entries in the file /etc/minor_perm such as

```
sd:* 0640 root sys
```

where sd represents the disk device node name, 0640 represents the file permission, root represents the owner, and sys represents the group.

You may be wondering how logical device names can be derived from their physical device names. The answer is that they need to be explicitly mapped to each other, just like the mapping between an Ethernet (hardware) address and an IP (logical) address for a network interface. The mappings between the two device representations are stored in the /etc/path_to_inst file. Storing them in this file allows for the settings to be preserved between system boots: if the system dynamically reconfigured them, the mappings might change and a previous mapping may be erroneous. The following example shows the mapping for device to instance names for a SPARC SBUS-based server:

```
"/sbus@3,0" 1 "sbus"
"/sbus@3,0/SUNW,fas@3,8800000" 0 "fas"
"/sbus@3,0/SUNW,fas@3,8800000/sd@4,0" 34 "sd"
"/sbus@3,0/SUNW,fas@3,8800000/sd@0,4" 273 "sd"
"/sbus@3,0/SUNW,fas@3,8800000/sd@1,5" 281 "sd"
"/sbus@3,0/SUNW,fas@3,8800000/sd@2,6" 289 "sd"
"/sbus@3,0/SUNW,fas@3,8800000/sd@3,7" 297 "sd"
"/sbus@3,0/SUNW,fas@3,8800000/sd@5,1" 305 "sd"
"/sbus@3,0/SUNW,fas@3,8800000/sd@6,2" 313 "sd"
"/sbus@3,0/SUNW,fas@3,8800000/sd@5,0" 35 "sd"
"/sbus@3,0/SUNW,fas@3,8800000/sd@0,5" 274 "sd"
"/sbus@3,0/SUNW,fas@3,8800000/sd@1,4" 280 "sd"
"/sbus@3,0/SUNW,fas@3,8800000/sd@2,7" 290 "sd"
"/sbus@3,0/SUNW,fas@3,8800000/sd@3,6" 296 "sd"
"/sbus@3,0/SUNW,fas@3,8800000/sd@4,1" 298 "sd"
```

8

```
"/sbus@3,0/SUNW,fas@3,8800000/sd@6,3" 314 "sd"
"/sbus@3,0/SUNW,fas@3,8800000/sd@6,0" 36 "sd"
"/sbus@3,0/SUNW,fas@3,8800000/sd@0,6" 275 "sd"
"/sbus@3,0/SUNW,fas@3,8800000/sd@1,7" 283 "sd"
"/sbus@3,0/SUNW,hme@3,8c00000" 0 "hme"
```

The SBUS ("/sbus@3,0" 1 "sbus") has several devices attached to it, including the network interface ("/sbus@3,0/SUNW,hme@3,8c00000" 0 "hme"). Peripheral Component Interconnect (PCI)-based systems have different mappings, as shown in the following output:

```
"/pci@2f,0" 0 "pcipsy"
"/pci@2f,0/isa@7" 0 "ebus"
"/pci@2f,0/isa@7/power@0,800" 0 "power"
"/pci@2f,0/isa@7/dma@0,0" 0 "isadma"
"/pci@2f,0/isa@7/dma@0,0/parallel@0,378" 0 "ecpp"
"/pci@2f,0/isa@7/dma@0,0/floppy@0,3f0" 0 "fd"
"/pci@2f,0/isa@7/serial@0,2e8" 1 "su"
"/pci@2f,0/isa@7/serial@0,3f8" 0 "su"
"/pci@2f,0/pmu@3" 0 "pmubus"
"/pci@2f,0/pmu@3/i2c@0" 0 "smbus"
"/pci@2f,0/pmu@3/i2c@0/temperature@30" 0 "max1617"
"/pci@2f,0/pmu@3/i2c@0/card-reader@40" 0 "scmi2c"
"/pci@2f,0/pmu@3/i2c@0/dimm@a0" 0 "seeprom"
"/pci@2f,0/pmu@3/fan-control@0" 0 "grfans"
"/pci@2f,0/pmu@3/ppm@0" 0 "grppm"
"/pci@2f,0/pmu@3/beep@0" 0 "grbeep"
"/pci@2f,0/ebus@c" 1 "ebus"
"/pci@2f,0/usb@c,3" 0 "ohci"
"/pci@2f,0/usb@c,3/mouse@2" 0 "hid"
"/pci@2f,0/usb@c,3/keyboard@4" 1 "hid"
"/pci@2f,0/firewire@c,2" 0 "hci1394"
"/pci@2f,0/ide@d" 0 "uata"
"/pci@2f,0/ide@d/dad@0,0" 0 "dad"
"/pci@2f,0/ide@d/sd@1,0" 0 "sd"
"/pci@2f,0/sound@8" 0 "audiots"
"/pci@2f,0/SUNW,m64B@13" 0 "m64"
"/pci@2f,0/network@c,1" 0 "eri"
"/pci@2f,0/pci@5" 0 "pci_pci"
"/options" 0 "options"
"/SUNW,UltraSPARC-IIe@0,0" 0 "us"
"/pseudo" 0 "pseudo"
```

8.2 Map Physical Device References

The PCI bus in this example (`"/pci@2f,0"` 0 `"pcipsy"`) has several devices attached to it, including the parallel port (`"/pci@2f,0/isa@7/dma@0,0/parallel@0,378"` 0 `"ecpp"`) and the floppy disk controller (`"/pci@2f,0/isa@7/dma@0,0/floppy@0,3f0"` 0 `"fd"`). If you are unsure how to relate logical device names and physical device names, a useful script called *whencedev*, written by Fred True, can be useful. For example, to display configuration details for *sd0*, the following command can be used:

```
$ whence.pl sd0
Information for sd0 ("/sbus@3,0/QLGC,isp@0,10000/sd@0,0"):
        -> SBus I/O board in cardcage slot 1
        -> Q-Logic SCSI controller in I/O board slot 0 (SBus slot)
        -> SCSI disk target 0 LUN 0
```

The *whencedev* script uses Perl and can be downloaded from **http://www.eng.auburn.edu/pub/mail-lists/ssa-managers.Aug97/msg00030.html**.

In addition to physical devices, Solaris also needs to refer to logical devices: for example, physical disks may be divided into many different slices, so the physical disk device will need to be referred to using a logical name. Logical device files in the */dev* directory are symbolically linked to physical device names in the */devices* directory. Most user applications will refer to logical device names.

A typical listing of the */dev* directory includes numerous entries that look like this:

aadmin1	nrst55	ptyre	ptyve	ptyze	rst53	tty	ttysd	ttywd
admin1	nrst60	ptyrf	ptyvf	ptyzf	rst54	ttya	ttyse	ttywe
arp	nswcol2	ptys0	ptyw0	qe	rst55	ttyb	ttysf	ttywf
bd.off	nswcol4	ptys1	ptyw1	qfe	rst60	ttyp0	ttyt0	ttyx0
c1	nswcol4a3	ptys2	ptyw2	rawip	rts	ttyp1	ttyt1	ttyx1
canon01	nswhp01	ptys3	ptyw3	rdsk	sad	ttyp2	ttyt2	ttyx2
chief	nswhp02	ptys4	ptyw4	rmt	sd193a	ttyp3	ttyt3	ttyx3
conslog	null	ptys5	ptyw5	rsd193a	sd193b	ttyp4	ttyt4	ttyx4
console	openprom	ptys6	ptyw6	rsd193b	sd193c	ttyp5	ttyt5	ttyx5
cua	osa	ptys7	ptyw7	rsd193c	sd193d	ttyp6	ttyt6	ttyx6
d1	pcmcia	ptys8	ptyw8	rsd193d	sd193e	ttyp7	ttyt7	ttyx7

8

These device names are designed to be easy to interpret. For example, */dev/console* represents the console device that is used by system services and other applications for status messages. The console is also used to boot the system and/or run a windowing system from, in the case of a common desktop environment (CDE). Some of the more common device names are listed here:

- */dev/qfe* represents a quad interface Ethernet device
- */dev/null* is a special device to which output can be piped when it needs to be discarded
- */dev/dsk* is a directory containing block disk device entries
- */dev/rdsk* is a directory containing raw disk device entries
- */dev/tty*i represent *i* terminal devices
- */dev/pty*i represent *i* pseudo terminal devices
- */dev/random* is a random number device that has many uses in security applications that utilize cryptography

1-Minute Drill

- What are the two types of device files supported by Solaris?
- Where are physical device files stored?
- Where are logical device files stored?

8.3 Map Logical Device References

Although it's possible to review the devices installed on the system by traversing the */dev* and */devices* directories, an easier way to do this is to use the `prtconf` command. Details of the system architecture peripherals will be displayed, with each section giving details on devices attached to buses, logical device names,

---

- Physical device files and logical device files
- The */devices* directory
- The */dev* directory

and driver status. Let's examine the output of `prtconf` for an Ultra SPARC system:

```
# prtconf
System Configuration:  Sun Microsystems  sun4u
Memory size: 512 Megabytes
```

Here, we can see that the system architecture is in *sun4u*, representing all Ultra series workstations. In addition, 512MB of RAM is installed. The next sections displayed show the list of buses and peripherals attached to each bus, arranged in a hierarchy. For example, Ultra 5 systems use a PCI bus, so devices are naturally attached to the PCI node, in the following order:

```
System Peripherals (Software Nodes):
SUNW,Ultra-5_10
    packages (driver not attached)
        terminal-emulator (driver not attached)
        deblocker (driver not attached)
        obp-tftp (driver not attached)
        disk-label (driver not attached)
        SUNW,builtin-drivers (driver not attached)
        sun-keyboard (driver not attached)
        ufs-file-system (driver not attached)
    chosen (driver not attached)
    openprom (driver not attached)
        client-services (driver not attached)
    options, instance #0
    aliases (driver not attached)
    memory (driver not attached)
    virtual-memory (driver not attached)
    pci, instance #0
        pci, instance #0
            ebus, instance #0
                auxio (driver not attached)
                power, instance #0
                SUNW,pll (driver not attached)
                se, instance #0
                su, instance #0
                su, instance #1
                ecpp (driver not attached)
                fdthree, instance #0
                eeprom (driver not attached)
```

8

```
            flashprom (driver not attached)
            SUNW,CS4231 (driver not attached)
        network, instance #0
        SUNW,m64B (driver not attached)
        ide, instance #0
            disk (driver not attached)
            cdrom (driver not attached)
            dad, instance #0
            sd, instance #30
    pci, instance #1
        scsi, instance #0
            disk (driver not attached)
            tape (driver not attached)
            sd, instance #0 (driver not attached)
            sd, instance #1 (driver not attached)
            sd, instance #2 (driver not attached)
            sd, instance #3
            sd, instance #4 (driver not attached)
            sd, instance #5 (driver not attached)
            sd, instance #6 (driver not attached)
            sd, instance #7 (driver not attached)
            sd, instance #8 (driver not attached)
            sd, instance #9 (driver not attached)
            sd, instance #10 (driver not attached)
            sd, instance #11 (driver not attached)
            sd, instance #12 (driver not attached)
            sd, instance #13 (driver not attached)
            sd, instance #14 (driver not attached)
        scsi, instance #1
            disk (driver not attached)
            tape (driver not attached)
            sd, instance #15 (driver not attached)
            sd, instance #16 (driver not attached)
            sd, instance #17 (driver not attached)
            sd, instance #18 (driver not attached)
            sd, instance #19 (driver not attached)
            sd, instance #20 (driver not attached)
            sd, instance #21 (driver not attached)
            sd, instance #22 (driver not attached)
            sd, instance #23 (driver not attached)
            sd, instance #24 (driver not attached)
            sd, instance #25 (driver not attached)
```

```
        sd, instance #26 (driver not attached)
        sd, instance #27 (driver not attached)
        sd, instance #28 (driver not attached)
        sd, instance #29 (driver not attached)
  SUNW,UltraSPARC-IIi (driver not attached)
  SUNW,ffb, instance #0
  pseudo, instance #0
```

8.4 Administer Solaris File Systems

We've previously looked at the general mapping of physical to logical device names. In this section, we'll examine the relationship between disk block and raw devices as they are implemented with Solaris file systems. By default, Solaris file systems are created as UFS (UNIX File System) file systems; however, this can be modified by changing the default setting in /etc/default/fs if required.

Each file system has entries in the /dev/dsk and /dev/rdsk directories, which correspond to the raw and block device interfaces respectively. Although raw and block logical devices refer to the same physical device, raw devices support low-level operations, while block devices support buffering and high-level I/O. Thus, system applications and servers that require low-level access use raw devices, while most user applications use the high-level access provided through the block device.

Disk partitions are referred to in Solaris by using their controller (c), target (t), disk (d) and slice (s) characteristics. Thus, the partition /dev/dsk/c1t2d3s4 refers to slice 4 on disk 3 at target 2 on controller 1. This nomenclature allows a large number of controllers, targets, and disks to be supported on a single system. UFS file systems comprise four key components: a boot block that stores data to boot a system; super blocks that store inode location data, size of the file system, number of disk blocks available, and their status; inodes that contain details of files; and blocks that actually store data. UFS file systems can be created on disks that have been partitioned using the format command by using the newfs command. For example, to create a new UFS file system on the partition c0t0d0s5, the following command could be used:

```
# newfs /dev/rdsk/c0t0d0s5
```

1-Minute Drill

- How are disks referred to in Solaris?
- Where is the default file system type set?

Since `newfs` just calls the `mkfs` command with the appropriate parameters, the following command is equivalent:

```
# mkfs -F ufs /dev/rdsk/c0t0d0s5
```

The `mkfs` command is generally used to create non-UFS file systems.

8.5 Monitor Disk Device Usage

File systems are generally referred to by their block device name, such as */dev/rdsk/c0t0d0s5*, rather than their physical device name, such as *name/pci@2f, 0/pci@1,1/ide@3/dad@0,5*. Linux uses disk device names that are easy to remember (*/dev/sda* and */dev/sdb* for SCSI disks) as does Windows (C:, D:, E:, and so on). However, the additional abstraction between physical and logical devices allows different hardware types to be supported, including multiple controllers. It's also easy to identify from a logical device name what physical device it represents. For example, disk partitions on different controllers can be identified by checking the disks installed on the system using the `df` command:

```
$ df -k
Filesystem         1k-blocks      Used Available Use% Mounted on
/dev/dsk/c0t0d0s0     482455    128023    306187  29% /
/dev/dsk/c0t0d0s3    1489367    840991    588802  59% /usr
/dev/dsk/c0t0d0s5    6314806    898162   5353496  14% /var
/dev/dsk/c3t4d0s0     962571    688097    216720  76% /export/root
/dev/dsk/c0t0d0s4    4032142   1061192   2930629  27% /opt
/dev/dsk/c0t0d0s6     962571      5631    899186   1% /tmp
/dev/dsk/c3t4d0s4    3291666      3281   3255469   0% /tools
/dev/dsk/c3t4d0s3    9075677   2455796   6529125  27% /usr/local
```

- By using their controller (c), target (t), disk (d), and slice (s) numbers
- */etc/default/fs*

Here, we can see that */dev/dsk/c0t0d0s0* and */dev/dsk/c0t0d0s3* are slice 0 and slice 3 of the disk */dev/dsk/c0t0d0*. The df command is commonly used to display the amount of used (and free) space available on mounted file systems, in terms of the total capacity of disk blocks expressed in kilobytes. The df command supports a number of options. For example, the df –a command displays disk usage on each file system:

```
# df -a
Filesystem           1k-blocks       Used Available Use% Mounted on
/dev/dsk/c0t0d0s0       482455     128023    306187  29% /
/dev/dsk/c0t0d0s3      1489367     840991    588802  59% /usr
/dev/dsk/c0t0d0s5      6314806     898162   5353496  14% /var
/dev/dsk/c3t4d0s0       962571     688097    216720  76% /export/root
/dev/dsk/c0t0d0s4      4032142    1061192   2930629  27% /opt
/dev/dsk/c0t0d0s6       962571       5631    899186   1% /tmp
/dev/dsk/c3t4d0s4      3291666       3281   3255469   0% /tools
/dev/dsk/c3t4d0s3      9075677    2455796   6529125  27% /usr/local
```

Using df –a ensures that, even when the *ignore* option is for a file system in the table of mounted file systems (/etc/mnttab), its status is displayed. A set of sample */etc/mnttab* entries is shown here:

```
# cat /etc/mnttab
/proc                /proc  proc  rw,suid,dev=2ec0000  1014754016
/dev/dsk/c0t0d0s0  /        ufs   rw,suid,dev=1d80010,logging,
    largefiles 1014754016
/dev/dsk/c0t0d0s3 /usr      ufs   rw,suid,dev=1d80013,logging,
    largefiles 1014754016
fd                   /dev/fd fd   rw,suid,dev=2f80000  1014754016
/dev/dsk/c0t0d0s5 /var      ufs   rw,suid,dev=1d80015,
    ignorelogging,largefiles 1014754016
/dev/dsk/c3t4d0s0 /export/root ufs  largefiles,logging,
    dev=1d80000 1014754046
```

Thus, even though */dev/dsk/c0t0d0s5* is set to *ignore*, its status is displayed. To display only file systems that are local to the server, the df –l command can be used:

```
# df -l
Filesystem           1k-blocks       Used Available Use% Mounted on
/dev/dsk/c0t0d0s0       482455     128023    306187  29% /
/dev/dsk/c0t0d0s3      1489367     840991    588802  59% /usr
/dev/dsk/c0t0d0s5      6314806     898162   5353496  14% /var
```

```
/dev/dsk/c3t4d0s0     962571     688097    216720  76% /export/root
/dev/dsk/c0t0d0s4    4032142    1061192   2930629  27% /opt
/dev/dsk/c0t0d0s6     962571       5631    899186   1% /tmp
/dev/dsk/c3t4d0s4    3291666       3281   3255469   0% /tools
/dev/dsk/c3t4d0s3    9075677    2455796   6529125  27% /usr/local
/dev/dsk/c2t5d0s3   78207672   16483194  60942402  21% /usr/local/src
```

This prevents waiting for NFS servers to respond with the status of exported file systems that have been locally mounted. Alternatively, an individual file system's status can be checked by passing it on the command line, as shown for the file system /users:

```
# df /users
Filesystem           1k-blocks      Used Available Use% Mounted on
/dev/dsk/c2t5d4s0     52126800  46979552   4625980  91% /users
```

An alternative method for obtaining disk space consumption data is to use the du command. The du command iteratively displays the number of bytes consumed by each directory, starting from a parent directory specified on the command line. For example, to display the number of blocks occupied by file in the /etc directory, the following command would be used:

```
# du /etc
22        ./default
7         ./cron.d
7         ./dfs
8         ./dhcp
225       ./fs/hsfs
801       ./fs/nfs
1         ./fs/proc
241       ./fs/ufs
1269      ./fs
24        ./inet
158       ./init.d
358       ./lib
240       ./mail
3         ./net/ticlts
3         ./net/ticots
3         ./net/ticotsord
10        ./net
153       ./opt/licenses
6         ./opt/SUNWdat/config
```

```
7         ./opt/SUNWdat
161       ./opt
3476      .
```

This output indicates that a total of 3476 blocks are used by files stored under the /etc directory. Each child directory displays the number of blocks stored in its own top-level directory and its child directories. Thus, files in the /etc/net directory and its child directories occupy 10 blocks, while files in the /etc/net/ticots directory occupy only 3 of those blocks.

8.6 Layout Disk Devices

A Solaris disk is divided into a number of logical partitions known as *slices*—some administrators still call them *partitions*, even though Sun documentation refers to them as slices. Each slice may contain an individual file system. File systems created for SPARC systems typically have eight slices, although only some of these are typically used for individual file systems. Solaris uses UFS file systems, and these have the same features that you'd expect to see on all modern file systems: hierarchical directory structures of arbitrary depth; support for system calls to create, read, update and delete files; and support for advanced features such as journaling.

The root directory for a Solaris file system is designated by a forward slash (/): all other directories must lie under the root directory. This rule applies to directories that are created on the same slice as the root, such as /etc, as well as directories that are stored on different slices. In the latter case, a directory referred to as a *mount point* must be created for users to be able to access files on the file system. Thus, if the root directory is stored on the partition c0t0d0s0, and /usr is stored in c0t0d0s5, the directory /usr will need to be created on the file system stored on c0t0d0s0 before files stored on c0t0d0s5 can be accessed by using the path /usr. No restrictions are placed on the local of mount points—they don't need to be mounted in the root directory. Indeed, modern practice usually involves mounting NFS-exported volumes on mount points in the /mnt directory, as this reduces the number of mount points created in the root directory. By default, a number of different system directories, such as /etc and /var, are created on the same slice as the root directory during installation.

8

A mount point can be created manually by using the `mkdir` command. For example, to create the mount point on *data*, the following command would be used:

```
# mkdir /data
```

Generally, all files on a single file system must be created on the same slice. However, if you use metadevices created using DiskSuite to implement a Redundant Array of Inexpensive Disks (RAID), a single logical disk may be created that spans multiple partitions. This can be useful if you need a single file system that is larger than any of your individual partitions, such as database files. However, coverage of RAID configuration is beyond the scope of this book.

Disks have eight slices, numbered 0 through 7. The file systems that are placed on each slice are subject to convention, but each can be individually assigned by the administrator. Although the defaults assigned by the installation program generally suit the system files, it may be necessary to use specific slices for specific types of partitions. For example, a site policy may specify that all database partitions use the slices that have the fastest seek times to optimize performance.

Ask the Expert

Question: Should I use RAID file systems?

Answer: You should use RAID file systems only if you need failover between file systems, and/or file systems that are larger than any of your existing disk capacities. For example, you may need to *mirror* file systems if they contain critical data. This reduces your disk capacity by 50 percent because data is written twice, once to each of the mirrored partitions. Alternatively, *striping* allows large partitions to be created using multiple disks. Database administrators often use RAID 5 because it combines the redundancy of mirroring with the extra capacity of striping, even though both are expensive in terms of disk space. Most production systems should use RAID.

Figure 8-1 shows the recommended layout for SPARC file system slices. The slices can be summarizes as follows:

Slice 0	Root partition
Slice 1	Virtual memory
Slice 2	Whole disk
Slice 3	*/export*
Slice 4	Shared swap space
Slice 5	*/opt*
Slice 6	*/usr*
Slice 7	*/export/home*

8.7 Format Disk Devices

For disk slices to be used to host file systems, they must be formatted using the `format` command. This process identifies defective disk blocks and marks them as bad so that data is not corrupted when written. If a new disk is installed in a system, a reconfiguration reboot should be performed, unless the system is a highly available server. The reconfiguration reboot can be performed by using the following commands from the shell:

```
# touch /reconfigure
# sync
# init 6
```

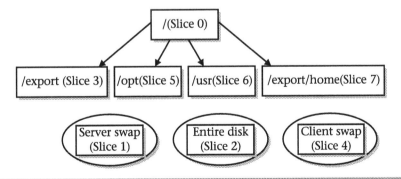

| **Figure 8-1** | Recommended SPARC filesystem layout |

Alternatively, the system can be shut down to the OpenBoot PROM monitor and booted from the *ok* prompt by using the following command:

```
ok boot -r
```

For SCSI disks, you should ensure that no conflicts exist between the ID associated with the new device and any existing devices on the chain. After the system has booted, new device files should have been created for the new disk. The format command can then be used to format the disk's partitions:

```
# format
```

When invoked, the format command displays the currently installed disks it can detect:

```
Searching for disks...done
AVAILABLE DISK SELECTIONS:
0. c0t1d0 <SUN2.10 cyl 4072 alt 2 hd 14 sec 72>
/iommu@f,e0000000/sbus@f,e0001000/espdma@f,400000/esp@f,800000/
sd@1,0
1. c0t2d0 <SUN1.05 cyl 2036 alt 2 hd 14 sec 72>
/iommu@f,e0000000/sbus@f,e0001000/espdma@f,400000/esp@f,800000/
sd@2,0
Specify disk (enter its number):
```

Ask the Expert

Question: Should I use SCSI- or IDE-based disks?

Answer: With the introduction of 10,000 RPM fast SCSI disks under Solaris, there's no reason why anyone would use IDE, even though it's possible with some Ultra SPARC architectures. If using an IDE-based system for applications that require fast data throughput, consider buying an external RAID array.

At this point, you need to specify which disk you intend to format. This just brings up the main menu—it doesn't destroy any data on the disk. If the selected disk contains data, the following output will be printed:

```
[disk formatted]
```

The main menu is then displayed:

```
FORMAT MENU:
        disk       - select a disk
        type       - select (define) a disk type
        partition  - select (define) a partition table
        current    - describe the current disk
        format     - format and analyze the disk
        fdisk      - run the fdisk program
        repair     - repair a defective sector
        show       - translate a disk address
        label      - write label to the disk
        analyze    - surface analysis
        defect     - defect list management
        backup     - search for backup labels
        verify     - read and display labels
        save       - save new disk/partition definitions
        volname    - set 8-character volume name
        !<cmd>     - execute <cmd>, then return
        quit
format>
```

To format the disk, simply use the format command from the main menu:

```
format> format
Ready to format. Formatting cannot be interrupted
and takes 15 minutes (estimated). Continue? yes
```

After formatting has been completed, new slices can be laid out by using the partition command from the main menu. This allows the size of individual slices to be specified. After the partitions have been created, a label must be written for the disk. This allows the disk to be identified by the operating system. The disk label can be viewed at any time by using the `prtvtoc` command:

```
# prtvtoc /dev/dsk/c0t0d0s2
* /dev/dsk/c0t0d0s2 partition map
*
* Dimensions:
*     512 bytes/sector
*      63 sectors/track
*     255 tracks/cylinder
*   16065 sectors/cylinder
*    1020 cylinders
*    1018 accessible cylinders
*
* Flags:
*   1: unmountable
*  10: read-only
*
*                          First     Sector    Last
* Partition  Tag  Flags    Sector    Count     Sector   Mount Directory
          0    2   00       48195    160650    208844    /
          1    7   00      208845     64260    273104    /var
          2    5   00           0  16354170  16354169
          3    3   01      273105    321300    594404
          6    4   00      594405   1317330   1911734    /usr
          7    8   00     1911735  14442435  16354169    /export/home
```

As you can see, the complete partition table is stored in the disk label. This can also be viewed using the `print` command in the format main menu:

```
format> print
Part Tag Flag Cylinders Size Blocks
0 root wm 0 0 (0/0/0) 0
1 swap wu 0 0 (0/0/0) 0
2 backup wm 0 - 3732 (3732/0/0) 2089920
3 unassigned wm 0 0 (0/0/0) 0
4 unassigned wm 0 0 (0/0/0) 0
5 home wm 0 - 3732 1075MB (3732/0/0) 2089920
6 usr wm 0 0 (0/0/0) 0
7 unassigned wm 0 0 (0/0/0) 0
```

Project 8-1: Adding a New File System

This project shows you how to add a new file sytsem (*/dev/dsk/c0t3d0s1*) to a server and mount it on the */users* mount point. This is necessary every time a new disk is added to the system.

Step-by-Step

1. Perform a reconfiguration boot:

```
# touch /reconfigure; sync; boot -r
```

2. Format the disk and lay out the partitions as required:

```
# format
```

3. Create a new UFS file system:

```
# newfs /dev/dsk/c0t3d0s1
```

4. Create a mount point:

```
# mkdir /users
```

5. Mount the file system:

```
# mount /dev/dsk/c0t3d0s1 /users
```

8

Summary

Using the touch, format, newfs, mkdir, and mount commands will prepare a disk for use as a file system.

After using the format command, the newfs command should be used to create a new UFS file system, and a mount point for each slice on the new disk should be created. The mount command can then be used to mount the disk on the mount point. For example, to mount the file system */dev/dsk/c0t3d0s6* on the mount point */data*, the following command would be used:

```
# mount /dev/dsk/c0t3d0s6 /data
```

To ensure that this file system is mounted at boot time, an entry should be created in the */etc/vfstab* file as follows:

```
/dev/dsk/c0t3d0s6 /dev/rdsk/c0t3d0s6 /data ufs 2 yes -
```

This entry associates the slice's raw and block devices with a mount point, specifies the file system type (UFS), a file system checking flag, a flag to force mounting at boot, and a - (hyphen) to indicate no further options.

☑ *Mastery Check*

1. What command is used to format disks in Solaris?

 A. mkdir

 B. format

 C. fmat

 D. chkdsk

2. What command is used to print a disk's label?

 A. print

 B. label

 C. prtvtoc

 D. prtlabel

3. What command can be used to create only UFS file systems?

 A. newfs

 B. ufs_fs

 C. newfs_ufs

 D. mknewfs

☑ Mastery Check

4. What command is used to display the number of disk blocks used by each directory?

   A. blocks

   B. df

   C. free

   D. D.du

5. In what directory are physical device names stored?

   A. /devices

   B. /dev

   C. /etc

   D. /usr

6. In what directory are logical device names stored?

   A. /devices

   B. /dev

   C. /etc

   D. /usr

7. What are /dev/tty1 and /dev/pty1?

   A. Terminal and pseudo-terminal devices

   B. Terminal and pseudo-terminal device drivers

   C. Login windows

   D. Terminal types

8

☑ Mastery Check

8. What form do physical device arguments always take?

A. *address@driver:arguments*

B. *driver@address:arguments*

C. *address:arguments@driver*

D. *driver:arguments@address*

9. What command is used to display a system's configuration?

A. `displayconf`

B. `writeconf`

C. `prtconf`

D. `confprint`

10. What command creates a new file system?

A. `createfs`

B. `createfilesystem`

C. `newfilesystem`

D. `newfs`

11. What command is used to create a mount point?

A. `mkdir`

B. `mkfile`

C. `mkmount`

D. `mkpoint`

☑ *Mastery Check*

12. What command prints the volume table of contents?

    A. `toc`

    B. `vtoc`

    C. `prtvtoc`

    D. `dispvtoc`

13. What slice should hold the root partition?

    A. 0

    B. 1

    C. 2

    D. 3

14. What slice should hold the export partition?

    A. 0

    B. 1

    C. 2

    D. 3

15. What slice should hold the virtual memory partition?

    A. 0

    B. 1

    C. 2

    D. 3

8

Module 9

Managing Users and Groups

Critical Skills

All operations on Solaris systems must be performed under the auspices of a specific user account. Also known as a user ID or a user login, every Solaris account has a unique username (such as "paul") and a unique user ID number (such as "128"), which distinguishes one user's account from those of other users. In addition, every user account is associated with a primary group (such as "staff"), which allows organizational structures to be mapped onto the system. Because Solaris permissions separate users and members of their primary group from other users on the system, in terms of file access, managing groups is an important aspect of system design. In this module, we examine how to create new users and groups and manage existing accounts. We also discuss the security implications of user accounts and groups.

9.1 Manage Users

All processes and files on a Solaris system are owned by a specific user account. This account may not correspond physically to a person, although that is certainly a common practice. In general, two types of accounts are created on a Solaris system: system accounts, which are used to run services, and user accounts, which are assigned to specific individuals. User accounts are commonly used for the following purposes:

- Executing commands and third-party applications, such as StarOffice

- Writing new software

- Running shells and scripts

Users generally log into their accounts and issue commands interactively. In contrast, system accounts are generally not logged into by any specific user; instead, they are used to manage discrete aspects of system operation, including the following:

- Managing system resources

- Installing and configuring devices and drivers

- Supporting such network services as mail, Internet access, and news groups

- Controlling processes and threads

1-Minute Drill

- What can be used to run shells and scripts?
- What can be used to manage system resources?

Although it is useful to distinguish between system and user accounts, Solaris assigns special privileges only to the super-user account, also known as *root*, which has a UID of 0 (zero). The root user has similar powers to the root account on Linux or the Administrator account on Windows. The root user has complete control over the system, including the ability to read files created and owned by other users and terminate or otherwise signal processes spawned by other users. This makes the root user very powerful—the target of most attacks on Solaris systems is access to the root account.

Every user on a Solaris system is associated with a primary group. Based on the system of UNIX file permissions, users can assign file access to themselves, to members of their primary group, or to all other users. This gives members of a group potential shared access to files that is distinguished from all other users. For example, members of the sales group may be allowed to read and update a spreadsheet containing sales data (sales.xls), but this should not be available for reading or writing to members of the helpdesk group. Alternatively, members of the helpdesk group maintain a journal of inquiries that they can read and write to (journal.txt), with members of the group managers granted only read access. Members of the sales group would not be able to read this file.

Figure 9-1 shows how the concept of primary groups manages file access.

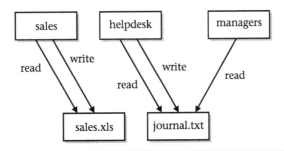

| **Figure 9-1** | Group-based file access |

- A user account.
- A system account.

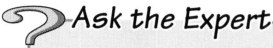

Ask the Expert

Question: How many groups should I create?

Answer: You should create as many groups as you need. One of the main problems with the UNIX group structure is that it's not hierarchical, as normal organizations have with their workgroups. For example, you might belong to Department X-Ray in Division Science in Location Boston: potentially, you want to share some data with all members of X-Ray and Science simply because they are located in Boston. A mechanism for inheritance of this kind is not available with UNIX groups. This is why the Lightweight Directory Access Protocol (LDAP) is becoming popular.

9.2 Administer Accounts

Several properties are associated with each user account, including the following:

- **username**, consisting of eight characters or less, which is unique on the system. Some usernames, such as root for the super-user, are reserved by the system.

- **password**, consisting of eight characters or less, which is not necessarily unique on the system, since different users can have the same password.

- **user ID (UID)**, a number greater than 0 that is unique on the system. The UID distinguishes user activities on the system. Some UIDs are reserved, such as UID 0, which is associated with the super-user.

- **group ID (GID)**, a number greater than 0 that uniquely identifies a group. Different users can share the same GID if they have primary membership of the associated group.

- **login shell**, which is spawned every time a user logs into the system. The most common shells are discussed in Module 6.

- **GECOS (comment)**, which is a description of the user. This can be generic, such as "Database Administrator," but it can also indicate a specific person, such as "George Goldsmith." This field has a historical relationship with the General Electric Computer Operating System

(GECOS), since early UNIX versions stored credentials for interacting with GECOS systems in this field.

●   **home directory**, which is a directory that the user owns, and under which the user's files are stored by default. This directory can be either a physical directory on a local file system or a directory exported from a server by using NFS and the automounter (see Module 21 for instructions on how to set up the automounter).

The definition of each parameter for each user is contained within the */etc/passwd* database, with one line being allocated to each user. In addition, each user should have a corresponding entry in the */etc/shadow* database, which contains the user's encrypted password string.

1-Minute Drill

●   What is the username?

●   What is the home directory?

A sample */etc/passwd* file is shown here:

```
$ cat /etc/passwd
root:x:0:1:Super-User:/:/sbin/sh
daemon:x:1:1::/:
bin:x:2:2::/usr/bin:
sys:x:3:3::/:
adm:x:4:4:Admin:/var/adm:
lp:x:71:8:Line Printer Admin:/usr/spool/lp:
uucp:x:5:5:uucp Admin:/usr/lib/uucp:
nuucp:x:9:9:uucp Admin:/var/spool/uucppublic:/usr/lib/uucp/uucico
listen:x:37:4:Network Admin:/usr/net/nls:
nobody:x:60001:60001:Nobody:/:
noaccess:x:60002:60002:No Access User:/:
```

Note that these are the standard system accounts that are created after installation. Many can be safely removed if they are not being used. For example, the *uucp* and *nuucp* accounts are used to manage the Unix-to-Unix

9

● A string of eight characters or less, which is unique on the system.
● A directory that the user owns and under which the user's files are stored by default.

Question: Why should I use password shadowing?

Answer: Password shadowing protects your encrypted password strings from a dictionary attack. Unlike a brute-force attack, dictionary attacks are much faster because the cracker can use some information about the targeted user to crack his or her password.

Copy Program (UUCP), a service that has been largely superseded by FTP and similar file transfer programs. If you don't intend to use UUCP, you should remove these accounts. The corresponding /etc/shadow database is shown here:

```
# cat /etc/shadow
root:f87gfg9ff:11033::::::
daemon:NP:6445::::::
bin:NP:6445::::::
sys:NP:6445::::::
adm:NP:6445::::::
lp:NP:6445::::::
uucp:*LK*:6445::::::
nuucp:*LK*:6445::::::
listen:NP:::::::
nobody:NP:6445::::::
noaccess:NP:6445::::::
```

Here, we can see that most of the system accounts have no password *NP* meaning that they cannot be logged into directly. Processes can be executed with the effective UID of these accounts. However, the exceptions are the UUCP accounts (*uucp* and *nuucp*), which have been locked, meaning that they are completely disabled. No processes may be spawned by using their corresponding UIDs.

9.3 Authenticate Users

Access to a user account can be granted only by authentication. Solaris provides a number of different authentication methods, although most are based on the presentation of two tokens by a prospective user: the username of the account to which access is required, and the corresponding password. User account information is stored in the */etc/passwd* database, while passwords are stored in encrypted form in the */etc/shadow* database. While all users can read the entries in */etc/passwd*, only the root user can read the entries in */etc/shadow*. This protects the encrypted passwords from being obtained by an unprivileged user who may attempt to "crack" the passwords. When a password is entered by the user, the *crypt* function is applied to the password: if this encrypted string matches the string contained within the */etc/shadow* database for that user, the user is authenticated and access to the account is granted. If the encrypted strings do not match, the user cannot be authenticated, and the login attempt is rejected. Other authentication methods are available, including those based on the Network Information Service (NIS/NIS+, which is discussed in Module 20) and the Lightweight Directory Access Protocol (LDAP; see Module 22).

One of the benefits of password security in Solaris is that passwords are encrypted with a one-way function: there is no corresponding "decrpyt" function that can translate these passwords into plaintext. Thus, most password cracking programs attempt to guess the password entries by encrypting a set of the most likely passwords to be entered by users. This list can include usernames, real names, birth dates, pet names, country names, and any other word in the dictionary. Remembering a password is difficult for users when they have to remember 20 other passwords for their bank account, share trading account, home alarm code, and so on, so most users will choose easy-to-remember passwords. Unfortunately, these are also likely to be easy-to-guess passwords! An ideal password consists of a combination of numbers, letters, and punctuation that is hard to guess but easy to remember. For example, substituting numbers in place of letters is a common practice. Thus, the password *pembroke* could be modified to *p3mbr0k3*—easy to remember but hard to guess. Another alternative is to use a password generation program, such as Van Vleck's *gpw*, which can be downloaded from **http://www.multicians.org/thvv/tvvtools.html**. The key benefit of *gpw* is that it produces non-words, generated randomly, that can be easily pronounced, making them easy to remember. For example, the passwords *stradion*, *allerish*, and *nathamen* might be produced by *gpw*.

Adding New Users

New user accounts can be added to the system by using the `useradd` command. The `useradd` command has the following format:

```
# useradd -u UID -g GID -d home_dir_path -s shell \
  -c comment login_name
```

The following example adds a user called *oliver* to the system, with a UID of 1025, GID of 25, home directory */home/oliver*, Bourne shell as the login shell, and the description "Oliver Goldsmith":

```
# useradd -u 1025 -g 25 -d /home/oliver -s /bin/sh \
  -c "Oliver Goldsmith" oliver
```

To verify that the user has been added to the system correctly, we can check the */etc/passwd* database:

```
# grep oliver /etc/passwd
oliver:x:1025:25:Oliver Goldsmith:/home/oliver:/bin/sh
```

Although these basic user characteristics are sufficient for most users, the useradd command allows a number of optional parameters to be set including the following:

-e *exp_date*	Sets the expiry date of the account to *exp_date* (e.g., "November 1, 2002"). This will prevent the user from logging in after that date.
-f *num_days*	Sets to *num_days* the number of days allowed between user logins before the account is suspended.
-G *grp*	Adds a secondary group membership for the user to the *grp* group.
-k *dir*	Specifies a new skeleton directory from which to create user login files. The default is */etc/skel*, but most sites modify these to suit local environments. For example, Oracle users may have a skeleton created under */etc/skel/oracle*.
-m	Creates the user's home directory if it doesn't already exist.
-P *file*	Sets the user's profile to file.
-p *file*	Sets the user's project to file.

Project 9-1: Creating a User's Home Directory Manually

This project shows you how to create a user's home directory manually. To create the home directory */home/paul* for the user paul of the group sales, the commands shown in this project could be used.

Step-by-Step

1. Create the directory and any other higher-level directories that don't exist in the path:

```
# mkdir -p /home/paul
```

2. Change the ownership of the directory to paul:

```
# chown paul /home/paul
```

3. Change the group membership of the directory to sales:

```
# chgrp sales /home/paul
```

Summary

The mkdir, chown, and chgrp commands can be used to create a user's home directory manually.

Deleting Existing Users

Existing user accounts can be deleted from the system by using the userdel command. The userdel command will either remove only account information or account information plus the user's home directory. For example, to remove the user oliver's account but not his home directory, the following command would be used:

```
# userdel oliver
```

Alternatively, to remove the account information and home directory, the following command would be used:

```
# userdel -r oliver
```

9

Note that while this removes the home directory and user information for oliver, it's possible that he may own files outside his home directory. Thus, a search should be performed using find to ensure that oliver no longer owns any files on any mounted file system:

```
# find / -user oliver -print
```

Modifying Existing Users

Existing user accounts can be modified on the system by using the usermod command. For example, if we wanted to change the user oliver's primary group from 25 to 10, the following command would be used:

```
# usermod -g 10 oliver
```

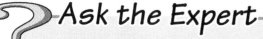

Ask the Expert

Question: What alternatives do I have to locking accounts?

Answer: Because files are owned by UID, it's possible to simply modify the username and change the account password. Thus, if user joe leaves the company and is replaced by gail, then gail can resume joe's work without interruption.

The change could be verified by checking the */etc/passwd* database:

```
# grep oliver /etc/passwd
oliver:x:1025:10:Oliver Goldsmith:/home/oliver:/bin/sh
```

All the options used with the useradd command can be used with the usermod command. However, note that if you change a user's properties, such as group membership or UID, permissions will need to be updated manually, as no automatic conversion process is performed by the usermod command.

9.4 Manage User Passwords

New passwords can be entered on the system by using the passwd command. In addition, existing passwords can also be modified by using the passwd command. While individual users are able to change their own passwords, the super-user is able to change the password for any user on the system or lock a user's password so that login access is denied. The super-user generally changes a user's password after the account has been created by using useradd. To change the password for oliver, for example, the super-user would enter the following command:

```
# passwd oliver
New password:
Re-enter new password:
passwd (SYSTEM): passwd successfully changed for oliver
```

On entering and re-entering the password, the super-user must type in the same password for the user's account to be modified. This reduces the chance of the super-user entering a password incorrectly. Each user must also enter his or her password twice when modifying a password entry. If two different passwords are entered, the following error message is displayed:

```
# passwd oliver
New password:
Re-enter new password:
passwd(SYSTEM): They don't match; try again.
New password:
Re-enter new password:
passwd (SYSTEM): passwd successfully changed for oliver
```

In the second half of this code, the two passwords entered for oliver matched, and the user's account was updated accordingly. Once a new password has been created, it can be verified by checking the */etc/shadow* database:

```
# grep oliver /etc/shadow
oliver:fg8d99cjds9f::::::::
```

Users can enter the `passwd` command with no arguments to change their own passwords. However, a super-user can use a number of options with the `passwd` command to perform account-related actions:

`-f` *user_id*	Requires the user *user_id* to change the user's password next time he or she logs in. Useful if a security breach has occurred.
`-l` *user_id*	Locks the *user_id* account, preventing any logins. Useful when a user leaves an organization suddenly, and the account cannot be removed without examining which of a user's files need to be transferred.
`-n` *days*	Sets the number of days before a password change is allowed. Should never be set because a user may need to change his or her password at any time if someone else discovers it.
`-x` *days*	Sets the number of days after which a password change is mandatory. Should be used in high-security installations in which a regular password change policy is enforced. Users should be given a warning by using the −w option at least one day before the change is required.
`-d` *user_id*	Removes the password for the *user_id* account. Should never be used because all accounts should have a password.

9

Checking Effective UID

The effective UID of the current user can be checked by using the id command. For the user oliver, the display for id would look like this:

```
$ id
uid=1025(oliver) gid=25(staff)
```

If the user has secondary group memberships, the following output would be displayed:

```
$ id
uid=1025(oliver) gid=25(staff) groups=0(root)
```

The id command always shows the real UID and the effective UID if it is different from the real UID. For example, if the user oliver had the effective UID of 0, by using su, the following output would be displayed:

```
$ id
uid=1025(oliver) gid=25(staff) euid=0(root)
```

Alternatively, if the newgrp command had changed the effective group to have a GID of 1, the following output would be displayed:

```
$ id
uid=1025(oliver) gid=25(staff) egid=1(other)
```

The id command is useful when you need to verify that your effective UID has been modified as a result of using the su command (discussed in the next section, "Changing Effective the UID") or after using the newgrp command (covered later in the section "Changing Groups").

Changing the Effective UID

The effective UID can be modified using the su command. By entering the password for the account that is going to be accessed, one user can literally "become" another. In addition, the user may choose to retain his/her own environment by failing to pass the - character or inherit the environment of the effective user by passing the - character with the su command.

For example, if the user oliver has responsibility for managing the Apache Web Server, he would normally use the su facility to assume the effective UID of the apache account, rather than logging out from the oliver account, and logging in again as apache. The following command sequence would occur:

```
$ su - apache
password:
$
```

If the apache account had a UID of 25, the following output would be displayed from the command line:

```
$ id
uid=1025(oliver) gid=25(staff) euid=25(apache)
```

Supplying the - ensures that the environment from the account being assumed is inherited by the user while using the assumed shell. However, if oliver didn't want to inherit this environment, he could have used the following command (sans -):

```
$ su apache
password:
$
```

9.5 Manage the Password Database

9

The /etc/passwd and /etc/shadow files can be edited manually, although any syntax errors in the file may render some user accounts unusable. However, Solaris provides the pwconv command to at least ensure that the password data in the password and shadow databases is consistent. The pwconv command performs one of three actions when invoked: First it checks that the shadow password database exists, and if the file is not found, a shadow password database is created. This involves writing new entries in /etc/shadow, reading and removing the encrypted password entries from /etc/passwd, and transferring them to /etc/shadow. This step is usually taken when manually upgrading a system from a previous version of Solaris that may not have supported password shadowing.

Second, if the /etc/shadow file does exist, pwconv verifies that all the user entries in /etc/passwd have a corresponding entry in /etc/shadow. If they don't, an entry is created in /etc/shadow and the user's encrypted password is transferred from /etc/passwd to /etc/shadow. This situation can occur if a set of new entries is manually created in *etc/passwd* by using a script to generate a large number of new entries, each with a default password. For example, the following shell script creates a set of 10 user accounts for a specific department, with a default password:

```
#!/bin/sh
# create_acct.sh: Creates a set of ten user accounts
#                 for department $1 gid $2
for user in 0 1 2 3 4 5 6 7 8 9
do
  echo "$1$user:C4dMH8As4bGTM:100$user:$2:"
  echo "User $1$user:/home/$1$user:/bin/sh"
done
```

This program could be run like this for the Sales Department (GID 25):

```
# cp /etc/passwd /etc/passwd.new
# create_acct.sh sales 25 >> /etc/passwd.new
```

The last five lines of *etc/passwd.new* should now look like this:

```
staff5:C4dMH8As4bGTM:1005:10:User staff5:/home/staff5:/bin/sh
staff6:C4dMH8As4bGTM:1006:10:User staff6:/home/staff6:/bin/sh
staff7:C4dMH8As4bGTM:1007:10:User staff7:/home/staff7:/bin/sh
staff8:C4dMH8As4bGTM:1008:10:User staff8:/home/staff8:/bin/sh
staff9:C4dMH8As4bGTM:1009:10:User staff9:/home/staff9:/bin/sh
```

It's good practice to verify the *etc/passwd.new* file before moving it to *etc/passwd.new*, after copying *etc/passwd* to *etc/passwd.orig*. If the *etc/passwd.orig* file is maintained as a working backup, it should be set to read-only by the root user. After pwconv is run, 10 new entries will be created in *etc/shadow* and the passwords removed from *etc/passwd*. The users created would then be able to change their passwords by using the passwd command.

Third and finally, if entries in *etc/shadow* do not exist in *etc/passwd*, these entries are removed from *etc/shadow*. This can occur if an entry has been manually removed from *etc/passwd*, but the corresponding entry in *etc/shadow* has been overlooked. Running pwconv will remove any entries that are no longer required. In practice, it's better to lock the user account rather than removing it entirely, as processes, files, and directories could still be owned by a user when it is deleted. Solaris does not perform this check automatically, although the find command can be used to list all files owned by a particular user. For example, to find all files belonging to the user jasmine on all mounted file systems, the following command could be used:

```
# find / -user jasmine -print
```

A regular check of all files that are not owned by an extant user (or an extant group) should be performed regularly:

```
# find / -nouser -print
# find / -nogroup -print
```

Another useful command is vipw. This ensures that the password file retains its schema and is not erroneously modified.

9.6 Manage Groups

A user's group memberships can be displayed by using the groups command. For example, to display the group members for the user jade, the following command would be used:

```
$ groups jade
jade : sales
```

Although users can belong to a primary and optionally a number of secondary groups, the user jade is a member only of the group sales. All group information is stored in the /etc/group database. A sample /etc/group database is shown here:

```
# cat /etc/group
root::0:root
other::1:
bin::2:root,bin,daemon
sys::3:root,bin,sys,adm
adm::4:root,adm,daemon
uucp::5:root,uucp
mail::6:root
tty::7:root,tty,adm
```

9

```
lp:h57fhgy5585jfd:8:root,lp,adm
nuucp::9:root,nuucp
staff::10:charles,oliver,george,alice
daemon::12:root,daemon
nobody::60001:
noaccess::60002:
nogroup::65534:
```

In this example, some groups like *root* have only a single member (*root*), while others have several members (*sys*, for example, has the members *root*, *bin*, *sys*, and *adm*). Note also that the *lp* group has a password associated with it. This means that when members of the group use `newgrp` to assume the group, they must enter the required password. Most groups are not password protected.

Adding New Groups

New groups can be added to the system by using the `groupadd` command. The GID and group name must be unique. For example, to create a group called developr (GID 165) on the local system, the following command would be used:

```
# groupadd -g 165 developr
```

The new entry could then be verified in the */etc/group* database by using the following command:

```
# grep developr /etc/group
developr::165:
```

Another restriction is that new groups must have a GID greater than 100, as low numbered groups are used by the operating system.

Deleting Existing Groups

Existing groups can be deleted from the system by using the `groupdel` command. Groups should be removed if they are no longer required and if no users are members of the group. In the following example, we'll remove the group guests. Firstly, check that no users are members of the group:

```
# grep guests /etc/passwd
```

If this returns nothing, the following command would be issued:

```
# groupdel guests
```

Modifying Existing Groups

Existing groups can be modified on the system by using the groupmod command. Both the name of a group and its GID can be modified. This action is typically performed when a mismatch occurs between the group definitions for files exported from a NFS volume and the client system. To modify the GID to 185 for the group developr, the following command would be used:

```
# groupmod -g 185 developr
```

Alternatively, to rename the developr group to softengr, the following command would be used:

```
# groupmod -n softengr developr
```

Changing Groups

The newgrp command is used to change a user's effective group while working in the shell. Because you are always logged in with your primary GID, you will need to use newgrp to change to any of your secondary GIDs or change back again. For example, if the user jade needs to change from her primary group developr to her secondary group admin, her ID would look like this before the change:

```
$ id
uid=1024(jade) gid=10(developr)
```

To change her effective GID, the following command would be used:

```
$ newgrp admin
```

To verify that the effective GID has been set correctly, the id command can again be used:

```
$ id
uid=1024(jade) gid=10(developr) egid=58(admin)
```

9

Changing the effective GID means that all files created, or processes spawned, will be associated with the new group. For example, prior to changing the effective GID, creating a new file (*database.txt*) would have had the following characteristics:

```
$ touch database.txt
$ ls -l database.txt
-rw-r--r--   1 jade  developr  0 Feb 10 11:17 database.txt
```

After changing the effective GID, re-creating the same file would result in the following characteristics:

```
$ touch database.txt
$ ls -l database.txt
-rw-r--r--   1 jade  admin  0 Feb 10 11:20 database.txt
```

Manual Changes and Conversion

The */etc/group* file can be modified manually, as required, without using the `groupadd`, `groupmod`, or `groupdel` command. While this is risky, because a syntax error could render some group definitions unusable, the `grpck` command can be used to verify the validity of the */etc/group* file. The following errors can be detected by `grpck`:

Too many/few fields	At least one line has too many or not enough fields.
No group name	At least one group name is missing.
Bad character(s) in group name	Group names can contain only letters and numbers.
Invalid GID	At least one GID supplied is not in the range 0–65535.
Null login name	At least one username is missing.
Logname not found in password file	At least one entry contains a username that's not defined in */etc/passwd*.
Line too long	Group entries can contain a maximum of 512 bytes, effectively limiting the size of groups. If your group definitions require more characters, you may need to use NIS/NIS+.
Duplicate logname entry	At least one entry has a username entered twice.

9.7 Monitor Users

After users are active on a system, it's useful to keep tabs on various aspects of user activity. The purpose is twofold—to ensure that system activity does not exceed capacity (checking for CPU "hogs"), and to ensure that user activity is consistent with its normal profile. If a specific user is hogging the CPU, that user' processes can have their priorities reset by using the `nice` command, as described in Module 10. In terms of security, monitoring user activity may reveal unauthorized or uncharacteristic activity. For example, while the local IRC client may have been removed because of an organization's acceptable use policy, a user might decide to compile a client and run it from her own home directory. In this case, examining what the user is doing may reveal these activities. In addition, checking out the locations from which users are logging in may reveal unauthorized access, particularly if the originating hostname or IP address is unusual or unexpected. In such cases, requesting a "talk" session and challenging the user should reveal whether the user is authentic or an intruder. In any case, accounts can be locked using the `passwd -l` command if there is any suspicion of illegal or unauthorized activity.

Three useful commands can be used for monitoring user activity: `who`, `w`, and `finger`.

who

The `who` command prints a list of all users who are currently logged into the system. Several fields can be displayed by the `who` command, including usernames, the connecting line, login date, idle time, process ID (PID), and a comment, as shown here:

```
$ who
root         console       Feb 10 12:39
yukio        pts/0         Jan 10 21:05     (sakura.acollege.ac.jp)
```

w

The w command provides a more detailed look at the list of currently logged in users, which includes foreground process data for each user as well as the connection origin data provided by `who`. In addition, the w command provides an overview of system activity, in the form a system load average that shows CPU loads for the previous 1-minute, 5-minute, and 15-minute intervals. These figures are tallied from the number of jobs processed in the run queue. The total uptime for the system is also displayed.

The following example shows the w output for the users root and jasmine:

```
root         console       Thu1pm  2days      6        6   /bin/sh
jasmine      pts/15        Fri2pm  5:45       9            /bin/ksh
```

9

In this example, the root user has been connected since Thursday at 1 P.M., while the user jasmine has been connected since Friday at 2 P.M.

finger

The `finger` command prints a list of currently logged in users, including their username, full name, connecting TTY, time idle, login time, and login location, as shown in the following example:

```
$ finger
Login       Name              TTY       Idle    When       Where
jade        Jade Goldsmith    pts/1     1d Tue  09:22      wollombi
jasmine     Jasmine Goldsmith pts/2     5 Sat   10:45      barrabra
```

User Messaging

Solaris provides a number of tools that can be used for communicating in real time to logged-in users. One way to provide information to users who are logging in is to modify the */etc/motd* file—*motd* stands for message of the day. For example, if you need to warn users of a scheduled system outage, the */etc/motd* file might contain a message like this:

```
This system will be shut down for scheduled maintenance today
Expected outage: 0300-0800 10th February 2002.
Contact: System Manager (sysadmin) for more information.
```

Even though systems are often maintained outside of normal business hours, it's essential to give users advance notice of at least 24 hours for any downtime.

Imagine, however, that an emergency has occurred and the system needs to be bought down immediately. A disk might have failed, that cannot be hot swapped because volume management is not enabled. To preserve data integrity, it may be necessary to shut down as soon as possible, and run `diskscan` and `fsck` to determine the extent of any damage. In this instance, all users can be warned of such a shutdown by using the `wall` command (*wall* stands for *write all* users). The following is an example of an emergency message:

```
# wall
This system will be shut down for emergency maintenance now
You have five minutes to save your work and log out.
Contact: System Manager (sysadmin) for more information.
```

Pressing CTRL-D will send the message.

If you want to communicate with a single user, two options are available: the `write` command sends a message directly to the terminal of a logged-in user. For example, if a user ignores the *wall* message, you may want to write him or her an individualized message:

```
# write jade
Dear jade,
This system is being shut down immediately.
Any work not saved now will be lost.
Yours Sincerely,
System Manager (sysadmin)
```

If you need to be persistent, the `talk` command disrupts the user with a beep and a request to talk. To talk to the user jade, the following command would be used:

```
# talk jade
```

Of course, `talk` and `write` can be used between individual users for normal communication as well.

☑ *Mastery Check*

9

1. What is a username?

    A. An authentication token that is encrypted

    B. A string of eight characters or less that identifies a user

    C. A number greater than 0 that is used to distinguish group activities on the system

    D. A number greater than 0 that is used to distinguish user activities on the system

2. What is a password?

    A. An authentication token that is encrypted

    B. A string of eight characters or less that identifies a user

☑ *Mastery Check*

    C. A number greater than 0 that is used to distinguish group activities on the system

    D. A number greater than 0 that is used to distinguish user activities on the system

3. What is a UID?

    A. An authentication token that is encrypted

    B. A string of eight characters or less that identifies a user

    C. A number greater than 0 that is used to distinguish group activities on the system

    D. A number greater than 0 that is used to distinguish user activities on the system

4. What is a GID?

    A. An authentication token that is encrypted

    B. A string of eight characters or less that identifies a user

    C. A number greater than 0 that is used to distinguish group activities on the system

    D. A number greater than 0 that is used to distinguish user activities on the system

5. What command checks which users are logged in?

    A. `who`

    B. `write`

    C. `wall`

    D. `finger`

6. What command writes a message to all logged in users?

    A. `who`

    B. `write`

Mastery Check

C. wall

D. finger

7. What command writes a message to a single user?

C. who

D. write

E. wall

F. finger

8. What command displays a load average?

A. who

B. write

C. wall

D. finger

9. What command adds new users to the system?

A. useradd

B. userdel

C. usermod

D. passwd

10. What command deletes users from the system?

A. useradd

B. userdel

C. usermod

D. passwd

11. What command modifies existing users on the system?

A. useradd

B. userdel

9

☑ Mastery Check

C. `usermod`

D. `passwd`

12. What command changes the password for users on the system?

    A. `useradd`

    B. `userdel`

    C. `usermod`

    D. `passwd`

13. Which of the following does `grpck` NOT detect?

    A. Too many/few fields—at least one line has too many or not enough fields

    B. No group name—at least one group name is missing

    C. Bad character(s) in group name—group names can contain only letters and numbers

    D. User over quota

14. What `passwd` command locks an account preventing logins?

    A. `passwd -L`

    B. `passwd -l`

    C. `passwd lock`

    D. `passwd -n`

15. What password command sets the number of days before a password change is allowed?

    A. `passwd -L`

    B. `passwd -l`

    C. `passwd lock`

    D. `passwd -n`

Module 10

Processes, Jobs, and Signals

Critical Skills

Processes lie at the heart of all modern multi-user operating systems. By dividing system tasks into small, discrete elements, which are uniquely identified by a process identifier (PID), Solaris is able to manage all of the applications that may be concurrently executed by many different users. In addition, individual users may execute more than one application at any one time. Each Solaris process is associated with a user identifier (UID) and a group identifier (GID), just like a standard file. This means that only users may send signals to their own processes, except for the super-user, who may send signals to any process on the system. Signals are typically used to restart or terminate processes. The multi-user, multitasking process model in Solaris ensures that system resources can be shared equally among all competing processes, or allocated preferentially to the most important applications. For example, a firewall application would probably take precedence over all other system processes. Individual users and the super-user may allocate a priority level to active processes in real time.

Module 10 examines the concepts of understanding processes and managing system file system, CPU, and memory resources. In this module, you will learn how to interpret process displays, trace system calls for processes that are resident in memory, and send signals to processes. In addition, you'll learn about such tools as top, which can be used for online monitoring of process activity, and you'll review the */proc* file system tools, which are used to extract real-time data about lightweight processes (LWPs) running on your system. Finally, you'll learn how to schedule processes to run at specific times by using at or cron.

10.1 Interpret Process Displays

Most users obtain information about processes by using the ps command, which has a number of options shown in Table 10-1. By default, the ps command displays only the processes that are owned by the current user; however, it can also be configured to display details of all processes on a system. This is one reason why it is prudent to check your process list to determine whether or not sensitive information is available to other users. For example, if a user executed a database client and passed the username and password on the command line, another user may be able to extract this information from the process list. Thus, even less privileged users may sometimes be able to extract useful information about processes being run by other users.

Parameter	Description
-a	Displays most frequently requested processes
-A, -e	Displays all processes
-c	Displays processes in scheduler format
-d	Displays all processes
-f	Displays comprehensive process information
-g	Displays process information on a group basis for a single group
-G	Displays process information on a group basis for a list of groups
-j	Displays SID and PGID (Process Group ID) in printout
-l	Displays complete process information
-L	Displays LWP details
-p	Displays process details for list of specified process
-P	Displays the CPU ID to which a process is bound
-s	Displays session leaders
-t	Displays all processes associated with a specific terminal
-u	Displays all processes for a specific user

Table 10-1   Commonly Used Options for the ps Command

One alternative to the ps command that has a graphical-user interface (GUI) is the CDE Process Manager, shown in Figure 10-1. It presents a snapshot of all processes on a system and includes columns for PID, command name, user, CPU time consumed, physical RAM used, virtual RAM used, date the process was started, and full command string. The display can be configured to refresh every 30 seconds or less, so that you can monitor process activities continuously.

10

1-Minute Drill

● What command displays process session leaders?

● What command displays processes for the user walrus?

● What command displays all processes in scheduler format?

● ps -s
● ps -u walrus
● ps -cd

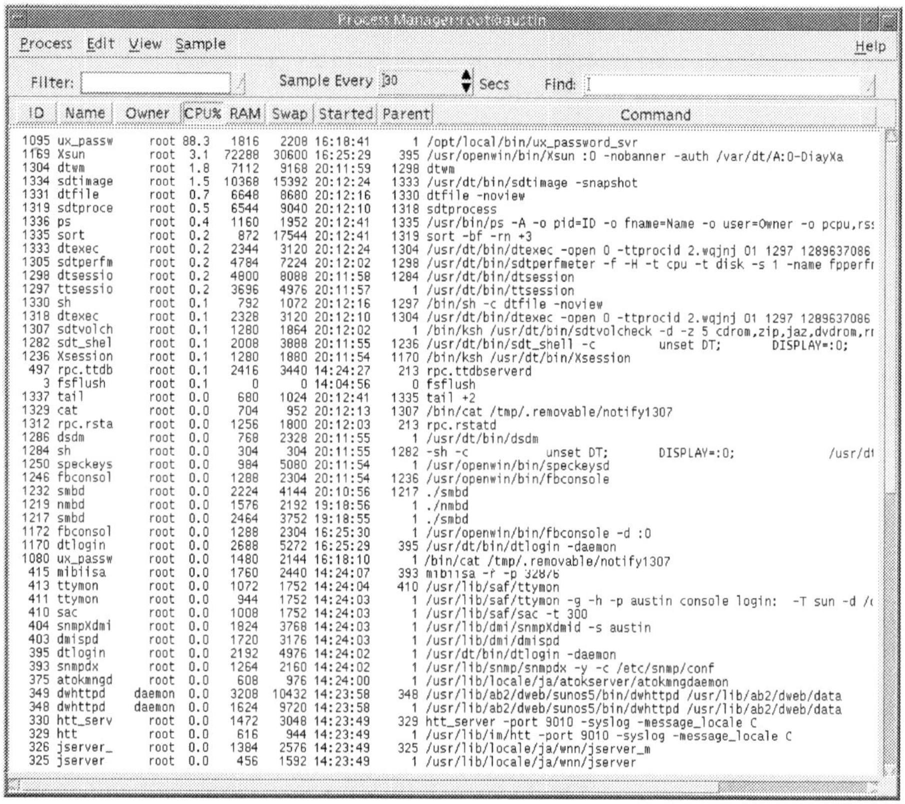

Figure 10-1 CDE Process Manager

In the following sections, we will examine the most commonly used process listings and review their utility in light of process and user management issues. In many ways, the CDE Process Manager is just a graphical representation of *top* (more about *top* in section 10.4).

Listing Frequently Requested Processes

The `ps -a` command lists most frequently requested processes, as shown in the following example:

```
$ ps -a
  PID TTY       TIME CMD
 1511 pts/2     0:00 sh
 1531 pts/2     0:00 ttsessio
 1532 pts/2     0:01 dtsessio
 2878 pts/2     0:00 dtfile
 3243 pts/3     0:00 netscape
 3242 pts/3     0:22 netscape
 2877 pts/2     0:00 sh
 6809 pts/7     0:00 man
 6824 pts/7     0:00 sh
 6825 pts/7     0:00 more
 6835 pts/5     0:00 dtterm
 6640 pts/7     0:00 bash
 6832 pts/5     0:00 ksh
 6840 pts/8     0:00 ps
```

The results here are unsurprising: the most frequently requested process has a PID of 1511 and is the Bourne shell, *sh*, running on the terminal *pts/2*. We can also see several other processes spawned from the terminal *pts/2*, including CDE session and file management utilities. The *TIME* column here displays the number of CPU minutes and seconds that a particular process has consumed since being spawned. The *netscape* application (*PID 3242*) has consumed the most CPU time in this example.

Ask the Expert

10

Question: What is the most useful process display for system monitoring?

Answer: I always use `ps -eaf` to provide comprehensive information on all user processes.

10.2 List All Processes

To obtain a list of all processes currently running on a system, you use the ps -A command. In the example shown next, the first process spawned after booting is the scheduler, followed by the *init* process, which is ultimately the parent process for all user processes spawned on the system. Indeed, if you examine the Parent PID (PPID) for processes whose parents have been killed, you will find that the PPID reverts to PID 1. In the *TTY* column, a question mark (?) is displayed wherever a process is not bound to a specific terminal. In this example, the process consuming the highest amount of CPU time is the file system flush process (*fsflush*), PID 3.

```
$ ps -A
   PID TTY       TIME CMD
     0 ?         0:00 sched
     1 ?         0:00 init
     2 ?         0:00 pageout
     3 ?         5:09 fsflush
   410 ?         0:00 sac
   179 ?         0:00 ss_timed
   413 ?         0:00 ttymon
    66 ?         0:00 devfseve
    68 ?         0:00 devfsadm
   290 ?         0:00 automoun
   243 ?         0:00 keyserv
   121 ?         0:04 skipd
   178 ?         0:00 ss_logd
   298 ?         0:01 syslogd
   282 ?         0:00 lockd
   286 ?         0:00 statd
   361 ?         0:00 vold
```

Scheduler Format

The ps -c command lists processes in the scheduler format. This includes two extra columns: priority class (*CLS*) and process priority (*PRI*). In this case, the ps command and the Korn shell (*ksh*) are both members of the Time Sharing class, meaning that a priority value may be assigned to each process. In the case of the ps process, this has a higher priority value than the Korn shell process, and thus it has greater access to the system's resources.

Ask the Expert

Question: At what priority should I set processes to run?

Answer: Unless a job should have more or less priority, you should leave the prioritized allocation of resources to the kernel. However, if you're running a slow batch job, or you need to get some results quickly, then you'll need to set the nice value directly.

```
$ ps -c
   PID  CLS PRI TTY       TIME CMD
  6842   TS  45 pts/8    0:00 ps
  6837   TS  35 pts/8    0:00 ksh
```

If you wanted to give priority to the Korn shell process, you could use the nice command to reduce the priority granted to the ps process:

```
$ nice -20 ps
```

However, a super-user may actually increase the priority of a process by using this command:

```
# nice --10 ps
```

This command would result in the priority of the ps command being increased directly by 10.

10

10.3 List Full Process Data

If you're an administrator, you'll typically want to keep an eye on all processes that are being run on your system. A number of good reasons for developing this kind of monitoring as a habit are listed here:

- **Performance**   It's critical to determine, during a general lag being experienced by interactive users on a system, which of the hundreds (or thousands) of processes are causing the bottleneck.

● **Security**   It's important to get an idea for the commands and applications
that are typically executed by users on your system. Unusual and/or
conspicuous activity may indicate a break-in attempt by a rogue user.
You may decide, in an emergency, to suspend a process that appears
suspicious and activate it again once its authenticity has been verified.

The most comprehensive process information can be obtained by running
the ps -f command, as shown in the following example:

```
$ ps -f
     UID    PID  PPID  C     STIME TTY     TIME CMD
    root   6846  6837  0 13:12:03 pts/8   0:00 ps -f
    root   6837  6835  0 13:10:42 pts/8   0:00 /bin/ksh
```

Here, we can see that several extra columns are printed in addition to the
standard process listing, including the *PPID*, and the processor utilization
column (*C*), which is retained only for historical purposes (this means that
scripts which expect to see the *C* column will not crash just because the data
is no longer available).

The ps -f command may be combined with the -e option to form the
command ps -ef, which prints comprehensive details on all processes
running on a system.

Group Process Information

Often, it's important that you keep track of what a specific group of users is
doing. For example, if you're running a student system at a college, you may
wish to check only the processes run by members of the group student to check
for password cracking programs or other prohibited applications. Fortunately,
the ps -G command prints group process data for a specified GID. In the
following code, we display process information on a group basis for members
of the group GID 1, which includes the root user:

```
$ ps -G 1
   PID TTY       TIME CMD
  1511 pts/2    0:00 sh
  1531 pts/2    0:00 ttsessio
  1475 ?        0:00 fbconsol
  1532 pts/2    0:01 dtsessio
  1544 ?        0:00 sdtvolch
```

```
 1539 ?          0:04 dtwm
 1541 ?          0:00 sdtperfm
 1515 ?          0:00 dsdm
 3207 ?          0:00 miniserv
```

Full Process Listing

If you haven't been satisfied by any of the process displays we've reviewed so far, the next command, ps -1, will print every piece of information that is collected about each individual process on the system. In the next example, each of the following characteristics is reported:

- Command name (CMD)
- CPU time consumed
- Memory address (ADDR)
- Memory address for sleeping processes (WCHAN)
- Memory size (SZ)
- Nice value (NI)
- Parent process ID (PPID)
- Process flags (F)
- Process ID (PID)
- Process priority (PRI)
- Process state (S), including running processes *R* and sleeping processes *S*
- Processor utilization (C)

In this example, the sleeping process PID 6837 has a parent PID of 6835, a priority of 63, a nice value of 24, a memory address of e0f85050, with a total size of 373K, a WCHAN of e0f850bc, and negligible CPU time consumed:

```
$ ps -1
 F S   UID   PID  PPID  C PRI NI     ADDR   SZ    WCHAN TTY    TIME CMD
 8 0     0  6861  6848  0  53 24 e1053780  196          pts/8  0:00 ps
 8 R     0  6848  6837  0  63 24 e128e098  501          pts/8  0:00 bash
 8 S     0  6837  6835  0  63 24 e0f85050  373 e0f850bc pts/8  0:00 ksh
```

Combining Process Options

One of the most useful features of the ps command is the ability to combine different process options into a single command. For example, if we wanted to print the list of all LWPs (threads) associated with every process on the system, we could use the command ps -eL. This produces a long listing showing all LWPs, with the LWP number shown in the column *LWP*:

```
$ ps -eL
  PID   LWP TTY      LTIME CMD
    0     1 ?         0:00 sched
    1     1 ?         0:00 init
    2     1 ?         0:00 pageout
    3     1 ?         5:09 fsflush
  410     1 ?         0:00 sac
  179     1 ?         0:00 ss_timed
  413     1 ?         0:00 ttymon
   66     1 ?         0:00 devfseve
  144     1 ?         0:00 httpd
  144     2 ?         0:00 httpd
  144     6 ?         0:00 httpd
  144     7 ?         0:00 httpd
  144     8 ?         0:00 httpd
  144     9 ?         0:00 httpd
  144    11 ?         0:00 httpd
  144    12 ?         0:00 httpd
  144    13 ?         0:00 httpd
```

Ask the Expert

Question: Why do some applications use threads and not processes?

Answer: The process lifecycle is expensive in terms of CPU and memory resources. Creating a process and killing it is much slower than spawning a lightweight process and managing it. Threads can be used to perform discrete tasks and then be killed off. Alternatively, they can be pooled and reused for optimal performance.

Obviously, the Apache Web Server daemon (*httpd*) has many LWPs associated with it. Another way to extract this information is to use the `pgrep` command, which displays a list of all processes with the same name and displays their PIDs:

```
$ pgrep httpd
144
3610
3611
2901
3612
3603
3604
3605
3607
3608
3609
3606
```

10.4 Monitor System Resources

In the previous section, we examined how to use the `ps` command to obtain interactive data about the number and type of processes being run on a Solaris system. However, to obtain real-time process information, many administrators prefer to use the *top* program, which is not supplied with Solaris 9, but which can be downloaded from **http://www.sunfreeware.com/**. If you prefer to build from source, the current *top* version is available from **ftp://ftp.groupsys.com/pub/top**.

A typical display from *top* is shown here:

```
last pid:  6911;  load averages:  0.05,  0.02,  0.02          13:16:05
74 processes:  73 sleeping, 1 on cpu
CPU states:     % idle,     % user,     % kernel,     % iowait,     % swap
Memory: 128M real, 9396K free, 106M swap in use, 137M swap free

  PID USERNAME THR PRI NICE  SIZE   RES STATE   TIME   CPU COMMAND
 6911 root       1  26    4 1264K  884K cpu     0:00 0.44% top
 6614 root       1  46    4 5924K 3780K sleep   0:00 0.13% dtterm
 6640 root       1  36    4 2008K 1456K sleep   0:00 0.02% bash
 6835 root       1  46    4 5940K 3840K sleep   0:00 0.01% dtterm
    1 root       1  58    0  628K  108K sleep   0:00 0.01% init
 6848 root       1  36    4 2004K 1412K sleep   0:00 0.01% bash
  669 root       1  59    0   15M   13M sleep   0:43 0.00% Xsun
```

10

```
3242 root      1  57   4   15M   12M sleep  0:21  0.00% netscape
 317 root      7  51   0 2900K 2108K sleep  0:04  0.00% nscd
 245 root      3  58   0 1776K 1144K sleep  0:04  0.00% nis_cachemgr
 121 root      1  58   0 4616K  968K sleep  0:03  0.00% skipd
1539 root      8  59   0 7576K 5064K sleep  0:03  0.00% dtwm
 376 root      1   1  19 2396K  408K sleep  0:01  0.00% sendmail
 298 root      9  58   0   13M 2588K sleep  0:01  0.00% syslogd
1583 root      1  12   0  760K  540K sleep  0:00  0.00% cat
```

The *top* display is updated every few seconds, so that all values reflect the current state of the system. We can see at 1:16.05 P.M., the last PID used was 6911, and that the 1-, 5-, and 15-minute load averages on the system were 0.05, 0.02, and 0.02, respectively. These values represent 5, 2, and 2 percent system load, respectively, meaning that the system is presently underutilized. A total of 74 processes were active, with all but one process (the *top* process) sleeping. The system in question has 128MB of physical RAM, of which almost 10MB is free. The system also has a total of 243MB of virtual RAM, of which approximately 106MB is being used. The process display is similar to the columns and values displayed in the ps examples earlier in the module: many of the processes, for example, have a number of LWPs associated with a single process (for example, *nscd*, the name service cache daemon, has seven LWPs, while the *top* program only has one).

1-Minute Drill

● What load average indicates that a uniprocessor system is operating at full capacity?

10.5 Trace System Calls

When developing applications, it is often useful to be able to examine what is going on "behind the scenes" in terms of processes being spawned and system calls being executed. Solaris provides the *truss* utility, which is able to track all of these details and which can be displayed interactively or dumped to a file. In addition, *truss* is often used by system administrators to determine why an application is failing to run. For example, if an application is attempting to read data from a configuration file that does not exist, or if it is trying to locate a

● 1.0

library whose location does not exist in the PATH of the runtime user, *truss* can reveal the calls that are failing.

In the following example, we trace the system calls involved in using the `ls` command. The first system call made is to the `execve()` function, which is called with the full name of the application that needs to be executed, a pointer to the list of arguments passed to the application (*0xEFFFF740*), and an environment pointer (*0xEFFFF74C*). Next, memory mapping operations are performed, followed by four attempts to open the library *libc.so.1*, which is checked against paths listed in the *LD_LIBRARY_PATH* environment variable. In this case, the library is not found in the */usr/local/lib/*, */usr/openwin/lib/*, or */usr/dt/lib/* directory, but it is finally located in the */usr/lib* directory. At the end of the *truss*, we can see the names of some of the files in the current directory being printed, including *filesync, man, script,* and *zipinfo*.

```
$ truss ls
execve("/usr/bin/ls", 0x08047BB0, 0x08047BB8)   argc = 1
open("/dev/zero", O_RDONLY)                     = 3
mmap(0x00000000, 4096, PROT_READ|PROT_WRITE|PROT_EXEC,
MAP_PRIVATE, 3, 0) = 0xDFBE1000
xstat(2, "/usr/bin/ls", 0x0804792C)             = 0
sysconfig(_CONFIG_PAGESIZE)                     = 4096
open("/usr/local/lib/libc.so.1", O_RDONLY)      Err#2 ENOENT
open("/usr/openwin/lib/libc.so.1", O_RDONLY)    Err#2 ENOENT
open("/usr/dt/lib/libc.so.1", O_RDONLY)         Err#2 ENOENT
open("/usr/lib/libc.so.1", O_RDONLY)            = 4
fxstat(2, 4, 0x0804776C)                        = 0
mmap(0x00000000, 4096, PROT_READ|PROT_EXEC, MAP_PRIVATE, 4, 0)
= 0xDFBDF000
mmap(0x00000000, 598016, PROT_READ|PROT_EXEC, MAP_PRIVATE, 4, 0)
= 0xDFB4C000
mmap(0xDFBD6000, 24392, PROT_READ|PROT_WRITE|PROT_EXEC,
MAP_PRIVATE|MAP_FIXED, 4, 561152) = 0xDFBD6000
mmap(0xDFBDC000, 6356, PROT_READ|PROT_WRITE|PROT_EXEC,
MAP_PRIVATE|MAP_FIXED, 3, 0) = 0xDFBDC000
close(4)                                        = 0
open("/usr/local/lib/libdl.so.1", O_RDONLY)     Err#2 ENOENT
open("/usr/openwin/lib/libdl.so.1", O_RDONLY)   Err#2 ENOENT
open("/usr/dt/lib/libdl.so.1", O_RDONLY)        Err#2 ENOENT
open("/usr/lib/libdl.so.1", O_RDONLY)           = 4
fxstat(2, 4, 0x0804776C)                        = 0
...
write(1, " f i l e                    ".., 59)   = 59
```

```
filesync          man           script          zipinfo
write(1, " f i l e s y n c        ".., 62)      = 62
llseek(0, 0, SEEK_CUR)                          = 100860
_exit(0)
```

10.6 Manage Multiple CPUs

In addition to the ps and top commands, Solaris provides several different utilities that can be used to profile system performance on multiple CPU systems, including the mpstat and psrinfo commands, which print real-time process statistics on a per-processor basis and the uptime of individual CPUs, respectively. The mpstat command prints statistics for major (*mjf*) and minor (*minf*) faults experienced, the number of calls passed between the two CPUs (*xcal*), the number of interrupts (*intr*), the percentage of CPU time consumed by user processes (*wt*), and the percentage of CPU time taken up by system processes (*sys*).

```
$ mpstat
CPU minf mjf xcal  intr ithr  csw icsw migr smtx  srw syscl  usr sys  wt idl
  0   46   1  205   330  260  114   92   35   97    0    62   30  13   8  48
  1   45   1   35    50  138   89   89   35   94    0   256   35  13   8  45
```

In the following psrinfo output, we can see that both CPUs came online together and have not ceased operating since that time:

```
$ psrinfo
0          on-line    since 05/16/00 18:35:23
1          on-line    since 05/16/00 18:35:26
```

The /proc File System

One of the key differences between Solaris and other network operating systems is the */proc* file system: by representing all of the LWPs running on a system within a file system-like hierarchy, standard system calls may be used to retrieve information about these processes. Each LWP is associated with a PID, which is represented by a directory entry under the */proc* directory. Each subdirectory then contains a number of different files in which runtime process data is stored.

The information that can be retrieved from /proc about LWPs is based on files that contain the following information:

● Address space (*as*)

● Address space references (*pagedata*)

● Control file (*ctl*)

● Credential data (*cred*)

● Current working directory (*cwd*)

● File descriptor (*fd*)

● Local descriptor table (*ldt*)

● Process information (*psinfo*)

● Reserved memory map (*rmap*)

● Root directory (*root*)

● Signals data (*sigact*)

● Status file (*status*)

● Virtual memory map (*map*)

Solaris provides a number of different "proc tools" that can be used to extract process state information from the /proc file system in a form that is easily accessible to developers and administrators. In the following sections, each of these tools is examined along with how they can be used to identify important run-time information about active LWPs.

10

1-Minute Drill

● What is the purpose of the /proc file system?

● It represents all lightweight processes running on a system within a file system-like hierarchy.

Tracing Flags

The pflags command is used to display tracing flags, the data model, and any pending signals for a specified process. In the following example, the data model is revealed at __IP32, the tracing flag is *PR_PCINVAL*, and two pending signals are identified:

```
$ pflags 11635
11635:  bash
        data model = _ILP32
 /1:    flags = PR_PCINVAL
  sigmask = 0x00020002,0x00000000
```

Process Credentials

The pcred command displays process credentials, which are evaluated by applications with respect to access and file permissions. The credentials that can be determined by the pcred command are the effective, real, and saved UIDs, and the effective, real, and saved GIDs of the target process. In the following example, the effective, real, and saved UID of the process is 501, while the effective, real, and saved GID of the process is 100. If the process being executed was setuid or setgid (that is, where the UID or GID was set to be something different than the executing user), the effective, real, and saved UIDs and GIDs would be distinct:

```
$ pcred 11635
11635:  e/r/suid=501  e/r/sgid=100
        groups: 100 101
```

Address Space Map

The pmap command is used to display a map of the address space associated with each process. It can be quite revealing to examine exactly what memory chunks are being consumed by an application and its associated files. In the following example, the Bourne again shell (bash) occupies memory directly, but system libraries, such as the *nsl* and *socket* libraries, are called by the shell and therefore require memory of their own:

```
$ pmap 11635
11635:  bash
```

```
00010000    488K read/exec          /usr/local/bin/bash
00098000     32K read/write/exec    /usr/local/bin/bash
000A0000    144K read/write/exec     [ heap ]
FF100000    656K read/exec          /usr/lib/libc.so.1
FF1B2000     32K read/write/exec    /usr/lib/libc.so.1
FF1BA000      8K read/write/exec     [ anon ]
FF200000    512K read/exec          /usr/lib/libnsl.so.1
FF28E000     40K read/write/exec    /usr/lib/libnsl.so.1
FF298000     32K read/write/exec     [ anon ]
FF2B0000      8K read/write/exec     [ anon ]
FF2C0000     16K read/exec          /usr/lib/locale/en_AU/en_AU.so.2
FF2D2000     16K read/write/exec    /usr/lib/locale/en_AU/en_AU.so.2
FF2E0000     16K read/exec          /usr/platform/sun4u/lib/libc_psr.so.1
FF2F0000     16K read/exec          /usr/lib/libmp.so.2
FF302000      8K read/write/exec    /usr/lib/libmp.so.2
FF320000     32K read/exec          /usr/lib/libsocket.so.1
FF336000     16K read/write/exec    /usr/lib/libsocket.so.1
FF340000    168K read/exec          /usr/lib/libcurses.so.1
FF378000     40K read/write/exec    /usr/lib/libcurses.so.1
FF382000      8K read/write/exec     [ anon ]
FF390000      8K read/exec          /usr/lib/libdl.so.1
FF3A0000      8K read/write/exec     [ anon ]
FF3B0000    120K read/exec          /usr/lib/ld.so.1
FF3DC000      8K read/write/exec    /usr/lib/ld.so.1
FFBEC000     16K read/write/exec     [ stack ]
 total     2448K
```

Libraries in Use

The `pldd` command displays a list of the libraries that are being currently used by a process. In combination with the `pmap` command, `pldd` provides a complete picture of the libraries that are being used at any one time by a process and may help to determine which system libraries are retained or backed up, or whose file size is monitored to detect Trojan horses in critical libraries.

```
$ pldd 11635
11635:  bash
/usr/lib/libcurses.so.1
/usr/lib/libsocket.so.1
/usr/lib/libnsl.so.1
/usr/lib/libdl.so.1
/usr/lib/libc.so.1
/usr/lib/libmp.so.2
/usr/platform/sun4u/lib/libc_psr.so.1
/usr/lib/locale/en_AU/en_AU.so.2
```

Current Process Signals

The psig command displays all the signals that are associated with the current process. Entries for the first nine process signals are displayed (for more information about these signals, see Table 10-2), including *SIGHUP*, *SIGINT*, *SIGILL*, *SIGTRAP*, *SIGABRT*, *SIGEMT*, *SIGFPE*, and *SIGKILL*.

```
$ psig 11635
11635:  bash
HUP        caught  0          HUP,INT,ILL,TRAP,ABRT,EMT,FPE,BUS,SEGV,
SYS,PIPE,ALRM,TERM,USR1,USR2,VTALRM,PROF,XCPU,XFSZ,LOST
INT        blocked,caught  0
QUIT       ignored
ILL        caught  0          HUP,INT,ILL,TRAP,ABRT,EMT,FPE,BUS,SEGV,
SYS,PIPE,ALRM,TERM,USR1,USR2,VTALRM,PROF,XCPU,XFSZ,LOST
TRAP       caught  0          HUP,INT,ILL,TRAP,ABRT,EMT,FPE,BUS,SEGV,
SYS,PIPE,ALRM,TERM,USR1,USR2,VTALRM,PROF,XCPU,XFSZ,LOST
ABRT       caught  0          HUP,INT,ILL,TRAP,ABRT,EMT,FPE,BUS,SEGV
,SYS,PIPE,ALRM,TERM,USR1,USR2,VTALRM,PROF,XCPU,XFSZ,LOST
EMT        caught  0          HUP,INT,ILL,TRAP,ABRT,EMT,FPE,BUS,SEGV,
SYS,PIPE,ALRM,TERM,USR1,USR2,VTALRM,PROF,XCPU,XFSZ,LOST
FPE        caught  0          HUP,INT,ILL,TRAP,ABRT,EMT,FPE,BUS,SEGV,
SYS,PIPE,ALRM,TERM,USR1,USR2,VTALRM,PROF,XCPU,XFSZ,LOST
KILL       default
```

Symbolic Stack Trace

The pstack command is used to print a symbolic stack trace for the LWPs associated with the named process. In the following example, the symbols identified include *waitid*, *_waitpid*, and *waitchld*.

```
$ pstack 11635
11635:  bash
 ff198038 waitid   (7, 0, ffbef4c8, 7)
 ff157084 _waitpid (ffffffff, ffbef5ac, 4, 7, ff1b3968, 3d30c) + 54
 0003d30c waitchld (0, 0, ff00, 9a000, 1, 3661) + 78
 0003c4cc wait_for (3661, 0, ffffffff, 0, 0, bafd0) + 150
 00031020 execute_command_internal (0, 9a000, 5, ffffffff, 0,
  ff198140) + 768
 00031e54 execute_pipeline (bae90, 0, 5, ffffffff, c2b50, 0) + 254
 00032094 execute_connection (bb1d0, 0, ffffffff, ffffffff,
  c2b50, ab831) + 20c
 0003127c execute_command_internal (0, 0, ffffffff, ffffffff,
```

```
  0, 0) + 9c4
0003069c execute_command (bb1d0, 73, 99c00, a6414, bb1d0, a) + 48
00027144 reader_loop (99c00, 1, 1, 1, ffbefb48, 1) + 1c4
0002568c main      (0, ffbefa24, ffbefa2c, a0598, 0, 0) + 82c
00024d7c _start    (0, 0, 0, 0, 0, 0) + 5c
```

Open Files

The pfiles command reports details about all of the files that have been opened by a specified process. In the following example, several files have been opened, with a number of different file permissions, including 0444, 0620, and 0644.

```
$ pfiles 11635
11635:  bash
  Current rlimit: 64 file descriptors
   0: S_IFCHR mode:0620 dev:136,0 ino:208102 uid:501 gid:7 rdev:24,3
      O_RDWR
   1: S_IFCHR mode:0620 dev:136,0 ino:208102 uid:501 gid:7 rdev:24,3
      O_RDWR
   2: S_IFCHR mode:0620 dev:136,0 ino:208102 uid:501 gid:7 rdev:24,3
      O_RDWR
   3: S_IFDOOR mode:0444 dev:176,0 ino:367 uid:0 gid:0 size:0
      O_RDONLY|O_LARGEFILE FD_CLOEXEC  door to nscd[184]
   4: S_IFDOOR mode:0644 dev:176,0 ino:373 uid:0 gid:0 size:0
      O_RDONLY  door to keyserv[106]
  63: S_IFCHR mode:0620 dev:136,0 ino:208102 uid:501 gid:7 rdev:24,3
      O_RDWR FD_CLOEXEC
```

Current Working Directory

The pwdx command is just like the pwd: it prints the current working directory of the LWP, except that the data is derived from the */proc* file system.

```
$ pwdx 11635
11635:  /etc/rc2.d
```

Process Tree

The ptree command displays a hierarchical diagram of all parent processes, with their child processes displayed beneath them. This pictorial representation makes it easy for you to obtain a quick snapshot of how all processes on the system are related to each other. In the following example, we can see that a telnet session (13961) spawned a Korn shell (13963), which then spawned a

Bash shell (13978), which was then used to execute the `ptree` command (14012). Of course, some processes like rpcbind (104) have no child processes but are still displayed as they are potential parent processes.

```
$ ptree
47     /usr/lib/devfsadm/devfseventd
49     /usr/lib/devfsadm/devfsadmd
104    /usr/sbin/rpcbind
106    /usr/sbin/keyserv
108    /usr/sbin/nis_cachemgr
150    /usr/sbin/inetd -s
  596    rpc.ttdbserverd
  10966 in.rlogind
    10968 -ksh
  13961 in.telnetd
    13963 -ksh
      13978 bash
        14012 ptree
149    /usr/lib/nfs/lockd
152    /usr/lib/nfs/statd
154    /usr/lib/autofs/automountd
166    /usr/sbin/syslogd
169    /usr/sbin/cron
184    /usr/sbin/nscd -S passwd,yes -S group,yes
190    /usr/lib/lpsched
204    /usr/lib/power/powerd
213    /usr/sbin/vold
215    /usr/lib/utmpd
219    /usr/local/sbin/sshd
223    /usr/lib/sendmail -bd -q15m
235    /usr/local/samba/bin/smbd -D -l /var/adm/smblogs/log -s
  /usr/local/samba/
  10483 /usr/local/samba/bin/smbd -D -l /var/adm/smblogs/log -s
  /usr/local/samb
  10678 /usr/local/samba/bin/smbd -D -l /var/adm/smblogs/log -s
  /usr/local/samb
```

Process Timing

The `ptime` command is similar to the `time` command: it displays the real, user, and system time required to execute a process. The difference between `ptime` and `time` is that the former uses the */proc* file system to obtain its data. In the following example, the `ls` command consumed 0.039 real seconds to execute, including 0.003 user seconds and 0.006 system seconds.

```
$ ptime /bin/ls /etc/rc3.d
README          S15nfs.server   S76snmpdx       S77dmi

real            0.039
user            0.003
sys             0.006
```

10.7 Send Signals

Earlier, we saw that the `psig` command was used to display signals associated with LWPs. In this context, a *signal* is a message sent between processes by using the interprocess communication facilities of Solaris. Signals allow a process like the shell to communicate with child processes, telling them to start, stop, or suspend their activity, among other things. These kinds of signals can also be sent directly from C programs, using the `signal()` system call.

Solaris supports all of the standard System V signal types, as shown in Table 10-2.

Signals are typically used in the shell to manage jobs that have been executed from the shell. In Microsoft Windows, a list of running processes may

Signal	Code	Action	Description
SIGHUP	1	Exit	Hang up
SIGINT	2	Exit	Interrupt
SIGQUIT	3	Core	Quit
SIGILL	4	Core	Illegal instruction
SIGTRAP	5	Core	Trace or breakpoint trap
SIGABRT	6	Core	Abort
SIGEMT	7	Core	Emulation trap
SIGFPE	8	Core	Arithmetic exception
SIGKILL	9	Exit	Killed
SIGBUS	10	Core	Bus error
SIGSEGV	11	Core	Segmentation fault
SIGSYS	12	Core	Bad system call
SIGPIPE	13	Exit	Broken pipe
SIGALRM	14	Exit	Alarm clock
SIGTERM	15	Exit	Terminated

Table 10-2   Solaris Process Signals

10

be obtained from the Task Manager, and a kill-like signal may be sent by clicking on the End Process button. Sending signals within the shell to kill a process performs a similar function; however, the many different signals are used for different purposes.

To launch a number of applications from a single shell, it is necessary to execute each application "in the background" by including an ampersand (&) on the command line, leaving the shell interface free to issue new commands. This kind of multiprocessing is made possible because all processes that are sent into the background are associated with a specific job number, in addition to their process number. Once a job is in the background, it may be bought into the foreground by using the fg command within the shell and by specifying the job number that needs to be brought to the foreground. An alternative method for sending a process into the background is to launch it normally in the foreground, then suspend the process by sending a signal, and then using the bg command to send the process into the background. The suspend signal is issued by using the CTRL-Z key combination.

There are no limits to the number of applications that may be run in the background, but only one application may be run in the foreground at any one time. In the following example, we begin by executing an application in the foreground (bash), then suspending it, and then sending it into the background. The process may be bought back into the foreground by using the fg command with the job number, after some other process (ls) has been run in the foreground and has exited.

Project 10-1: Running Jobs in the Background and Foreground

This project shows you how to suspend a job, run it in the background, and then bring it to the foreground again. This is an important task for running multiple jobs from a single terminal.

Step-by-Step

1. Run a new process from an existing shell:

```
csh% bash
bash-2.03$
```

2. Suspend the new process:

```
^z
```

3. Send the new process into the background:

```
csh% bg
[1]  1024
```

4. Perform other tasks in the foreground:

```
csh% ls
data1.txt    data2.txt    data3.txt
```

5. Bring the background process into the foreground:

```
csh% fg
bash-2.03$
```

Summary

Processes can be sent into the background by using bg, and then they can be sent back into the foreground by using fg.

To send a signal to a process, other than to suspend, background, or foreground, you need to use the kill command. Does the command name sound fatal? Well, signals sent by kill are usually sent to restart, terminate a process gracefully, or terminate a process ungracefully. The signal that you decide to send to a process will obviously depend on the urgency of the situation and the integrity of data being operated on by the process in question. For example, a database server process may be restarted by sending a kill –1 command, which should cause it to restart after shutting down gracefully and rereading its configuration file. This process could take a long time. Alternatively, if you urgently need to shut down a process and don't care about the consequences, you could issue a kill –9 command. Finally, if you need to kill a parent and all of its child processes, a kill –15 is often the most appropriate command.

As an example, if you wanted to kill the Samba server with a PID of 666, then typing

```
$ kill -1 666
```

10

would restart the Samba server, with its configuration updated from disk. However, if you issued the `kill` signal to the process with this command

```
$ kill -9 666
```

the process would be stopped immediately and not restarted automatically.

10.8 Schedule Jobs

In the previous examples, we've examined how to spawn processes from a shell by executing them from the command line. However, in many situations, a process needs to be started (or killed) when a system administrator is not available. For example, the Solaris security package called *aset* is often used at its low level to perform a security scan every week or each night. Typically, CPU-intensive tasks like searching or security audits are performed at times of low system load (such as midnight). Thus, *aset* can be scheduled to run once per week, at any required time, or several times per week, depending on the level of threat posed to the system. Alternatively, you may want to run a task only once at some future time. For example, you may decide to initiate a complete system backup using *ufsdump* in preparation for a system upgrade. This could be scheduled to be performed once at 2 A.M. the following morning.

Jobs can be scheduled to occur regularly by using the `cron` command. Alternatively, once-off jobs can be scheduled to occur at a specific date and time by using the `at` command. In the following sections, we examine how to schedule jobs by using `cron` and `at`.

The at Command

A single job can be scheduled to occur by using the `at` command. The job can be composed of a single command to be executed or a list of commands to be processed sequentially, much like a script. Once a job has been submitted, it is stored in a file within the */var/spool/cron/atjobs* directory, which contains some `at`-specific wrapping around the commands to be executed.

As an example, consider a service that is to be switched on late at night, such as a Web server that releases exam results at a college. If the time is quite specific, it's important that the service not be available before the advertised time. In addition, administrators may not be available to switch on the service.

Fortunately, the at command can be used to set up the server to run—if the server is started by a script called */opt/scripts/start_exam_server.sh*, for example, the following command would execute the script at 10:30 P.M.:

```
$ at 2230
at> /opt/scripts/start_exam_server.sh
at> <EOT>
commands will be executed using /bin/sh
job 234563467.a at Mon Jan 21 22:30:00 2002
```

To verify that the job has been submitted correctly, we can check to see whether its command file is in the *atjobs* queue:

```
$ ls -l /var/spool/cron/atjobs
total 8
-r-Sr--r--    1 apache       www         3045 Jan  21 12:35 234563467.a
```

We can also verify that the job contains the appropriate commands by using the cat command:

```
$ cat /var/spool/cron/atjobs/234563467.a
: at job
: jobname: stdin
: notify by mail: no
export PWD; PWD='/home/apache'
export _; _='/usr/bin/at'
cd /home/apache
umask 22
ulimit unlimited
/opt/scripts/start_exam_server.sh
```

After the job has been successfully completed, an e-mail message is sent to the user who submitted the job, verifying that the command executed correctly or than an error occurred.

Let's examine the message received after the execution of job *234563467.a*:

```
From apache Mon Jan 21 22:30:00 2002
Date: Mon Jan 21 22:30:00 +1000 (EST)
From: apache <Apache User>
To: apache
Subject: Output from "at" job
```

10

```
Your "at" job on webserver
"/var/spool/cron/atjobs/234563467.a"
produced the following output:
/bin/sh[5]: Webserver started successfully
```

The cron Command

Since the `at` command submits jobs to be processed only once, the `cron` command must be used to process jobs that occur on a regular basis. Every user on the system has access to a *crontab* file, which lists all of the jobs that have been submitted and the schedule that they are to follow for execution. To schedule a job, a user must issue the `crontab` command. For example, to run the *aset* check every day, the root user would submit the following job by using the `crontab -e` command, which invokes the default editor:

```
0 2 * * * /usr/sbin/aset
```

This command would execute the *aset* utility every morning at 2:00 A.M. Once submitted, the job is stored in a file in the */var/spool/cron/cronjobs* directory. To verify that a job has been submitted correctly, the following command can be used:

```
# crontab -l root
0 2 * * * /usr/sbin/aset
```

Here, you can see that the entry has been inserted correctly. In addition to the command name to be executed, five columns define the time and date of execution: the minute of execution (0–59), the hour of execution (0–23), the day of the month of execution (1–-31), the month of execution (1–12), and the day of execution (0–6). A wildcard character indicates that all values will be used; thus, wildcard entries in the day of the month, year, and week columns indicate that the application should execute daily. In addition, command-delimited entries in each column denote multiple times/dates of execution. Thus, if a command was to be executed only on the second and tenth day of each month, the string 2,10 would be inserted into the dates column.

☑ *Mastery Check*

1. What ps command displays all processes?

    A. ps –a

    B. ps –e

    C. ps –c

    D. ps -f

2. What ps command displays the most frequently requested processes?

    A. ps –a

    B. ps –e

    C. ps –c

    D. ps -f

3. What ps command displays all processes in scheduler format?

    A. ps –a

    B. ps –e

    C. ps –c

    D. ps -f

4. What ps command displays comprehensive process information?

    A. ps –a

    B. ps –g

    C. ps –G

    D. ps -f

10

☑ Mastery Check

5. What ps command displays the SID and PGID in the printout?

   A. ps -j

   B. ps -G

   C. ps -g

   D. ps -P

6. What ps command displays process information on a group basis for a list of groups?

   A. ps -j

   B. ps -G

   C. ps -g

   D. ps -P

7. What ps command displays process information on a group basis for a single group?

   A. ps -j

   B. ps -G

   C. ps -g

   D. ps -P

8. What ps command displays the CPU ID to which a process is bound?

   A. ps -j

   B. ps -G

   C. ps -g

   D. ps -P

✓ Mastery Check

9. What is the integer code for a *SIGILL*?

   A. 1

   B. 2

   C. 3

   D. 4

10. What is the integer code for a *SIGQUIT*?

   A. 1

   B. 2

   C. 3

   D. 4

11. What is the integer code for a *SIGINT*?

   A. 1

   B. 2

   C. 3

   D. 4

12. What is the integer code for a *SIGHUP*?

   A. 1

   B. 2

   C. 3

   D. 4

10

☑ Mastery Check

13. What is the integer code for a *SIGABRT*?

    A. 5

    B. 6

    C. 7

    D. 8

14. What is the integer code for a *SIGEMT*?

    A. 5

    B. 6

    C. 7

    D. 8

15. What is the integer code for a *SIGFPE*?

    A. 5

    B. 6

    C. 7

    D. 8

Module 11

Package and Patch Management

Critical Skills

11.1   Manage packages

11.2   Review package contents

11.3   Verify package validity

11.4   Install and remove packages

11.5   Create new packages

11.6   Manage file compression

11.7   Build source software

All Solaris software that is installed as part of the operating environment comes packaged in an archive known as a *package*. Solaris packages provide an easy way to bring together application binaries, configuration files, and documentation for distribution to other systems. In addition to the Solaris packaging system, Solaris also supports standard UNIX archiving and compression tools, such as *tar* (tape archive) and *compress*. This module examines how to manage packages by using the standard Solaris packaging tools. Operations reviewed include installing packages, displaying information about packages, removing packages, and creating new packages.

Not all Solaris software is supplied in precompiled binary format, which is why this module also examines how to build software distributions from source distributions, such as those provided by the GNU project. Although building large projects from source may seem daunting initially, the use of GNU configure scripts and the *Makefile* utility makes it as easy as typing a few commands. Although building software from source is time consuming, local optimizations may be performed by manipulating *Makefiles*, and sources can be checked for Trojan horses if the source of the software is unknown.

Because the operating system is supplied in binary format, whenever changes are made to key system files as a result of bugs being identified or security risks being determined, a patch is released. The patch file updates these system files without having to rebuild them from source. It's important to keep your system's "patch level" up to date by installing the latest patches on a regular basis to ensure that your system will not fall victim to a known vulnerability or previously identified issue.

11.1 Manage Packages

A package contains a set of files that are concatenated to permit easy transport among Solaris systems. Each package contains enough information about file ownership, group membership, expected permissions, path to install, and checksums to enable the easy installation of an application. A package can store both text and binary data in the same file. Although tape archives (described later in the section "Creating Archives") can also be used to store sets of files, only packages ensure that applications can be easily managed once installed. For example, packages can be added and installed by using the *admintool*, whereas applications installed from a tape archive cannot be centrally managed in this way. Command-line relatives of *admintool* include *pkgadd*, which installs a package, and *pkgrm*, which removes a package. These commands are described in Table 11-1.

Command	Action
pkgadd	Installs a new package onto the system
pkgchk	Checks the status of an installed file
pkginfo	Displays a file listing for a package
pkgmk	Makes a new package directory
pkgproto	Makes a new prototype file that defines the files to be stored in a package
pkgrm	Uninstalls a package from the system
pkgtrans	Translates a package directory into a package file

Table 11-1   Solaris Package Management Commands

Alternatively, package information can be obtained by running the */usr/bin/prodreg* command to view the Solaris Product Registry directly. Installations based on tape archives require that administrators keep track of where files are installed. One convention involves storing these installations under the */usr/local* directory—thus, the source for Apache Web Server 1.3.12 would be stored in the directory */usr/local/apache-1.3.12*. However, no centralized management tool is available for managing these kinds of installations. Installations can be automated through an install script in conjunction with a Web Start Wizard.

All files installed as part of the Solaris installation process are associated with a specific package. For example, to determine which package an installed file belongs to, as well as its characteristics, the pkgchk command can be used:

```
# pkgchk -l -p /usr/bin/rmdir
Pathname: /usr/bin/rmdir
Type: regular file
Expected mode: 0555
Expected owner: bin
Expected group: bin
Expected file size (bytes): 9576
Expected sum(1) of contents: 39875
Expected last modification: Nov 05 06:22:21 PM 2001
Referenced by the following packages:
        SUNWcsu
Current status: installed
```

11

In the following sections, the use of the package management commands will be reviewed in detail.

1-Minute Drill

- What command installs a new package?
- What command displays a list of files in package?
- What command uninstalls a package from the system?

11.2 Review Package Contents

At any time, we can examine which packages have been installed on a system by using the `pkginfo` command:

```
# pkginfo
application GNUlstdc        libstdc++
application GNUmake         make
system      NCRos86r        NCR Platform Support
system      SFWaalib        ASCII Art Library
system      SFWaconf        GNU autoconf
system      SFWamake        GNU automake
system      SFWbison        GNU bison
system      SFWemacs        GNU Emacs
system      SFWflex         GNU flex
system      SFWfvwm         fvwm virtual window manager
system      SFWgcc          GNU compilers
system      SFWgdb          GNU source-level debugger
system      SFWgimp         GNU Image Manipulation Program
system      SFWglib         GLIB - Library of C routines
system      SFWgm4          GNU m4
system      SFWgmake        GNU make
system      SFWgs           GNU Ghostscript
system      SFWgsfot        GNU Ghostscript Other Fonts
system      SFWgsfst        GNU Ghostscript Standard Fonts
system      SFWgtk          GTK - The GIMP Toolkit
system      SFWjpg          The Independent JPEG Groups JPEG software
system      SFWlxrun        lxrun
system      SFWmpage        mpage - print multiple pages per sheet
system      SFWmpeg         The MPEG Library
system      SFWncur         ncurses library
system      SFWolvwm        OPEN LOOK Virtual Window Manager
system      SFWpng          PNG reference library
```

- `pkgadd`
- `pkginfo`
- `pkgrm`

This system has quite a few packages installed in both the system and application categories, including *lxrun*, the application that allows Linux binaries to be executed on Solaris Intel, and the *Gimp*, a graphics manipulation program. There are no restrictions on the kinds of files and applications that can be installed by using packages, as long as they are ordinary files or directories. Note that most packages supplied by Sun have the package prefix *SUNW*.

11.3 Verify Package Validity

Some important conventions are used by packages (especially those downloaded from the popular package site **http://www.sunfreeware.com**) that can be used to determine whether a package will work on your system. For example, SPARC and Intel packages can be distinguished by the string *sparc* or *intel*, respectively, appearing in filenames. In addition, some packages are compressed by the compress or gzip program, with a *.Z* or *.gz* extension, respectively, meaning that they need to be uncompressed before being installed. Typically, package names and version numbers will also appear in the filename. For example, if a version of Apache was built and packaged into a file called *apache-1.3.12-sol9-sparc-opt.gz*, the filename would suggest that the package contained the gzip compressed binaries for Apache 1.3.12 for Solaris 9 on the SPARC platform for installation into the */opt* directory.

Before installing a package, it's a good idea for you to verify that the contents will actually be readable by the package program. This can be achieved by first uncompressing the package and checking the file headers:

```
$ gzip -d apache-1.3.12-sol9-sparc-opt.gz
$ head apache-1.3.12-sol9-sparc-opt
# PaCkAgE DaTaStReAm
APCHweb 1 150
# end of header
NAME=apache
ARCH=sparc
VERSION=1.3.12
CATEGORY=application
VENDOR=Apache Consortium
EMAIL=postmaster@apache.org
```

Since this header contains the *PaCkAgE DaTaStReAm* directive, and several key descriptors (such as *VERSION*, *CATEGORY* and *VENDOR*), the file appears to be a genuine package.

11.4 Install and Remove Packages

To add a package to the system, the pkgadd command is used. In the following example, we add the package *apache-1.3.12-sol9-sparc-opt* to the system:

```
# pkgadd -d apache-1.3.12-sol9-sparc-opt
```

We would then see the following output:

```
The following packages are available:
  1  APCHweb      apache
                  (sparc) 1.3.12

Select package(s) you wish to process (or 'all' to process
all packages). (default: all) [?,??,q]:  all
```

By entering **all** (or simply pressing ENTER), the files contained in the package will be extracted and installed to the */opt* directory:

```
Processing package instance <APCHweb> from
  </var/spool/apache-1.3.12-sol9-sparc-opt>

apache
(sparc) 1.3.12
Apache Consortium
Using </opt> as the package base directory.
## Processing package information.
## Processing system information.
   2 package pathnames are already properly installed.
## Verifying disk space requirements.
## Checking for conflicts with packages already installed.
## Checking for setuid/setgid programs.

Installing apache as <APCHweb>

## Installing part 1 of 1.
/usr/local/apache-1.3.12/bin/httpd
/usr/local/apache-1.3.12/bin/apachectl
...
 [ verifying class <none> ]

Installation of <APCHweb> was successful.
```

Before installing the package, the `pkgadd` command ensures that no conflicts will occur with existing files and that sufficient disk space exists on the system to store all the package files. In addition, existing packages are checked to ensure that the package has not already been installed, and failed or partial installations are searched for. Any installation dependencies must be met prior to installation, and an optional copyright may be displayed by some packages.

As an alternative to `pkgadd`, the *admintool* can also be used to install packages. Acting as a GUI wrapper, *admintool* simply composes a `pkgadd` command to execute in a separate terminal window from the parameters supplied by the administrator. Linux administrators may prefer to learn the command-line tools, while Windows administrators may feel more comfortable with *admintool*.

Removing Packages

An installed package can be removed from the system by using the `pkgrm` command. For example, if we wanted to remove the Apache package after it was installed under the */opt* directory, we would use the following command:

```
# pkgrm APCHweb

The following package is currently installed:
  APCHweb            apache
                     (sparc) 1.3.12

Do you want to remove this package?
```

After answering y, the files that comprise the package will be removed:

```
## Removing installed package instance <APCHweb>
## Verifying package dependencies.
## Processing package information.
## Removing pathnames in class <none>
/usr/local/apache-1.3.12/bin/httpd
/usr/local/apache-1.3.12/bin/apachectl
...
## Updating system information.
Removal of <APCHweb> was successful.
```

11

If you're unsure of the target package name, or if you want to remove multiple packages, the pkgrm command can also be executed in interactive mode:

```
# pkgrm

The following packages are available:
   1  GNUlstdc      libstdc++
                    (i86pc) 2.8.1.1
   2  GNUmake       make
                    (i86pc) 3.77
   3  NCRos86r      NCR Platform Support, OS Functionality (Root)
                    (i386) 1.1.0,REV=1998.08.07.12.41
   4  SFWaalib      ASCII Art Library
                    (i386) 1.2,REV=1999.11.25.13.32
   5  SFWaconf      GNU autoconf
                    (i386) 2.13,REV=1999.11.25.13.32
   6  SFWamake      GNU automake
                    (i386) 1.4,REV=1999.11.25.13.32
   7  SFWbison      GNU bison
                    (i386) 1.28,REV=1999.11.25.13.32
   8  SFWemacs      GNU Emacs
                    (i386) 20.4,REV=1999.11.25.13.32
   9  SFWflex       GNU flex
                    (i386) 2.5.4,REV=1999.11.25.13.32
  10  SFWfvwm       fvwm virtual window manager
                    (i386) 2.2.2,REV=1999.11.25.13.32

... 288 more menu choices to follow;
<RETURN> for more choices, <CTRL-D> to stop display:
```

At this point, the number of the package that you wish to remove may be entered. As an alternative to pkgrm, packages can be removed by using *admintool*. After highlighting the name of the package that you want to remove, choose Edit | Delete and confirm the removal when prompted.

11.5 Create New Packages

Creating a package is easy if you following a few simple steps. In this example, we compile and build the Apache Web Server from source, which is then customized for our local environment. Instead of rebuilding Apache on every Web server from source, if we compile it once and then distribute it as a package to all of the local systems, we can save valuable time and CPU cycles.

The first step is to download the Apache source and build it according to the instructions supplied with the source package. After compiling the application into the source directory (for example, */usr/local/apache*), local customizations should be made as appropriate. Next, we need to create the two files that are used to create the package: the *prototype* file, which contains a list of all the files to be stored in the archive and their file permissions, and the *pkginfo* file, which contains all of the descriptive information regarding the package, including the creator, architecture, and base directory.

To create the *pkginfo* file, we use the find command to create a list of all of the files below the base directory of the package installation. In the case of Apache, the base directory will be */usr/local/apache*, if that is where the source was compiled:

```
# cd /usr/local/apache
# find . -print | pkgproto > prototype
```

This command will produce the *prototype* file in */usr/local/apache*. It contains entries like this:

```
d none bin 0755 nobody nobody
f none bin/httpd 0755 nobody nobody
f none bin/ab 0755 nobody nobody
f none bin/htpasswd 0755 nobody nobody
f none bin/htdigest 0755 nobody nobody
f none bin/apachectl 0755 nobody nobody
f none bin/dbmmanage 0755 nobody nobody
f none bin/logresolve 0755 nobody nobody
f none bin/rotatelogs 0755 nobody nobody
f none bin/apxs 0755 nobody nobody
d none libexec 0755 nobody nobody
d none man 0755 nobody nobody
d none man/man1 0755 nobody nobody
f none man/man1/htpasswd.1 0644 nobody nobody
f none man/man1/htdigest.1 0644 nobody nobody
f none man/man1/dbmmanage.1 0644 nobody nobody
d none man/man8 0755 nobody nobody
f none man/man8/httpd.8 0644 nobody nobody
f none man/man8/ab.8 0644 nobody nobody
f none man/man8/apachectl.8 0644 nobody nobody
```

Each entry is either a *f* (file) or a *d* (directory), with the octal permissions code, user, and group ownership also being displayed. After verifying that all

11

the files that you wish to package are listed in the *pkginfo* file, you need to manually add an entry for the *pkginfo* file itself into the *pkginfo* file:

```
i pkginfo=./pkginfo
```

The *pkginfo* contains a description of your archive. Adding this entry will ensure that the *pkginfo* file is added to the archive. Next, you need to create the *pkginfo* file in the base directory of the package (that is, */usr/local/apache* for this example). The file needs to contain several customized entries such as the following:

```
PKG="EDapache"
NAME="Apache"
ARCH="sparc"
VERSION="1.3.12"
CATEGORY="application"
VENDOR="Cassowary Computing Pty Ltd"
EMAIL="paul@cassowary.net"
PSTAMP="Paul Watters"
BASEDIR="/usr/local/apache"
CLASSES="none"
```

Although these tags are self-explanatory, Table 11-2 contains a description of each of the options available for the *pkginfo* file.

Command	Description
PKG	The name of the package
NAME	The name of the application contained in the package
ARCH	The target system architecture (SPARC or Intel)
VERSION	The package version number
CATEGORY	A package contains either an application or a system application
VENDOR	The supplier of the software
EMAIL	The e-mail address of the vendor
PSTAMP	The package builder's name
BASEDIR	The base directory where package files will be installed

Table 11-2 Command Options for *pkginfo* Files

Once the *pkginfo* file has been created, we're ready to begin building the package. After changing into the package base directory, the following command should be executed:

```
# pkgmk -o -r /usr/local/apache
## Building pkgmap from package prototype file.
## Processing pkginfo file.
## Attempting to volumize 362 entries in pkgmap.
part  1 -- 6631 blocks, 363 entries
## Packaging one part.
/var/spool/pkg/EDapache/pkgmap
/var/spool/pkg/EDapache/pkginfo
/var/spool/pkg/EDapache/reloc/.bash_history
/var/spool/pkg/EDapache/reloc/.profile
/var/spool/pkg/EDapache/reloc/bin/ab
/var/spool/pkg/EDapache/reloc/bin/apachectl
/var/spool/pkg/EDapache/reloc/bin/apxs
/var/spool/pkg/EDapache/reloc/bin/dbmmanage
/var/spool/pkg/EDapache/reloc/bin/htdigest
/var/spool/pkg/EDapache/reloc/bin/htpasswd
```

A directory called *EDapache* will have been created in */var/spool/pkg*, containing a copy of the source files that are now ready to be packaged in the archive, by using the `pkgtrans` command:

```
# cd /var/spool/pkg
# pkgtrans -s /var/spool/pkg /tmp/EDapache-1.3.12.tar

The following packages are available:
  1  EDapache      Apache
                   (sparc) 1.3.12

Select package(s) you wish to process (or 'all' to process
all packages). (default: all) [?,??,q]:
```

You need to select the *EDapache* package to be built, by pressing the ENTER key:

```
Transferring <EDapache> package instance
```

11

The package (*EDapache-1.3.12*) has now been successfully created in the */tmp* directory:

```
-rw-r--r--   1 root      other      3163648 Oct 18 10:09
  EDapache-1.3.12.tar
```

To reduce the size of the package file, the `gzip` command may be used to compress its contents:

```
# gzip EDapache-1.3.12
# ls -l EDapache-1.3.12.gz
-rw-r--r--   1 root      other       816536 Oct 18 10:09
  EDapache-1.3.12.gz
```

The compressed package file may now be distributed to other users and installed using the `pkgadd` command.

11.6 Manage File Compression

Using packages gives administrators the greatest level of control over how an archive is distributed and installed. However, creating the *pkginfo* and prototype files can be a time-consuming process for creating packages that are simply designed for a tape backup or for temporary use. In this case, it may be appropriate to create a tape archive (a *tar* file) rather than a package. Another advantage of using a tar file is that it can be distributed to colleagues using operating systems other than Solaris (such as Microsoft Windows and Linux) and unpacked with ease.

Creating Archives

Creating a tar file is easy: For example, to create a tape archive containing the Apache distribution that we packaged in the previous section, we would use this command:

```
# tar cvf /tmp/apache.tar *
a bin/ OK
a bin/httpd 494K
a bin/ab 28K
a bin/htpasswd 39K
```

```
a bin/htdigest 16K
a bin/apachectl 7K
a bin/dbmmanage 7K
a bin/logresolve 10K
a bin/rotatelogs 7K
a bin/apxs 20K
a cgi-bin/ 0K
a cgi-bin/hello.c 1K
a cgi-bin/printenv 1K
a cgi-bin/test-cgi 1K
a cgi-bin/hello 7K
a cgi-bin/hello.cgi 7K
a cgi-bin/hello.sh 1K
a cgi-bin/prt 1K
a conf/ 0K
```

The `cvf` part of the `tar` command can be read as "create file using verbose mode and copy to a file." Originally, the `tar` command was designed to copy archive to a tape device; thus, an extra modifier is required to specify that the archive should be copied to a file instead. Table 11-3 summarizes the main modifiers used with the `tar` command.

The `tar` command takes either function letters or functions modifiers. The main function letters used with `tar` to specify operations are presented in the following sections, along with examples.

Modifier	Name	Description
b	Blocking factor	Specifies the number of tape blocks to be used during each read and write operation.
e	Error	Specifies that tar should exit if an error is detected.
f	File	Writes output to a file, rather than a tape drive.
h	Symbolic Links	Archives files accessed through symbolic links.
I	Ignore	Ignores checksum errors during archive creation.
k	Kilobytes	Specifies the size of the archive in kilobytes. If an archive is larger than this size, it will be split across multiple archives.
o	Ownership	Modifies the user and group ownership of all archive files to the current owner.
v	Verbose	Displays information about all files extracted or added to the archive.

Table 11-3   Tape Archive Function Modifiers

11

Replacing Files

The function letter *r* is used to replace files in an existing archive. The named files are written at the end of the tar file, as shown in this example:

```
# tar rvf /tmp/apache.tar *
a bin/ OK
a bin/httpd 494K
a bin/ab 28K
a bin/htpasswd 39K
a bin/htdigest 16K
a bin/apachectl 7K
a bin/dbmmanage 7K
a bin/logresolve 10K
a bin/rotatelogs 7K
a bin/apxs 20K
a cgi-bin/ OK
a cgi-bin/hello.c 1K
a cgi-bin/printenv 1K
a cgi-bin/test-cgi 1K
a cgi-bin/hello 7K
a cgi-bin/hello.cgi 7K
a cgi-bin/hello.sh 1K
a cgi-bin/prt 1K
```

Ask the Expert

Question: I want to create archives that may be restored on Linux as well as Solaris. What format should I use to create them?

Answer: Solaris packages can be used only on Solaris, much like Windows CAB files are designed for Windows, and RedHat Linux RPM files are used for Linux. The most portable format for exchanging data between Solaris and Linux is *tar*, compressed by *gzip*. For exchanging data with Windows systems, *zip* files are an alternative, although applications like *WinZip* can also read and extract data from a tar file.

Displaying Contents

The function letter *t* is used to extract the table of contents of an archive, which lists all the files that have been archived within a specific file, as shown in this example:

```
# tar tvf /tmp/apache.tar *
drwxr-xr-x 1003/10        0 Mar 30 13:45 2000 bin/
-rwxr-xr-x 1003/10   505536 Mar 30 13:45 2000 bin/httpd
-rwxr-xr-x 1003/10    27896 Mar 30 13:45 2000 bin/ab
-rwxr-xr-x 1003/10    38916 Mar 30 13:45 2000 bin/htpasswd
-rwxr-xr-x 1003/10    16332 Mar 30 13:45 2000 bin/htdigest
-rwxr-xr-x 1003/10     7065 Mar 30 13:45 2000 bin/apachectl
-rwxr-xr-x 1003/10     6456 Mar 30 13:45 2000 bin/dbmmanage
-rwxr-xr-x 1003/10     9448 Mar 30 13:45 2000 bin/logresolve
-rwxr-xr-x 1003/10     6696 Mar 30 13:45 2000 bin/rotatelogs
-rwxr-xr-x 1003/10    20449 Mar 30 13:45 2000 bin/apxs
drwxr-xr-x 1003/10        0 Oct  5 14:36 2000 cgi-bin/
-rwxr-xr-x 1003/10      279 Oct  5 15:04 2000 cgi-bin/hello.c
-rwxr-xr-x 1003/10      274 Mar 30 13:45 2000 cgi-bin/printenv
-rwxr-xr-x 1003/10      757 Mar 30 13:45 2000 cgi-bin/test-cgi
-rwxr-xr-x 1003/10     7032 Oct  5 15:04 2000 cgi-bin/hello
-rwxr-xr-x 1003/10     6888 Oct  5 14:31 2000 cgi-bin/hello.cgi
-rwxr-xr-x 1003/10      179 Oct  5 15:09 2000 cgi-bin/hello.sh
-rwxr-xr-x 1003/10      274 Oct  5 14:34 2000 cgi-bin/prt
```

Extracting Files

The function letter *x* is used to extract files from an archive, as shown in this example:

```
# tar xvf apache.tar
x bin, 0 bytes, 0 tape blocks
x bin/httpd, 505536 bytes, 988 tape blocks
x bin/ab, 27896 bytes, 55 tape blocks
x bin/htpasswd, 38916 bytes, 77 tape blocks
x bin/htdigest, 16332 bytes, 32 tape blocks
x bin/apachectl, 7065 bytes, 14 tape blocks
x bin/dbmmanage, 6456 bytes, 13 tape blocks
x bin/logresolve, 9448 bytes, 19 tape blocks
x bin/rotatelogs, 6696 bytes, 14 tape blocks
x bin/apxs, 20449 bytes, 40 tape blocks
x cgi-bin, 0 bytes, 0 tape blocks
```

11

```
x cgi-bin/hello.c, 279 bytes, 1 tape blocks
x cgi-bin/printenv, 274 bytes, 1 tape blocks
x cgi-bin/test-cgi, 757 bytes, 2 tape blocks
x cgi-bin/hello, 7032 bytes, 14 tape blocks
x cgi-bin/hello.cgi, 6888 bytes, 14 tape blocks
x cgi-bin/hello.sh, 179 bytes, 1 tape blocks
x cgi-bin/prt, 274 bytes, 1 tape blocks
```

Project 11-1: Creating a Home Directory Archive

This project shows you how to create an archive of a user's home directory. This can be used as a form of temporary backup for users to ensure that their files are not accidentally overwritten.

Step-by-Step

1. Change to the user's home directory:

```
# cd ~user
```

2. Create the archive in the temporary area:

```
# tar cvf /tmp/user.tar *
```

3. Compress the archive to conserve disk space:

```
# gzip -9 /tmp/user.tar
```

Summary

The `tar` and `gzip` commands can be used to create tape archives that save disk space through compression.

Compressing Files

Archives and other files can occupy a large amount of disk space if they contain data that is redundant. For example, text files often have large segments of empty space, and images with segments of the same color are clearly redundant. Solaris provides tools to exploit this redundancy by allowing files to be stored in a compressed format. When tape archives are created as shown in the preceding section, it's wise to maximize the availability of disk space to other applications by compressing archives before they are moved to offline storage, such as backup tapes.

Two compression commands are typically used under Solaris: the compress command, which creates compressed files with a *.Z* extension, and the GNU gzip command, which creates compressed files with a *.gz* extension. Because compress and gzip use different compression algorithms to pack data, the size of a file compressed by gzip or compress can be different. In general, gzip can achieve a higher compression ration than compress. Solaris 9 also provides the bzip command, which provides compression through the lossless Burrows-Wheeler compression system.

To compress an archive called *backup.tar*, the following command would be used:

```
$ compress backup.tar
```

Once the compressed file *backup.tar.Z* has been created, the original file *backup.tar* will be deleted. Alternatively, the following command could be used to compress *backup.tar* using the gzip command:

```
$ gzip backup.tar
```

Again, once the gzip compressed file *backup.tar.gz* has been created, the original file *backup.tar* will be deleted. To perform repeat packing on the file to achieve maximum compression, the following command can be used:

```
$ gzip -9 backup.tar
```

Keep in mind that repeat packing is a CPU-intensive and lengthy process. To restore a file that has been compressed by using the *compress* program, the uncompress command is used:

```
$ uncompress backup.tar.Z
```

Once the file *backup.tar* has been restored, the *backup.tar.Z* file will be automatically removed. Alternatively, to restore a file compressed using gzip, the following command will be used:

```
$ gzip -d backup.tar.gz
```

Once again, after the file *backup.tar* has been restored, the *backup.tar.gz* file will be removed automatically.

11

1-Minute Drill

- What command is used to operate on tape archives?
- What command is used to decompress *gzip* files?
- What command is used to decompress compressed files?

11.7 Build Source Software

In the previous sections, we have examined how to create a Solaris package from compiled source and how to create a tape archive from source. However, many administrators who are new to Solaris may be unable to compile from source without some guidance. In this section, we walk through the compilation and building of a GNU package (the Text Utilities), and explain the procedure for downloading, configuring, compiling, and installing software supplied as source.

One of the most confusing aspects of building applications under Solaris is the lack of a C compiler, which is considered standard across all UNIX systems. Solaris used to have a C compiler; however, it is now sold separately by Sun. Fortunately, the GNU C compiler (GCC) is completely free and is supplied with Solaris. Alternatively, you can download the latest version from **http://www.sunfreeware.com**.

Be sure that you obtain the latest version of the GCC software before installing it. After you have a compiler installed, you can check to see that it works by typing the following command:

```
$ gcc -v
Reading specs from /usr/local/lib/gcc-lib/sparc-solaris2.9/
2.95.2/specsgcc version 2.95.2 20020101 (release)
```

Alternatively, try writing a simple Hello World program to see whether the source code can be compiled and linked appropriately:

```
$ cat hello.c
#include <stdio.h>
main()
{
```

- `tar`
- `gzip -d`
- `uncompress`

```
        printf("Hello World!\n");
}
$ gcc hello.c -o hello
```

Once compiled, the program can be run as usual:

```
$ ./hello
Hello World!
```

If you received any errors at this point, check that GCC can be found in your *PATH* environment variable, and that the *LD_LIBRARY_PATH* contains the path to the GCC libraries directory.

Next, you will need to download the source code that you wish to compile. In this case, we downloaded the text utilities source file from **http://www.gnu.org** (*textutils-2.0.tar.gz*). The first step is to uncompress the source file:

```
# gzip -d textutils-2.0.tar.gz
```

At this point, the MD5 checksum of the file should be computed and compared to that stored on the originating site. This will tell you whether the file is authentic. The tar file should then be extracted using the command

```
# tar xvf textutils-2.0.tar
```

After changing to the source directory,

```
# cd textutils-2.0
```

the following files should be visible:

```
# ls
ABOUT-NLS     config.sub     INSTALL        Makefile.maint  src
acconfig.h    configure      install-sh     man             stamp-h.in
aclocal.m4    configure.in   intl           missing         tests
AUTHORS       COPYING        lib            mkinstalldirs   THANKS
ChangeLog     djgpp          m4             NEWS            TODO
config.guess  doc            Makefile.am    po
config.h.in   GNUmakefile    Makefile.in    README
```

Most source distributions are accompanied by a README file that contains all the information that you need to know about a program, including what it's designed to do, what platforms it can be executed upon, and what its system requirements are. The first step to installing a source distribution is to read the README file:

```
# more README
These are the GNU text file (actually, file contents) processing
utilities.  Most of these programs have significant advantages over
their Unix counterparts, such as greater speed, additional options,
and fewer arbitrary limits.

The programs that can be built with this package are: cat, cksum, comm,
csplit, cut, expand, fmt, fold, head, join, md5sum, nl, od, paste, pr,
ptx, sort, split, sum, tac, tail, tr, tsort, unexpand, uniq, and wc.

See the file NEWS for a list of major changes in the current release.

See the file INSTALL for compilation and installation instructions.
```

As the README file suggests, reading the INSTALL file will instruct you (often step-by-step) how to configure, make, and install the source package:

```
# more INSTALL
Basic Installation
==================

   These are generic installation instructions.

   The `configure' shell script attempts to guess correct values for
various system-dependent variables used during compilation.  It uses
those values to create a `Makefile' in each directory of the package.
It may also create one or more `.h' files containing system-dependent
definitions.  Finally, it creates a shell script `config.status' that
you can run in the future to recreate the current configuration, a file
`config.cache' that saves the results of its tests to speed up
reconfiguring, and a file `config.log' containing compiler output
(useful mainly for debugging `configure').
```

To create an appropriate *Makefile* that matches the local system architecture, you must run the *configure* script, which has been generated by the GNU *Configure* utility:

```
# ./configure
creating cache ./config.cache
checking host system type... i386-pc-solaris2.8
checking for a BSD compatible install... ./install-sh -c
checking whether build environment is sane... yes
checking whether make sets ${MAKE}... yes
checking for working aclocal... missing
```

```
checking for working autoconf... missing
checking for working automake... missing
checking for working autoheader... missing
checking for working makeinfo... missing
checking for gnutar... no
checking for gtar... no
```

After several pages of checking that various packages exist on your system, a series of *Makefiles* will then be created:

```
creating ./config.status
creating Makefile
creating doc/Makefile
creating intl/Makefile
creating lib/Makefile
creating man/Makefile
creating m4/Makefile
creating po/Makefile.in
creating src/Makefilecreating djgpp/Makefile
```

If no problems are encountered, the source can then be built by using the make command (remember that */usr/ccs/bin* must be in your path for this to work):

```
# make
make  all-recursive
make[1]: Entering directory `/tmp/textutils-2.0'
Making all in lib
make[2]: Entering directory `/tmp/textutils-2.0/lib'
gcc -DHAVE_CONFIG_H -I. -I.. -I.. -I.. -I. -I../intl     -g -02 -c argmatch.c
gcc -DHAVE_CONFIG_H -I. -I.. -I.. -I.. -I. -I../intl     -g -02 -c closeout.c
gcc -DHAVE_CONFIG_H -I. -I.. -I.. -I.. -I. -I../intl     -g -02 -c diacrit.c
gcc -DHAVE_CONFIG_H -I. -I.. -I.. -I.. -I. -I../intl     -g -02 -c full-write.c
gcc -DHAVE_CONFIG_H -I. -I.. -I.. -I.. -I. -I../intl     -g -02 -c getopt.c
gcc -DHAVE_CONFIG_H -I. -I.. -I.. -I.. -I. -I../intl     -g -02 -c getopt1.c
gcc -DHAVE_CONFIG_H -I. -I.. -I.. -I.. -I. -I../intl     -g -02 -c hard-locale.c
gcc -DHAVE_CONFIG_H -I. -I.. -I.. -I.. -I. -I../intl     -g -02 -c human.c
gcc -DHAVE_CONFIG_H -I. -I.. -I.. -I.. -I. -I../intl     -g -02 -c linebuffer.c
gcc -DHAVE_CONFIG_H -I. -I.. -I.. -I.. -I. -I../intl     -g -02 -c long-options.c
gcc -DHAVE_CONFIG_H -I. -I.. -I.. -I.. -I. -I../intl     -g -02 -c md5.c
gcc -DHAVE_CONFIG_H -I. -I.. -I.. -I.. -I. -I../intl     -g -02 -c memcasecmp.c
gcc -DHAVE_CONFIG_H -I. -I.. -I.. -I.. -I. -I../intl     -g -02 -c memcoll.c
gcc -DHAVE_CONFIG_H -I. -I.. -I.. -I.. -I. -I../intl     -g -02 -c obstack.c
gcc -DHAVE_CONFIG_H -I. -I.. -I.. -I.. -I. -I../intl     -g -02 -c quotearg.c
gcc -DHAVE_CONFIG_H -I. -I.. -I.. -I.. -I. -I../intl     -g -02 -c readtokens.c
gcc -DHAVE_CONFIG_H -I. -I.. -I.. -I.. -I. -I../intl     -g -02 -c safe-read.c
gcc -DHAVE_CONFIG_H -I. -I.. -I.. -I.. -I. -I../intl     -g -02 -c version-etc.c
gcc -DHAVE_CONFIG_H -I. -I.. -I.. -I.. -I. -I../intl     -g -02 -c xmalloc.c
gcc -DHAVE_CONFIG_H -I. -I.. -I.. -I.. -I. -I../intl     -g -02 -c xstrdup.c
gcc -DHAVE_CONFIG_H -I. -I.. -I.. -I.. -I. -I../intl     -g -02 -c xstrtod.c
gcc -DHAVE_CONFIG_H -I. -I.. -I.. -I.. -I. -I../intl     -g -02 -c xstrtol.c
gcc -DHAVE_CONFIG_H -I. -I.. -I.. -I.. -I. -I../intl     -g -02 -c xstrtoul.c
```

11

```
gcc -DHAVE_CONFIG_H -I. -I.. -I.. -I.. -I. -I../intl    -g -02 -c xstrtoumax.c
gcc -DHAVE_CONFIG_H -I. -I.. -I.. -I.. -I. -I../intl    -g -02 -c mktime.c
gcc -DHAVE_CONFIG_H -I. -I.. -I.. -I.. -I. -I../intl    -g -02 -c strtoumax.c
gcc -DHAVE_CONFIG_H -I. -I.. -I.. -I.. -I. -I../intl    -g -02 -c regex.c
gcc -DHAVE_CONFIG_H -I. -I.. -I.. -I.. -I. -I../intl    -g -02 -c getline.c
gcc -DHAVE_CONFIG_H -I. -I.. -I.. -I.. -I. -I../intl    -g -02 -c stpcpy.c
gcc -DHAVE_CONFIG_H -I. -I.. -I.. -I.. -I. -I../intl    -g -02 -c error.c
```

Again, after several pages of building, the source should be compiled, and you may then install the binaries:

```
# make install
Making install in lib
make[1]: Entering directory `/tmp/textutils-2.0/lib'
make[2]: Entering directory `/tmp/textutils-2.0/lib'
make[2]: Nothing to be done for `install-exec-am'.
make[2]: Nothing to be done for `install-data-am'.
make[2]: Leaving directory `/tmp/textutils-2.0/lib'
make[1]: Leaving directory `/tmp/textutils-2.0/lib'
Making install in intl
make[1]: Entering directory `/tmp/textutils-2.0/intl'
if test "textutils" = "gettext" \
    && test '' = 'intl-compat.o'; then \
  if test -r ./mkinstalldirs; then \
    ./mkinstalldirs /usr/local/lib /usr/local/include; \
  else \
    ../mkinstalldirs /usr/local/lib /usr/local/include; \
  fi; \
```

Patches

After releases of individual applications and entire operating environments, it's inevitable that bugs will be identified in production that were not found during testing. This reflects the limited number of possible test cases that can be examined in a test lab compared to an operating environment with more than a million licensees. Thus, once bugs are reported and fixes have been produced, a system for distributing code updates is required. Because Solaris administrators typically do not have the source code for the current production release of Solaris, they must rely on binary patches to update binary files. Once applied to binary files, these patches ensure that the modified version of the application tested in the lab that has been shown to fix a bug, matches the contents of a locally installed file. While it is possible for entire applications to be distributed in binary format, this is impractical given the small code footprint of many bug fixes relative to the size of full applications.

1-Minute Drill

- What is a package?
- What is a patch?
- What are the two most common compression programs?

In addition to releasing patches for bugs, patches are also released to combat security exploits that have been identified in Solaris software. While these vulnerabilities may or may not result from a bug, they typically need to be fixed quickly to prevent unauthorized system access or other forms of attack from occurring. For example, many Solaris daemons in the past have been affected by buffer overflow vulnerabilities that allow system services to be crashed or that allow remote access to be gained. These vulnerabilities arise from the absence of boundary checking on some forms of input; thus, it has been possible for rogue users, for example, to write past array boundaries thereby corrupting kernel and system data, if the effective user of the process was root (many services, such as *inetd*, have the effective user ID of *root*). It is imperative that exploits that enable rogue users to remotely gain access of a system be countered as soon as possible by installing a patch.

Two types of patches are typically released: single patches and jumbo patches. Single patches address only an individual issue that has been identified as a bug. For example, patch 108435-01 provided a fix for BugId 4318566 that affected Sun's C++ compiler. Jumbo patches, in contrast, are clusters of recommended patches for a particular operating system release and should be applied to all new installations. This approach is similar to the Windows Service Packs, where fixes to a wide variety of problems can be applied concurrently. Details of the latest single patches and recommended patches can be obtained from **http://sunsolve.sun.com**. The SunSolve Patch Report, available at **ftp://sunsolve.sun.com/pub/patches/Solaris9.PatchReport**, provides a list of all patches released for Solaris 9 and details any changes or updates for existing patches.

11

- A package is a text file that contains a complete application ready for installation.
- A patch is a binary file that allows applications to be modified without requiring recompilation.
- `compress` and `gzip`

Ask the Expert

Question: What's the best place to find out about new security vulnerabilities?

Answer: The Common Vulnerabilities and Exposures database (**cve.mitre.org**) issues alerts catalogued by their CVE number. Vendor patches are also hyperlinked from the CVE page. The CERT team (**http://www.cert.org**) also releases details of security-related exploits.

Each identified vulnerability will contain a hyperlink back to the CVE database, so that information displayed about every issue is updated directly from the source. New patches and bug fixes are also listed.

Reviewing Patches

To work out whether a patch is required for your system, or to see whether it has already been installed, the showrev command should be used:

```
# showrev -p
Patch: 107430-01 Obsoletes:  Requires:  Incompatibles:  Packages: SUNWwsr
Patch: 108029-01 Obsoletes:  Requires:  Incompatibles:  Packages: SUNWwsr
Patch: 107437-03 Obsoletes:  Requires:  Incompatibles:  Packages: SUNWtiu8
Patch: 107316-01 Obsoletes:  Requires:  Incompatibles:  Packages: SUNWploc
Patch: 107453-01 Obsoletes:  Requires:  Incompatibles:  Packages: SUNWkvm
Patch: 106541-20 Obsoletes: 106832-03, 106976-01, 107029-01, 107030-01,
   107334-01, 107031-01, 107117-05, 107899-01, 108752-01, 107147-08,
   109104-04 Requires: 107544-02 Incompatibles:  Packages: SUNWkvm,
   SUNWcsu, SUNWcsr, SUNWcsl, SUNWcar, SUNWesu, SUNWarc,
   SUNWatfsr, SUNWscpu, SUNWcpr, SUNWdpl, SUNWhea, SUNWipc,
   SUNWtoo, SUNWnisu, SUNWpcmci, SUNWpcmcu, SUNWtnfc,   SUNWvolu
```

In this example, patches including 106541-20, 107453-01, 107316-01, 107437-03, 108029-01, and 107430-01 have been installed. In addition, most patches are new, since they do not obsolete any existing packages and are not incompatible with any patches. The exception is patch 106541-20, which obsoletes many previous patches and affects several different packages.

Patch Installation

Patches can be installed by using the patchadd command. For example, the following command would add patch 106541-20 to the system, assuming it was stored in the /tmp directory:

```
# patchadd /tmp/106541-15
```

Ask the Expert

Question: OK, I've added a patch to the system. How do I know that it was installed properly?

Answer: You can always check that a specific patch has been installed by reviewing all installed patches using the showrev command, and grepping for the entry you're interested in. For example, to verify that the patch 108453-10 has been installed successfully, use the following command:

```
# showrev -p | grep 108453-10
```

Alternatively, if a number of patches are to be installed, they can be added on the command line. The following command would add the patches 107453-01, 107316-01, and 107437-03 to the system:

```
# patchadd 107453-01 107316-01 107437-03
```

Patch Removal

If a patch does not fix the bug it should have fixed, or if it causes further problems on a system, it may be necessary for you to back out the patch by using the patchrm command. For example, to back out the patch 107453-01, the following command would be used:

```
# patchrm 107453-01
```

If you attempt to back out a patch that does not exist, the following error message will be printed:

```
Checking installed packages and patches...
Patch 107453-01 has not been applied to this system.
patchrm is terminating.
```

11

☑ Mastery Check

1. What command is used to verify that a package has been installed?

   A. pkginfo

   B. pkgchk

   C. pkgadd

   D. pkgprint

2. What command is used to create tape archives?

   A. tapes

   B. archives

   C. tar

   D. tarchives

3. What is the default package spooling directory?

   A. /spool

   B. /dev/spool

   C. /var/spool

   D. /tmp/spool

4. What command is used to remove installed packages?

   A. pkgrm

   B. pkgdel

   C. pkgdelete

   E. pkguninstall

☑ Mastery Check

5. What `tar` modifier should be used to specify the number of tape blocks to be used during each read and write operation?

A. *b*

B. *e*

C. f

D. *h*

6. What `tar` modifier should be used to specify that `tar` should exit if an error is detected?

A. *b*

B. *e*

C. *f*

D. *h*

7. What `tar` modifier should be used to specify that output is written to a file, rather than a tape drive?

A. *b*

B. *e*

C. *f*

D. *h*

8. What `tar` modifier should be used to archive files accessed through symbolic links?

A. *b*

B. *e*

C. *f*

D. *h*

11

☑ Mastery Check

9. What `tar` modifier should be used to ignore *checksum* errors during archive creation?

A. *i*

B. *k*

C. *o*

D. *v*

10. What `tar` modifier should be used to specify the size of the archive in kilobytes?

A. *i*

B. *k*

C. *o*

D. *v*

11. What `tar` modifier should be used to modify the user and group ownership of all archive files to the current owner?

A. *i*

B. *k*

C. *o*

D. *v*

12. What `tar` modifier should be used to display information about all files extracted or added to the archive?

A. *i*

B. *k*

C. *o*

D. *v*

☑ Mastery Check

13. What command can be used to display file headers?

    A. headers

    B. header

    C. head

    D. tail

14. What is the first step to create a *pkginfo* file?

    A. Initialize pkgchk

    B. Use the find command

    C. Use the tail command

    D. Use the pkginfo command

15. What GCC option is used to specify an executable name with gcc?

    A. *–name*

    B. *–n*

    C. *–o*

    D. *–N*

11

Module 12

Backup and Restore

Critical Skills

The ability to store data reliably is one of the key purposes of an information system. However, physical devices such as hard disk drives have a *mean time to failure* (MTTF): that is, every device attached to your system has an average life span that must be considered when building reliable systems. The significance of the MTTF is that you must always plan for the day that your system is not available because of a hardware fault. For example, if a hard disk fails, causing a service failure, you need to have a strategy in place to restore services as quickly as possible.

In a production system, this may involve using a Redundant Array of Inexpensive Disks (RAID) to ensure that if a single disk fails, users can still operate uninterrupted while a new disk is installed. However, if key system components fail because of a power surge or similar catastrophic event, RAID won't save you. In this event, you need to revert to backups and restore data manually. If the disk failure occurs on a server, many clients are dependent on continued service for their operation, so a speedy recovery process is essential. In this module, we examine how to implement backups using standard Solaris tools and restore volumes to disks when a failure has occurred.

12.1 Implement Backup Strategies

Backup strategies should be designed around specific scenarios, which can include the following:

- Single disk failure

- Multiple disk failure

- Complete system failure

Single disk failures are generally the easiest of all to fix, as a new disk can be installed and files restored from a backup device. Alternatively, if sufficient disk space is available on another partition, a symbolic link created between the original mount point of the failed disk and the spare partition may allow service to be resumed more quickly. This is particularly true if the failed disk hosted temporary disk space. However, in the case of a multiple disk failure, it may be necessary for you to install multiple new disks, in which case, you won't have any spare partitions to play with. In this instance, it will be necessary for you to install the files from the affected partitions from a backup device.

Both of these scenarios can potentially be remedied with RAID mirroring, as long as sufficient mirrors and state databases exist on nonfailing partitions to allow data to be read and written. A complete system failure, irrespective of RAID, will require that existing partitions be restored to new disks on a new system. Fortunately, total system failures are rare. In addition to installing a software RAID product, such as Solaris DiskSuite, many enterprise administrators employ external RAID storage systems, such as the T3 storage array.

Clearly, speed of recovery is the key parameter in minimizing downtime due to disk or system failure. The total recovery speed is dependent on the amount of data to be restored and the speed of the backup/restore device used. This implies that partitions should be kept normalized as much as possible; simply backing up all partitions in a single set may mean a tape drive spends a long time searching for the blocks to be restored. In addition, it's wise to invest in a fast backup/restore device—digital tapes running on Digital Audio Tape (DAT) drives are much faster and have higher storage capacities than Quarter Inch Cartridge (QIC) tapes, even though DATs are more expensive. If speed of recovery is critical, it's worth spending the extra money on a fast backup/restore device. The fastest and greatest capacity tape system is now the Linear Tape Open (LTO) standard—more information can be found at **http://www.lto-technology.com/newsite/html/about.html**.

Although speed of recovery is important, most businesses would find that the integrity of restored data is just as important. Integrity of data is related to its contemporary nature: data restored from a week ago may not be useful today. For example, if a bank lost one day's worth of data because of a failed disk, since a restore could only be made from the previous day's backup, many customers will be out of pocket, since the payments they made against bills will have been made but not recorded. Alternatively, the bank may ultimately lose if a large number of customer withdrawal records are lost. In this context, ensuring that data is both accurate and up to date after a restore is critical.

Another issue to consider is the integrity of data as it is backed up. For example, if a user has a file open and is making changes to it, it may be available for read for backup, even though new changes have not been written to the file. This might result in data being lost if the file has not been closed before the backup occurs. For this reason, it's preferable that backups be performed when users are not actively using the system and when databases have been shut down. If this is not possible—because, for example, a database application is in use 24×7—a "warm dump" should be taken at regular intervals so that the time at which the data was current can be easily established.

12

It's important to ensure that indexes, data files, and rollback segments are synchronized if the database is to be correctly restored to an operational state. When planning to invest in third-party backup software, it's best to consult with your database vendor about the appropriate backup strategies that should be employed.

Two types of backups can be used to store files for possible recovery: an incremental dump or a full dump. The incremental dump strategy involves trading off the amount of data recorded every day against the total time that a system must be backing up data: only the files that have been changed during the previous backup epoch (usually one day) need to be written to a tape. Usually, an incremental strategy is matched up with a weekly full dump, where all files on a file system are written to disk. This ensures that a single tape or small set of tapes can be used to restore all the files from a file system. Using the incremental approach, the full dump set plus one tape for each day of incrementation is required to fully restore data.

The main problem with maintaining large sets of incremental dump tapes is that if you lose one tape from the set, you may not be able to restore some files. The best way to deal with the lost tape problem is to ensure that you utilize an off-site storage facility to store at least one full dump once a week. This will ensure that you always have a fallback position if your current tape set is lost or destroyed. Remember that full dumps can be slow, so they should not be performed each day. This strategy can be summarized in the following table:

Monday	Tuesday	Wednesday	Thursday	Friday	Saturday	Sunday
Incremental	Incremental	Incremental	Incremental	Incremental	Incremental	Full

Let's consider an example: if a disk failure were to occur on a Wednesday morning, the full dump from Sunday and the incremental dump tapes from Monday and Tuesday would be required for backup.

Many Sun systems are supplied with their own tape backup device, such as a Digital Data Storage-3 (DDS-3) tape drive. This means that if a network goes down, the local host can still back up its own files. However, it is also possible for systems without a tape drive to remotely mount a tape drive on a central server to perform backups. This allows different systems to make the best use of a single backup device. If client systems are untrusted by the server, it may be more appropriate for the server to mount an NT File System (NFS)-exported volume from the client and write that data to the server's local tape drive. This replaces the client/server trust dependency with a server/client trust dependency—if the client doesn't trust the server, the client shouldn't be writing sensitive data to the server's tape.

Ask the Expert

Question: What types of backup media should I be using?

Answer: Unless you have time to spare, and extremely small file systems, a QIC tape is useless. A DDS-3 DAT drive should provide several gigabytes of storage, which is sufficient for most partitions. CD-R (Readable) and CD-RW drives are also good for exchanging data between systems that do not have tape drives.

Of course, more complex backup solutions are available for data centers and the like. For example, customized tape libraries can be built and controlled by a Solaris system. Alternatively, Storage Area Network (SAN) technology may be used to build redundant, highly available distributed storage systems for performing network-wide backups. This approach has the advantage of being able to share storage resources and centralize management of separate resources. Sun has developed Java-based Jiro technology that uses the Federated Management Architecture (FMA) to implement network-centric distributed storage, with key hardware manufacturers such as Hitachi, Quantum, Veritas, and Fujitsu developing Jiro-based products. Details on Jiro and FMA can be downloaded from **http://www.jiro.com/**.

Instead of centralizing all backups to a single tape device, it's wise to have at least one standby tape drive attached to another system, so that a hardware failure on the main tape drive will not prevent backups from being taken for all systems on the network. Individual hosts may also employ more than one backup device: a CD-RW (Read-Writable) drive may supplement tape-based backups, for example, maximizing redundancy while reducing common points of failure.

1-Minute Drill

- What are the two main types of backups?
- What tapes are required to perform a recovery using an incremental dump?
- What tapes are required to perform a recovery using a full dump?

12

- Incremental dump and full dump.
- The full dump set plus one tape for each day of incrementation.
- The full dump set only.

12.2 Backup and Restore Data

Solaris supports many standard UNIX backup and restore programs, as well as more complex third-party freeware and commercial applications. Which application you decide to use for backups depends on a number of factors. For example, if you require that your backup tapes be read by a different operating system, you may need to use one of the standard tools. If you want more flexibility and the ability to support multiple clients and backup sets from a single interface, you may need to use a commercial product like Veritas NetBackup or Legato Networker.

The most commonly used Solaris tools include *tar, dd, cpio, ufsdump,* and *ufsrestore.* These tools are typically used for backing up single machines that have access to multiple backup devices, such as DAT drives and CD-RW drives. For backing up multiple machines from a single server, Legato Networker is highly recommended. For implementing a distributed storage system, Veritas NetBackup is commonly used. The following sections will review the standard Solaris tools.

12.3 Create Tape Archives

The most common backup command is the `tar` command, which creates tape archives that can be stored on hard disks, tapes, or CDs. One of the greatest benefits of using tar files for backups is their portability: a tar file created on Solaris can be unpacked onto a Linux or Windows system. This makes it easy to share data with users on other platforms. Tar files can also be used to restore files in an emergency onto a PC. For example, if a full rebuild is being performed on a central server from backups, but a few critical files are required instantly, they can be retrieved from a PC using a tar file. However, tar does not feature inbuilt compression like the Zip file format; tar files were originally designed to write to tape devices, and they can be compressed using third-party compression to save space and be stored on a normal disk. Indeed, it is common for source distributions to be disseminated using tar files. This distribution can be made over the network as well, by using FTP or a secure copy program.

Let's look at how tape archives can be created and extracted by using the `tar` command. In the following example, we'll create a tape archive of the directory */opt/netscape/communicator-4.36.* As a first step, we can gauge the amount of disk space an archive will require by using `du` to count the number of disk blocks consumed by the target directory, its files, and the files contained within its subdirectories:

```
$ du /opt/netscape/communicator-4.36
39       ./movemail-src
1468     ./plugins
209      ./dynfonts
5        ./talkback
66       ./java/classes/aix
195      ./java/classes/hpux
86       ./java/classes/irix
6815     ./java/classes
6816     ./java
58       ./nethelp/netscape/composer
28       ./nethelp/netscape/home
92       ./nethelp/netscape/messengr
52       ./nethelp/netscape/navigatr
38       ./nethelp/netscape/news
23       ./nethelp/netscape/shared
26       ./nethelp/netscape/trouble
26       ./nethelp/netscape/Collabra
344      ./nethelp/netscape
641      ./nethelp
330      ./spell
2        ./lib
916      ./plugins.old
26142    .
```

We can see that the total size of the tape archive should be approximately 26,142 disk blocks; thus we need to ensure that the file system where the tar file will be stored can accommodate the new file. (The standard block size is 512 bytes on UNIX File Systems, or UFSs.) To create a tar file called *netscape.tar* in the */tmp* directory, the following command would be used, by passing the options *cvf* on the command line (*c* meaning *create*):

```
$ tar cvf /tmp/netscape.tar *
bookmark.htm
default-netscape-preferences.js
dynfonts/
dynfonts/libTrueDoc.so
java/
java/classes/
java/classes/awt.properties
java/classes/font.properties
```

12

```
java/classes/font.properties.cs
java/classes/font.properties.el
java/classes/font.properties.hu
java/classes/font.properties.ja
java/classes/font.properties.ko
java/classes/font.properties.lt
java/classes/font.properties.lv
java/classes/font.properties.pl
java/classes/font.properties.ru
java/classes/font.properties.tr
java/classes/font.properties.zh
java/classes/font.properties.zh_GB2312
java/classes/font.properties.zh_TW
java/classes/font.properties.zh_TW_Big5
...
```

An entry for every file and directory to be stored in the archive will be displayed. Once the tar file has been created, it can be easily extracted by passing the options *xvf* on the command line (*x* meaning *extract*), as shown here:

```
$ tar xvf netscape.tar
bookmark.htm
default-netscape-preferences.js
dynfonts/
dynfonts/libTrueDoc.so
java/
java/classes/
java/classes/awt.properties
java/classes/font.properties
java/classes/font.properties.cs
java/classes/font.properties.el
java/classes/font.properties.hu
java/classes/font.properties.ja
java/classes/font.properties.ko
java/classes/font.properties.lt
java/classes/font.properties.lv
java/classes/font.properties.pl
java/classes/font.properties.ru
java/classes/font.properties.tr
java/classes/font.properties.zh
java/classes/font.properties.zh_GB2312
java/classes/font.properties.zh_TW
java/classes/font.properties.zh_TW_Big5
...
```

Unlike programs that create Zip file archives, tar does not automatically compress files. This must be performed by a third-party program, such as *compress, pack,* or *gzip.* These applications give varying rates of compression accompanied by faster or slower execution times. Tar files compressed with *compress* have the extension *.Z,* while tar files compressed with *pack* have the extension *.z.* Alternatively, *gzip*ped tar files have the extension *.gz.* To compress the *netscape.tar* file, the following command would be used:

```
$ compress /tmp/netscape.tar
```

After compression has been completed, the original file will be removed, in this case leaving only */tmp/netscape.tar.gz.* To uncompress the tar file, the following command would be used:

```
$ uncompress /tmp/netscape.tar.gz
```

12.4 Copy Tape Archives

In the previous section, we examined how to create tar files. In the examples presented, archives were written to files rather than to tape devices. This is because tar, while being the traditional file archiving tool, has been superseded by more modern tools, such as cpio. The `cpio` command allows archives to be written across multiple volumes, unlike tar, which is restricted to a single volume. cpio supports two modes: copy in mode (`cpio -i`), which uses a data stream obtained from standard input, and copy out mode (`cpio -o`), which uses a list of files specified on the command line for input. Generally, most applications use copy out mode to pass a list of files to be archived, in conjunction with other filters and pipes on the command line. For example, to create an archive called *netscape.ar,* containing all of the files under */opt/netscape/communicator-4.36,* the following commands would be used:

```
$ find . -name '/opt/netscape/communicator-4.36' -print |\
   cpio -oc > /tmp/netscape.ar
```

12

The archives are stored as plaintext—thus, by using text processing utilities like head and tail, it's possible to filter and display their contents. For example, to review the header of the *netscape.ar* file, the following command could be used:

```
$ head /tmp/netscape.ar
070701004a3ac1000041ed0000071a00000064000000043caa9a7700000
```

```
000000000970000004000000c400000aea0000000d00000000.dt/sess
ions070701004a3ac3000081a40000071a0000006400000013cabe96b0
000001400000097000000400000000000000000000000001900000003.dt/
sessions/lastsession/usr/dt/bin/Xsession070701004a3ac600008
1a40000071a0000006400000013c86ef5b0000094f0000009700000040
00000000000000000000001400000003.dt/sessions/dtperfSdtperfm
eter*swap.MinMax:    4
```

To retrieve files from the archive, the following command could be used:

```
$ cat /tmp/netscape.ar| cpio -icd "*"
```

To extract a specific file, such as *java/classes/awt.properties*, the following command would be used:

```
$ cat /tmp/netscape.ar | \
  cpio -ic "java/classes/awt.properties"
```

12.5 Copy Disks

To create an exact, byte-by-byte copy of raw disk or tape blocks, the dd command can be used. It effectively allows disk slices to copied, where an input file (*if*) and an output file (*of*) are specified on the command line. For example, to create an exact copy of the */dev/rdsk/c1t0d0s5* slice on */dev/rdsk/c1t0d1s5*, the following command could be used:

```
# dd if=/dev/rdsk/c1t0d1s5 of=/dev/rdsk/c1t0d0s5 bs=64k
```

In this example, a block size (*bs*) of *64k* is specified. It is also possible to create a copy of a slice to a disk by specifying an output file of the tape device (*/dev/rmt/0h*):

```
# dd if=/dev/rdsk/c1t0d1s5  of=/dev/rmt/0h
```

Project 12-1: Copying a File System to a Disk-Based Archive

This project shows you how to copy a file system to a disk-based archive in */store*. This is useful for backing up one file system to a storage facility on another.

Step-by-Step

1. Obtain the device name for the file system you wish to copy to tape:

```
# df | grep "/staff"
.../dev/dsk/c1t0d0s5...
```

2. Create a file list by using the `find` command:

```
# find /staff -name '*' -print > /tmp/filelist.txt
```

3. Generate the archive in */spool*:

```
# cat /tmp/filelist.txt | cpio -oc > /store/staff.ar
```

Summary

The `find`, `cat`, and `cpio` commands can be used to archive entire disks to a storage area.

The `ufsdump` and `ufsrestore` commands are common to all UNIX systems, and they allow full dumps and incremental backups to be performed and restored when required. Typically, `ufsdump` is run every night during times of low system and/or network utilization, when resources can be devoted to compressing and writing data to a tape or other backup device. If all goes well, `ufsrestore` is never used—except when an emergency arises, during which time it is run during the single user run level prior to booting into the multi-user run levels.

The key parameter supplied to `ufsdump` is the "dump level" being performed during a specific backup activity. A full dump is always the dump level of zero. However, incremental dump levels are quite arbitrary, although members of an incremental dump set have an ordinal relationship to each other. The scheme works like this: a low numbered dump level (such as 1) should be used at the beginning of the week (Sunday), increasing by one each day until the end of the week (Saturday) with a dump level of 7. When the lower numbered is encountered on Sunday, the dumping cycle begins anew. Cycling through tapes this way ensures that tapes are used consistently across different weeks. Thus, for a weekly incremental dump, you'll need a set of seven tapes—preferably two sets of seven that can be used on a week-in, week-out basis, with the set not being used stored off-site.

12

Ask the Expert

Question: What backup programs are used in industry?

Answer: Most commercial organizations use commercial software like Veritas NetBackup and Legato Networker. These are specialized products that require extensive configuration. Using ufsdump is probably standard on most workstations, even if larger companies might take a more integrated approach to data management.

12.6 Create Backups (ufsdump)

Before creating a dump, it's important to know whether or not the tape has sufficient capacity to store all the data from the target file system. The total dump can be estimated by using the ufsdump command in the following way:

```
# ufsdump S /dev/rdsk/c0t0d1s1
100765536
```

In this example, approximately 100MB of data needs to be written, meaning that a single QIC, DLT, or DAT tape would be able to store all the data on the partition. Let's examine the output of a full dump of */dev/rdsk/c0t0d1s1*—here, we pass the dump level of 0, using a cartridge and updating the dump record in */etc/dumpdates* (*0cu*):

```
# ufsdump 0cu /dev/rmt/0 /dev/rdsk/c0t0d1s1
  DUMP: Writing 63 Kilobyte records
  DUMP: Date of this level 0 dump: Wed Apr 03 13:26:33 2002
  DUMP: Date of last level 0 dump: the epoch
  DUMP: Dumping /dev/rdsk/c0t0d1s1 (solaris:/) to /dev/rmt/0.
  DUMP: Mapping (Pass I) [regular files]
  DUMP: Mapping (Pass II) [directories]
  DUMP: Estimated 201531072 blocks (98.4MB).
  DUMP: Dumping (Pass III) [directories]
  DUMP: Dumping (Pass IV) [regular files]
  DUMP: 201531072 blocks (98.4MB) on 1 volume at 1167 KB/sec
  DUMP: DUMP IS DONE
  DUMP: Level 0 dump on Wed Apr 03 15:12:02 2002
```

We can verify that the dump was performed correctly by checking the
/etc/dumpdates file:

```
# cat /etc/dumpdates
/dev/rdsk/c0t0d1s1          0 Wed Apr 03 15:12:02 2002
/dev/rdsk/c0t0d1s3          0 Wed Apr 03 17:22:06 2002
/dev/rdsk/c0t0d1s4          0 Wed Apr 03 18:02:12 2002
/dev/rdsk/c0t0d1s5          0 Wed Apr 03 18:24:55 2002
/dev/rdsk/c0t0d1s6          0 Wed Apr 03 17:54:23 2002
```

ufsdump can be used to perform bulk file copying tasks even on other file
systems. For example, to copy all the files from the /dev/rdsk/c0t0d0s1 slice to
the directory /data, the following command sequence could be used:

```
# mkdir /data
# ufsdump 0f - /dev/rdsk/c0t0d0s1 | (cd /data; ufsrestore xf -)
```

Project 12-2: Performing a Full Dump

This project shows you how to perform a full dump of a file system
(/dev/rdsk/c0t3d0s1) using ufsdump to an external tape drive. This is the
traditional backup performed daily at many sites.

Step-by-Step

1. Check the size of the file system and verify that it will fit on your tape:

```
# ufsdump S /dev/rdsk/c0t3d0s1
```

2. Perform the full dump:

```
# ufsdump 0cu /dev/rmt/0 /dev/rdsk/c0t3d0s1
```

3. Check the dumpdates file to be sure that it completed OK:

```
# grep c0t3d0s1 /etc/dumpdates
```

Summary

The ufsdump and grep commands can be used to create a tape archive and
verify that it was written at a specific time.

12

12.7 Restore Backups (ufsrestore)

The ufsrestore program is easy to use. In it simplest form, the *xf* parameters can be used to extract files from a specified tape device. In the following example, files will be extracted from the tape */dev/rmt/0*:

```
# ufsrestore xf /dev/rmt/0
You have not read any volumes yet.
Unless you know which volume your file(s) are on you should start
with the last volume and work towards the first.
Specify next volume #: 1
set owner/mode for '.'? [yn] y
```

In this example, we've specified that volume 1 should be extracted. It is possible (although not recommended) to store multiple ufsdump volumes on one tape. This is because volumes are not labeled, and it's easy to confuse the different volume numbers. In an emergency, it's easier to restore all volume 1's from the available tapes. Again, if you're not sure what's on a tape, you can print a file listing to the screen by issuing the following command:

```
# ufsrestore tf /dev/rmt/0
12   ./java/classes/font.properties.cs
13   ./java/classes/font.properties.el
16   ./java/classes/font.properties.hu
12   ./java/classes/font.properties.ja
12   ./java/classes/font.properties.ko
11   ./java/classes/font.properties.lt
10   ./java/classes/font.properties.lv
22   ./java/classes/font.properties.pl
```

In addition to executing ufsrestore non-interactively, a menu-driven interactive mode can also be used to extract files manually:

```
# ufsrestore I
ufsrestore > help
Available commands are:
        ls [arg] - list directory
        cd arg - change directory
```

```
      pwd - print current directory
      add [arg] - add `arg' to list of files to be extracted
      delete [arg] - delete `arg' from list of files to be extracted
      extract - extract requested files
      setmodes - set modes of requested directories
      quit - immediately exit program
      what - list dump header information
      verbose - toggle verbose flag (useful with ``ls'')
      help or `?' - print this list
If no `arg' is supplied, the current directory is used
ufsrestore >
```

It is most useful to use the interactive version of ufsrestore when you need to perform multiple operations on a tape. For example, you may wish to extract files from several different directories, or examine the header information for the dump. Scripts will typically call ufsrestore in its non-interactive form.

1-Minute Drill

● What command is used to restore files from tape?

● What command is used to back up files to tape?

● What command is used to create an exact, byte-by-byte copy of raw disk or tape blocks?

● ufsrestore
● ufsdump
● dd

☑ *Mastery Check*

1. What command is used to create tape archives?

   A. tar cvf

   B. tar create

   C. tar make

   D. ctar

2. What command is used to extract tape archives?

   A. tar xvf

   B. tar extract

   C. tar unmake

   D. xtar

3. What command allows archives to be written across multiple volumes?

   A. tar

   B. dd

   C. cpio

   D. mv

4. Which of the following commands does *not* compress data?

   A. tar

   B. compress

   C. gzip

   D. pack

5. What command is used to display the table of contents for tape archives?

   A. tar tvf

   B. tar table

   C. tar display

   D. xtar -t

☑ Mastery Check

6. What is the purpose of the `ufsrestore tf` command?

A. Display tape table of contents

B. Perform a backup on an old tape

C. Perform a non-interactive restore

D. Perform a time-limited restore

7. What is LTO?

A. Latent Tape Optimization

B. Linear Tape Open standard

C. Laser Type Origination

D. Latent Tape Organization

8. What does the `dd` command do?

A. Creates a file-by-file copy of all files on a file system

B. Creates an exact, byte-by-byte copy of raw disk or tape blocks

C. Displays disk usage

D. Reads fragmented files from disk

9. What command allows archives to be written across multiple volumes?

A. `tar`

B. `dd`

C. `df`

D. `cpio`

10. What `ufsrestore` command is used to add a file to a list of files to be restored?

A. `attach`

B. `submit`

C. `do`

D. `add`

12

☑ Mastery Check

11. What `ufsrestore` command is used to list files?

    A. `dir`

    B. `ls`

    C. `attach`

    D. `arg`

12. What `ufsrestore` command is used to change?

    A. `chdir`

    B. `cd`

    C. `change`

    D. mv

13. What `ufsrestore` command is used to list header dump information?

    A. header

    B. dump

    C. what

    D. which

14. What `ufsrestore` command is used to set directory modes?

    A. `setmodes`

    B. `setmode`

    C. modeset

    D. sm

15. What `ufsrestore` command is used to extract files?

    A. `attach`

    B. submit

    C. do

    D. `extract`

Part 4

Managing Internet Services

Module 13

Electronic Mail

Critical Skills

Electronic mail (e-mail) is one of the foundation services offered by Solaris and other network operating systems such as Linux and Microsoft Windows. Solaris e-mail services allow the delivery of local messages for single standalone systems, as well as company intranets and the global Internet. Solaris provides both Mail Transport Agents (MTAs), such as the popular Sendmail program, as well as Mail User Agents (MUAs), using a network protocol to retrieve mail from a Solaris server for display on a client system. For example, a Windows-based client network might use Qualcomm's Eudora program to read and send e-mail through the Internet by connecting to a Solaris Sendmail server and using the Post Office Protocol (POP). Alternatively, in a mixed-platform environment, client systems may all use the Pine program ("Pine is not elm"), making use of the more advanced Internet Message Access Protocol (IMAP). A further option for Solaris users is to access their e-mail by using one of the standard command-line clients, such as mailx or elm (which may be installed separately); these clients can be executed from any of the standard shells and do not require support for a third-party mail exchange protocol between client and server, as mail folders are accessed directly from the local file system.

This module will examine how to configure and install GUI and command-line e-mail clients and review the major configuration options for the Sendmail MTA. It also examines how to retrieve and install the latest version of Sendmail, which may fix bugs that have been identified in the vendor-supplied version provided by Sun. Finally, we will explore some of the options for sending multimedia objects through e-mail messages by using Metamail.

13.1 Manage Electronic Mail Systems

Until relatively recently, many vendor-specific electronic messaging products used nonstandard, proprietary protocols for exchanging data. For example, UNIX systems often transferred e-mail using the Unix-to-Unix Copy Program (UUCP), while some systems designed for Microsoft Windows made use of the X.400 protocol. This made the exchange of e-mail among systems problematic because systems implementing these protocols could not communicate with each other.

RFC 821 suggested that a standard protocol should be implemented on all e-mail servers, and that the protocol should use a human-friendly command set so that troubleshooting could be simplified. The Simple Mail Transfer Protocol (SMTP) is now the world standard for exchanging e-mail among hosts, although a more enhanced version of SMTP (known as ESMTP, or Extended Simple Mail Transfer Protocol) is supported by many different MTAs. SMTP delivery problems can be easily diagnosed by using standard tools such as Telnet.

Exchange of e-mail messages using SMTP operates using a client/server model: The sender of a message passes the text of the message, along with a recipient address to the local MTA. That MTA then establishes a client session with a remote mail server (possibly via an intermediate mail relay). After verifying that mail for the recipient can be accepted by the remote server, the server then requests that the message be passed, and it is delivered locally by a mail handler (such as procmail). Delivery is then acknowledged by the server to the client. The exchange of data between the local e-mail client and the local MTA usually occurs by using POP or IMAP. The exchange of data between the local MTA and the remote MTA uses SMTP. Finally, the exchange of data between the remote MTA and the local e-mail client also occurs by using POP or IMAP. This configuration is shown in Figure 13-1.

1-Minute Drill

● What port is used to exchange SMTP data?

● What protocol is used to transfer mail among MTAs?

13.2 Sending and Receiving Mail

Let's look at a concrete example of how mail exchange works in real life. Imagine that the local user **pwatters@cassowary.paulwatters.com** wanted to send a message to the remote user **yasunari@paulwatters.com**—we can examine the process as it occurs by using the test facility of the Sendmail program. Although we wouldn't normally use Sendmail in this way as a

---

● Port 25
● Sendmail

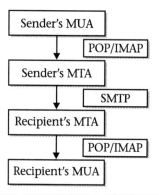

Figure 13-1 Mail exchange process

normal mail client, we can more easily examine the steps taken when mail is being transferred.

1. This command takes the contents of the file *message.txt* and sends it using Sendmail to the remote user **yasunari@paulwatters.com**.

```
$ /usr/lib/sendmail -v yasunari@paulwatters.com < message.txt
```

2. This line documents the attempt to make a TCP connection on port 25 from **cassowary.paulwatters.com** to the mailhost for **paulwatters.com**.

```
yasunari@paulwatters.com... Connecting to mail-incoming.hostsave.com
(TCP)...
```

3. This line is the acknowledgment returned from the mail server for the domain **paulwatters.com** (**lmg.ahnet.net**). It also announces that the remote server speaks ESMTP as well as SMTP, and that the current local time is 8:45 A.M.

```
220 lmg.ahnet.net ZMailer Server 2.99.38 #1 ESMTP ready at Mon,
21 Jan 2002 08:45:01 -0700
```

4. The HELO command allows the local sender's host to be identified to the recipient's mail host:

```
>>> HELO cassowary.paulwatters.com
```

5. The remote host acknowledges the local host:

```
250 lmg.ahnet.net Hello cassowary.paulwatters.com
```

6. The local server announces a message from the local user **pwatters@cassowary.paulwatters.com** by using the MAIL command:

```
>>> MAIL From:<pwatters@cassowary.paulwatters.com>
```

7. The remote server acknowledges receipt of the request and notes that that the sending user is remote relative to its domain:

```
250 (verified non-local) Ok
```

8. The local server sends the RCPT command, which indicates the remote user to whom the mail is addressed:

```
>>> RCPT To:<yasunari@paulwatters.com>
```

9. The remote server acknowledges receipt of the request and notes that that the recipient is a user local to the domain:

```
250 (verified local) Ok
```

10. The DATA command is sent by the client to indicate that the message data will be now be uploaded:

```
>>> DATA
```

11. The message upload request is acknowledged, and the message body may now be sent.

```
354 Start mail input; end with <CRLF>.<CRLF>
```

12. The message body is transferred and terminated by a single period at the end of the message:

```
testing
>>> .
```

13. Receipt of the message is acknowledged:

```
250 2.6.0 Roger
```

13

14. The local server requests a disconnection:

```
>>> QUIT
```

15. The remote server accepts the disconnection and confirms delivery of the message:

```
221 2.0.0 lmg.ahnet.net Out
yasunari@paulwatters.com... Sent
```

1-Minute Drill

● What SMTP command designates a mail recipient?

Using a Relay

Of course, not every Solaris system is going to have a mail system running locally: in large organizations, a typical Internet gateway system may perform packet filtering, Web serving, and mail serving for an entire site. This means that mail originating from Solaris systems, in this situation, must be relayed through the gateway system. The domains that are accepted for relaying are defined in the */etc/mail/relay-domains* file. Thus, relaying mail for a local domain would require the local domain name to be entered. Alternatively, if remote sites within an organization wish to use the mail relay, their domain names may also be entered.

Mail relaying used to be the norm with respect to handling e-mail. However, the growth of Unsolicited Commercial Email (UCE—or spam) that abused the e-mail relay system has seen relaying decrease in popularity over the years. The following example mirrors the direct mail approach shown earlier but uses a mail relay:

```
$ /usr/lib/sendmail -v yasunari@paulwatters.com < message.txt
yasunari@paulwatters.com... Connecting to relay.paulwatters.com.
 via relay...
220 relay.paulwatters.com ESMTP Sendmail 8.11.0/8.11.0;
```

● RCPT

```
Mon, 21 Jan 2002 08:45:01 -0700 (EST)
>>> EHLO cassowary.paulwatters.com
250- relay.paulwatters.com Hello pwatters@cassowary.
paulwatters.com [10.64.128.16], pleased to meet you
250-EXPN
250-VERB
250-8BITMIME
250-SIZE 10000000
250-DSN
250-ONEX
250-ETRN
250-XUSR
250 HELP
>>> MAIL From:<pwatters@cassowary.paulwatters.com> SIZE=6819
250 <pwatters@cassowary.paulwatters.com >... Sender ok
>>> RCPT To:<yasunari@paulwatters.com>
250 <yasunari@paulwatters.com>... Recipient ok
>>> DATA
354 Enter mail, end with "." on a line by itself
message
>>> .
250 NAA13535 Message accepted for delivery
yasunari@paulwatters.com... Sent (NAA13535 Message
accepted for delivery)
Closing connection to relay.paulwatters.com.
>>> QUIT
221 relay.paulwatters.com closing connection
```

13.3 Manual Testing

If you're not on a system that has Sendmail (such as a Windows 2000 server), but you want to test whether a mail connection can be made with a remote host, the Telnet utility may be used to make a connection directly on the SMTP port (port 25). Using this technique, SMTP commands and message data may be entered manually and transmitted to the remote server. The remote server doesn't really care that you aren't a Sendmail server; it simply responds to the commands it receives. In the following example, a message is manually entered by a user from the system sender to a user on the system receiver. After exchanging the usual acknowledgments, the sender and recipients are identified and the message data is forwarded. The message is delivered and acknowledged.

13

Project 13-1: Testing ESMTP Mail Transactions Manually

This project shows you how to test the mail exchange process manually. This is an important procedure to use when a problem occurs while transferring mail from one MTA to another.

Step-By-Step

1. Telnet to port 25 on the server to which you want to connect:

```
$ telnet receiver 25
Trying 204.68.12.36 ...
Connected to receiver.paulwatters.com.
Escape character is '^]'.
220 receiver.paulwatters.com ESMTP Sendmail 8.8.8+Sun/8.8.8;
Mon, 21 Jan 2002 08:45:01 -0700(EST)
```

2. Enter the EHLO command:

```
EHLO sender
250-receiver.paulwatters.com Hello sender.paulwatters.com
[203.64.12.36], pleased to meet you
```

3. Enter the MAIL command:

```
MAIL FROM: <pwatters@sender.paulwatters.com>
250 <pwatters@sender.paulwatters.com>... Sender ok
```

4. Identify the recipient:

```
RCPT TO: <pwatters@receiver.paulwatters.com>
250 <pwatters@receiver.paulwatters.com>... Recipient ok
```

5. Enter the data:

```
DATA
354 Enter mail, end with "." on a line by itself
Testing...
.
250 MAA18353 Message accepted for delivery
```

6. Exit the transaction:

```
QUIT
221 receiver.paulwatters.com closing connection
Connection closed by foreign host.
```

Summary
The `telnet` command can be used to connect to the SMTP port directly, and SMTP commands can simply be typed in by the tester.

13.4 Explain the Different Client Protocols

Using the manual testing technique, it is possible to enter all SMTP and ESMTP commands interactively. To determine which SMTP commands are available from a particular server, you can simply type the HELP command once connected:

```
HELP
214-This is Sendmail version 8.8.8+Sun
214-Topics:
214-    HELO    EHLO    MAIL    RCPT    DATA
214-    RSET    NOOP    QUIT    HELP    VRFY
214-    EXPN    VERB    ETRN    DSN
214-For more info use "HELP <topic>".
214-To report bugs in the implementation contact Sun Microsystems
214-Technical Support.
214-For local information send email to Postmaster at your site.
214 End of HELP info
```

These SMTP commands perform the following functions:

Command	Description
DATA	Indicates that the data being sent is message data
EHLO	Indicates that the host speaks ESMTP
EXPN	Lists local members of a mailing list
HELO	Indicates that the host speaks SMTP
MAIL	Contains the address of the sender

13

Command	Description
QUIT	Ends a session
RCPT	Contains the address of the recipient
VRFY	Verifies that a recipient address exists as a user account on the system

Alternatively, if you want to obtain a list of ESMTP commands that are available from an ESMTP server, you must use the EHLO command:

```
$ telnet receiver 25
Trying 204.68.12.36 ...
Connected to receiver.paulwatters.com.
Escape character is '^]'.
220 receiver.paulwatters.com ESMTP Sendmail 8.8.8+Sun/8.8.8;
Mon, 21 Jan 2002 08:45:01 -0700 (EST)
EHLO sender
250-receiver.paulwatters.com Hello sender.paulwatters.com
[203.64.12.36], pleased to meet you
250-EXPN
250-VERB
250-8BITMIME
250-SIZE
250-DSN
250-ONEX
250-ETRN
250-XUSR
250 HELP
```

These commands perform the following functions:

Command	Description
VERB	Starts verbose mode
8BITMIME	Uses 8-bit data
DSN	Delivery status notification
SIZE	Declares size of message
ONEX	Single message transmission
ETRN	Initializes remote message queue
XUSR	Submits data for user

13.5 Investigating E-mail Headers

Every time an MTA generates a mail message and transmits it to a recipient at another system, a set of identifying lines are added to the top of the message. These identifiers are known as *headers*, and they can be used to trace the origin of a message, the date it was sent, and other similar types of imformation. Historically, headers could be trusted to provide authoritative information. However, since many MTAs do not prevent fake or incorrect information from being inserted into e-mail headers, companies that generate large volumes of spam mail are able to exploit the "open" nature of Sendmail and other standard MTAs.

A number of mandatory and optional e-mail headers must be generated to ensure that a message is delivered correctly. These include the following:

Header	Description
Content-Length	Contains the number of lines in the message.
Content-Type	States the MIME type that the body of the message contains. This may be text or any one of the multimedia types supported by MIME.
Date	Contains the time and date that the message was received.
From	States the name and e-mail address of the sender.
Message-Id	Contains a random string that uniquely identifies the message.
Received	States how the message was received, including the name of the mailserver.
Subject	Contains the topic of the message, as inserted by the sender.
To	States the name and e-mail address of the recipient.

13

These headers are used by mail clients to extract data for display about every message in each user's mailbox, as follows:

```
From someone@mcgraw-hill.com Mon Jan 21 08:45 2002
Received: from birds.paulwatters.com
(root@birds.paulwatters.com [137.111.216.12])
        by emu.birds.paulwatters.com (8.9.1a/8.9.1) with ESMTP id MAA07956
        for <pwatters@emu.birds.paulwatters.com>;
        Mon, 21 Jan 2002 08:45:01 -0700 (EST)
Received: from animals.paulwatters.com
        (animals.paulwatters.com [137.111.1.11])
        by birds.paulwatters.com (8.8.8/8.8.8) with ESMTP id MAA12227
        for <pwatters@cassowary.paulwatters.com>;
        Mon, 21 Jan 2002 08:45:01 -0700 (EST)
Received: from corp148mr.mcgraw-hill.com (corp148mr.mcgraw-hill.com [198.45.18.131])
        by animals.paulwatters.com (8.10.2/8.10.2)
        with ESMTP id e901YAP07532
        for <pwatters@paulwatters.com>; Mon, 21 Jan 2002 08:45:01 -0700
Message-Id: <200010240134.e901YAP07532@animals.paulwatters.com>
From: Someone <someone@mcgraw-hill.com>
To: WATTERS Paul Andrew <pwatters@cassowary.paulwatters.com>
Subject: Solaris Book
Date: Mon, 21 Jan 2002 08:45:00 -0700
MIME-Version: 1.0
X-Mailer: Internet Mail Service (5.5.2650.21)
Content-Type: text/plain;
        charset="iso-8859-1"
Content-Length: 956

[Charset iso-8859-1 unsupported, filtering to ASCII...]
[You can also use 'v' to view or save this part.]
```

These headers indicate that the user *Someone* from the domain **mcgraw-hill.com** sent a message on January 21 at 8:45 A.M to *pwatters* in the domain **paulwatters.com**. The message passed through several relay hosts, including **animals.paulwatters.com**, to arrive at the destination. The message had 956 lines, included the subject "Solaris Book," and had the message ID 200010240134.e9O1YAP07532. The MIME version was 1.0, used the ISO-8859-1 character set, and the content-type was text/plain.

MIME

The MIME type found in the previous example is typical of mail messages that contain plaintext. The Multipurpose Internet Mail Extensions (MIME) were first outlined in RFC 2045, with the intention of providing a text-based encoding system by which multimedia documents (word processing documents, images, and movies) could be transmitted by e-mail. MIME is required because e-mail is an inherently text-based system for passing messages—but few restrictions apply to the content of these messages. This freedom can often be seen at work in the viruses that are passed through e-mail to infect host systems, where the mail reader has super-user privileges (a good reason never to execute an attachment as root!). Since many MTAs have limitations on the size of messages that are accepted, MIME has the ability to encode multimedia content across different messages of a fixed size, so that they may be reassembled at the destination.

As we saw in the preceding code, a MIME type is associated with every e-mail message, which is stated in the header with a line like this:

```
Content-Type: text/plain; charset=us-ascii
```

This line specifies that the message was composed and sent in plaintext and that there are no multimedia attachments. However, let's have a look at a message that does contain an encoded multimedia attachment:

```
This is a multi-part message in MIME format.

------=_NextPart_000_0008_01C033D3.0A46C4E0
Content-Type: text/plain;
        charset="iso-8859-1"
Content-Transfer-Encoding: 7bit

Gentlemen, Please find attached our current business plan.

-Paul W.

------=_NextPart_000_0008_01C033D3.0A46C4E0
Content-Type: application/msword;
        name="business.doc"
Content-Disposition: attachment;
        filename="business.doc"
Content-Transfer-Encoding: base64

OM8R4KGxGuEAAAAAAAAAAAAAAAAAAAAPgADAP7/CQAGAAAAAAAAAAAAAAABAAAAQgAAAAAAAAA
EAAARAAAAAEAAAD+////AAAAAEEAAAD//////////////////////////////////////////
//////////////////////////////////////////////////////////////////////////
//////////////////////////////////////////////////////////////////////////
//////////////////////////////////////////////////////////////////////////
/////////////////////////////////////////////////////////////////////////
```

As we can see from the MIME encoding definitions, this message contains an attachment of the *application/msword* format (Microsoft Word), which is called *business.doc*. To extract the Word file from the message, we need to either use

13

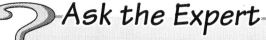

Ask the Expert

Question: Why should you use Metamail and not uuencode?

Answer: Metamail is designed specifically for use with e-mail and is designed to work across platforms. Uuencode was originally designed for UNIX and may not work on systems that do not support its type of encoding.

a mail program that handles MIME or save the file as text and run it through Metamail:

```
$ metamail business.meta
This message contains data in an unrecognized format, application/msword,
which can either be viewed as text or written to a file.

What do you want to do with the application/msword data?
1 -- See it as text
2 -- Write it to a file
3 -- Just skip it

2
Please enter the name of a file to which the data should be written
(Default: business.doc) >
Wrote file business.doc
```

13.6 Review the Configuration of the Sendmail MTA

Sendmail (**http://www.sendmail.org**) is the MTA supplied with Solaris. It has been developed over many years on all UNIX platforms, making it the de facto standard for mail transport. However, Sendmail configuration performed by hand is one of the most difficult operations that can be undertaken by a Solaris system administrator. As mailer systems and networks have become more varied over the years, Sendmail configuration has increased in complexity.

The main configuration file for running Sendmail is called *sendmail.cf*. It is a large file that dictates how Sendmail operates in all conceivable scenarios, according to various rule sets. Fortunately, a number of macros can be used to configure *sendmail.cf* for local use, rather than directly modifying the file. This ensures that rule sets and other parameters are internally consistent. The macros are written in the m4 language, which is easy to learn.

In this section, we cover some key functions of Sendmail, especially those supporting aliases and local mailing groups. In addition, we examine how to obtain the latest Sendmail distribution that you can build locally. You may need to do this if a major security flaw is exposed and a vendor-supplied patch is not available.

Sendmail Distribution

The latest version of Sendmail is always available at **ftp.sendmail.org**. In addition to the source files, the **ftp.sendmail.org** login banner always contains the latest information about the current Sendmail release. The main issue to consider when upgrading Sendmail is the compatibility of your existing *sendmail.cf* configuration file with the requirements of the new installation. Fortunately, most of the tags have remained constant throughout the various incarnations of Sendmail, especially since the first V8 release.

Running Sendmail

The Sendmail daemon is generally started at boot time by a script in */etc/init.d*, which is symbolically linked to a script in */etc/rc2* or */etc/rc3* (multi-user startup). If Sendmail needs to be halted at any time, the following command can be used:

```
# /etc/init.d/sendmail stop
```

To restart Sendmail, the following command can be used:

```
# /etc/init.d/sendmail start
```

To verify that the Sendmail daemon is running, the `pgrep` command can be used:

```
# pgrep sendmail
```

13

If Sendmail is running, the Parent PID (PID) of the Sendmail daemon process will be returned. However, if no PID is returned, the Sendmail daemon will need to be restarted.

Sendmail Configuration

The *sendmail.cf* file is divided into a number of sections:

- **Local info** contains configuration information for the local host, including its official domain name, masquerading name, administrator's e-mail address, and mail hub.

- **Options** records Sendmail-specific parameters, including 7- and 8-bit mail support, maximum message sizes, alias database options, and error modes.

- **Message precedence** defines the delivery priorities of different message types.

- **Trusted users** defines the list of users who may administer the mail system.

- **Format of headers** defines exactly how the headers discussed earlier are to be printed on each e-mail.

- **Rewriting rules** determine how to find the host on which a particular user account exists, so that a message may be successfully delivered.

Each line in the *sendmail.cf* file contains either a comment, a rule, a macro, an option, or a mail header. The most common commands used in a *sendmail.cf* file are listed here:

Command	Description
C	Prefixes a macro with more than one option
D	Prefixes a simple macro
E	Defines an environment variable
H	Prefixes a mail header used to construct mail message
M	Contains the name and path of the local mail delivery agent (e.g., the standard */bin/mail* or the third-party *procmail*)
O	Prefixes an option
P	Specifies the message precedence options
R	Specifies an address rewriting rule
S	Prefixes the definition of a rule set

Note

When generated by m4 macros, administrators should never need to edit the *sendmail.cf* file directly.

m4 Configuration

The m4 macro language can be used to create a *sendmail.cf* file by making use of a set of predefined macros that have been developed for use with Sendmail. To create a *sendmail.cf* file using m4 macros, a text file containing a list of macros to run and the appropriate parameter values for your site must be created in a text file; this is typically called *sendmail.mc*. Once this file has been installed into the *cf/cf* subdirectory under the main *sendmail* directory, the following command can be used from that directory to build a new *sendmail.cf* file:

```
# cp /etc/sendmail.cf /etc/sendmail.orig
# m4 ../m4/cf.m4 sendmail.mc > /etc/sendmail.cf
```

The first command backs up the current production *sendmail.cf* file, while the next command builds a new production *sendmail.cf* file. Once Sendmail has been started, it will be running with the new configuration.

Let's take a closer look at the macros and parameters that can be used to configure Sendmail before examining a sample *sendmail.mc* file.

Macros

The following macros are defined for use with *sendmail.mc*:

Macro	Description
DOMAIN	Used to define common elements for mail servers with the same domain name
EXPOSED_USER	Prevents domain masquerading for specific users
FEATURE	Enable a specific Sendmail feature
MAILER	Specifies the mail delivery program to use on the server (local, smtp, or procmail)
MASQUERADE_AS	Inserts an effective domain on all outgoing e-mail rather than the real domain
OSTYPE	Defines the host operating system type

Features

After the basic domain and operating system parameters have been generated, the next step is to enable specific Sendmail features by using the FEATURE macro. One instance of FEATURE is required for every feature that is to be enabled. Commonly used features include the following:

13

Feature	Description
accept_unqualified_senders	Accepts messages for delivery from users with e-mail addresses that do not have a fully qualified domain name.
accept_unresolvable_domains	Accepts messages for delivery from users with e-mail addresses whose fully qualified domain name is not resolvable.
access_db	Enables a database of senders and domains to be maintained from whom mail is automatically bounced or rejected.
always_add_domain	Inserts domain onto all e-mails sent through Sendmail, even those that are being delivered to local users.
blacklist_recipients	Defines a list of recipients who are not allowed to receive e-mail.
domaintable	Substitutes a new domain name for a previous domain name.
mailertable	Allows a different mail server to be associated with each virtual domain supported.
nullclient	Allows local Sendmail instances to forward all messages to a single outbound Sendmail server for delivery.
promiscuous_relay	Allows relaying of mail from any site through the local server. This should never be used because of the risk that spam merchants will find your server and use it to relay spam, thereby obscuring its true origin.
redirect	Redirects messages destined for users who no longer exist on the system. Requires a corresponding entry in */etc/aliases* with the name of the former user and his/her new e-mail address.
relay_based_on_mx	Uses the MX record defined in DNS to determine if the local Sendmail server is the correct server to relay messages from other servers.
relay_entire_domain	Permits all hosts within the local domain to route e-mail through the local Sendmail server.
smrsh	A functionally limited shell that can be used to restrict system access by the Sendmail daemon.
use_ct_file	Prevents users from changing the username part of their e-mail addresses on outbound e-mails.
use_cw_file	Contains a list of all DNS aliases for the mail server.

Feature	Description
virtusertable	Supports routing of e-mail for user accounts with the same username that belongs to different virtual domains. Thus, **joe@domainone.com** is not confused with **joe@domaintwo.com**, even though both domains use the same Sendmail instance.

Parameters

Specific parameters can be set for Sendmail's operation with the m4 `define` command. Although most of the values set by default within Sendmail will be satisfactory for normal use, you may occasionally need to change a value. Sendmail defines a large number of parameters; however, we'll examine only some of the most commonly modified parameters:

Parameter	Description
confDOMAIN_NAME	If your DNS server is unreliable, you might want to set the default domain name here.
confLOG_LEVEL	Specifies the logging level for Sendmail from 0 (minimal) to 13 (everything).
confMAILER_NAME	The alias used for returning messages and other automatically generated mails sent by the system. This is generally set to MAILER-DAEMON, which is typically aliased to root. So, it's possible to just set the value to root.
confMAX_MESSAGE_SIZE	The maximum size, in bytes, of any message that is accepted for delivery. Although large attachments are common these days, an upper limit of a few megabytes should be set to prevent a denial of service attack.
confSMTP_LOGIN_MSG	Replaces the standard Sendmail version banner with a local (usually nondescript) message. Can be useful in preventing would-be crackers from attempting an exploit that is specific to your version of Sendmail.

Sample sendmail.mc File

Here we define a sample *sendmail.mc* file that contains some of the parameters, features, and macros just discussed:

```
OSTYPE('solaris2')
define('confDOMAIN_NAME', 'cassowary.net')
define('confLOG_LEVEL', '13')
define('confMAILER_NAME', 'root')
```

13

```
define('confMAX_MESSAGE_SIZE', '1048576')
define('confSMTP_LOGIN_MSG', 'No Name Mail Server')
FEATURE('smrsh','/usr/sbin/smrsh')
FEATURE(redirect)
FEATURE(always_add_domain)
FEATURE(blacklist_recipients)
FEATURE('access_db')
```

More extensive examples for many different configuration files are supplied with the Sendmail source. In particular, Eric Allman's excellent README file should be read by anyone who is seriously contemplating extensive Sendmail configuration.

Aliases

One of the useful features of Solaris mail-handling is its ability to define aliases that correspond to single users or mailing lists composed of multiple users. For example, the user *pwatters* might also be the local webmaster, so it makes sense to redirect all mail sent to **webmaster@some.host.com** to **pwatters@some.host.com** using the aliases database. Similarly, if the users *paul*, *maya*, *miki*, and *moppet* are members of the coffee drinking club, club announcements could be sent to **coffee@some.host.com** if an alias was set up in the database containing the users *paul*, *maya*, *miki*, and *moppet*.

To set up an alias for the webmaster account, we would enter the following line into the */etc/aliases* database:

```
webmaster: pwatters
```

Similarly for the coffee group, we would enter the following line into the */etc/aliases* database:

```
coffee: paul, maya, miki, moppet
```

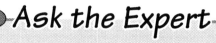

Ask the Expert

Question: Isn't using macros "cheating"?

Answer: Yes, but 99 percent of Sendmail configuration can be done by using macros. Leave the other 1 percent to Sendmail experts.

When a new alias like this is inserted into the aliases database, the `newaliases` command must be executed to update the files */etc/aliases.dir* and */etc/aliases/pag*. A sample */etc/aliases* file is shown here:

```
Postmaster: root
MAILER-DAEMON: postmaster
nobody: /dev/null
staff:paul, brad, fred, jim
solaris-users: paul, tim
help:          tim
helpdesk:      tim
support:          moppet
manager:          miki
```

When new aliases are added, the `newaliases` (or Sendmail –bi) command should be run to ensure that the aliases database is updated.

Spam Control

One of the most effective forms of spam control is to use the access_db feature. Using this feature allows a database to be maintained in */etc/mail/access* of offending sites, domains, and users—basically, as soon as one of these is identified as an offender, all mail can be blocked from entering your site. Thus, the list of all users in your domain, purchased by a would-be spammer, will be useless after the first time the spammer begins spamming your site since an effective block can be put in place. In addition, messages can be bounced back directly to the originating site or user with various offensive or polite remarks about spam and its uses. (Note that the spam being discussed here has nothing to do with the delicious ham product of the same name.)

For example, to reject all messages that are sent from a specific e-mail address, such as **spam@somesite.com**, the following entry would be inserted into */etc/mail/access*:

```
spam@somesite.com    REJECT
```

This would result in the message being bounced back to its sender. Alternatively, to send a customized message, the following command could be used:

```
spam@somesite.com    550 Take your dirty spam and ...
```

13

Often, spammers change the usernames from which they send messages. Examples might be **marketing@spamme.com**, **sales@spamme.com**, and the like, so it's sometimes necessary to block every message from a spammer's domain:

```
spamme.com    REJECT
```

Alternatively, some spammers deliberately mangle mail headers to prevent messages from being bounced back to them. In this case, it is possible to discard the message rather than delivering it or bouncing it. The following command would drop all e-mail from the **spamme.com** domain:

```
spamme.com    DISCARD
```

Managing the Mail Queue

In high-volume mail environments, it is often necessary for Sendmail to queue mail messages prior to delivery. This is because mail acceptance from a remote server is paradoxically often faster than local delivery. This leads to a mismatch between sending and delivery times—although some delivery times are very fast, others can be quite slow, depending on the number of other messages to be processed in the queue.

If mail cannot be delivered from the queue, the number of messages being delayed will obviously grow. This may occur because the /var partition becomes too full to spool mail messages, due to unrotated log files, large prints jobs, or

Ask the Expert

Question: Can Solaris systems transmit virii?

Answer: Yes. Since many MTAs around the world run Sendmail on Solaris, the virii can pass through the MTA without affecting the system. Clients that extract and execute attachments from Windows-based clients are susceptible. However, a number of anti-virus products are available that detect virii in messages at the Sendmail level and reject the message. This protects Windows clients, since the message containing a virus is never sent past the Solaris MTA.

even undeleted core files. If a user complains that messages are not being received, the mail queue can be checked by using the `mailq` command:

```
# mailq
```

This command prints a list of all messages, sorted by date received, including the sender, recipient, and message ID. If you identify a message that has been sitting in the queue for a few days, check its size by matching the message ID with the corresponding file in */var/spool/mqueue*. If the message is too large to be delivered, it can be deleted manually by the super-user.

You may also want to increase the rate at which Sendmail checks the queue from the typical default of 15 minutes to something like 1 minute. This can be achieved by modifying the *–q* parameter in */etc/init.d/sendmail* to check for each minute (`-q1m`) rather than every 15 minutes (`-q15m`).

Reading Mail

Several different mail clients are available for Solaris. Some mail clients, such as mailx, elm, and pine, access mail directly from the local file system. Other clients, such as Netscape Mail, may use POP or IMAP to retrieve messages from a remote server. One advantage of using a mail client on the local mail server is that users can take advantage of such programs as vacation, which sends a courtesy message to all users who e-mail you when you are away from your office. On the other hand, GUI clients are often the easiest to use for novice users or those who wish to read their mail from a remote system.

POP

The Post Office Protocol (POP) is a straightforward method of delivering e-mail to clients from a server system. As described in RFC 1725, POP is designed to facilitate offline delivery of mail to remote clients who may or may not have a permanent Internet connection. Using POP allows mail messages to be received and stored on a SMTP server, where a separate POP server listens for client connections on port 110. After a request for a connection has been received, an exchange of commands and their arguments ensues, in a similar fashion to

13

SMTP. The following commands are typically issued by a client application to the POP server in response to a series of requests:

Command	Description
USER *username*	Sends a valid *username* on the remote server system
PASS *password*	Sends a valid *password* for the *username* specified on the remote system
LIST	Generates a list of available mail messages to be downloaded
RETR *n*	Retrieves the body of message *n* from the user's remote mailbox
DELE *n*	Deletes the message *n* from the user's remote mailbox
QUIT	Ends the POP session

If a command is accepted by the server, an +*OK* response is issued. However, if an error condition is encountered, the server responds with an *ERR* message.

POP is commonly used by GUI clients that make it easy for users to read and manage their e-mail and send new messages, without ever logging into a shell and using a command-line client like elm or mailx. The protocol allows large capacity mail servers to manage all back-end mail operations, providing high availability and performance, without using any client resources. However, a number of security issues related to POP make it unsuitable for deployment across the Internet. For example, the user's username and password are transmitted in cleartext across the Internet—any rogue user with a packet sniffer can filter the packets searching for strings like *USER* and *PASS*, and extract the corresponding username and password.

One of the most popular POP mail user agents is Eudora (**http://www.qualcomm.com**), which runs on both the Microsoft Windows and MacOS platforms. Eudora is able to send and receive messages with attachments, and it has extensive folder-based management of received and sent messages. One of its best features is a "chili pepper" rating system for message content—if you receive an office joke with three chilis, it may be best to read it when your boss isn't nearby!

IMAP

One of the performance issues associated with POP is the fact that it is largely offline: the POP client must make a connection to the server, usually every 10 minutes, to determine whether new messages have been received. This process is wasteful if you rarely receive messages, particularly if hundreds of clients are connecting simultaneously to the server.

An alternative is to use a server that supports the Internet Message Access Protocol (IMAP), as described in RFC 2060. IMAP is designed to connect clients and servers in real time, providing instant access to new messages and to mail delivery facilities. In addition, IMAP is much more efficient, because message parts can be requested for download selectively, unlike POP, which requires that the entire message be downloaded upon request. For example, a user could search his/her mailbox for all messages received by a particular user, just by retrieving the header files. Because all of this activity occurs on the server, the client is not burdened. Like POP, IMAP clients are generally GUI in nature, although some old favorites (like pine) are now available for use in their standard form with Microsoft Windows, using IMAP.

13.7 Examine How to Use the elm Mail Client

Like other System V operating systems, Solaris has the standard mailx client, which may be executed by typing **mailx** on the command line. The mailx program has only basic message-handling facilities, and many users prefer to use a full-featured system such as pine or elm (**ftp://ftp.virginia.edu/pub/elm/elm2.5.6.tar.gz**). One advantage of using a command-line client is that mail can be easily accessed by making a Telnet (or secure shell) connection to the mail server and spawning the client from the shell. This means that a simple terminal is all that is required to read e-mail.

The elm interface is shown in Figure 13-2. Many of the single keystroke commands used in elm are listed on the bottom half of the screen. The elm program can be executed from the command line by using this command:

```
$ elm
```

From the main menu, a number of different commands may be used to send mail, retrieve messages, and use mail folders, as listed here:

Command	Description
a	Inserts an alias for the user associated with the current message into the Address Book
b	Returns the messages to the sender appearing as if delivery was unsuccessful

13

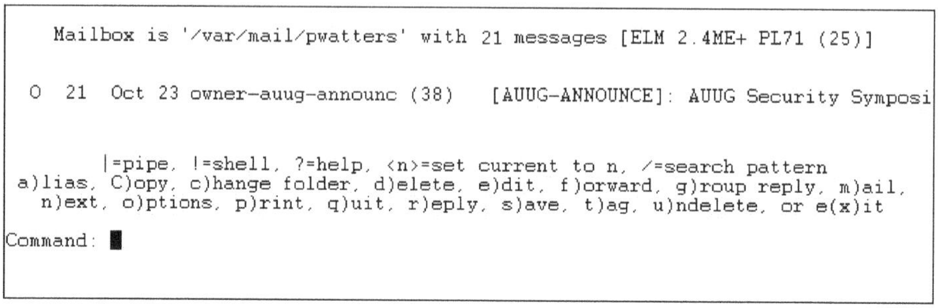

```
Mailbox is '/var/mail/pwatters' with 21 messages [ELM 2.4ME+ PL71 (25)]

O  21  Oct 23 owner-auug-announc (38)    [AUUG-ANNOUNCE]: AUUG Security Symposi


        |=pipe, !=shell, ?=help, <n>=set current to n, /=search pattern
 a)lias, C)opy, c)hange folder, d)elete, e)dit, f)orward, g)roup reply, m)ail,
   n)ext, o)ptions, p)rint, q)uit, r)eply, s)ave, t)ag, u)ndelete, or e(x)it
Command: █
```

Figure 13-2 The elm mail user agent

Command	Description
c	Opens a folder
d	Removes the current message from the mailbox
f	Sends the current message to another user
m	Makes a new mail message
o	Changes options that are saved in ~/.elm/elmrc
p	Sends the current message to a printer
q	Quits elm
s	Copies the current message to a folder
x	Exits elm

Most users include a signature at the end of their e-mail message, which includes contact information. Here's my signature, for example:

```
--
Paul A. Watters
Managing Directory, Cassowary Computing Pty Ltd
Sydney NSW Australia
md@cassowary.net
```

This signature should be contained in the file ~/.signature. The elm user's guide can be downloaded from **http://www.instinct.org/elm/doc/Users.txt**.

An alternative to using elm is a GUI-based client, such as Eudora, which is shown in Figure 13-3. This interface is particularly useful for administrators and users from a Microsoft Windows background, as they will already be familiar with the interface and commands used by the Eudora client.

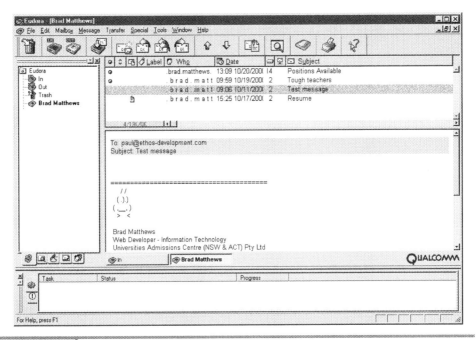

Figure 13-3 Eudora mail client

☑ *Mastery Check*

1. What is the purpose of the DATA command?

   A. Indicates that the data being sent is message data

   B. Indicates that the host speaks ESMTP

   C. Lists local members of a mailing list

   D. Indicates that the host speaks SMTP

2. What is the purpose of the EHLO command?

   A. Indicates that the data being sent is message data

   B. Indicates that the host speaks ESMTP

13

☑ Mastery Check

    C. Lists local members of a mailing list

    D. Indicates that the host speaks SMTP

3. What is the purpose of the EXPN command?

    A. Indicates that the data being sent is message data

    B. Indicates that the host speaks ESMTP

    C. Lists local members of a mailing list

    D. Indicates that the host speaks SMTP

4. What is the purpose of the HELO command?

    A. Indicates that the data being sent is message data

    B. Indicates that the host speaks ESMTP

    C. Lists local members of a mailing list

    D. Indicates that the host speaks SMTP

5. The MAIL command is used for what purpose?

    A. Contains the address of the sender

    B. Ends a session

    C. Contains the address of the recipient

    D. Verifies that a recipient address exists as a user account on the system

6. The QUIT command is used for what purpose?

    A. Contains the address of the sender

    B. Ends a session

    C. Contains the address of the recipient

    D. Verifies that a recipient address exists as a user account on the system

Mastery Check

7. The RCPT command is used for what purpose?

   A. Contains the address of the sender

   B. Ends a session

   C. Contains the address of the recipient

   D. Verifies that a recipient address exists as a user account on the system

8. The VRFY command is used for what purpose?

   A. Contains the address of the sender

   B. Ends a session

   C. Contains the address of the recipient

   D. Verifies that a recipient address exists as a user account on the system

9. In ESMTP, what is the role of the VERB command?

   A. Starts verbose mode

   B. Uses 8-bit data

   C. Delivers status notification

   D. Declares size of message

10. In ESMTP, what is the role of the 8BITMIME command?

   A. Starts verbose mode

   B. Uses 8-bit data

   C. Delivers status notification

   D. Declares size of message

11. In ESMTP, what is the role of the DSN command?

   A. Starts verbose mode

   B. Uses 8-bit data

13

☑ Mastery Check

      C. Delivers status notification

      D. Declares size of message

12. In ESMTP, what is the role of the `SIZE` command?

      A. Starts verbose mode

      B. Uses 8-bit data

      C. Delivers status notification

      D. Declares size of message

13. In elm, what is the purpose of the `d` command?

      A. Opens a folder

      B. Removes the current message from the mailbox

      C. Sends the current message to another user

      D. Makes a new mail message

14. In elm, what is the purpose of the `f` command?

      A. Opens a folder

      B. Removes the current message from the mailbox

      C. Sends the current message to another user

      D. Makes a new mail message

15. In elm, what is the purpose of the `m` command?

      A. Opens a folder

      B. Removes the current message from the mailbox

      C. Sends the current message to another user

      D. Makes a new mail message

Module 14

Domain Name Services

Critical Skills

To identify hosts connected to the Internet in a unique way, an IP address must be allocated to each host. This 32-byte number consists of four individual numbers in the range [0,255] and can be allocated permanently to a host (a *static* address) or leased to a host whenever a host is "live" and connected to the Internet (a *dynamic* address). While this addressing scheme is sufficient for differentiating hosts, from the perspective of TCP/IP applications such as Telnet and FTP, it is difficult for humans to remember IP addresses—and it's even more difficult to associate addresses with specific tasks. This is where the Domain Name Service (DNS) plays a significant role in making Internet services easier for humans: organizations can map their subnets to domain names, and individual hosts can be mapped to hostnames that are unique within a specific domain or subdomain. For example, the Web server with the domain name **http://www.sun.com** has an IP address of 192.18.97.241. The hostname of the server in this example is **www**, and its domain is **sun.com**.

This module examines how you configure a DNS server for Solaris and how you can make the best use of the client tools supplied with the system. In addition, we examine how to build and configure the latest version of the Berkeley Internet Daemon (BIND) from source, if security issues leave your existing BIND service vulnerable to attack.

14.1 Design Domain Name Services

Humans are not good at remembering numbers, especially the 32-bit numbers that comprise addresses used to identify hosts using the Internet Protocol (IP). However, humans can remember names quite well, so in the early days of the Internet, a listing of all hostnames, domains, and their mappings was distributed to hosts in the form of a flat text file called *HOSTS.TXT*. A hostname, such as *mail* uniquely identifies a host on the local network, while a domain like **cassowary.net** distinguishes local hosts from those belonging to other domains. This hierarchical approach allows subdomains to be created, such as **users.cassowary.net** and **admins.cassowary.net**, if functional or geographical segmentation is required.

While this modular approach was quite efficient, since no precious network bandwidth was consumed during hostname and IP address lookups, it also meant that as new hosts and networks were added to the Internet at an exponential rate, it was necessary to implement a new solution. Requiring clients to refresh their *HOSTS.TXT* file on a regular basis was certainly not a scalable solution! Solaris also implemented (and still retains) a version of the *HOSTS.TXT* file in the form of the */etc/hosts* file, which can be used on small networks to match IP addresses with hostnames.

Some Solaris applications still use the */etc/hosts* file, especially where common logging is performed between hosts on the local network. In this case, the local logging hostname (the *loghost*) is often defined in */etc/hosts*:

```
203.128.16.23    johnson    samuel.cassowary.net            loghost
```

However, for every new entry or change made to the file, an update must be performed on every host on the network, which is clearly inefficient.

Early approaches to solving this dilemma involved the development of a distributed database of hostname-to-address mappings, whereby a single host was designated for each domain as the "authoritative" host, as proposed in RFC 882 and 883. Thus, if a new host was added to an existing network, remote hosts would automatically be able to look up the relevant address by contacting the so-called "name server" of that domain. Only when new networks were added to the Internet would a new entry be required to register with so-called "root" domains. These name servers also provided data to initialize local caches of DNS data, so that lookups to remote servers did not need to be performed constantly. This significantly reduced Internet traffic being generated by DNS lookups.

Of course, for DNS clients operating on each Solaris system to determine which remote name server to connect to, to allow lookups of hostnames that are controlled by the remote server, the IP address of that remote server must be known. For example, if the name server that is authoritative for **www.cassowary.net** is **ns.paulwatters.com**, how would a client determine this relationship, as **cassowary.net** is obviously a second-level domain different from **paulwatters.com**. After the IP address of the remote DNS server is known, the IP addresses for any clients that are managed by that server can be easily looked up. These domain name servers can be identified by contacting a root name server, which manages top-level domains for the U.S., including the traditional *.edu* (educational organizations), *.com* (commercial organizations), and *.net* (network) domains.

In addition to distinctions based on organizational purpose (commercial or educational), many nations also have their own top-level domains, such as *.au* (Australia), *.fj* (Fiji) and *.nz* (New Zealand). Under these top-level geographic domains are a number of second-level domains that match the generic top-level

14

domains defined in the U.S.: for example, Australia has *.com.au* (Australian commercial organizations), *.edu.au* (Australian educational organizations), and *.asn.au* (Australian non-profit associations) domains.

Some new top-level domains have been recently defined by InterNIC, including *.biz*, *.info*, *.name*, *.museum*, *.coop*, *.aero*, and i. A list of registrars that are permitted by InterNIC to register names can be found at **http://www.internic.net/regist.html**. A competitive regime determines the operation of domain name registrars; thus, it's advisable to "shop around" for the best price and service, particularly if you manage many second-level domains.

To support domain-name resolution, a client/server architecture is used. On the server side, Solaris provides an implementation of BIND as well as client libraries and tools to perform DNS resolution, including nslookup, which performs name resolution on the command line. While Sun ships a tailor-made edition of BIND with Solaris 9, administrators can download, build, install, and configure a native BIND version, from **http://www.isc.org/**.

1-Minute Drill

- What is DNS?
- How is DNS different from NIS?

Let's look at an example of how a DNS architecture operates in practice: Imagine an insurance company called LInsurance that registered the domain name **linsurance.com**. LInsurance would need to install a master DNS server for the domain and register its IP address with the DNS registrar used. In addition, a slave DNS server is required, which can be co-located with the master DNS server, or preferably located on a different site. A commercial DNS provider, such as **http://www.zoneedit.com/** will provide slave lookup facilities. The master and slave DNS servers may be authoritative for subdomains like **sales.linsurance.com** and **admin.linsurance.com**, or these third-level domains could have their own master and slave DNS servers. This configuration is shown in Figure 14-1.

- The Domain Name Service.
- DNS manages only hostname–IP address mapping; NIS manages many different types of information about resources such as users, groups, and passwords. DNS is scalable for the WWW, but NIS is not.

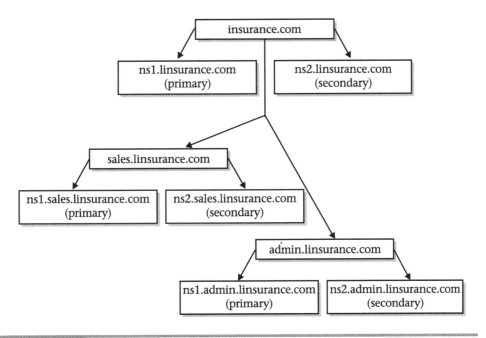

Figure 14-1   Typical second- and third-level DNS server configuration

Ask the Expert

Question: Do I need to use DNS if I have already installed NIS and I want to connect to the Internet?

Answer: Yes. While it is not mandatory for naming local hosts in a local network, using DNS is required if your servers or clients are connected to the Internet. Although you technically could get away without DNS, you would need to know the IP addresses of all remote hosts to which you intend to connect.

14.2 Administer the WHOIS Database

The servers ns1.linsurance.com and ns2.linsurance.com rely on the list of authoritative root servers to perform external resolutions correctly, which is found in the WHOIS database (**ftp://ftp.rs.internic.net/domain/named.root**):

```
;       This file holds the information on root name servers needed to
;       initialize cache of Internet domain name servers
;       (e.g. reference this file in the "cache  .  <file>"
;       configuration file of BIND domain name servers).
;
;       This file is made available by InterNIC registration services
;       under anonymous FTP as
;           file                /domain/named.root
;           on server           FTP.RS.INTERNIC.NET
;       -OR- under Gopher at    RS.INTERNIC.NET
;           under menu          InterNIC Registration Services (NSI)
;               submenu         InterNIC Registration Archives
;           file                named.root
;
;       last update:    Aug 22, 1997
;       related version of root zone:   1997082200
.                               3600000  IN  NS    A.ROOT-SERVERS.NET.
A.ROOT-SERVERS.NET.             3600000      A     198.41.0.4
.                               3600000      NS    B.ROOT-SERVERS.NET.
B.ROOT-SERVERS.NET.             3600000      A     128.9.0.107
.                               3600000      NS    C.ROOT-SERVERS.NET.
C.ROOT-SERVERS.NET.             3600000      A     192.33.4.12
.                               3600000      NS    D.ROOT-SERVERS.NET.
D.ROOT-SERVERS.NET.             3600000      A     128.8.10.90
.                               3600000      NS    E.ROOT-SERVERS.NET.
E.ROOT-SERVERS.NET.             3600000      A     192.203.230.10
.                               3600000      NS    F.ROOT-SERVERS.NET.
F.ROOT-SERVERS.NET.             3600000      A     192.5.5.241
.                               3600000      NS    G.ROOT-SERVERS.NET.
G.ROOT-SERVERS.NET.             3600000      A     192.112.36.4
.                               3600000      NS    H.ROOT-SERVERS.NET.
H.ROOT-SERVERS.NET.             3600000      A     128.63.2.53
.                               3600000      NS    I.ROOT-SERVERS.NET.
I.ROOT-SERVERS.NET.             3600000      A     192.36.148.17
.                               3600000      NS    J.ROOT-SERVERS.NET.
J.ROOT-SERVERS.NET.             3600000      A     198.41.0.10
.                               3600000      NS    K.ROOT-SERVERS.NET.
K.ROOT-SERVERS.NET.             3600000      A     193.0.14.129
```

```
.                          3600000    NS    L.ROOT-SERVERS.NET.
L.ROOT-SERVERS.NET.        3600000    A     198.32.64.12
.                          3600000    NS    M.ROOT-SERVERS.NET.
M.ROOT-SERVERS.NET.        3600000    A     202.12.27.33
; End of File
```

To allow DNS resolution on the client side, this data should be stored in the *named.root* file, since it permits client systems that do not host a DNS server to perform their own lookups. If an external client wished to determine out the IP address of the host **www.admin.linsurance.com**, a request for the authoritative DNS server for the **linsurance.com** domain (**ns1.linsurance.com**) could be made to one of the root servers. The server ns1.linsurance.com would then either be able to resolve the address or pass the request to the server that is authoritative for the **admin.linsurance.com** subdomain. Many of the details of how DNS resolution is performed can be configured by the administrator and may depend on alignments with other naming services (such as the Network Information Service described in Module 20).

14.3 Configure DNS Servers

Solaris uses BIND to provide DNS services. When configured correctly, BIND is both reliable and scalable. The key configuration file for the modern version of BIND (including the version shipped with Solaris 9) is */etc/named.conf*, while

Ask the Expert

Question: I've heard that DNS is bad because all of the IP addresses on your local network can be looked up by writing a shell script calling *nslookup* repetitively. Is that true?

Answer: No. This is where firewalls and proxy servers come in. The only hosts whose IP addresses should be externally visible from your network are your DNS server and your Web server. Many sites run an internal DNS server that uses addresses in the 10.0.0.0 range that are nonroutable through the Internet to protect against external access. Using a proxy server allows local clients to sit behind a firewall and yet still gain access to the Web.

14

previous versions (BIND 4 and earlier) used the */etc/named.boot* file (not to be confused with *named.root*!). If you are still running BIND 4 on some of your systems, you should upgrade using the procedure outlined in this section.

The BIND configuration file (*/etc/named.conf*) controls many aspects of how DNS servers operate, including the creation of zones and setting configurable operations like logging. The following statement types are legal in */etc/named.conf*:

Statement Type	Description
acl	Specifies an access control list that lists the clients who may access the server.
include	Loads an external file that accommodates any kind of statement that is legal in */etc/named.conf*. This allows the different sections of */etc/named.conf*, which can grow very large, to be effectively partitioned.
logging	Specifies what log level is set for the server's operations. Can be useful for security purposes.
options	Specifies various administrator-configurable options for the DNS server.
server	Specifies various administrator-configurable options for other servers.
zone	Sets up DNS zones for the local domain.

The following sections, will review how each of these statements can be applied, including examples.

acl

An access control list (ACL) determines which hosts can access the server. For example, to allow only DNS requests from the network 206.43.58.0, the following acl statement should be inserted into */etc/named.conf*:

```
acl local_network {
204.43.58/24
};
```

Prefix notation is used to describe the netmask (that is, 24 specifies a Class C network with the mask 255.255.255.0). As an alternative to specifying which network address ranges may have access to the server, it's also possible for you to define an ACL that permits hosts and networks to be explicitly denied access. This is useful when users from a specific host and/or network have been detected trying to hack the DNS server by using denial-of-service (DoS) or some other method. For example, to deny access from the Web server host 204.43.58.16 to the internal DNS server, we would use the following entry:

```
acl local_network {
!204.43.58.16; 204.43.58/24
};
```

According to the lexical rules for parsing /etc/named.boot, any negation of individual hosts in a subnet must precede a rule that would otherwise permit access.

include

For sites with large DNS installations, it's sometimes necessary to configure a set of external files that typically correspond to the different sections of the /etc/named.conf file. Thus, some /etc/named.conf files might just consist of a series of include statements, naming files that corresponded to the individual sections of /etc/named.conf. For example, a large zone section could be placed into a separate file called zones.conf, and included with the following statement:

```
include "/var/named/zone.conf"
```

Other common include statements may be composed of the following:

```
include "/var/named/acl.conf"
include "/var/named/options.conf"
include "/var/named/server.conf"
```

options

The options section is concerned with the real-time operation of the BIND server by setting administrator configurable parameters. These include the directory in which BIND files are stored and the file in which the process ID (PID) of the BIND server process is stored. A set of typical options is shown here:

```
options {
directory "/usr/local/named";
pid-file "/usr/local/named/pid";
}
```

14

server

The server statement permits configuration for communication with remote DNS servers, largely concerned with data transfer details. For example, the local server can be set up to allow invalid data and whether or not compound queries can be answered within a single solicitation. A sample server statement is shown here for the remote server 208.56.43.21:

```
server 208.56.43.21
{
        bogus no;
        transfer-format many-answers;
}
```

14.4 Create Zone Files

For every subdomain or network for which name services are managed by a local server, a zone must be created in the /etc/named.conf file that defines its operational properties. These parameters include whether or not the server is a master or slave server for the domain, as well as all of the definitions for IP-to-name and name-to-IP mappings for all hosts on the network.

A zone must be created for each network or subdomain that your DNS server manages. Zones can be created either as master or slave, depending on which server is authoritative for a particular domain. Entries for zones must also be included to resolve both IP address and domain names correctly. For the domain **paulwatters.com**, the following zone entries would need to be created:

```
zone "paulwatters.com"
{
        type master;
        file "paulwatters.com.db";
}
zone "24.58.206.in-addr.arpa"
{
        type master;
        file "paulwatters.com.rev";
}
```

This defines two files */var/named/paulwatters.com.db* and */var/named/paulwatters.com.rev* that need to be modified to contain host data for matching names to IP addresses and vice versa. A typical */var/named/paulwatters.com.db* file would contain SOA entries as follows:

```
@       IN    SOA     paulwatters.com.    root.paulwatters.com.    (
        2002011103          ;serial number
              10800          ;refresh every three hours
          1800;retry every 30 mins
        1209600     ;Two week expiry
        604800)     ;Minimum one week expiry
        IN    NS     annarbor.paulwatters.com.
        IN    MX     10    firewall.paulwatters.com.
        firewall    IN    A     206.58.24.1    ;firewall
        newyork       IN    A    206.58.24.2     ;webserver
        richmond      IN    A    206.58.24.3     ;webserver
        boston    IN    A    206.58.24.4    ;kerberos
        secure    IN    CNAME    boston
```

Here, we can see that the nameserver *NS annarbor* is part of a network that also contains the hosts *firewall* (a firewall), *newyork* (a Web server), *richmond* (also a Web server), and *boston* (a Kerberos server). In addition, the host *boston* has the alias *secure*. The corresponding */var/named/paulwatters.com.rev* file would contain entries with the mappings reversed:

```
@   IN    SOA    24.58.206.in-addr.arpa.    root.paulwatters.com.    (
        2002011103     ;serial number
        10800     ;refresh every three hours
        1800;retry every 30 mins
        1209600     ;Two week expiry
        604800)     ;Minimum one week expiry
        IN    NS     annarbor.paulwatters.com.
1       IN    PTR     firewall.paulwatters.com.
2       IN    PTR     newyork.paulwatters.com.
3       IN    PTR     richmond.paulwatters.com.
4       IN    PTR     boston.paulwatters.com.
```

Here, the 1, 2, 3, and 4 listed in the left column correspond to IP address from the 206.58.24.0 network. The records typically contained in the zone files include the following:

- Address records (A)
- Pointer records (PTR)

14

- Mail exchanger records (MX)

- Canonical name records (CNAME)

Project 14-1: Adding a Host to DNS

This project shows you how to add a new host to a server that is authoritative for a specific domain (**paulwatters.com**). This is necessary every time you add a new host to the local network.

Step-By-Step

1. Choose an IP address that has not already been used:

```
206.58.24.5
```

2. Choose a hostname that has not already been used on the local network:

```
clash
```

3. Insert the appropriate entry into the */var/named/paulwatters.com.db* file:

```
clash    IN    A    206.58.24.5
```

4. Insert the appropriate entry into the */var/named/paulwatters.com.rev* file:

```
5    IN    PTR    clash.paulwatters.com.
```

Summary

Hosts can be added to DNS by inserting the appropriate records in */var/named/ paulwatters.com.db* and */var/named/paulwatters.com.rev*, where *paulwatters.com* is replaced by your local domain name.

14.5 Use DNS Clients

To set up a Solaris system to use DNS as the default naming service, the name service switch file (*/etc/nsswitch.conf*) must first be configured. The following line specifies that the name resolution service to use is DNS followed by a file based lookup (from *etc/hosts*) if the server based lookup fails:

```
/etc/nsswitch.conf hosts:        dns [NOTFOUND=return] files
```

Alternatively, if you use NIS/NIS+ for local network names, you may need to use the following:

```
/etc/nsswitch.conf hosts:        dns nisplus nis [NOTFOUND=return] files
```

To make use of DNS, you also need to ensure that the BIND package was installed during installation or installed directly from the source. The next step involves defining the local domain for the client, which should be entered into the file */etc/defaultdomain*. For example, for the host **www.paulwatters.com**, the following entry should be inserted into */etc/defaultdomain*:

```
paulwatters.com
```

The final step is to configure the resolver, through the */etc/resolv.conf* file, to define the master and slave DNS servers for the local domain. Using a slave as well as a master server ensures continuity of DNS service for remote and local site lookups even when one of the servers is not available due to technical problems. The */etc/resolv.conf* file would contain the following entries for the domain **linsurance.com**:

```
domain linsurance.com
domain admin.bigbank.com
domain sales.bigbank.com
nameserver 206.45.34.1
nameserver 206.45.34.2
```

Name servers are always listed in the order in which they should be contacted.

14.6 Administer nslookup

While many applications use standard library routines to resolve IP addresses and domain names, users can also perform these operations on the command line. The key command-line tool for performing DNS resolutions is nslookup, which can resolve both local and remote addresses. In addition, nslookup allows

14

local users to connect directly to a remote name server to perform host or IP address lookups on the remote network.

Let's examine how nslookup works by retrieving the IP address for the host **www.paulwatters.com**.

Once the client resolver is configured in this way, we can use a number of tools to test whether DNS is working and also to further examine how IP addresses are resolved. The most important tool for performing DNS resolutions is nslookup, which can be used in a simple command-line mode to look up fully qualified domain names from IP addresses and vice versa. However, nslookup also features an interactive mode that is useful for retrieving name server characteristics for a particular domain and for determining which DNS servers are authoritative for a specific host or network.

Let's look at a simple example—if we wanted to determine the IP address of the host **www.paulwatters.com**, using a client on the host **client.paulwatters.com**, we would use the following command:

```
$ nslookup www.paulwatters.com

Server:   ns.paulwatters.com
Address:  206.68.216.16

Name:     delta.paulwatters.com
Address:  206.68.216.20
Aliases:  www.paulwatters.com
```

Here, the client system contacts **ns.paulwatters.com** to obtain the IP address for the host with the canonical name **delta.paulwatters.com**, which has an alias of www. Passing the IP address of 206.68.216.20 on the command line would have resulted in the canonical (real) name being returned (**delta.paulwatters.com**) rather than the alias (**www.paulwatters.com**).

If you are contacting a remote server and you want to ensure that you obtain the most authoritative data available, you can specify the name of the remote name server to which you want to connect. For example, if we wanted to look up the IP address of the host **jaws.someschool.edu**, we could simply use the following command:

```
$ nslookup jaws.someschool.edu
Server:   ns.paulwatters.com
Address:  206.68.216.16
```

```
Name: www.someschool.edu
Address:  129.78.64.2
Aliases:  jaws.someschool.edu
```

To ensure that this data was authoritative, we could point the DNS client to the remote DNS server, as shown in the next example:

```
$ nslookup
Default Server:  ns.paulwatters.com
Address:  206.68.216.16
> server ns.someschool.edu
Default Server:  ns.someschool.edu
Address:  129.78.64.2
> jaws.someschool.edu
Server:  ns.someschool.edu
Address:  129.78.64.2
Name:    www.someschool.edu
Address:  129.78.64.24
Aliases:  jaws.someschool.edu
```

Here, we've used the *server* keyword to specify a different DNS server, and we've then entered the hostname to be resolved. Since we've now connected to the authoritative DNS server for the **someschool.edu** domain, we needn't pass the fully-qualified hostname (**jaws.someschool.com**) in our query; it would have been sufficient to pass *jaws* alone. This is possible only if **ns.someschool.edu** allows you to query with respect to an ACL.

If we wanted to obtain some administrative data related to the remote host, we could use the `nslookup` command to retrieve the Start of Authority (SOA) record, which contains entries for the remote administrator's e-mail address, among others:

```
$ nslookup
Default Server:  ns.paulwatters.com
Address:  206.68.216.16

> server ns.someschool.edu
Default Server:  ns.someschool.edu
Address:  129.78.64.2
> set q=soa
> jaws.someschool.edu
```

14

```
Server:  ns.someschool.edu
Address:  129.78.64.2

jaws.someschool.edu canonical name = www.someschool.edu
ns.someschool.edu
        origin = ns.someschool.edu
        mail addr = root.ns.someschool.edu
        serial = 318
        refresh = 1800 (30 mins)
        retry   = 3600 (1 hour)
        expire  = 18000 (5 hours)
        minimum ttl = 18000 (5 hours)
```

The SOA record for the host **jaws.someschool.edu** reveals the following information:

- The actual (canonical) name of the host **jaws.someschool.edu** is actually **www.someschool.edu**.

- The **ns.someschool.edu** server is authoritative for the host **www.someschool.edu**.

- The current record's serial number is 318, which must be incremented after each DNS entry is added, deleted, or modified.

- The refresh rate is half an hour.

- The retry rate is one hour.

- The time of expiry is five hours.

- The TTL is also five hours.

1-Minute Drill

- What command is used to perform name service lookups?

- `nslookup`

As we saw in the "Configure a DNS Server" section, each of these parameters can be set within the */etc/named.conf* file for each zone. Another tool that is useful for resolving IP addresses and hostnames is the `whois` command, which retrieves details of DNS registration from the InterNIC registry database, including the authoritative name servers for a specific domain name. For example, the record for **cassowary.net** shows the master and slave name servers for the domain:

```
$ whois cassowary.net

Whois Server Version 1.3

Domain names in the .com, .net, and .org domains can now be registered
with many different competing registrars. Go to http://www.internic.net
for detailed information.

    Domain Name: CASSOWARY.NET
    Registrar: NETWORK SOLUTIONS, INC.
    Whois Server: whois.networksolutions.com
    Referral URL: http://www.networksolutions.com
    Name Server: NS1.HOSTSAVE.COM
    Name Server: NS2.HOSTSAVE.COM
    Updated Date: 28-feb-2002


>>> Last update of whois database: Sun, 24 Mar 2002 17:12:10 EST <<<

The Registry database contains ONLY .COM, .NET, .ORG, .EDU domains and
Registrars.
```

Ask the Expert

Question: Is DNS setup during the Solaris installation program yet? I still have nightmares from performing manual configuration in previous versions...

Answer: Yes. And you can set up support for other naming services like NIS and LDAP (how's that for progress!).

14.7 Build a DNS Server

Most Solaris systems already run BIND, so why upgrade? A number of new features in the new version will be of particular interest to Solaris users:

- Improved DNS security, with support for digitally signed zones as well as DNS requests.

- Support for IP6, the new standard for IP networking.

- Multiple views of a network's namespace, depending on whether the client is behind or in front of a firewall.

- Support for symmetric multiprocessing. As many Solaris systems are multiprocessor, this greatly improves resolution performance.

To compile BIND, you need to download the source, uncompress the source archive, and use `tar` to extract its contents. Next, you need to run the `configure` command, which will produce output like the following:

```
# ./configure
creating cache ./config.cache
checking host system type... i386-sparc-solaris2.9
checking whether make sets ${MAKE}... yes
checking for ranlib... ranlib
checking for a BSD compatible install... ./install-sh -c
checking for ar... /usr/ccs/bin/ar
checking for etags... no
checking for emacs-etags... no
checking for perl5... no
checking for perl... /usr/local/bin/perl
checking whether byte ordering is bigendian... yes
checking for compatible OpenSSL library... using private library
checking for gcc... gcc
checking whether the C compiler (gcc  ) works... yes
checking whether the C compiler (gcc  ) is a cross-compiler... no
checking whether we are using GNU C... yes
checking whether gcc accepts -g... yes
```

Next, you build the application binaries using the `make` command:

```
# make
making all in /tmp/bind-9.0.0/make
make[1]: Entering directory `/tmp/bind-9.0.0/make'
make[1]: Leaving directory `/tmp/bind-9.0.0/make'
making all in /tmp/bind-9.0.0/lib
make[1]: Entering directory `/tmp/bind-9.0.0/lib'
making all in /tmp/bind-9.0.0/lib/isc
make[2]: Entering directory `/tmp/bind-9.0.0/lib/isc'
making all in /tmp/bind-9.0.0/lib/isc/include
make[3]: Entering directory `/tmp/bind-9.0.0/lib/isc/include'
making all in /tmp/bind-9.0.0/lib/isc/include/isc
make[4]: Entering directory `/tmp/bind-9.0.0/lib/isc/include/isc'
make[4]: Leaving directory `/tmp/bind-9.0.0/lib/isc/include/isc'
make[3]: Leaving directory `/tmp/bind-9.0.0/lib/isc/include'
making all in /tmp/bind-9.0.0/lib/isc/unix
```

Finally, you test the binaries by building the testing programs:

```
# make test
make[1]: Entering directory `/tmp/bind-9.0.0/bin/tests/db'
S:./t_db:Friday 03 November 12:23:27 2000
T:dns_db_load:1:A
A:A call to dns_db_load(db, filename) loads the
contents of the database in file name into db.
I:testing using file dns_db_load_1.data and name a.
R:PASS
T:dns_db_iscache:2:A
A:When the database db has cache semantics, a call
to dns_db_iscache(db) returns  ISC_TRUE.
I:testing using file dns_db_iscache_1.data
R:PASS
T:dns_db_iscache:3:A
A:When the database db has zone semantics, a call
 to dns_db_iscache(db) returns ISC_FALSE.
I:testing using file dns_db_iscache_2.data
R:PASS
T:dns_db_iszone:4:A
A:When the database db has zone semantics, a call
 to dns_db_iszone(db) returns I SC_TRUE.
I:testing using file dns_db_iszone_1.data
R:PASS
```

If all tests pass, you may perform a "make install" to install the new binaries.

14

☑ *Mastery Check*

1. What file is used to configure a DNS server?

    A. */etc/named.conf*

    B. */etc/name.conf*

    C. */etc/named/named.conf*

    D. */etc/name/name.conf*

2. Which ACL entry would prevent the client 204.43.58.16 from connecting to the local DNS server?

    A. *204.43.58.16

    B. !204.43.58.16

    C. >204.43.58.16

    D. ~204.43.58.16

3. What file is used to configure the resolver?

    A. */usr/local/resolv.conf*

    B. */etc/resolver/resolver.conf*

    C. */etc/resolver.conf*

    D. */etc/resolv.conf*

4. What file is used to configure the name service switch?

    A. */etc/nameservice.conf*

    B. */etc/switch.conf*

    C. */etc/nsswitch.conf*

    D. */etc/bind.conf*

5. What does the file *named.root* contain?

    A. Root name server IP addresses

    B. Root name server routes

☑ *Mastery Check*

    C. Domain name authority for the local domain

    D. Cache settings for the local root DNS cache

6. In *named.conf*, what is the purpose of the keyword *acl*?

    A. Specifies an access control list that lists the clients who may access the server

    B. Loads an external file that accommodates any kind of statement that is legal

    C. Specifies what log level is set for the server's operations

    D. Specifies various administrator-configurable options for the DNS server

7. In *named.conf*, what is the purpose of the keyword *include*?

    A. Specifies an access control list that lists the clients who may access the server

    B. Loads an external file that accommodates any kind of statement that is legal

    C. Specifies what log level is set for the server's operations

    D. Specifies various administrator-configurable options for the DNS server

8. In *named.conf*, what is the purpose of the keyword *logging*?

    A. Specifies an access control list that lists the clients who may access the server

    B. Loads an external file that accommodates any kind of statement that is legal

    C. Specifies what log level is set for the server's operations

    D. Specifies various administrator-configurable options for the DNS server

9. In *named.conf*, what is the purpose of the keyword *options*?

    A. Specifies an access control list that lists the clients who may access the server

    B. Loads an external file that accommodates any kind of statement that is legal

14

☑ Mastery Check

C. Specifies what log level is set for the server's operations

D. Specifies various administrator-configurable options for the DNS server

10. In *named.conf*, what is the purpose of the keyword *server*?

A. Specifies what log level is set for the server's operations

B. Specifies various administrator-configurable options for the DNS server

C. Specifies various administrator-configurable options for other servers

D. Sets up DNS zones for the local domain

11. In *named.conf*, what is the purpose of the keyword *zone*?

A. Specifies what log level is set for the server's operations

B. Specifies various administrator-configurable options for the DNS server

C. Specifies various administrator-configurable options for other servers

D. Sets up DNS zones for the local domain

12. What command retrieves the authoritative name servers for a specific domain name and the details of DNS registration?

A. whois

B. bind

C. query

D. nsquery

13. In a SOA for a rev file, what does the *A* parameter denote?

A. Address records

B. Pointer records

C. Mail exchanger records

D. Canonical name records

☑ Mastery Check

14. In a SOA for a rev file, what does the *PTR* parameter denote?

   A. Address records

   B. Pointer records

   C. Mail exchanger records

   D. Canonical name records

14. In a SOA for a rev file, what does the *MX* parameter denote?

   A. Address records

   B. Pointer records

   C. Mail exchanger records

   D. Canonical name records

15. In a SOA for a rev file, what does the *CNAME* parameter denote?

   A. Address records

   B. Pointer records

   C. Mail exchanger records

   D. Canonical name records

Module 15

Network Services

Critical Skills

Sun's often-quoted motto is "The Network Is The Computer." For Solaris administrators, this means that understanding the fundamentals of networking is one of the most important foundation topics required to support higher-level services like remote access (see Module 16). In this module, we review the general Open System Interconnect (OSI) networking model, and the more specific Transmission Control Protocol (TCP), User Datagram Protocol (UDP), and Internet Protocol (IP), which form the basis of "TCP/IP networking." We'll then examine how TCP/IP is implemented on Solaris, including the configuration of network interfaces, daemons, addresses, ports, and sockets. Finally, we'll configure the Internet daemon (inetd) to support a number of separate network services that are centrally managed.

15.1 Design Networks

A network is a combination of hardware and software that enables computers to communicate with each other. At the hardware level, building a network involves installing a network interface into each system ("host") to be networked, and implementing a specific network topology by using cables, such as Ethernet, or wireless. At the software level, representations of network devices must be created, and protocols must be implemented for exchanging data between hosts. Data is exchanged by dividing it into packets that have a specific structure, enabling large data elements to be exchanged between hosts by using a small amount of wrapping. This wrapping, based on various protocols, contains information about the order in which packets should be assembled when transmitted from one host to another.

By supporting many different types of hardware devices and connection technologies, and by implementing standards-based networking software, Solaris provides a flexible platform for supporting high-level network services and applications.

15.2 Design Networking Topologies

The two most common forms of network topology are the star network and the ring network. The ring topology, as shown in Figure 15-1, is a peer-to-peer topology, where neighboring hosts are connected and data is exchanged between distant hosts by passing data from the source host to the target host through all intermediate hosts. Ring networks are most suitable for networks where long distances separate individual hosts.

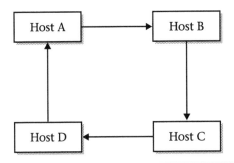

Figure 15-1 Ring network topology

Caution

If only one of the links between hosts is broken, data transmission between all hosts can be interrupted.

In contrast, a star network has a centralized topology, where all hosts connect to a central point and exchange data at that point, as shown in Figure 15-2. This has the advantage of minimizing the number of hops that data must travel from a source to a target host, compared to a ring network. In addition, if one link is broken, only data originating from or sent to the host on that link will be disrupted.

Caution

If the point at which hosts are connected breaks down, all data transmission will cease.

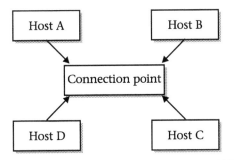

Figure 15-2 Star network topology

In practice, most modern high-speed networks are based on star topologies. When connecting local area networks together to form internets, a star topology has the advantage of being able to interconnect networks by their central connection points. This means that data sent from a host on one network must travel to its central point, which then sends the data to the connection point on a remote network, which then passes the data to the remote target host. Thus, only three hops are required to exchange data between hosts on two networks when using a star topology. This data flow is shown in Figure 15-3.

Let's look at a specific example of how an internet can be laid out before examining how OSI and the Solaris implementation of TCP/IP make this possible. Imagine that a Web server runs on the host 203.54.68.21 while a Web client (such as Netscape Navigator) runs on the host 203.54.67.122. Since these two hosts are located on two different local area (Class C) networks, they must be interconnected by a router. In the star topology, a connection point must allow a link to each host on the local network—in this example, a hub or switch is used to connect each host, as well as forwarding all data bound for nonlocal addresses to the router. Thus, when a high-level HTTP request is sent from the client 203.54.67.122 to the server 203.54.68.21, a packet is sent to the hub, which detects that the destination is nonlocal and forwards the packet to the router. The router then forwards the packet to the router for the remote network, which detects that the destination is local and passes it to the hub, which in turn passes it to the server. Since HTTP is a request/response protocol, the backwards path is traced when a response to the request is generated by the server. The configuration for this example is shown in Figure 15-4.

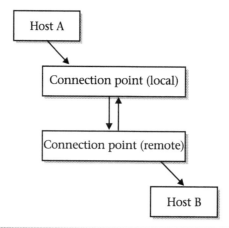

Figure 15-3 Interconnecting networks

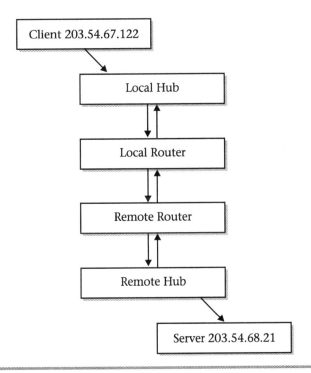

1-Minute Drill

● What is the main advantage of a star topology?
● When is a ring network most suitable?

If this example seems complex, you'll be pleased to know that the implementation of many of these services is hidden from users, and most often from developers. This makes implementing networking applications very simple when using high-level protocols like HTTP. For example, consider the following Java code, which uses HTTP to make a connection to a remote server running an application called StockServer. After passing the name of a stock in the URL, the current price should be returned by the server. The code fragment

---

● A star topology has the advantage of being able to interconnect networks by their central connection points.
● A ring network is most suitable where long distances separate individual hosts.

shows the definition for the URL, a declaration for an input stream, reading a line from the stream and assigning the result to a variable (stockPrice), and closing the stream. If this code was contained in an applet, for example, the stockPrice for SUNW could then be displayed.

```
String stockURL="http://data.cassowary.net/servlet/StockServer?
  code=SUNW";
URL u = new URL(stockURL);
BufferedReader in = new BufferedReader(new InputStreamReader
  (u.openStream()));
String stockPrice=in.readLine();
in.close();
```

15.3 Utilize OSI Networking

Building networks is complex, given the wide array of hardware and software that can be used to implement them. The OSI networking model, as shown in Figure 15-5, provides a framework for defining the scope of different layers of networking technology, which can be used to understand how different protocols and suites (such as TCP/IP) operate. Each layer of the model, starting from the bottom, supports the functionality required by the top levels. Moving from bottom to top, operations become more and more abstracted from their physical implementation. It is this abstraction that allows HTTP and other high-level protocols to operate without being concerned about low-level implementations. It also allows for different instantiations of lower levels, without higher-level code needing to be rewritten.

Starting from the bottom, the first level is the physical layer, which defines how data is exchanged at its very basic level (bits and bytes), as well as cabling requirements. The second level is the data link layer, which defines the apparatus for transferring data, including error checking and synchronization. The third

Ask the Expert

Question: Should I use a ring or star topology?

Answer: Most modern network use star topologies because of their superior fault tolerance.

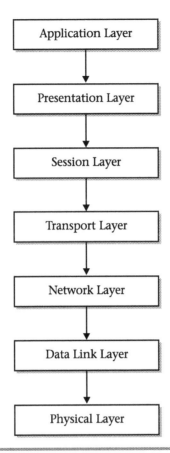

Figure 15-5 The Open System Interconnect (OSI) networking model

level is the network layer, which specifies operational issues such as how networks can exchange data, as shown in Figures 15-3 and 15-4. The fourth level, the transport layer, specifies how individual computers are to interpret data received from the network. The fifth level is the session layer, which determines how data from different sources can be separated and how associations between hosts can be maintained. The sixth level is the presentation layer, which specifies how different types of data are formatted and how they should be exposed. The seventh level is the application layer, which describes how high-level applications can communicate with each other in a standard way.

15

15.4 Implement TCP/IP Services

The TCP/IP suite of protocols forms the basis of all Internet communications, and was originally devised as part of the Defense Advanced Research Projects Agency (DARPA) for the ARPANET. While TCP/IP is the default networking protocol supported by Solaris, other operating systems also support TCP/IP, even if it is not their primary protocol. For example, Microsoft Windows networks support NetBEUI and IPX/SPX, while MacOS supports AppleTalk.

Note

Linux administrators should already be familiar with TCP/IP.

TCP/IP presents a simpler interface than OSI, since only the Application, Transport, Network and Link layers need to be addressed. This can be seen in the following packet intercept performed by the snoop application, which reads raw packet data from a network interface operating in promiscuous mode. The following example shows ETHER (Link), IP (Network), TCP (Transport) and TELNET (Application) sections, respectively:

```
# snoop -v tcp port 23
Using device /dev/hme0 (promiscuous mode)
ETHER:  ----- Ether Header -----
ETHER:
ETHER:  Packet 1 arrived at 14:13:22.14
ETHER:  Packet size = 60 bytes
ETHER:  Destination = 1:58:4:16:8a:34,
ETHER:  Source      = 2:60:5:12:6b:35, Sun
ETHER:  Ethertype = 0800 (IP)
ETHER:
IP:    ----- IP Header -----
IP:
IP:    Version = 4
IP:    Header length = 20 bytes
IP:    Type of service = 0x00
IP:          xxx. .... = 0 (precedence)
IP:          ...0 .... = normal delay
IP:          .... 0... = normal throughput
IP:          .... .0.. = normal reliability
IP:    Total length = 40 bytes
IP:    Identification = 46864
IP:    Flags = 0x4
IP:          .1.. .... = do not fragment
```

```
IP:        ..0. .... = last fragment
IP:    Fragment offset = 0 bytes
IP:    Time to live = 255 seconds/hops
IP:    Protocol = 6 (TCP)
IP:    Header checksum = 11a9
IP:    Source address = 64.23.168.76, moppet.paulwatters.com
IP:    Destination address = 64.23.168.48, miki.paulwatters.com
IP:    No options
IP:
TCP:   ----- TCP Header -----
TCP:
TCP:   Source port = 62421
TCP:   Destination port = 23 (TELNET)
TCP:   Sequence number = 796159562
TCP:   Acknowledgement number = 105859685
TCP:   Data offset = 20 bytes
TCP:   Flags = 0x10
TCP:        ..0. .... = No urgent pointer
TCP:        ...1 .... = Acknowledgement
TCP:        .... 0... = No push
TCP:        .... .0.. = No reset
TCP:        .... ..0. = No Syn
TCP:        .... ...0 = No Fin
TCP:   Window = 8760
TCP:   Checksum = 0x8f8f
TCP:   Urgent pointer = 0
TCP:   No options
TCP:
TELNET: ----- TELNET:   -----
TELNET:
TELNET: "a"
TELNET:
```

Ask the Expert

Question: Hey! Can you really spy on other people's packets using snoop?

Answer: Yes, but consider the legal consequences if you do. After all, your boss might not be too happy if you present him or her with a list of all of his or her passwords. A better approach would be to ensure that—for remote access, for example—secure shell (SSH) is used in preference to telnet.

15

TCP/IP is layered, just like the OSI reference model. Thus, when a client application needs to communicate with a server, a process is initiated of passing data down each level on the client side from the application layer to the physical layer, and up each level on the server side from the physical layer to the application layer. Data is passed between layers in service data units. However, it's important to note that each client layer logically only ever communicates with the corresponding server layer, as demonstrated by the Java code presented earlier: the application layer is not concerned with logically communicating with the physical layer, for example.

Note

Abstraction is the core benefit of TCP/IP in development and communication terms, since each level is logically isolated, while methods for supporting service data are also well defined.

The ETHER header defines many of the characteristics of the packet. In the snoop example, the packets' arrival time and size (in bytes), and destination and source addresses (Ethernet format), are all noted. In addition, the network type is also supplied. This leads into the IP header, which shows the IP version (IPv4), the length of the header (in bytes), destination and source addresses (IP format), and a checksum to ensure data integrity. Also, the protocol for transport is defined as TCP. The TCP header shows the port on which the data is being sent and on which it should be received, in addition to the application type (TELNET). The sequence and acknowledgement numbers determine how packets are ordered at the receiving end, since TCP is connection-oriented and guarantees data delivery—unlike other transport protocols like UDP, which are connectionless and do not guarantee the delivery of data. Finally, the data being transported is displayed—"a".

Note

In addition to TELNET, other application protocols include the Simple Mail Transfer Protocol (SMTP), File Transfer Protocol (FTP), and the Network File System (NFS).

We'll now review each of these layers as they are implemented in the Solaris TCP/IP stack.

Ethernet Layer

Ethernet is the most commonly used link technology supported by Solaris and comes in five different speeds, including the following:

10BASE-2	2 Mbps
10BASE-5	5 Mbps
10BASE-T	10 Mbps
100BASE-T	100 Mbps
1000BASE-FX	1 Gbps

Solaris systems are typically supplied with a single Ethernet card, supporting 10/100 Mbps, however, server systems (such as the 420R) are supplied with quad Ethernet cards, supporting four interfaces operating at 10/100 Mbps. Although Ethernet (specified by the IEEE 802.3 standard) is the most common link type, other supported link types on Solaris include the Fiber Distributed Data Interface (FDDI) and Asynchronous Transfer Mode (ATM). FDDI networks use a ring topology based on a transmitting and receiving ring, using high-quality fiber-optic cable to support high-speed redundant connections. However, FDDI is expensive compared to Ethernet, and gigabit FDDI is not available. ATM is designed for high quality of service applications, like video and audio streaming, which require a constant amount of bandwidth to operate. Data is transmitted in fixed-size cells of 53 bytes, and a connection is maintained as long as required between client and server.

Tip

Although ATM does not approach the speeds of Gigabit Ethernet, it's quality of service provisions benefit certain types of data transmission.

Note that the address used in the ETHER is the hardware address, otherwise known as the Media Access Control (MAC) address. This address is used to distinguish hosts at the link level, and is mapped to an IP address at the network level by using the Address Resolution Protocol (ARP). You can check the table of IP address to MAC address mappings by using the `arp` command:

```
$ arp -a
Net to Media Table
Device IP Address            Mask            Flags Phys Addr
------ --------------------- --------------- ----- ---------------
hme0   www.cassowary.net     255.255.255.255       00:19:cd:e3:05:a3
hme0   mail.cassowary.net    255.255.255.255       08:11:92:a4:12:ee
hme0   ftp.cassowary.net     255.255.255.255 SP    08:12:4e:4d:55:a2
hme0   BASE-ADDRESS.MCAST.NET 240.0.0.0      SM    01:01:4e:00:00:00
```

15

Here, the network device is shown with the fully qualified hostname (or IP address), the netmask, any flags, and the MAC address. The flags indicate the status of each interface, including "SP" for the localhost, where an entry will be published on request, and "SM" for the localhost, supporting multicast. Alternatively, a specific host can be queried by passing its name on the command line:

```
$ arp mail
mail (204.67.34.12) at 08:11:92:a4:12:ee
```

Conversely, the Reverse Address Resolution Protocol (RARP) is used to map MAC addresses to IP addresses. RARP is typically used to supply IP addresses from boot servers to diskless clients.

Note

A database of Ethernet addresses is maintained in the */etc/ethers* table to support this activity.

IP

The basic element of the Internet Protocol is the IP address, which is a 32-bit number (4 bytes) that uniquely identifies network interfaces on the Internet. For "single-homed" hosts, which have only one network interface, the IP address identifies the host. However, for "multihomed" hosts, which have multiple network interfaces, the IP address does not uniquely identify the host. Even the domain name assigned to a multihost can be different, depending on which network the interface is connected to.

The IP address is usually specified in dot decimal notation, where each of the bytes is displayed as an integer separated by a "dot." An example IP address is 192.205.76.123, which is based on a Class C network. There are five "classes" of network defined by IP (A, B, C, D, and E), although only three of these (A, B, and C) are actually used for the identification of hosts. Network classes can be identified by a discrete range of values; thus, if an address lies within a specific range, it can be identified as belonging to a network of a specific class. The following ranges are defined by IP:

Class A: 0.0.0.0	127.255.255.255
Class B: 128.0.0.0	191.255.255.255
Class C: 192.0.0.0	223.255.255.255
Class D: 224.0.0.0	239.255.255.255
Class E: 240.0.0.0	247.255.255.255

The different classes allow for ever-decreasing numbers of hosts in each network, starting from Class A, where networks can support millions of hosts, to Class C networks, which can only support up to 254 hosts. Some address ranges have special purposes. The following network address ranges are reserved for private use, and are commonly used to define IP address for internal networks:

10.0.0.0	10.255.255.255
172.16.0.0	172.31.255.255
192.168.0.0	192.168.255.255

Private addresses are not resolvable from the Internet. In addition, the 127.0.0.0 addresses are used to refer to the localhost, with the most commonly used value being 127.0.0.1.

Subnets allow large networks to be divided up into smaller logical networks, by using a subnet mask. For Class A networks, the mask is 255.0.0.0; for Class B networks, the mask is 255.255.0.0; and for Class C networks, the mask is 255.255.255.0.

Note

Solaris 9 now provides complete support for IPv6 and IPSec. These innovations are designed to increase the capacity of the Internet, and secure packets transmitted by using transport protocols. Discussion of their implementation is beyond the scope of this book.

TCP

TCP is a connection-oriented protocol that guarantees delivery of packets, where data has been segmented into smaller units. The benefit of transmitting small units in a guaranteed delivery scheme is that, if checksum errors are detected or some data is not received, the amount of data that needs to be transmitted is very small. In addition, if packet delivery "times out," packets can then be retransmitted.

15

By using sequence numbers, TCP always manages to reassemble packets in their correct order. Port numbers for TCP (and UDP) services are defined in the */etc/services* database. A sample database is shown below:

```
tcpmux          1/tcp
echo            7/tcp
echo            7/udp
discard         9/tcp           sink null
discard         9/udp           sink null
systat          11/tcp          users
daytime         13/tcp
daytime         13/udp
netstat         15/tcp
chargen         19/tcp          ttytst source
chargen         19/udp          ttytst source
ftp-data        20/tcp
ftp             21/tcp
telnet          23/tcp
smtp            25/tcp          mail
time            37/tcp          timserver
time            37/udp          timserver
name            42/udp          nameserver
whois           43/tcp          nicname
domain          53/udp
domain          53/tcp
bootps          67/udp
bootpc          68/udp
hostnames       101/tcp         hostname
pop2            109/tcp         pop-2
pop3            110/tcp
sunrpc          111/udp         rpcbind
sunrpc          111/tcp         rpcbind
imap            143/tcp         imap2
ldap            389/tcp
ldap            389/udp
ldaps           636/tcp
ldaps           636/udp
tftp            69/udp
rje             77/tcp
finger          79/tcp
link            87/tcp          ttylink
supdup          95/tcp
```

Reading from left to right are the service name, port number transport type, and service aliases. For example, the sunrpc service is also known as rpcbind, and is essential for supporting remote procedure call (RPC) applications like NFS. Other services defined above include the echo service, which simply sends back the segment transmitted to it; daytime, which returns the current local time at the server; ftp, which supports the File Transfer Protocol (FTP) service; and smtp, which supports the Simple Mail Transfer Protocol (SMTP). If services are not to be supported on the localhost, their entries should be commented in the service database. For example, to disable the service definition for the finger service, which allows remote users to check local user details, the finger entry would be modified as follows:

```
#finger          79/tcp
```

Port numbers 1–1024 are standard, as defined by Request For Comment (RFC) memos (**http://www.rfc-editor.org/rfc.html**).

Note

Nonstandard services should always be run on ports above 1024.

Application Protocols

Services are implemented by daemons that listen for connections and generate responses based on specific requests. Many of the TCP service definitions match up with an application supported by a daemon (server) process. There are two types of daemons supported by Solaris: standalone daemons and inetd daemons. Standalone daemons internally manage their own activities, while inetd allows daemons to be run through a single central server. This allows for centralization of administration and reduced need for processes running on a system, because inetd can listen for connections and invoke daemon processes as required. Definitions for services are contained in the */etc/inetd.conf* file. A sample */etc/inetd.conf* file is shown here:

```
ftp      stream  tcp   nowait  root   /usr/sbin/in.ftpd      in.ftpd -l
telnet   stream  tcp   nowait  root   /usr/sbin/in.telnetd   in.telnetd
name     dgram   udp   wait    root   /usr/sbin/in.tnamed    in.tnamed
shell    stream  tcp   nowait  root   /usr/sbin/in.rshd      in.rshd
login    stream  tcp   nowait  root   /usr/sbin/in.rlogind   in.rlogind
exec     stream  tcp   nowait  root   /usr/sbin/in.rexecd    in.rexecd
```

15

```
comsat   dgram   udp    wait    root    /usr/sbin/in.comsat    in.comsat
talk     dgram   udp    wait    root    /usr/sbin/in.talkd     in.talkd
uucp     stream  tcp    nowait  root    /usr/sbin/in.uucpd     in.uucpd
tftp     dgram   udp    wait    root    /usr/sbin/in.tftpd     in.tftpd -s
tftpboot
finger   stream  tcp    nowait  nobody  /usr/sbin/in.fingerd   in.fingerd
systat   stream  tcp    nowait  root    /usr/bin/ps            ps -ef
netstat  stream  tcp    nowait  root    /usr/bin/netstat       netstat -f inet
time     stream  tcp    nowait  root    internal
time     dgram   udp    wait    root    internal
echo     stream  tcp    nowait  root    internal
echo     dgram   udp    wait    root    internal
discard  stream  tcp    nowait  root    internal
discard  dgram   udp    wait    root    internal
daytime  stream  tcp    nowait  root    internal
daytime  dgram   udp    wait    root    internal
chargen  stream  tcp    nowait  root    internal
chargen  dgram   udp    wait    root    internal
```

Reading from left to right are the service name, socket type, transport protocol, flags, executing user, and daemon program to execute upon request. Socket types include streams or datagrams, transports include TCP and UDP, and flags include wait (wait after response) and nowait (exit after response).

A sample inetd application is the talk service. By examining its definition in */etc/inetd.conf*, we can see that it uses datagram sockets, runs on UDP, waits until timeout, is run by root, is implemented by the command /usr/sbin/in.talkd, and has the name in.talkd. The talk service supports instant communications between users on the local system, or between any two systems on the Internet. To issue a talk request to a remote user, a local user would issue the talk command followed by the user's username and fully qualified domain name. For example, to talk to the user shusaku at the host *users.cassowary.net*, the following command would be used:

```
$ talk shusaku@users.cassowary.net
```

If the host *users.cassowary.net* is running inetd, and inetd supports in.talkd, the following talk request would appear on the user shusaku's login shell:

```
Message from Talk_Daemon@db.cassowary.net at 10:50 ...
talk: connection requested by yasuanri@db.cassowary.net.
talk: respond with:   talk yasunari@db.cassowary.net
```

If the user shusaku wished to "talk" with yasunari, the following command would be used by shusaku:

```
$ talk yasunari@db.cassowary.net
```

If a service is to be disabled for security purposes, its entry can simply be commented out—just like for the services database. For example, to disable the finger service, the finger entry would be commented as follows:

```
#finger  stream  tcp     nowait  nobody  /usr/sbin/in.fingerd    in.fingerd
```

Once changes have been made in *inetd.conf*, a SIGHUP signal should be sent to the inetd process, causing it to reread the *inetd.conf* file. To restart inetd with a PID of 186, the following command would be used:

```
# kill -1 186
```

Many of the services supported by inetd support remote access, which is covered in Module 16.

15.5 Configure Network Interfaces

Because all network operations require access to a network interface, it's important to understand how to manage the interface and troubleshoot it when necessary. In the following sections, we examine how to configure a network interface, manually stop and start interfaces, and set key transmission parameters. In addition, we investigate the use of the `netstat` command to troubleshoot network configurations with respect to the IP, TCP, UDP, and ICMP protocols.

Interface Configuration

The current configuration for a network interface can always be displayed by using the `ifconfig` command. For example, to display the parameters for all of the interfaces installed on a local system, the following command could be used:

```
# ifconfig -a
lo0: flags=849<UP,LOOPBACK,RUNNING,MULTICAST> mtu 8232
        inet 127.0.0.1 netmask ff000000
hme0: flags=863<UP,BROADCAST,NOTRAILERS,RUNNING,MULTICAST> mtu 1500
        inet 192.68.24.16 netmask ffffff00 broadcast 192.68.24.255
```

This example shows two interfaces: the loopback interface, which handles internal connections, and the hme0 interface, which handles all external connections. The hme0 interface has the IP address 192.68.24.16, clearly belonging to the Class C network 192.68.24.0. Thus, a Class C netmask is specified in hex

15

(ffffff00), and the broadcast address is given as the highest numbered slot in the 192.68.24.0 network (that is, 192.68.24.255). In addition, the interface is noted as UP as opposed to DOWN. To display information for a specific interface, the following command could be used:

```
# ifconfig hme0
hme0: flags=863<UP,BROADCAST,NOTRAILERS,RUNNING,MULTICAST> mtu 1500
        inet 192.17.128.16 netmask ffffff00 broadcast 192.17.128.255
        ether 8:0:18:6:e1:b2
```

In this example, the /etc/ethers database contains an entry for 192.17.128.16, so a MAC address for the interface is also displayed. This may be a little confusing, since the interface address of the host itself need not (but could) be entered in the /etc/ethers database. The MAC address for all interfaces on SPARC boxes are the same—based on the setting in the PROM chip or if specified otherwise on the ifconfig command line. In addition to displaying the configuration and status of a network interface, the ifconfig command can be used to bring an interface up, or take it down. While this operation is typically performed manually at boot time, there are occasions where it is necessary to perform this operation manually. For example, if an attack is detected through a remote access connection, the interface can be disabled rapidly, after which patches can be applied or some other remedial action performed before the interface is bought back up. For example, to bring the hme0 interface down the following command is used:

```
# ifconfig hme0 down
```

To verify the status of the interface, the ifconfig command can be used once again:

```
# ifconfig hme0
hme0: flags=863<DOWN,BROADCAST,NOTRAILERS,RUNNING,MULTICAST> mtu 1500
        inet 192.68.24.16 netmask ffffff00 broadcast 192.68.24.255
```

The DOWN flag is now noted in the status, and no incoming or outgoing connections will be accepted. Bringing an interface down will impact on all services that use that interface. Some daemons will handle the disruption gracefully, while others may terminate after a connection timeout. To bring the interface back up again, the following command is used:

```
# ifconfig hme0 up
```

Again, the UP status of the network interface can be verified by using the `ifconfig` command:

```
# ifconfig hme0
hme0: flags=863<UP,BROADCAST,NOTRAILERS,RUNNING,MULTICAST> mtu 1500
        inet 192.68.24.16 netmask ffffff00 broadcast 192.68.24.255
```

Project 15-1: Bringing an Interface Up and Down Manually

This project shows you how to bring down a network interface and bring it up again. This is useful in a security context when an intruder is detected connecting on a specific interface, and you want to block their access quickly.

Step-by-Step

1. Check the network interface status:

```
# ifconfig hme0
hme0: flags=863<UP,BROADCAST,NOTRAILERS,RUNNING,MULTICAST> mtu 1500
        inet 192.68.24.16 netmask ffffff00 broadcast 192.68.24.255
```

2. Bring the interface down:

```
# ifconfig hme0 down
```

3. Check the network interface status again:

```
# ifconfig hme0
hme0: flags=863<DOWN,BROADCAST,NOTRAILERS,RUNNING,MULTICAST> mtu 1500
        inet 192.68.24.16 netmask ffffff00 broadcast 192.68.24.255
```

4. Bring the interface up:

```
# ifconfig hme0 up
```

5. Check the network interface status again:

```
# ifconfig hme0
hme0: flags=863<UP,BROADCAST,NOTRAILERS,RUNNING,MULTICAST> mtu 1500
        inet 192.68.24.16 netmask ffffff00 broadcast 192.68.24.255
```

Summary

The `ifconfig` command can be used to bring network interfaces up and down manually, as required.

15

If you want to modify the operational settings of the TCP device /dev/tcp, the ndd command can be used. A wide range of parameters can be set, including IP forwarding, various connection intervals and timeouts, and buffer sizes. To view the current values, the following command can be used:

```
# ndd /dev/tcp \?
```

Parameters can also be set to new values by using the −set option. For example, to disable IPv4 packet forwarding, the following command would be used:

```
# ndd -set /dev/ip ip_forwarding 0
```

If you make changes that need to be made permanent, the /etc/rc2.d/S69inet file should be modified to include the new ndd line.

15.6 Troubleshoot Networks

One of the most difficult issues in network troubleshooting is determining exactly where the problem lies. For example, a user may complain that they've lost Internet access, but there may potentially be 20 or 30 hosts lying between the client and server systems: how is it possible to determine where the fault lies? The first step is to use the ping command to see if a host is reachable. This command attempts to make a connection to a remote host by sending off an ICMP echo request and waiting 20 seconds for a response. If no response is received, an error message is reported. However, if the host is reachable, the following message will be displayed:

```
$ ping cyclops.cassowary.net
cyclops.cassowary.net is alive
```

It is also possible to examine relative response latencies by pinging the remote host every second and seeing if there is a lot of variability:

```
$ ping -s cyclops.cassowary.net
PING cyclops.cassowary.net: 56 data bytes
64 bytes from cyclops.cassowary.net (192.128.205.2):
icmp_seq=0. time=1. ms
64 bytes from cyclops.cassowary.net (192.128.205.2):
icmp_seq=1. time=0. ms
```

```
64 bytes from cyclops.cassowary.net (192.128.205.2):
icmp_seq=2. time=10. ms
...
---- cyclops.cassowary.net PING Statistics----
3 packets transmitted, 3 packets received, 0% packet loss
round-trip (ms) min/avg/max = 0/2/10
```

Here, we can see that there is a lot of variability in response times, with some taking up to ten times longer than others. This may indicate a high level of traffic that is causing collisions. One solution would be to upgrade the speed of the local cabling and network interfaces used. Alternatively, subnets could be created to reduce the amount of data being transmitted around the local network.

15.7 Use traceroute

If the connection is believed to be broken, then the `traceroute` command can be used to isolate which intermediate host is failing. The following `traceroute` command shows a successful connection to the Sun Web server:

```
$ traceroute www.sun.com
Tracing route to wwwseast.usec.sun.com [192.9.49.30]
over a maximum of 30 hops:
 1    184 ms    142 ms    138 ms   202.10.4.131
 2    147 ms    144 ms    138 ms   202.10.4.129
 3    150 ms    142 ms    144 ms   202.10.1.73
 4    150 ms    144 ms    141 ms   atm11-0-0-11 [202.139.32.17]
 5    148 ms    143 ms    139 ms   202.139.1.197
 6    490 ms    489 ms    474 ms   hssi9-0-0.sf1 [192.65.89.246]
 7    526 ms    480 ms    485 ms   g-sfd-br-02 [207.124.109.57]
 8    494 ms    482 ms    485 ms   core7-hssi6 [204.70.10.9]
 9    483 ms    489 ms    484 ms   corerouter2 [204.70.9.132]
10    557 ms    552 ms    561 ms   xcore3 [204.70.150.81]
11    566 ms    572 ms    554 ms   sun-micro [204.70.179.102]
12    577 ms    574 ms    558 ms   www.sun.com [192.9.49.30]
Trace complete.
```

If one or more intermediate hosts fail to respond within 5 seconds, a * would be displayed. For example, if the host xcore3.Boston.cw.net did not respond to three requests, that line of display would look like this:

```
10    * * *   xcore3.Boston.cw.net [204.70.150.81]
```

15

Alternatively, if the host was completely unreachable, the following output would be displayed:

```
10    * * !H  xcore3.Boston.cw.net [204.70.150.81]
```

The administrator of xcore3.Boston.cw.net should then be contacted to determine the nature of the problem.

If the connection fails on the first hop, the problem might be local. In this case, the netstat command should be used to determine the status of all network interfaces on the local system. Let's look at an example:

```
# netstat -i
Name  Mtu   Net/Dest        Address    Ipkts     Ierrs   Opkts
lo0   8232  loopback        localhost  434332    0       434332
hme0  1500  192.128.205.2   chaos      43234544  554533  43789077
```

This example shows the host chaos with the IP address 192.128.205.2. Although there were no outbound packet errors (Oerrs), there were a number of inbound packet errors (Ierrs). An alternative view is provided on a per-protocol basis for the TCP, ICMP, and UDP protocols:

```
# netstat -s
UDP
        udpInDatagrams    =502856     udpInErrors       =       0
        udpOutDatagrams   =459357
TCP     tcpRtoAlgorithm   =      4    tcpRtoMin         =     200
        tcpRtoMax         =240000     tcpMaxConn        =      -1
        tcpActiveOpens    = 33786     tcpPassiveOpens   = 12296
        tcpAttemptFails   =    324    tcpEstabResets    =     909
        tcpCurrEstab      =    384    tcpOutSegs        =19158723
        tcpOutDataSegs    =13666668   tcpOutDataBytes   =981537148
        tcpRetransSegs    = 33038     tcpRetransBytes   =41629885
        tcpOutAck         =5490764    tcpOutAckDelayed  =462511
        tcpOutUrg         =     51    tcpOutWinUpdate   =     456
        tcpOutWinProbe    =    290    tcpOutControl     = 92218
        tcpOutRsts        =   1455    tcpOutFastRetrans = 18954
        tcpInSegs         =15617893
        tcpInAckSegs      =9161810    tcpInAckBytes     =981315052
        tcpInDupAck       =4559921    tcpInAckUnsent    =       0
        tcpInInorderSegs  =5741788    tcpInInorderBytes =1120389303
        tcpInUnorderSegs  = 25045     tcpInUnorderBytes =16972517
```

```
            tcpInDupSegs           =4390218    tcpInDupBytes          =4889714
            tcpInPartDupSegs       =    375    tcpInPartDupBytes      =130424
            tcpInPastWinSegs       =     17    tcpInPastWinBytes      =1808990872
            tcpInWinProbe          =    162    tcpInWinUpdate         =    270
            tcpInClosed            =    313    tcpRttNoUpdate         = 28077
            tcpRttUpdate           =9096791    tcpTimRetrans          = 18098
            tcpTimRetransDrop      =     26    tcpTimKeepalive        =    509
            tcpTimKeepaliveProbe=        76    tcpTimKeepaliveDrop    =      1
            tcpListenDrop          =      0    tcpListenDropQ0        =      0
            tcpHalfOpenDrop        =      0
IP          ipForwarding           =      2    ipDefaultTTL           =    255
            ipInReceives           =16081438   ipInHdrErrors          =      8
            ipInAddrErrors         =      0    ipInCksumErrs          =      1
            ipForwDatagrams        =      0    ipForwProhibits        =      2
            ipInUnknownProtos      =    274    ipInDiscards           =      0
            ipInDelivers           =16146712   ipOutRequests          =19560145
            ipOutDiscards          =      0    ipOutNoRoutes          =      0
            ipReasmTimeout         =     60    ipReasmReqds           =      0
            ipReasmOKs             =      0    ipReasmFails           =      0
            ipReasmDuplicates      =      0    ipReasmPartDups        =      0
            ipFragOKs              =   7780    ipFragFails            =      0
            ipFragCreates          =  40837    ipRoutingDiscards      =      0
            tcpInErrs              =    291    udpNoPorts             =144065
            udpInCksumErrs         =      2    udpInOverflows         =      0
            rawipInOverflows       =      0
ICMP        icmpInMsgs             =  17469    icmpInErrors           =      0
            icmpInCksumErrs        =      0    icmpInUnknowns         =      0
            icmpInDestUnreachs     =   2343    icmpInTimeExcds        =     26
            icmpInParmProbs        =      0    icmpInSrcQuenchs       =      0
            icmpInRedirects        =     19    icmpInBadRedirects     =     19
            icmpInEchos            =   9580    icmpInEchoReps         =   5226
            icmpInTimestamps       =      0    icmpInTimestampReps    =      0
            icmpInAddrMasks        =      0    icmpInAddrMaskReps     =      0
            icmpInFragNeeded       =      0    icmpOutMsgs            = 11693
            icmpOutDrops           =140883     icmpOutErrors          =      0
            icmpOutDestUnreachs    =   2113    icmpOutTimeExcds       =      0
            icmpOutParmProbs       =      0    icmpOutSrcQuenchs      =      0
            icmpOutRedirects       =      0    icmpOutEchos           =      0
            icmpOutEchoReps        =   9580    icmpOutTimestamps      =      0
            icmpOutTimestampReps=        0     icmpOutAddrMasks       =      0
            icmpOutAddrMaskReps =        0     icmpOutFragNeeded      =      0
            icmpInOverflows        =      0
```

Again, specific error counters such as icmpOutErrors, udpInErrors, and tcpInDupBytes should be regularly reviewed to ensure that error rates do not approach the total number of packets being transferred in or out of an interface.

☑ *Mastery Check*

1. Which of the following is a valid network topology? (Choose one only)

   A. Star

   B. Box

   C. Square

   D. Circle

2. Which of the following is a valid network topology? (Choose one only)

   A. Cube

   B. Angle

   C. Cross

   D. Ring

3. What is OSI? (Choose one only)

   A. A network protocol

   B. A framework for defining the scope of different layers of networking technology

   C. A cube network

   D. A networking software package

4. What is the role of the physical layer? (Choose one only)

   A. Defines how data is exchanged at its very basic level

   B. Defines the apparatus for transferring data, including error checking and synchronization

   C. Defines specific operational issues, such as how networks can exchange data

   D. Specifies how individual computers are to interpret data received from the network

☑ Mastery Check

5. What is the role of the data link layer? (Choose one only)

   A. Defines how data is exchanged at its very basic level

   B. Defines the apparatus for transferring data, including error checking and synchronization

   C. Defines specific operational issues, such as how networks can exchange data

   D. Specifies how individual computers are to interpret data received from the network

6. What is the role of the session layer? (Choose one only)

   A. Defines how data is exchanged at its very basic level

   B. Determines how data from different sources can be separated

   C. Specifies how different types of data are formatted

   D. Describes how high-level applications can communicate with each other.

7. What is the role of the presentation layer? (Choose one only)

   A. Defines how data is exchanged at its very basic level

   B. Determines how data from different sources can be separated

   C. Specifies how different types of data are formatted

   D. Describes how high-level applications can communicate with each other.

8. What is the role of the application layer? (Choose one only)

   A. Defines how data is exchanged at its very basic level

   B. Determines how data from different sources can be separated

   C. Specifies how different types of data are formatted

   D. Describes how high-level applications can communicate with each other

☑ Mastery Check

9. What link speeds are supported by Solaris? (Choose one only)

    A. 10BASE-T - 10 Mbps

    B. 100BASE-T - 100 Mbps

    C. 1000BASE-FX - 1 Gbps

    D. 10000BASE-T - 10 Gbps

10. What command is used to modify /dev/tcp settings? (Choose one only)

    A. `tcp`

    B. `ar`

    C. `netstat`

    D. `ndd`

11. What command is used to disable IP forwarding? (Choose one only)

    A. `ndd -forwarding 0`

    B. `ndd -set /dev/ip ip_forwarding 0`

    C. `ndd -set /dev/ip ip_-forwarding +0`

    D. `ndd -noforward`

12. What command is used to verify the status of a network interface? (Choose one only)

    A. `netview`

    B. `netlook`

    C. `ifconfig`

    D. `hmelook`

13. What command is used to check the table of IP address to MAC address mappings? (Choose one only)

    A. `arp`

    B. `ar`

    C. `ndd`

    D. `netstat`

Module 16

Remote Access

Critical Skills

Providing interactive, remote access to clients is one of the key features of a multi-user system—since there is only one console, which is usually occupied by the super-user, or mounted in a rack, alternative access must be provided. Traditionally, two types of remote access have been devised, both of which have proven to be less than secure in the Internet age. Interactive access where a user can interact with a shell, such a C shell (/bin/csh), through a telnet client is provided by a DARPA protocol-compliant telnet server. Variations on this type of access are provided by the r-commands, which allow single commands to be issued, for example, without requiring interactive access to a remote shell. Alternatively, file transfer access is provided by clients and servers implementing the File Transfer Protocol (FTP). While telnet and FTP have proven beneficial over the years, they also have inherent security risks, because authentication tokens (username and password) are transmitted "in the clear" over the network. If the client and server are located on a local area network, which is protected by a firewall from external intrusion, then telnet and FTP are relatively safe— only interception on the local network must then be guarded against. However, since wide area shell access may need to be made available to employees, contractors, customers, and partners, a more secure system is required. With the release of Solaris 9, Sun has finally included the Secure Shell (ssh) and Secure Copy (scp) applications, which implement secure authentication based on public-key cryptography. These measures protect the exchange of authentication tokens and all packets exchanged between client and server. In this module, we examine how to manage remote access services that operate securely and openly.

16.1 Utilize telnet

The telnet protocol, originally developed at DARPA, is one of the most commonly used remote services. Solaris supports a telnet server that operates as part of the Internet daemon (inetd). telnet clients are available for most operating systems that support TCP/IP, including Solaris 9 (and previous versions), Linux, Windows, MacOS, and other UNIX systems, as shown in Figure 16-1.

Tip

Browser-based clients, written in Java, allow a Web browser to be used as a telnet client to the system from which a telnet applet is downloaded. This permits clients to access telnet services without requiring an external client, since the applet is downloaded to the local system directly from the server (see **http://srp.stanford .edu/~tjw/telnet.html** for more details).

16

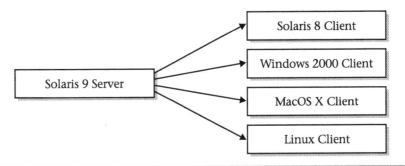

Figure 16-1 Supporting multiple telnet clients using a Solaris 9 Telnet server

Figure 16-2 shows the result of logging into a Solaris system by using a Windows telnet client. telnet clients typically support a standard terminal emulation type, such as VT-100 or VT-220. It's important to note that only clients that have support for the X Windowing System (X11) will be able to launch X11 GUI applications when logging into a remote server using Telnet.

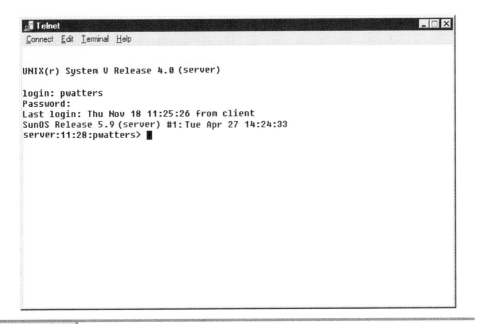

Figure 16-2 Logging into a Solaris 9 server using a Windows telnet client

Note

Although X11 servers are available for Windows, they are not supplied by Microsoft with the Windows distribution.

After printing a welcome banner, the user is prompted for a username and password. If the passwords match, a shell is spawned and the user may enter commands and interact with the shell. Alternatively, if the username and password do not match, the user's login attempt is rejected, and they will be given the opportunity to log in again after a short delay. This delay slows down brute force cracking attempts. This process is shown in Figure 16-3. Behind the scenes, a TCP connection is initially made from the client to the server, which the server responds to with the authentication challenge. This connection attempt may be blocked by a packet-filtering firewall at any router that lies on a network path between the two hosts.

Many users can have a telnet connection open to a Solaris server at any point in time. This allows multiple clients to make use of centralized computing resources, whether for mail, news, databases, or graphics. telnet does not support the execution of applications requiring CDE and/or X11, unless the client provides support for X11. All Solaris systems provide this support, as do many other UNIX and Linux systems. It is even possible to use an X11 server for Windows to remotely execute CDE-based applications with their displays set to the

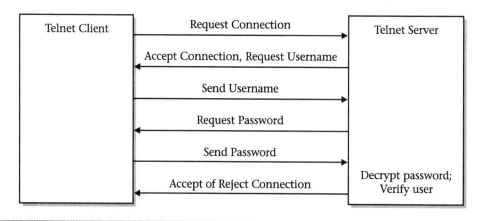

Figure 16-3 Login and authentication process

Windows desktop. Reflection X is one excellent product for Windows that is designed for this purpose.

Let's look at a sample telnet session between a system called brolga and a system called currawong, for the user pwatters:

```
$ telnet currawong
Trying 134.128.64.16...

Connected to currawong.cassowary.net.
Escape character is '^]'.


SunOS 5.9

login: pwatters
Password:

Last login: Thu Feb 21 10:03:02 from sparrow
Sun Microsystems Inc.   SunOS 5.9         Generic January 2002

You have new mail.
currawong:11:41:pwatters>
```

The sequence of events is straightforward: the user enters their username on the remote system when prompted, presses ENTER, and then enters their password on the remote machine. If the username and password are accepted, the session proceeds and the user's default shell is spawned. The user may now issue commands interactively on the command line as if they were sitting at the console.

1-Minute Drill

● What authentication tokens are required to log in?

The Solaris telnet client has an extensive help facility available, which can be viewed by keying the escape sequence (usually ^]), and typing the command **help**. The main telnet commands are shown in Table 16-1.

● Username and password

Command	Description
close	Quit telnet session.
logout	Close connection.
display	Print connection characteristics.
mode	Change mode.
open	Open connection.
quit	Quit telnet session.
send	Send special characters.
set	Set connection characteristics.
unset	Unset connection characteristics.
status	Display connection status.
toggle	Change connection characteristics.
slc	Toggle special character mode.
z	Suspend connection.
!	Spawn shell.
environ	Update environment variables.
?	Display help.
ENTER	Return to session.

Table 16-1   telnet Client Commands

As an example of how these commands work, the display command will print all of the current settings being used by your terminal:

```
telnet> display
will flush output when sending interrupt characters.
won't send interrupt characters in urgent mode.
won't skip reading of ~/.telnetrc file.
won't map carriage return on output.
will recognize certain control characters.
won't turn on socket level debugging.
won't print hexadecimal representation of network traffic.
won't print user readable output for "netdata".
won't show option processing.
won't print hexadecimal representation of terminal traffic.
echo            [^E]
escape          [^]]
rlogin          [off]
tracefile       "(standard output)"
```

```
flushoutput    [^O]
interrupt      [^C]
quit           [^\]
eof            [^D]
erase          [^?]
kill           [^U]
lnext          [^V]
susp           [^Z]
reprint        [^R]
worderase      [^W]
start          [^Q]
stop           [^S]
forw1          [off]
forw2          [off]
ayt            [^T]
```

1-Minute Drill

● What is the default telnet tracefile?

Alternatively, the `status` command reveals the characteristics of the current telnet connection:

```
telnet> status
Connected to currawong.cassowary.net.
Operating in single character mode
Catching signals locally
Remote character echo
Escape character is '^]'.
```

To resume the telnet session, simply hit the ENTER key at the `telnet>` prompt. telnet operates as a service of the Internet daemon (inetd), which runs the in.telnetd server when a request from a client is made. In order to permit telnet connections on the default port 23, the following line must appear in the services database (*/etc/services*):

```
telnet    23/tcp
```

● Standard output.

In addition, the following entry must appear in the inetd configuration file (*/etc/inetd.conf*):

```
telnet  stream  tcp     nowait  root    /usr/sbin/in.telnetd in.telnetd
```

16.2 Utilize FTP

Now that we have seen how telnet runs, we will examine some of the services that are provided through inetd in detail. One of the most commonly used inetd services is the File Transfer Program (FTP). FTP allows users to retrieve files from accounts on different systems on the local area network, or across the Internet. One popular variant of FTP is anonymous FTP, which is a convention by which remote access to a local file system is granted anonymously. This allows public users to download files from your system without having to provide any kind of authentication credentials.

Tip

Many public software archives support anonymous FTP.

Let's examine a sample FTP session for the user pwatters on a system called emu, who wants to transfer files to a system called cassowary using the remote account paul:

```
emu:/ $ ftp cassowary
Connected to cassowary.paulwatters.com.
220 cassowary FTP server (SunOS 5.9) ready.
Name (emu:pwatters): paul
331 Password required for paul.
Password:
230 User paul logged in.
ftp>
```

In this example, the user pwatters on emu connects to cassowary by using the standard ftp client program. However, pwatters could easily have used the FTP capacity of the Netscape Navigator program or the xftp application. The server cassowary responds to the client request by printing a welcome banner and asking for a valid username. Notice that the client's current username is displayed as part of the prompt—this means that if the account name on the

FTP server is the same as the FTP client, the user may just press ENTER to accept the proposed username. However, in the example shown, the client username is pwatters, but the server username is paul, so **paul** must be entered directly.

Next, the password for the paul account is requested. If this is entered correctly, the user will be logged into the server account, with the working directory root corresponding to the user's home directory. However, if the username and/or password are not correct, the following error message will be displayed:

```
530 Login incorrect.
Login failed.
ftp>
```

At the FTP prompt, it is possible to retry the authentication sequence without having to quit the FTP client, and restart by using the following commands:

```
ftp> user paul
331 Password required for paul.
Password:
230 User paul logged in.
ftp>
```

In this example, the correct password has been entered, and the remote user may then proceed to issue a number of commands through the FTP client. You can obtain a list of all supported commands on the FTP server by using the help command:

```
ftp> help
Commands may be abbreviated.  Commands are:

!           cr          macdef      proxy        send
$           delete      mdelete     sendport     status
account     debug       mdir        put          struct
append      dir         mget        pwd          sunique
ascii       disconnect  mkdir       quit         tenex
bell        form        mls         quote        trace
binary      get         mode        recv         type
bye         glob        mput        remotehelp   user
case        hash        nmap        rename       verbose
cd          help        ntrans      reset        ?
cdup        lcd         open        rmdir
close       ls          prompt      runique
```

Table 16-2 describes the most commonly used FTP commands. However, most users will typically use only three or four commands during a session. The first command is usually to verify the current working directory, for which the pwd command is used:

```
ftp> pwd
257 "/home/paul" is current directory.
```

Command	Description
!	Spawns a shell.
$	Runs a macro.
?	Displays help.
append	Appends data to a file.
ascii	Transfer files as ASCII.
bell	Sound upon completion.
bye	Quit FTP session.
case	Enable case mapping.
cd	Change directory.
cdup	Change directory to parent.
close	Quit FTP session.
cr	Enable RETURN key stripping.
delete	Remove file.
dir	Print directory listing.
disconnect	Quit FTP session.
form	Specify ASCII/binary format.
glob	Enable filename expansion.
hash	Enable hash printing.
help	Displays help.
lcd	Change working directory on client.
ls	Print directory listing.
macdef	Enter a macro.
mdelete	Delete files.
mdir	Multiple directory listing.
mkdir	Create directory.
mls	Multiple directory listing.
mput	Upload files.

Table 16-2   FTP Commands

16

Command	Description
nmap	Enable templates.
ntrans	Define translation table.
open	Open connection.
prompt	Toggle per-file prompting.
proxy	Enable proxying.
put	Upload file.
quit	Quit FTP session.
quote	Execute command.
remotehelp	Displays help.
rename	Change filename.
reset	Reset connection.
rmdir	Delete directory.
runique	Enable unique filenames.
send	Upload file.
sendport	Enable PORT command.
status	Display status.
struct	Define file transfer structure.
tenex	Toggle tenex file support.
trace	Display IP packet trace.
user	User login.
verbose	Display verbose messages.

Table 16-2   FTP Commands *(continued)*

Next, the target directory should be selected. To determine which directories exist underneath the current directory, or to verify what files already exist in the current directory, the dir command may be used:

```
ftp> dir
200 PORT command successful.
150 ASCII data connection for /bin/ls (64.16.128.48,44879) (0 bytes).
total 34
drwxr-xr-x    2 paul     staff      512 May 10 13:53 .
drwxr-xr-x    6 paul     staff      512 May 15 09:10 ..
-rw-r--r--    1 paul     staff     1987 May 10 13:50 _GoodDayStub.java
-rw-r--r--    1 paul     staff      411 May 10 13:50 GoodDay.java
-rw-r--r--    1 paul     staff     4649 May 10 13:50 GoodDayHelper.java
-rw-r--r--    1 paul     staff      877 May 10 13:50 GoodDayHolder.java
```

```
-rw-r--r--  1 paul    staff     414 May 10 13:50 GoodDayOperations.java
-rw-r--r--  1 paul    staff    2522 May 10 13:50 GoodDayPOA.java
-rw-r--r--  1 paul    staff    1227 May 10 13:50 GoodDayPOATie.java
226 ASCII Transfer complete.
637 bytes received in 0.03 seconds (20.46 Kbytes/s)
```

In this example, we can see that there are several Java source files in this directory. Now imagine that we wanted to download the *GoodDay.java* file to the local system. We would use the command

```
ftp> get GoodDay.java
200 PORT command successful.
150 Binary data connection for GoodDay.java
    (64.16.128.48,44879) (411 bytes).
226 Binary Transfer complete.
411 bytes received in 0.05 seconds (10.45 Kbytes/sec)
```

If we modified the file locally, added 4,000,000 bytes, and then wished to upload it back to the server, we could use the command

```
ftp> put GoodDay.java
200 PORT command successful.
150 Binary data connection for GoodDay.java (203.134.34.185,1036).
226 Transfer complete.
4000411 bytes sent in 0.6 seconds (10.45 Kbytes/sec)
```

Once a FTP session has been completed, the `quit` command may be used to terminate the client session.

16.3 Configure Anonymous

FTP is a useful client/server protocol for transferring individual files or groups of files of binary or plaintext data between hosts. So far, we've focused on the situation where the user attempting to log in from a remote host has a valid username and password on the FTP server; that is, they can be identified and authenticated using the standard Solaris username and password matching routines. However, one of the most widespread uses of FTP is not providing remote access to identifiable clients—in other words, the users of the FTP service remain anonymous because their credentials are not validated on the server side.

Anonymous FTP services are not supported by default in Solaris, unlike most Linux distributions—and also unlike Windows, where the Internet Information Server (IIS) provides anonymous FTP access. However, a simple procedure can be followed to enable anonymous FTP on Solaris, which we will review in this section. Firstly, we will examine the limitations and restrictions placed on anonymous FTP services by Solaris, and discuss various strategies that can be used to secure anonymous FTP.

Obviously, the greatest fear in opening up access to your system for anonymous users is that they will abuse the system, or find a way to penetrate the protective layers that you put in place to protect the system. For example, if you must provide anonymous FTP uploads, you run the risk of allowing users to upload very large files that could be used to literally fill the file system to capacity. Imagine further that the file system on which the anonymous FTP user's home directory resides was the same file system on which every other users' files were located. Authenticated users would not be able to create new files without deleting others first, making it very difficult to work effectively. One solution to this problem is to create a single partition with a capacity equal to the total estimated space required for uploads. Thus, if an anonymous user fills this partition with junk in order to deny service to other users, service will only be disrupted for other anonymous users. Most sites that provide anonymous FTP services only allow the anonymous downloading of files from an archive, rather than allowing unauthenticated write access to the remote file system.

Tip

If a remote user really does need to upload files, it's best to create a new account for them using admintool, and place a quota on their ability to create files on the file system.

Anonymous FTP is supported by all FTP clients, including the XFTP client developed by the Lawrence Livermore National Laboratory (available for download from **http://www.llnl.gov/ia/xftp.html**). XFTP allows a client to log in anonymously to a remote host—the files can be downloaded and uploaded according to the file permissions set for the FTP user's home directory and below. When logging in anonymously, users must use the username "ftp" or "anonymous"; in this way, the normal authentication mechanisms are bypassed.

Anonymous FTP works by setting the effective root directory of the anonymous FTP account to something other than the real root directory: this gives the remote user a view of the Solaris system that appears to have all of the normal system directories and mount points (such as */usr*, */etc*, and */lib*). However, this "virtual root" directory is actually located well below the root directory for authenticated users. For example, imagine that we created a 150MB slice, such as */dev/dsk/c1t1d1s7*, which was only to be used for anonymous FTP. If we created a mount point called */anon*, and mounted the file system */dev/dsk/c1t1d1s7* there, the root directory for the anonymous FTP user would actually be */anon*. Thus, if an anonymous FTP user typed **cd /**, they would literally be changing the working directory to */anon*.

The home directory of the anonymous FTP user would then be set to */anon*, and they would not be allowed to own files on other file systems. Provided that no symbolic links were created between the */anon* file system and directories on other file systems, the */anon* file system would be completely separate from every other user's files. Of course, it is necessary to provide copies of various system files and directories in the miniroot file system, such as a skeleton password file and the `ls` command. This allows files to be listed through the FTP client interface, and allows the files to be owned by a valid user defined in the skeleton password file (including the User ID and Group ID of accounts like root). Of course, no real passwords should be stored in this password file—all entries should be removed except for root, and password shadowing should be enabled. We will cover these steps later in this section.

Traditionally when you connect to an anonymous FTP server, you identify yourself as the user "ftp" or the user "anonymous", after which you are asked to enter your e-mail address:

```
$ ftp ftp.sun.com
Connected to ftp.sun.com.
220-Welcome to Sun Microsystems Corporate FTP Server.
220-
220 ftp FTP server (ftpd Thu Feb 21 23:31:06 PST 2002) ready.
Name (ftp.sun.com:pwatters): anonymous
331 Guest login ok, send your complete e-mail address as password.
Password:
230 Guest login ok, access restrictions apply.
```

However, some unscrupulous site administrators have been known to sell lists of all e-mail addresses that are entered into their anonymous FTP server so that companies can send "targeted" unsolicited commercial e-mail to the address entered. It is therefore wise to enter a fake e-mail address that contains at least one @ character, as this is typically used for validation.

Caution

You should never enter a valid password from your own system, as this could be recorded and used to break into your local account in the future.

An anonymous FTP session is almost exactly the same as a normal FTP session: the same commands are used to upload and download files (`get`, `put`, `mget`, `mput`), change directories (`cd`, `lcd`), print the current working directory (`pwd`), and get a directory listing (`dir`, `ls`). The main difference is that you will not be logged into the same system area as all other users, unless the home directory of the FTP user is set to / (that is, the root directory, would be a very bad idea!). Most anonymous FTP servers have a *README* or *INDEX* file that explains what files are available to download and what restrictions might be placed on anonymous users, such as download size and connect time limits.

If you experience any difficulties with setting up anonymous FTP on Solaris, you should consult the Anonymous FTP FAQ file available at **ftp://rtfm.mit .edu/pub/usenet/news.answers/computer-security/anonymous-ftp-faq**. In addition, security patches are released periodically for all Internet daemons, including in.ftpd, through SunSolve.

Tip

CERT advisories are available at **http://www.cert.org/**, and these contain important late-breaking news about vulnerabilities that have been discovered by vendors or that have been widely publicized on the Internet.

Solaris 9 provides the `ftpconfig` command to install anonymous FTP. If you encounter problems with anonymous FTP, it's often possible to determine what the problem is by examining the FTP status codes that are returned from all FTP commands sent to the server. The most likely cause of access problems is file permissions—you need to ensure that all anonymous FTP files are world readable, and that directories are world executable. A full list of error codes is given in Table 16-3.

Code	Description
110	Restart marker reply.
120	Service ready in *nnn* minutes.
125	Data connection already open; transfer starting.
150	File status okay; about to open data connection.
200	Command okay.
202	Command not implemented, superfluous at this site.
211	System status, or system help reply.
212	Directory status.
213	File status.
214	Help message.
215	NAME system type.
220	Service ready for new user.
221	Service closing control connection.
225	Data connection open; no transfer in progress.
226	Closing data connection.
227	Entering Passive Mode (h1,h2,h3,h4,p1,p2).
230	User logged in, proceed.
250	Requested file action okay, completed.
257	"PATHNAME" created.
331	Username okay, need password.
332	Need account for login.
350	Requested file action pending further information.
421	Service not available, closing control connection.
425	Can't open data connection.
426	Connection closed; transfer aborted.
450	Requested file action not taken.
451	Requested action aborted: local error in processing.
452	Requested action not taken.
500	Syntax error, command unrecognized.
501	Syntax error in parameters or arguments.
502	Command not implemented.
503	Bad sequence of commands.
504	Command not implemented for that parameter.
530	Not logged in.

Table 16-3   FTP Status Codes

Code	Description
532	Need account for storing files.
550	Requested action not taken.
551	Requested action aborted: page type unknown.
552	Requested file action aborted.
553	Requested action not taken.

Table 16-3   FTP Status Codes (*continued*)

For more information about how FTP operates, including anonymous FTP, see the following RFCs:

RFC 2640	Internationalization of the File Transfer Protocol
RFC 2389	Feature negotiation mechanism for the File Transfer Protocol
RFC 1986	Experiments with a Simple File Transfer Protocol for Radio Links using Enhanced Trivial File Transfer Protocol (ETFTP)
RFC 1440	SIFT/UFT: Sender-Initiated/Unsolicited File Transfer
RFC 1068	Background File Transfer Program (BFTP)
RFC 2585	Internet X.509 Public Key Infrastructure Operational Protocols: FTP and HTTP
RFC 2428	FTP Extensions for IPv6 and NATs
RFC 2228	FTP Security Extensions
RFC 1639	FTP Operation Over Big Address Records (FOOBAR)

Although Solaris comes with a standard FTP server, you may decide to install one of the many third-party FTP servers that are available on the Internet. This is because some third-party FTP servers offer some extra features that are useful for supporting anonymous FTP because they support upload/download quotas and sophisticated group access facilities. One of the most popular servers is the Washington University FTP server (WU-FTPD), which can be downloaded from **ftp://ftp.wu.edu/**. One of the nicest features of WU-FTPD is the ability to examine the source code and customize it to meet your own requirements. Thus, if you wanted to incorporate a new security feature into the FTP server, you could easily make the change. Unfortunately, giving the source code away to crackers on the Internet makes the system more vulnerable to attack because a weakness may be identified in the source. For example, many standard daemons (until recently) did not perform bounds checking on command parameter arrays, which meant that servers could easily be compromised by passing parameter strings greater than the declared size of the parameter array. However, these problems have been largely rectified in recent years, and having access to the source code can also help developers identify any potential weaknesses.

The Washington FTP daemon is very useful for managing anonymous FTP because file download limits can be set on a per-user basis or per-session basis, rather than just on the file system. This can be useful for preventing denial of service attacks, as well as allowing a more equitable distribution of download bandwidth from a public server during peak periods. Options for the WU-FTPD can be set for various options, including the ability to delete, overwrite, rename, change permissions, and set umasks for the anonymous FTP client:

```
delete      yes     guest,anonymous
overwrite   yes     guest,anonymous
rename      no      guest,anonymous
chmod       yes     anonymous
umask       no      anonymous
```

Once the WU-FTPD daemon has been installed and configured, it can be started by adding the following line to the *etc/inetd.conf* file:

```
ftp  stream  tcp  nowait  root  /usr/local/wu-ftpd/ftpd  ftpd -laio
```

The line that contains the original FTP daemon configuration should be commented out, and the inetd process should then be restarted.

Ask the Expert

Question: Should I allow anonymous FTP?

Answer: Before the advent of the WWW, anonymous FTP was the main method for downloading source file distributions. However, given the security risks of establishing a chroot jail to try and isolate anonymous FTP users from real users, it doesn't seem worth the effort, given that system users can place files for public retrieval using a Web server.

16.4 Perform Service Testing

If you're having trouble getting anonymous FTP to work, or any of the TCP/IP services supported by Solaris, you can always test the protocol commands manually by using a telnet client to make a TCP connection to the target port on the server. In the case of FTP, you can issue commands interactively to port 21, and verify the response accordingly. The port number can be specified on the command line after the server hostname. To test an anonymous FTP server, you could use the following command:

```
$ telnet server 21
Trying 203.64.22.1...
Connected to server.
Escape character is '^]'.
220 server FTP server (UNIX(r) System V Release 4.0) ready.
```

This means that the FTP server is ready to serve queries. If your FTP server needs to be highly available, it's easy to write a script that uses telnet to test that a server is operational 24×7. To test the availability of other remote access services, you simply need to specify the port number on the command line. For example, to test the sendmail service, you could use the command

```
$ telnet server 25
Trying 203.64.22.1...
Connected to server.
Escape character is '^]'.
220 server ESMTP Sendmail 9.0.0a/9.0.0; Sat,
11 Nov 2001 08:34:01 +1100 (EST)
```

In addition to testing connectivity, it is also possible to issue commands and test their responses. For example, if you're running a Web server that should always serve the same index page, you could write a script that used telnet to determine whether or not the Web page was actually being served by the server. A get command can be issued using the Hypertext Transfer Protocol (HTTP), and the contents of the returned page can be matched with the expected page (rather than a 404 error page, which would indicate that the page had not been found). To retrieve the default index.html page on the server, the following command could be used:

```
$ telnet server 80
Trying 203.64.22.1...
Connected to server.
Escape character is '^]'.
GET index.html
<!DOCTYPE HTML PUBLIC "-//IETF//DTD HTML 3.0//EN">
<HTML><HEAD>
<TITLE>Index Page</TITLE></HEAD>
<h1>Hopefully this is the page you wanted to see!</h1>
```

Project 16-1: Testing the FTP Service

This project shows you how to test for a specific service by using the `telnet` command. This approach is useful when a service is not responding and you need to begin the troubleshooting process.

Step-by-Step

1. Check */etc/services* for the port number for FTP:

```
$ grep ftp /etc/services
```

2. telnet to the appropriate port:

```
$ telnet localhost 21
```

3. If no result is returned, the service is not working. If the service is working, the following would be displayed:

```
Trying 127.0.0.1...
Connected to localhost.
Escape character is '^]'.
220 server FTP server (UNIX(r) System V Release 4.0) ready.
...
```

Summary

The FTP server can be tested by using the `telnet` command and connecting to the FTP port.

16.5 Utilize r-commands

So far, we've focused on the telnet and FTP commands to perform remote access operations; however, there is another set of remote access commands known as the "r-commands." These can be used to spawn remote shells, using the `rsh` command, and execute commands remotely using the `rlogin` command. The rsh application is used to execute commands remotely on a server that has the remote shell daemon running. The command that is to be executed can be specified on the command line—for example, if you want to run the who command on a remote server to see who is currently logged-in:

```
client$ rsh server who
```

The output from the command is piped to standard output, meaning that it can be redirected to a file on the client system. For example, if the above command was run once hourly as a security measure to log all active users every hour, the output could be redirected to a running logfile like the following:

```
client$ rsh server who >> /var/log/server.who.log
```

The */var/log/server.who.log* file would then contain all of the entries for the command, every time it is executed. A cron job could be created which schedules this command to run hourly, in which case all logged entries will appear sequentially in the file. Once the application has been executed on the remote server, terminal control returns to the client.

The `rlogin` command is different from `rsh`, because the client is remotely logged into a server after spawning a remote shell, as shown in Figure 16-4. Thus, the `rlogin` command does not terminate once a connection has been established and a shell has been spawned. To make a connection to a server running the rlogin daemon, you would need to use the following command:

```
client$ rlogin server
```

You would then be prompted to enter your password:

```
password:
```

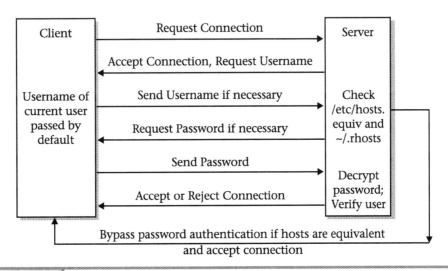

Figure 16-4   Authentication using rlogin

If the username and password can be authenticated, a shell will be spawned and you will be able to enter commands directly. Alternatively, if your remote username is different than your local username, you may pass it on the command line by using the -1 parameter. For example, the local user bill may have an account called william on the remote server, in which case the following command could be used:

```
bill@client$ rlogin server -l william
```

The r-commands are used as alternatives to telnet in a number of different situations. Using rlogin is typically faster than using telnet, and in some networks the telnet service may be completely disabled. Authentication in this case may rely on Kerberos or another distributed authentication mechanism. This means that each user would have a single password in the domain, meaning if the user authenticated at one server, he or she can rlogin to another without authentication. This is a very useful feature for managing large networks of hosts that have similar configurations and can be set by defining hosts as equivalent in the /etc/hosts.equiv file.

Another nice trick for servers running X11 is that it is possible to telnet from one system to another, and remotely execute applications whose display is set to the current system's console. For example, if we logged into the host chile on the console, but we wished to run a statistical analysis package on the host ecuador, we would simply telnet to ecuador from chile and execute the application. The application would run on the remote system, but all input and output would be redirected to the current terminal. However, two steps are usually required to get this process working properly. Firstly, you must set the DISPLAY environment variable on the server ecuador to be chile with the following command:

```
ecuador$ DISPLAY=chile:0.0; export DISPLAY
```

In addition, if you get a message like

```
Error: Can't open display: chile:0
```

you will need to explicitly allow connections from ecuador to chile's display by executing the following command:

```
chile$ xhost + ecuador
```

16

This procedure is very useful when a central server has many CPUs, lots of RAM, and all of the major applications installed, and your local client system is not powerful. An example is the Sun Ray thin client, which is the size of a small book and executes all processes on a central workgroup server, such as an Enterprise 450, as shown in Figure 16-5.

Using rlogin introduces a number of risks when used to jump between a large number of similar hosts, such as a Web farm. Administrators may be tempted to set up an */etc/hosts.equiv* file that permits users on different hosts with the same username to log in without a password (that is, hosts are designated as equivalent for authentication purposes). Inserting a "+" symbol into */etc/hosts.equiv* allows all remote users to log in to your system if an account with the same name that they are using exists on your system.

Caution

If a rogue user used the finger program to gain a list of all users on your system, they could simply create an account on their system with the same name, and rlogin.

A similar program exists with *.rhosts* files: this allows unchallenged logins to occur from the hosts defined in the file. Like */etc/hosts.equiv*, this is a very convenient, but ultimately dangerous, approach.

Tip

If distributed authentication is required, it's better to use the Network Information Service (NIS/NIS+) to perform the authentication.

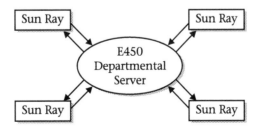

Figure 16-5 Sun Ray thin client architecture

16.6 Set Up Remote Access Security

As we have already seen, permitting remote access applications like rlogin to operate introduces a number of security risks. All remote access tools like telnet, ftp, and rsh are useful applications in their own right, which is why they continue to be supported under Solaris. In general, they can be used safely in a secure local area network. However, if you want to make a remote connection across the Internet, there is a possibility that someone is intercepting your telnet, rlogin, rsh, or ftp packets on an intermediate host. You can obtain an idea of how many potential sniffers could be capturing your data packets by examining a list of all intermediate hosts between the client and server, using the traceroute command:

```
$ traceroute www.sun.com
Tracing route to wwwwseast.usec.sun.com [192.9.49.30]
over a maximum of 30 hops:
  1    184 ms    142 ms    138 ms   202.10.4.131
  2    147 ms    144 ms    138 ms   202.10.4.129
  3    150 ms    142 ms    144 ms   202.10.1.73
  4    150 ms    144 ms    141 ms   atm11 [202.139.32.17]
  5    148 ms    143 ms    139 ms   202.139.1.197
  6    490 ms    489 ms    474 ms   hssi9 [192.65.89.246]
  7    526 ms    480 ms    485 ms   g-sfd [207.124.109.57]
  8    494 ms    482 ms    485 ms   core7 [204.70.10.9]
  9    483 ms    489 ms    484 ms   corerouter2 [204.70.9.132]
 10    557 ms    552 ms    561 ms   xcore3 [204.70.150.81]
 11    566 ms    572 ms    554 ms   sun-micro [204.70.179.102]
 12    577 ms    574 ms    558 ms   wwwsun.com [192.9.49.30]
Trace complete.
```

If your username and password are sent "in the clear" (that is, not encrypted)—as rlogin, rsh, telnet, and ftp all do—then these two authentication credentials could be intercepted by using the snoop command. You can see for yourself the power of the snoop command by running it on your local system to intercept all packets generated by telnet running on port 23:

```
# snoop tcp port 23
Using device /dev/hme0 (promiscuous mode)
moppet.paulwatters.com -> miki.paulwatters.com TELNET C port=62421
miki.paulwatters.com -> moppet.paulwatters.com TELNET R port=62421
```

```
Using device /dev/hme0
moppet.paulwatters.com -> miki.paulwatters.com TELNET C port=62421
miki.paulwatters.com -> moppet.paulwatters.com TELNET R port=62421
moppet.paulwatters.com ->
moppet.paulwatters.com -> miki.paulwatters.com TELNET C port=62421
miki.paulwatters.com -> moppet.paulwatters.com TELNET R port=62421
miki.paulwatters.com ->
moppet.paulwatters.com -> miki.paulwatters.com TELNET C port=62421
miki.paulwatters.com -> moppet.paulwatters.com TELNET R port=62421
miki.paulwatters.com ->
moppet.paulwatters.com -> miki.paulwatters.com TELNET C port=62421
miki.paulwatters.com -> moppet.paulwatters.com TELNET R port=62421
moppet.paulwatters.com ->
moppet.paulwatters.com -> miki.paulwatters.com TELNET C port=62421
miki.paulwatters.com -> moppet.paulwatters.com TELNET R port=62421
miki.paulwatters.com ->
moppet.paulwatters.com -> miki.paulwatters.com TELNET C port=62421
miki.paulwatters.com -> moppet.paulwatters.com TELNET R port=62421
moppet.paulwatters.com ->
moppet.paulwatters.com -> miki.paulwatters.com TELNET C port=62421
```

Here, we can see that telnet data is being transferred between the hosts miki and moppet. To actually see what data is being transmitted, such as a username and password, you simply switch to verbose mode by specifying the -v option on the command line:

```
# snoop -v tcp port 23
Using device /dev/hme0 (promiscuous mode)
ETHER:  ----- Ether Header -----
ETHER:
ETHER:  Packet 1 arrived at 14:13:22.14
ETHER:  Packet size = 60 bytes
ETHER:  Destination = 1:58:4:16:8a:34,
ETHER:  Source      = 2:60:5:12:6b:35, Sun
ETHER:  Ethertype = 0800 (IP)
ETHER:
IP:    ----- IP Header -----
IP:
IP:    Version = 4
IP:    Header length = 20 bytes
IP:    Type of service = 0x00
IP:          xxx. .... = 0 (precedence)
IP:          ...0 .... = normal delay
```

```
IP:          .... 0... = normal throughput
IP:          .... .0.. = normal reliability
IP:   Total length = 40 bytes
IP:   Identification = 46864
IP:   Flags = 0x4
IP:          .1.. .... = do not fragment
IP:          ..0. .... = last fragment
IP:   Fragment offset = 0 bytes
IP:   Time to live = 255 seconds/hops
IP:   Protocol = 6 (TCP)
IP:   Header checksum = 11a9
IP:   Source address = 64.23.168.76, moppet.paulwatters.com
IP:   Destination address = 64.23.168.48, miki.paulwatters.com
IP:   No options
IP:
TCP:  ----- TCP Header -----
TCP:
TCP:  Source port = 62421
TCP:  Destination port = 23 (TELNET)
TCP:  Sequence number = 796159562
TCP:  Acknowledgement number = 105859685
TCP:  Data offset = 20 bytes
TCP:  Flags = 0x10
TCP:          ..0. .... = No urgent pointer
TCP:          ...1 .... = Acknowledgement
TCP:          .... 0... = No push
TCP:          .... .0.. = No reset
TCP:          .... ..0. = No Syn
TCP:          .... ...0 = No Fin
TCP:  Window = 8760
TCP:  Checksum = 0x8f8f
TCP:  Urgent pointer = 0
TCP:  No options
TCP:
TELNET:  ----- TELNET:    -----
TELNET:
TELNET:  ""
TELNET:
```

The details listed above are only for a single packet, which is a lot of information being made available to all who are listening. One method for reducing the risk of exposing authentication credentials to public scrutiny is to use a remote access client that encrypts the exchange of username and password data between the client and the server. This means that although the username and password strings can still be captured, their contents would need to be "cracked" by using a brute force method. Such a method is extremely unlikely to succeed if a password is selected that is difficult to crack (for example, a password composed of eight random numbers and characters). Alternatively, the entire session may be encrypted, making it ever more difficult for an eavesdropper to determine what data is being exchanged.

16.7 Configure Secure Shell

One of the most popular applications for securing remote access is the Secure Shell (ssh), which is available in both freeware and commercially supported editions. If you wish to use the ssh developed as part of the OpenBSD project, you can download the latest portable release from **http://www.openssh.com/portable.html**. Alternatively, if your boss insists on commercial products, you can download and purchase a commercial ssh from **http://www.ssh.com/**. Both of these packages support the ssh1 (RSA-based) and ssh2 (DH/DSA-based) protocols, developed by the IETF (**http://www.ietf.org/html.charters/secsh-charter.html**), as well as supporting multiple encryption algorithms (for example, 3DES and Blowfish). In addition to using ssh as an alternative for shell-based interactive logins, the scp and sftp programs can be used as alternatives to rcp (remote copy) and FTP, respectively.

⎯⎜*Note* ⎯⎯⎯⎯⎯⎯⎯⎯⎯⎯⎯⎯⎯⎯⎯⎯⎯⎯⎯⎯⎯⎯⎯⎯⎯⎯⎯⎯⎯⎯⎯⎯⎯⎯⎯

Solaris 9 is distributed with OpenSSH for the first time.

ssh works by encrypting the contents of data transmitted between client and server. This includes authentication tokens as well as user data, which protects all data from interception by packet sniffing, as described in the section "Set Up Remote Access Security." Only a user with the appropriate key may decrypt the data and read its contents. To use ssh, both the client and server must have a public key and a private key: the public key is transmitted by the client to the server, where it is signed with a private key. This enables data to be transmitted from client to server, signed by the client's private key and the server's public key, which can only be unlocked with the server's private key. Having access to a public key does not allow any form of decryption. Figure 16-6 shows how ssh operates to establish a session between client and server.

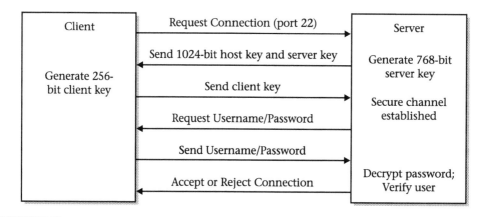

Figure 16-6   Securing remote access with secure shell

One alternative to ssh for authentication involves using a network authentication service like Kerberos to perform secure authentication for remote access. While this involves running another centralized service, Kerberized daemons are available not just for remote access tools like telnet, but for other types of applications that require authentication between client and server. Solaris 9 is supplied with a Kerberos v5 server and v5 clients. Although discussion of Kerberos configuration is beyond the scope of this chapter, readers can find out more in *Solaris 9: The Complete Reference*, published by McGraw Hill/Osborne, 2002.

☑ *Mastery Check*

1. What is the function of the telnet `close` command? (Choose one only)

   A. Quit telnet session

   B. Close connection

   C. Print connection characteristics

   D. Change mode

☑ Mastery Check

16

2. What is the function of the telnet `logout` command? (Choose one only)

   A. Quit telnet session

   B. Close connection

   C. Print connection characteristics

   D. Change mode

3. What is the function of the telnet `display` command? (Choose one only)

   A. Quit telnet session

   B. Close connection

   C. Print connection characteristics

   D. Change mode

4. What is the function of the telnet `mode` command? (Choose one only)

   A. Quit telnet session

   B. Close connection

   C. Print connection characteristics

   D. Change mode

5. What is the function of the telnet `open` command? (Choose one only)

   A. Open connection

   B. Quit telnet session

   C. Send special characters

   D. Set connection characteristics

☑ Mastery Check

6. What is the function of the telnet `quit` command? (Choose one only)

    A. Open connection

    B. Quit telnet session

    C. Send special characters

    D. Set connection characteristics

7. What is the function of the telnet `send` command? (Choose one only)

    A. Open connection

    B. Quit telnet session

    C. Send special characters

    D. Set connection characteristics

8. What is the function of the telnet `set` command? (Choose one only)

    A. Open connection

    B. Quit telnet session

    C. Send special characters

    D. Set connection characteristics

9. What is the function of the telnet `unset` command? (Choose one only)

    A. Unset connection characteristics

    B. Display connection status

    C. Change connection characteristics

    D. Toggle special character mode

☑ *Mastery Check*

10. What is the function of the telnet `status` command? (Choose one only)

    A. Unset connection characteristics

    B. Display connection status

    C. Change connection characteristics

    D. Toggle special character mode

11. What is the function of the telnet `toggle` command? (Choose one only)

    A. Unset connection characteristics

    B. Display connection status

    C. Change connection characteristics

    D. Toggle special character mode

12. What is the function of the telnet `slc` command? (Choose one only)

    A. Unset connection characteristics

    B. Display connection status

    C. Change connection characteristics

    D. Toggle special character mode

13. What is the function of the telnet `z` command? (Choose one only)

    A. Unset connection characteristics

    B. Suspend connection

    C. Spawn shell

    D. Update environment variables

☑ *Mastery Check*

14. What is the function of the telnet ! command? (Choose one only)

    A. Unset connection characteristics

    B. Suspend connection

    C. Spawn shell

    D. Update environment variables

15. What is the function of the telnet `environ` command? (Choose one only)

    A. Unset connection characteristics

    B. Suspend connection

    C. Spawn shell

    D. Update environment variables

Module 17

Web Services

Critical Skills

The World Wide Web (WWW) has become one of the most dominant Internet services provided by organizations and individuals worldwide. Everyone has a "home page" that they wish to share with the rest of the world; alternatively, many companies offer goods and services through the Internet. In this module, you will learn how to install and configure the popular Apache Web server, and write simple CGI applications using Perl. In addition, we will examine how to secure Web content by using the HTTPS protocol.

17.1 Install Apache

Apache is the de facto industry standard for Web servers, with 56 percent of Internet sites using Apache as their primary Web server according to the latest Netcraft survey (**http://www.netcraft.com/survey/**). Many Internet Web servers combine the functionality of Apache with the stability of Solaris to ensure 24x7 reliability. With the release of Solaris 9, Sun has finally bowed to pressure and included the Apache binaries with the operating environment distribution. This means that you won't need to build Apache from sources to get started with Apache. However, you may decide to recompile Apache from sources in the future, if you wish to take advantage of the different kinds of module support available for Apache.

Apache's main task is to serve files to clients using the Hypertext Transfer Protocol (HTTP). Web browsers typically make a TCP connection to port 80 on the Web server, issue a GET or POST request, and then parse the HTML tags—which are interpreted on the client side to produce the Web pages that we all know and love. Figure 17-1 shows a Netscape client on Solaris retrieving an HTML page from a Solaris server running Apache.

1-Minute Drill

● What operations are supported by HTTP?

Providing Web services through Apache is intended to be straightforward, with all administration performed by a single command (`apachectl`), and all configuration information now stored within a single configuration (previous versions split this data into multiple files). In addition to serving simple HTML

● GET and POST

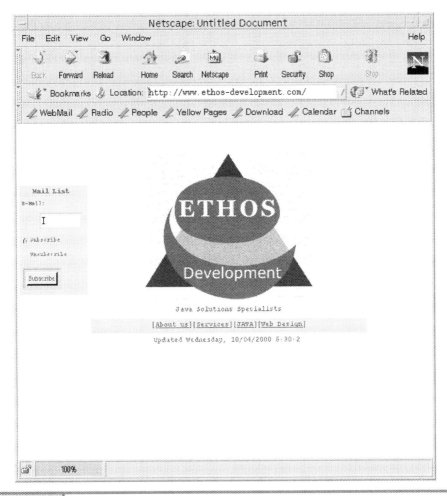

Figure 17-1 A Netscape client running on Solaris retrieves an HTML page from a Solaris server running Apache.

pages, Apache also supports a number of advanced features. Firstly, Apache provides support for more multiple virtual hosts residing on a single physical server. This allows ISPs and ASPs to increase efficiency and reduce costs by co-hosting multiple client sites on a single server. Each client can log in and update their own content without interfering with another client's content, and by using DNS aliases the correct target hostname is always resolved to the real host's IP address. An individual physical server could therefore host sites like **www.cassowary.net** and **www.paulwatters.com**, while keeping content separate.

Note

Rather than requiring one installation of Apache per client, running on different ports, Apache supports virtual hosting through a single installation running on one port.

Apache also provides a number of methods for running applications on the server, which can be accessed through a client browser. The default method for providing this access is the Common Gateway Interface (CGI). CGI applications can range from compiled applications, developed in C, C++, and Fortran, to interpreted scripts that execute in a shell (such as Bourne shell), or an interpreter such as Perl or Python. While CGI works best for CPU-intensive server tasks with few users, it fails to scale well where many users must be supported. This is because, for every user, a new process must be spawned to service the request: either a shell or interpreter process, or an application process. This can greatly reduce the performance of a server, unless a module like mod_perl is loaded that can run scripts inline. However, for applications with many users, Java servlets provide access to multiple threads servicing multiple user requests with very little overhead, because only a single process is ever required.

Security is a key concern for Internet users who routinely enter their credit card numbers to purchase goods and services. Rather than allowing a third party to "sniff" credit card details and authentication tokens from the Internet, Apache provides a Secure HTTP service (HTTPS) that makes use of a Secure Socket Layer (SSL) to improve transaction security. Although not enabled by default, SSL can easily be implemented by loading the mod_ssl module. This modular access to advanced features is one of the great architectural achievements of Apache: administrators only need to load the features that they wish to support, leading to efficient, fast Web serving.

Tip

Modules implement advances features such as a proxy/cache server, and user authentication.

Finally, Apache supports auditing through advanced logging features that can be customized for a specific format. While the default is the Common Log Format (CLF), specific fields can be included or omitted according to administrator requirements. These logs can be exported to reporting applications like WebTrends so that an overview of operational parameters, like peak load times, can be incorporated into Apache's configuration.

17.2 Configure Apache

The */etc/apache/httpd.conf* file is the main configuration file for Apache. It divides the configuration of the server into three sections: the Global Environment section, the Main Server Configuration section, and the Virtual Hosts Configuration section. The Global Environment section sets the basic parameters for the Web server's operation and management, including the base directory for all Apache files (*/usr/apache* by default), the number of client processes to start, and the timeout for receiving requests. The Main Server Configuration sections deal primarily with operational settings, such as setting the name of the directory where HTML documents are stored, the server name, and customizations for logging. Finally, the Virtual Hosts Configuration section allows settings for individual virtual hosts to be entered, including the virtual hostname, separate log file, server administrator's e-mail address, and the document root directory for the virtual host.

1-Minute Drill

● What are the main Apache configuration file sections?

In the following sections, we will review how each *httpd.conf* section is configured.

Configuring the Global Environment

In this section, we examine some the most common parameters that are set in the Global Environment section:

```
ServerType standalone
ServerRoot "/usr/apache"
PidFile /usr/apache/logs/httpd.pid
ScoreBoardFile /usr/apache/logs/apache_status
Timeout 300
KeepAlive On
MaxKeepAliveRequests 100
KeepAliveTimeout 15
MaxRequestsPerChild 0
LoadModule usertrack_module  modules/mod_usertrack.so
```

● The Global Environment section, the Main Server Configuration section, and the Virtual Hosts Configuration section

Like many daemons, Apache can work with the Internet super daemon (inetd), as discussed in Module 15, or it can run as a standalone process, as set by the *ServerType* parameter. Most administrators choose to run Apache as a standalone because a priority can be set in the individual *httpd* process, limiting its ability to interfere with other services provided through inetd. The *ServerRoot* parameter specifies the directory from which all Apache files are taken as relative. By default, this directory is */usr/apache*: however, if you decide to compile and install a new Apache version, a common practice is to name the Apache directory with its major and minor version number. Thus, the *ServerRoot* for Apache 1.39 would be */usr/apache-1.39*.

1-Minute Drill

● What would the *ServerRoot* be for Apache 1.45?

The *PidFile* parameter specifies the file which contains the process ID (PID) of the Apache server when it is running. This allows the *apachectl* script to determine whether or not a daemon is active when it attempts to start or stop the service. Although process information can be obtained by using the ps command, *apachectl* uses the *PidFile* to ensure that killing the *httpd* process for the current server does not interfere with any other "httpd" servers in the process list.

Tip

Since some servers operate more than one version of Apache, it's unwise to assume that all processes with the name "httpd" belong to a specific Apache instance.

The *ScoreBoardFile* parameters specifies a file that tracks Apache's status, while the *Timeout* setting determines how long clients should be kept running after receiving no requests. In addition, if your site typically serves pages with many images, it's good practice to enable *KeepAlive*, which allows a connection between a client and server to be maintained for a certain period while extra requests are made. This significantly reduces the time that clients wait for images and other included files to download. However, by setting it high, you may be locking other users out, as clients' processes simply wait for requests

---

● */usr/apache-1.45*

Ask the Expert

Question: I have a high volume Web site with the same users downloading many files at once. Should I use *KeepAlive*?

Answer: Yes. If you have a small number of users who sequentially download a large number of files, *KeepAlive* is suitable. However, if most of your users only retrieve a single page, and you must support a large number of users, then *KeepAlive* should be switched off.

that may (or may not) arrive. The maximum number of *KeepAlive* requests to honor is specified by the *MaxKeepAliveRequests* parameter. In this section, modules can also be loaded, as shown by the *LoadModule* request for the mod_usertrack module, which supports the use of cookies to store client-side data.

Configuring the Main Server

The Main Server configuration sets up key runtime configuration options for the main server. The following settings represent typical values for the main server:

```
Port 80
ServerAdmin paul@cassowary.net
ServerName www.cassowary.net
DocumentRoot "/usr/apache/htdocs"
<Directory />
    Options FollowSymLinks
    AllowOverride None
</Directory>
<Directory "/usr/apache/htdocs">
    Options Indexes FollowSymLinks MultiViews
    AllowOverride None
    Order allow,deny
    Allow from all
</Directory>
UserDir "/usr/apache/users/"
DirectoryIndex index.html
AccessFileName .htaccess
<Files .htaccess>
    Order allow,deny
    Deny from all
</Files>
UseCanonicalName On
```

Although this configuration may seem daunting, there are generally few parameters that need to be set by the server administrator. One example is the *Port* parameter, which is set to a default of port 80. This allows URLs of the form **http://www.cassowary.net/** to be used, since the port number does not have to be specified for this value. However, only privileged users like root can run services on ports less than 1024—so if an unprivileged user wanted to run Apache, the *Port* parameter would have to be set to a high value, like 8080. Thus, the URL to access the service would be **http://www.cassowary.net:8080/**.

The next parameter is the *ServerAdmin* definition, which contains the e-mail address of the Web server administrator. This is provided on error pages so that users can send in reports of missing pages and services. In addition, the fully qualified *ServerName* must be specified, including the *DocumentRoot* for the main server, where its HTML files will be stored, to support relative and absolute pathnames in URLs. While this is generally located underneath the Apache directory root, it can be located on a larger-capacity, higher-speed file system, such as a RAID array.

For the *DocumentRoot* directory, a number of options can be set, such as whether or not to follow symbolic links on the file system, and whether or not public access permissions will be granted on the directory. To protect the contents of a directory, a *.htaccess* file must be created, which contains a list of usernames and passwords. When attempting to access a protected directory, users will be challenged for authentication tokens, as shown here:

The *DirectoryIndex* specifies the name of the file that is retrieved when only a directory URL is supplied as opposed to a file URL. Thus, if *DirectoryIndex* is set to *index.html*, then the URL **http://www.cassowary.net/index.html** would be equivalent to **http://www.cassowary.net/**.

```
TypesConfig /usr/apache/conf/mime.types
DefaultType text/plain
HostnameLookups Off
ErrorLog /usr/apache/logs/error.log
LogLevel warn
LogFormat "%h %l %u %t \"%r\" %>s %b \"%{Referer}i\" \"%
{User-Agent}i\"" combined
LogFormat "%h %l %u %t \"%r\" %>s %b" common
LogFormat "%{Referer}i -> %U" referer
LogFormat "%{User-agent}i" agent
CustomLog /usr/apache/logs/access.log common
CustomLog /usr/apache/logs/access.log combined
ServerSignature On
Alias /icons/ "/usr/apache/icons/"
ScriptAlias /cgi-bin/ "/usr/apache/cgi-bin/"
<Directory "/usr/apache/cgi-bin">
    AllowOverride None
    Options None
</Directory>
IndexOptions FancyIndexing
AddIconByEncoding (CMP,/icons/compressed.gif) x-compress x-gzip
AddIconByType (TXT,/icons/text.gif) text/*
AddIconByType (IMG,/icons/image2.gif) image/*
AddIconByType (SND,/icons/sound2.gif) audio/*
AddIconByType (VID,/icons/movie.gif) video/*
AddIcon /icons/binary.gif .bin .exe
AddIcon /icons/binhex.gif .hqx
AddIcon /icons/tar.gif .tar
AddIcon /icons/world2.gif .wrl .wrl.gz .vrml .vrm .iv
AddIcon /icons/compressed.gif .Z .z .tgz .gz .zip
AddIcon /icons/a.gif .ps .ai .eps
AddIcon /icons/layout.gif .html .shtml .htm .pdf
AddIcon /icons/text.gif .txt
AddIcon /icons/c.gif .c
AddIcon /icons/p.gif .pl .py
AddIcon /icons/f.gif .for
AddIcon /icons/dvi.gif .dvi
AddIcon /icons/uuencoded.gif .uu
AddIcon /icons/script.gif .conf .sh .shar .csh .ksh .tcl
AddIcon /icons/tex.gif .tex
AddIcon /icons/bomb.gif core
AddIcon /icons/back.gif ..
AddIcon /icons/hand.right.gif README
AddIcon /icons/folder.gif ^^DIRECTORY^^
```

```
AddIcon /icons/blank.gif ^^BLANKICON^^
DefaultIcon /icons/unknown.gif
ReadmeName README
HeaderName HEADER
IndexIgnore .??* *~ *# HEADER* README* RCS CVS *,v *,t
AddEncoding x-compress Z
AddEncoding x-gzip gz tgz
AddLanguage da .dk
AddLanguage nl .nl
AddLanguage en .en
AddLanguage et .ee
AddLanguage fr .fr
AddLanguage de .de
AddLanguage el .el
AddLanguage it .it
AddLanguage pt .pt
AddLanguage ltz .lu
AddLanguage ca .ca
AddLanguage es .es
AddLanguage sv .se
AddLanguage cz .cz
LanguagePriority en da nl et fr de el it pt ltz ca es sv
```

The preceding parameters set a number of key variables associated with logging, languages, and the default icons used in the display of error pages and FTP screens. Logging can be specified using the common or combined log formats, or a customized format based on individual fields. In addition, hostname lookups on client names can be performed; otherwise, IP addresses will be logged. Production systems should never enable hostname lookups, because they are slow and can impact on server performance. Logs are recorded for both file access and errors. A sample set of entries for the access log is shown here:

```
205.64.56.22 - - [13/Feb/2002:18:23:01 +1000]
  "GET /cgi-bin/printenv HTTP/1.1" 200 1024
205.64.56.22 - - [13/Feb/2002:18:23:05 +1000]
  "GET /cgi-bin/Search.cgi?term=solaris&type=simple HTTP/1.1" 200 85527
205.64.56.22 - - [13/Feb/2002:18:23:10 +1000]
  "GET /index.html HTTP/1.1" 200 94151
205.64.56.22 - - [13/Feb/2002:18:23:25 +1000]
  "GET /pdf/money.pdf HTTP/1.1" 403 29
```

These examples show a number of connections being made from the client 205.64.56.22 on February 13, 2002 to various files on the local file system, as well as to two CGI scripts. On each request, a 200 success code is returned, except for the last request for the *money.pdf* file, which returned a 403 access forbidden message. A list of HTTP codes for transmission success, client failure, and server failure is shown in Table 17-1.

Code Type	Code	Description
Successful Transmission	200	OK
	201	Created
	202	Accepted
	203	Non-Authoritative Information
	204	No Content
	205	Reset Content
	206	Partial Content
Client Errors	400	Bad Request
	401	Unauthorized
	402	Payment Required
	403	Forbidden
	404	Not Found
	405	Method Not Allowed
	406	Not Acceptable
	407	Proxy Authentication Required
	408	Request Timeout
	409	Conflict
	410	Gone
	411	Length Required
	412	Precondition Failed
	413	Request Entity Too Large
	414	Request-URI Too Long
	415	Unsupported Media Type
	416	Expectation Failed
Server Errors	500	Internal Server Error
	501	Not Implemented
	502	Bad Gateway
	503	Service Unavailable

Table 17-1   HTTP Response Codes

Code Type	Code	Description
	504	Gateway Timeout
	505	HTTP Version Not Supported

Table 17-1 HTTP Response Codes (*continued*)

Support for specific languages can also be configured based on the top-level domains associated with clients. For example, clients connecting from ".it" domains are assumed to want to Italian language support.

Some commonly used MIME types supported by Apache are shown above. In addition, support for external applications, such as Java applets and RealPlayer audio, can be individually defined. Some examples of MIME types include application/x-javascript, representing the JavaScript language, and application/x-csh, representing C shell scripting.

```
AddType application/x-tar .tgz
BrowserMatch "Mozilla/2" nokeepalive
BrowserMatch "MSIE 4\.0b2;" nokeepalive downgrade-1.0
    force-response-1.0
BrowserMatch "RealPlayer 4\.0" force-response-1.0
BrowserMatch "Java/1\.0" force-response-1.0
BrowserMatch "JDK/1\.0" force-response-1.0
application/mac-binhex40        hqx
application/mac-compactpro      cpt
application/msword              doc
application/pdf                 pdf
application/postscript          ai eps ps
application/x-bcpio             bcpio
application/x-cdlink            vcd
application/x-chess-pgn         pgn
application/x-compress
application/x-cpio              cpio
application/x-csh               csh
application/x-director          dcr dir dxr
application/x-dvi               dvi
application/x-futuresplash      spl
application/x-gtar              gtar
application/x-gzip
application/x-hdf               hdf
application/x-javascript        js
application/x-koan              skp skd skt skm
```

Tip

By defining MIME types, administrators can determine how various file types are served to clients.

Configure Virtual Hosts

A sample virtual host configuration for Apache is shown below for the virtual host **www.paulwatters.com**, running on the main server **www.cassowary.net**. There is no practical limit to the number of virtual hosts that can be supported, as long as sufficient network, disk, and CPU resources are available to support each site. A *ServerAdmin* e-mail address, *DocumentRoot* and *ServerName* can also be set to be distinct from the main server. In addition, an error log and access log can be defined for each virtual host, so that entries for different sites don't overlap:

```
<VirtualHost www.paulwatters.com>
    ServerAdmin webmaster@www.paulwatters.com
    DocumentRoot /usr/apache/htdocs/www.paulwatters.com
    ServerName www.paulwatters.com
    ErrorLog /usr/apache/logs/www.paulwatters.com-error_log
    CustomLog /usr/apache/logs/www.paulwatters.com-access_log
  common
</VirtualHost>
```

17.3 Run Apache

Apache is supplied with a control program called *apachectl*, which can be used to start and stop the server, as well as restart, report on status, shut down gracefully, and test the syntax of the configuration file. In addition, a full description for each command can be obtained by using the `help` command:

```
$ apachectl help
usage: apachectl (start|stop|restart|fullstatus|
  status|graceful|configtest|help
start     - start httpd
stop      - stop httpd
restart   - restart httpd if running by sending
  a SIGHUP or start if not running
fullstatus - dump a full status screen; requires
  lynx and mod_status enabled
```

```
status     - dump a short status screen; requires
  lynx and mod_status enabled
graceful   - do a graceful restart by sending a
  SIGUSR1 or start if not running
configtest - do a configuration syntax test
help       - this screen
```

The Apache server can be started by using the following command:

```
$ apachectl start
```

The Apache server can be stopped by using the following command:

```
$ apachectl stop
```

The Apache server can be restarted by using the following command:

```
$ apachectl restart
```

A restart is required after changes to the *etc/apache/httpd.conf* file have been made.

17.4 Utilize Apache Modules

In recent times, Apache has grown to be more than a simple Web server. It has a number of modules that can be used to extend its features, including the following:

- **mod_access**   Allows or denies access to the Web server based on the originating IP address of the request.

- **mod_actions**   Associated MIME types of files requested by a specific CGI application.

- **mod_alias**   Rewrites URLs according to site specifications.

- **mod_auth**   Implements username/password authentication.

- **mod_autoindex**   Creates indexes for directory listings automatically.

- **mod_cgi**   Supports the Common Gateway Interface (CGI).

- **mod_dir**   Provides directory access support.

- **mod_env**   Handles environment variables.

- **mod_imap**   Supports image maps.

- **mod_info**   Prints information about the runtime configuration of the Apache server, including the number and type of modules loaded.

- **mod_mime**   Supports MIME types.

- **mod_proxy**   Supports proxy/cache operations for HTTP and FTP.

- **mod_setenvif**   Processes environment variables on the basis of HTTP headers.

- **mod_status**   Supports real-time status monitoring.

- **mod_unique_id**   Initializes a singular identity with each request.

- **mod_userdir**   Supports access by user directory.

- **mod_usertrack**   Supports the use of cookies to store client-side data.

For more information on modules, check the entry on managing modules in the Apache manual (**http://localhost/manual/mod**). Adding modules at run time is easy: to load the mod_usertrack, for example, you would need to include the following lines in the *httpd.conf* file:

```
LoadModule usertrack_module modules/mod_usertrack.so
AddModule mod_usertrack.c
```

17.5 Administer GUIs with Webmin

If you're a Windows administrator, you've probably cringed at the amount of configuration file editing required to configure the Apache Web server. Fortunately, there is an alternative to manual configuration, which comes in the form of a Webmin module. Webmin is a browser-based UNIX system configuration system, which comes with its own simplified Web server (*miniserv.pl*). The management interface consists of dynamically generated HTML on the client side, CGI applications on the server side, and Java applets. Although Webmin is the ideal tool to manage Apache services, it can also be used for user administration, boot management, the domain name service, and almost every kind of system management required on Solaris. The Webmin interface is shown in Figure 17-2.

To install Webmin, you need to download the source or binary archive from **http://www.webmin.com/webmin/**. Binary distributions are only available for Solaris Sparc, however, so you'll need to install Solaris Intel from source. The current source version is available at **http://www.webmin.com/webmin/ download/solaris-pkg/webmin-0.81.pkg.gz**. Many of the CGI scripts use Perl, which is included as part of the Solaris 8 distribution. To administer Apache, you will also require the Apache module, which can be downloaded at **http://www.webmin.com/webmin/download/modules/apache.wbm**. Once installed, the Apache interface will become available, as shown in Figure 17-3.

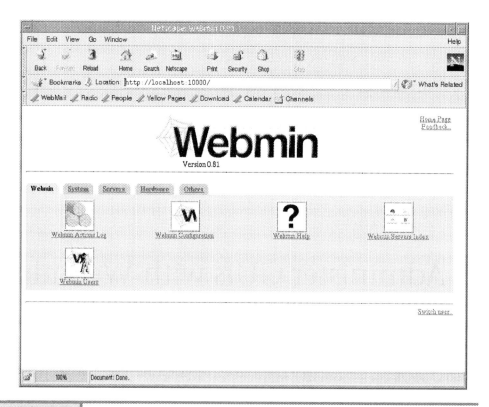

Figure 17-2 The Webmin administration interface

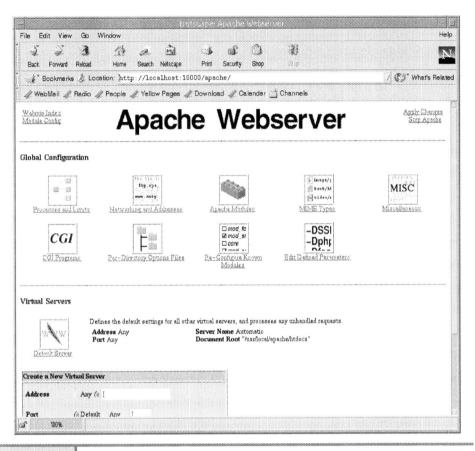

Figure 17-3   The Apache Webmin interface

The Apache Webmin interface allows you to configure all aspects of the Apache Web server without having to manually edit the configuration file. There are several different pages that are used to make configuration changes, and restart the server if necessary, including the following:

● Managing processes and server limits

● Setting network addresses

● Adding Apache modules

● Configuring MIME types

- Installing CGI programs
- Modifying module configuration

Each of these pages has a distinct purpose—for example, the Processes and Limits page shown in Figure 17-4 enables you to insert values for the following options:

- Maximum headers in request
- Maximum request line size

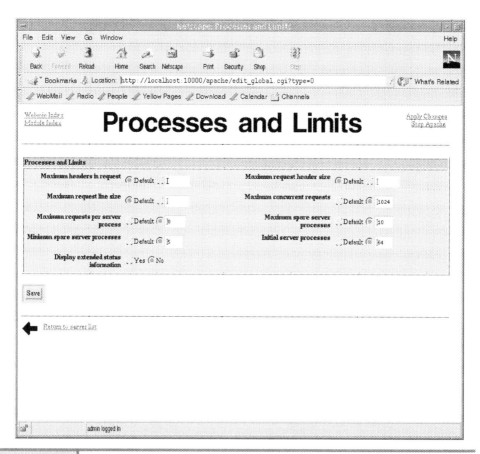

Figure 17-4   Managing processes and limits in Apache

- Maximum requests per server process

- Minimum spare server processes

- Maximum request header size

- Maximum concurrent requests

- Maximum spare server processes

- Initial server processes

Once installed, the Webmin Web server will be started, and you will be able to connect through to your local server on port 10000. In addition to administering Apache by using Webmin, you may also run Webmin through Apache, by running it as root and setting the *DocumentRoot* to the installation directory.

If you find Webmin useful, you can join the Webmin mailing list at **http://www.webmin.com/webmin/mailing.html**. There is also a very useful user's guide provided by Caldera at **http://www.calderasystems.com/ edesktop/usersguide/ch10.html**.

17.6 Write CGI Applications

Apache supports CGI applications natively, so there's no special configuration required to run CGI applications. The only two requirements are that a CGI application must have read and execute permissions on the script or application that is to be run, and that the "Content-type: text/html" string must be printed, followed by two newline characters. One of the nice features of the CGI standard is that a CGI application can be written in the language of your choice—C, C++, Perl, Bourne shell scripts—any language that your organization has expertise in. In addition, there are enhancements that speed up the sometimes slow execution of CGI applications. For example, there is a mod_perl Apache module that reduces overhead due to the invocation of the Perl interpreter by interpreting the Perl code within the Apache server itself.

Let's see what a CGI script can do. The *printenv* CGI script is supplied with Apache and can be used to print the set of environment variables that can be interpreted by CGI applications:

```
DOCUMENT_ROOT="/usr/apache/htdocs"
GATEWAY_INTERFACE="CGI/1.1"
```

```
HTTP_ACCEPT="image/gif, image/x-xbitmap,
  image/jpeg, image/pjpeg, application/vnd.ms-excel,
  application/msword, application/vnd.ms-powerpoint, */*"
HTTP_ACCEPT_ENCODING="gzip, deflate"
HTTP_ACCEPT_LANGUAGE="en-au"
HTTP_CONNECTION="Keep-Alive"
HTTP_HOST="www"
HTTP_USER_AGENT="Mozilla/4.75 (X11; I; SunOS 5.8)"
PATH="/usr/sbin:/usr/bin:/bin:/usr/ucb:/usr/local/binQUERY_STRING=""
REMOTE_ADDR="209.67.50.55"
REMOTE_PORT="3399"
REQUEST_METHOD="GET"
REQUEST_URI="/cgi-bin/printenv"
SCRIPT_FILENAME="/usr/apache/cgi-bin/printenv"
SCRIPT_NAME="/cgi-bin/printenv"
SERVER_ADDR="209.67.50.203"
SERVER_ADMIN="paul@paulwatters.com"
SERVER_NAME="www.paulwatters.com"
SERVER_PORT="80"
SERVER_PROTOCOL="HTTP/1.1"
SERVER_SIGNATURE="Apache/1.3.12 Server at www.
  paulwatters.com Port 80\n"
SERVER_SOFTWARE="Apache/1.3.12 (Unix)
  " TZ="Australia/NSW"
```

Let's examine how CGI works behind the scenes with a simple application that can be written in one of several different languages. The goal is to print out the following HTML:

```
<HTML>
<HEAD>
<TITLE>Essential Skills Example</TITLE>
</HEAD>
<BODY>
Hello Solaris Administrators!
</BODY>
</HTML>
```

This HTML code prints a simple message in the browser window, as well as in the title bar. We can easily write a CGI program in C to print out this HTML, by using the following code:

```
#include <stdio.h>
main()
{
```

```
    printf("Content-type: text/html\n\n");
    printf("<HTML>\n");
    printf("<HEAD>\n");
    printf("<TITLE>Essential Skills Example</TITLE>\n");
    printf("</HEAD>\n");
    printf("<BODY>\n");
    printf("Hello Solaris Administrators!\n");
    printf("</BODY>\n");
    printf("</HTML>\n");
}
```

To compile this code, you need to use gcc:

```
$ gcc hello_world.c -o hello.cgi
```

Next, copy the *hello.cgi* program to the Apache *cgi-bin* directory:

```
$ cp hello.cgi /usr/apache/cgi-bin/
```

Finally, you need to set the permissions correctly for the user who actually runs the Apache process:

```
$ chmod 755 hello.cgi
```

To execute the CGI program, you simply request the following URL:

```
http://localhost/cgi-bin/hello.cgi
```

Project 17-1: Executing a Perl CGI Program

This project shows you how to prepare a Perl script (*guestbook.pl*) for server-side execution. This procedure must be followed for each CGI script that you install.

Step-by-Step

1. Create the script:

```
$ guestbook.pl
```

2. Copy the script to the CGI directory:

```
$ cp guestbook.pl /usr/apache/cgi-bin/
```

3. Set the appropriate executable permissions:

```
$ chmod 755 guestbook.pl
```

4. Test the script:

```
$ netscape http://localhost/cgi-bin/guestbook.pl
```

Summary
The `cp` and `chmod` commands can be used to prepare a CGI script for execution.

17.7 Secure WWW Services

Web sites that just serve home pages and public content use the HTTP protocol, since the contents of pages being sent from client to server are publicly accessible. However, how can the contents of private sites be protected from access by rogue users and from interception by a third party? One possibility is to use mod_auth to protect individual pages and directories by requiring that users enter a username and password to access the site. This solves the problem of unauthorized users being able to access the site, but creates another problem: usernames and passwords can be intercepted by an intermediate user on the network by snooping the contents of packets. While this may not be an issue for sites that do not contain private user-specific data (such as an electronic magazine subscription), it poses strong risks for online banking, stock trading, and similar financial applications. In these cases, obtaining a username and password may well give a rogue user access to a user's bank account and stocks, and full control to transfer funds or liquidate securities. This risk is unacceptable, and a number of strategies have been devised to reduce the risk of interception of authentication tokens.

The most common solution involves implementing a Secure Socket Layer (SSL) between client and server by using the Secure HTTP (HTTPS) protocol, which uses public-key cryptography to ensure that request-response communications between client and server are encrypted. This implies that, while the communications can still be intercepted at the packet level, their contents cannot be easily understood without access to the private key of the recipient. Since both clients and servers have public keys that are exchanged with each other, encrypted data can be sent in both directions. Although it is theoretically possible to decrypt these communications, the amount of computing power required to do so (especially for larger key sizes) is technically infeasible.

Tip

While commercial encryption libraries usually cost a small fortune, OpenSSL (**http://www.openssl.org/**) is free.

In order to access a SSL service, a URL simply changes from "http" to "https". However, Apache requires the mod_ssl module to be installed and configured before secure services can be provided. This module can be downloaded from **http://www.modssl.org/**. Once its module loading entry has been placed in */etc/apache/httpd.conf*, Apache needs to be restarted, after being stopped, by using the following command:

```
$ apachectl startssl
```

To build SSL, you will need to download the Apache source from **www.apache.org**, the OpenSSL source from **www.openssl.org**, and the mod_ssl source from **www.modssl.org**. Assuming you have Apache 1.3.20, OpenSSL 0.9.5, and mod_ssl mod_ssl-2.8.6-1.3.20, the following command sequence will build the mod_ssl binaries, after all three distribution files have been unpacked into the same source directory:

```
$ cd openssl-0.9.5
$ ./config; make
$ cd ../mod_ssl-2.8.6-1.3.20
$ ./configure --with-apache=../apache_1.3.20 \
    --with-ssl=../openssl-0.9.5 --prefix=/usr/apache-1.3.20
$ cd ../apache_1.3.20
$ make; make certificate; make install
```

This installs the new Apache into */usr/apache-1.3.20*. Instructions for creating certificates and mod_ssl configuration can be found at **http://www.modssl.org/ source/exp/mod_ssl/pkg.mod_ssl/INSTALL**.

☑️Mastery Check

1. What is the correct description of the HTTP code 200?

    A. OK

    B. Created

    C. Accepted

    D. Non-Authoritative Information

2. What is the correct description of the HTTP code 201?

    A. OK

    B. Created

    C. Accepted

    D. Non-Authoritative Information

3. What is the correct description of the HTTP code 202?

    A. OK

    B. Created

    C. Accepted

    D. Non-Authoritative Information

4. What is the correct description of the HTTP code 203?

    A. OK

    B. Created

    C. Accepted

    D. Non-Authoritative Information

5. What is the correct description of the HTTP code 204?

    A. No Content

    B. Reset Content

☑ Mastery Check

    C. Partial Content

    D. Bad Request

6. What is the correct description of the HTTP code 205?

    A. No Content

    B. Reset Content

    C. Partial Content

    D. Bad Request

7. What is the correct description of the HTTP code 206?

    A. No Content

    B. Reset Content

    C. Partial Content

    D. Bad Request

8. What is the correct description of the HTTP code 400?

    A. No Content

    B. Reset Content

    C. Partial Content

    D. Bad Request

9. What is the correct description of the HTTP code 401?

    A. Unauthorized

    B. Payment Required

    C. Forbidden

    D. Not Found

☑ *Mastery Check*

10. What is the correct description of the HTTP code 402?

    A. Unauthorized

    B. Payment Required

    C. Forbidden

    D. Not Found

11. What is the correct description of the HTTP code 403?

    A. Unauthorized

    B. Payment Required

    C. Forbidden

    D. Not Found

12. What is the correct description of the HTTP code 404?

    A. Unauthorized

    B. Payment Required

    C. Forbidden

    D. Not Found

13. What is the correct description of the HTTP code 405?

    A. Unauthorized

    B. Method Not Allowed

    C. Not Acceptable

    D. Proxy Authentication Required

14. What is the correct description of the HTTP code 406?

    A. Unauthorized

    B. Method Not Allowed

✓ Mastery Check

C. Not Acceptable

D. Proxy Authentication Required

15. What is the correct description of the HTTP code 407?

A. Unauthorized

B. Method Not Allowed

C. Not Acceptable

D. Proxy Authentication Required

Module 18

Security

Critical Skills

Security is a central concern to system administrators of all network operating systems, because all services may potentially have inherent flaws or weaknesses revealed through undetected bugs, which may compromise a networked system. Solaris is no exception, and new Solaris administrators will find themselves revisiting similar issues they may have encountered with other operating systems. For example, Linux, Microsoft Windows, and Solaris all run database systems that have daemons that listen for connections coming through the Internet. These servers may be shipped with default user accounts with well-known passwords that are not inactivated by local administrators after configuration and administration. Consequently, exploits involving such services are broadcast on USENET newsgroups, cracking mailing lists and Web sites. Alternatively, some security issues are specific to Solaris: username and password sniffing while a remote user is using Telnet to spawn a local shell is unique to Solaris and other UNIX systems, because PC-based products that provide remote access (such as Symantec's pcAnywhere product) encrypt the exchange of authentication credentials by default.

In this module, we will focus on laying the groundwork for an understanding of the vulnerabilities of the Solaris operating system, as well as the techniques used by Solaris managers to reduce the risk of a successful attack by a rogue user. We also examine some of the many resources on the Internet that may be used to learn more about Solaris security, as well as implement specific Solaris security solutions.

18.1 Disable IP Ports

Perhaps the first step in preventing unauthorized access of the kind reported by SAINT as vulnerabilities is to disable access to specific IP ports, by disabling entries in the services database. This prevents services from operating, even if the inetd attempts to accept a connection for a service because it is still defined in */etc/inetd.conf*. In this section, we will examine how to disable specific services from inetd, in conjunction with the services database.

The following services are typically enabled in */etc/services*, and configured in */etc/inetd.conf*. Most sites will want to disable them, and install more secure equivalents. For example, the ftp and telnet services may be replaced by the encrypted secure copy and secure shell programs, respectively. To disable the ftp, telnet, shell, login, exec, comsat, talk, uucp, and finger services, we would "comment out" their entries in *etc/inetd.conf* by inserting a hash character "#" at the first character position of the line that defines the service. The following configuration enables these services in *etc/inetd.conf*:

```
ftp      stream  tcp    nowait  root    /usr/sbin/in.ftpd      in.ftpd -1
telnet   stream  tcp    nowait  root    /usr/sbin/in.telnetd   in.telnetd
shell    stream  tcp    nowait  root    /usr/sbin/in.rshd      in.rshd
login    stream  tcp    nowait  root    /usr/sbin/in.rlogind   in.rlogind
exec     stream  tcp    nowait  root    /usr/sbin/in.rexecd    in.rexecd
comsat   dgram   udp    wait    root    /usr/sbin/in.comsat    in.comsat
talk     dgram   udp    wait    root    /usr/sbin/in.talkd     in.talkd
uucp     stream  tcp    nowait  root    /usr/sbin/in.uucpd     in.uucpd
finger   stream  tcp    nowait  nobody  /usr/sbin/in.fingerd   in.fingerd
```

The following configuration disables the ftp, telnet, shell, login, exec, comsat, talk, uucp, and finger services in *etc/inetd.conf*:

```
#ftp      stream  tcp    nowait  root    /usr/sbin/in.ftpd      in.ftpd -1
#telnet   stream  tcp    nowait  root    /usr/sbin/in.telnetd   in.telnetd
#shell    stream  tcp    nowait  root    /usr/sbin/in.rshd      in.rshd
#login    stream  tcp    nowait  root    /usr/sbin/in.rlogind   in.rlogind
#exec     stream  tcp    nowait  root    /usr/sbin/in.rexecd    in.rexecd
#comsat   dgram   udp    wait    root    /usr/sbin/in.comsat    in.comsat
#talk     dgram   udp    wait    root    /usr/sbin/in.talkd     in.talkd
#uucp     stream  tcp    nowait  root    /usr/sbin/in.uucpd     in.uucpd
#finger   stream  tcp    nowait  nobody  /usr/sbin/in.fingerd   in.fingerd
```

By default, many of these services will be commented out already in the standard release. However, you should always verify that the appropriate services have been enabled or disabled after installation.

Similarly, the following configuration enables the ftp, telnet, shell, login, exec, comsat, talk, and uucp services in *etc/services*:

```
ftp           21/tcp
telnet        23/tcp
shell         514/tcp        cmd
login         513/tcp
exec          512/tcp
biff          512/udp        comsat
talk          517/udp
uucp          540/tcp        uucpd
```

Similarly, the following configuration disables the ftp, telnet, shell, login, exec, comsat, talk, uucp, and finger services in */etc/services*:

```
#ftp                21/tcp
#telnet             23/tcp
#shell              514/tcp         cmd
#login              513/tcp
#exec               512/tcp
#biff               512/udp         comsat
#talk               517/udp
#uucp               540/tcp         uucpd
#finger  stream  tcp      nowait   nobody  /usr/sbin/in.fingerd   in.fingerd
```

1-Minute Drill

● What database defines services in Solaris?

● What configuration file specifies the services enabled by inetd?

● What port does FTP run on?

Project 18-1: Removing Service Definitions

This project shows you how to remove service definitions for the ftp service. This is important to ensure that ftp services cannot be run where Secure Copy (scp) is provided as a secure alternative.

Step-by-Step

1. Edit the */etc/services* file:

```
# vi /etc/services
```

2. Insert a hash symbol (#) as the first character of the line containing the ftp entry:

```
#ftp                21/tcp
```

3. Edit the */etc/inetd.conf* file:

```
# vi /etc/inetd.conf
```

● /etc/services
● /etc/inetd.conf
● port 21

4. Insert a hash symbol (#) as the first character of the line containing the ftp entry:

```
# ftp  stream  tcp  nowait  root  /usr/sbin/in.ftpd  in.ftpd -l
```

5. Send a SIGHUP to inetd (assuming inetd has PID of 256):

```
# kill -1 256
```

18

Summary

After removing the appropriate service definitions, the `kill` command should be used to restart inetd without FTP support.

18.2 Filter IP Packets

The basic idea behind many firewall products is to "filter" the IP packets that arrive at a router, selectively permit them to be processed by the kernel, and then passed through the router or explicitly rejected. This is useful for allowing external users to send mail on port 25, or retrieve Web pages on port 80, while preventing secure shell access on port 22. Conversely, IP packets that arrive from behind a firewall may also be blocked on specific ports. This allows local users to ping external hosts, or establish an FTP connection to a remote archive, while preventing them from using services that are not sanctioned. Firewall systems are also available for both Microsoft Windows and Linux systems: while the former tend to be GUI-oriented, such as Checkpoint's Firewall-1 (**http://www.checkpoint.com/**), Linux firewalls are typically configured from the command line. An example is the IP Filter program, available from **http://cheops.anu.edu.au/~avalon/ip-filter.html**, which works with both Solaris and Linux. Note that in order to operate as a firewall and router, a system must have two network interfaces installed and configured.

The best system for users who are new to Solaris is Sun's own SunScreen firewall (**http://www.sun.com/software/securenet/lite/download.html**). It comes in both a free and a commercial edition, with the latter more than adequate for protecting small networks. The current release version for SPARC is 3.1, which supports Gigabit Ethernet, SNMP management, and direct editing of security policy tables. However, it does not currently support IPv6. The firewall may be administered locally or remotely by using a secure session.

There are several important limitations that are placed on the Lite version of SunScreen:

- It is designed to work with a system that is already acting as a router (if it wasn't, why would you want SunScreen anyway?).

- It does not operate in the special "stealth" mode employed by the commercial edition.

- It does not support any of the High Availability features of the commercial version.

- It does not support more than two network interfaces. However, as most routers only have two interfaces, this should not be an issue for small networks.

- It does not provide support for proxying.

SunScreen can be operated in either GUI mode, through a standard Web browser such as Netscape, or by directly editing the system's configuration files. It is easy to install using the Web Start Wizard, which is provided with the installation package.

To install the software, you need to run the */opt/SUNWicg/SunScreen/bin/ss_install* script. There are several options that need to be configured for SunScreen to operate as desired:

- Routing or stealth mode operation

- Local or remote administration

- Restrictive, secure, or permissive security level

- Support for DNS resolution

After choosing the appropriate option for your system, the following message will be displayed:

```
--Adding interfaces & interface addresses
--Initialize 'vars' databases
--Initialize 'authuser' & 'proxyuser' databases
--Initialize 'logmacro' database
--Applying edits
```

```
--Activating configuration
loading skip keystore.
Successfully initialized certificate database in /etc/skip/certdb
starting skip key manager daemon.
Configuration activated successfully on cassowary.
Reboot the machine now for changes to take effect.
```

After rebooting the system, the firewall software will be loaded into the kernel, and you will then need to add rules to the firewall, by using your browser to set the appropriate administration options. Figure 18-1 shows the browser starting on port 3852 on the localhost.

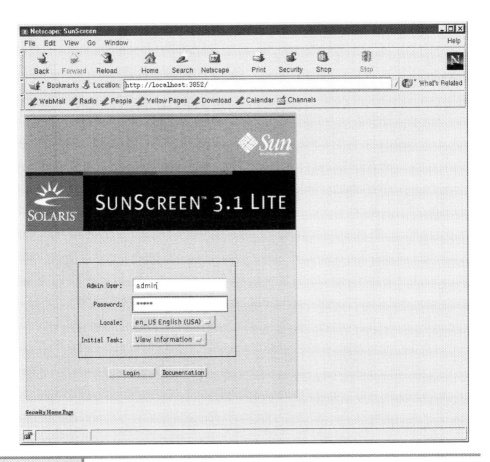

Figure 18-1   Starting the SunScreen administrative interface

When first installed, the SunScreen username and password will be admin and admin, respectively. These should be entered into the Admin User and Password fields. After clicking the Login button, the SunScreen Information page is displayed, as shown in Figure 18-2. There are several options available at this point: firewall logs may be viewed, as may connection statistics. However, most users will want to create a set of security policies immediately upon starting the firewall service.

Security policies are based on rules that either ALLOW or DENY a packet to be transmitted from a source to a destination address. Alternatively, an address

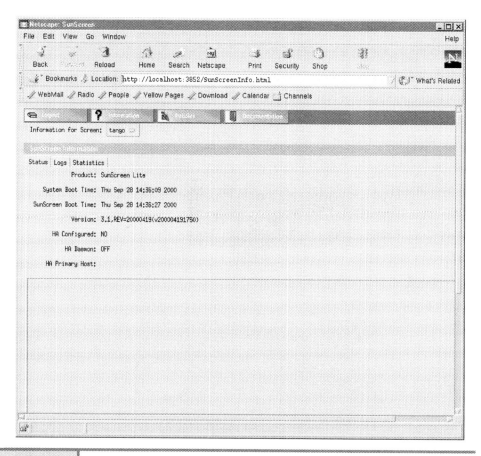

Figure 18-2 SunScreen Information interface

class may be specified by using wildcards. The main actions associated with ALLOW rules are listed here:

LOG_NONE   LOG_SUMMARY   LOG_DETAIL   SNMP_NONE   SNMP

The main actions associated with DENY rules are listed here:

LOG_NONE	LOG_SUMMARY	LOG_DETAIL
SNMP_NONE	SNMP	ICMP_NONE
ICMP_NET_UNREACHABLE	ICMP_HOST_UNREACHABLE	ICMP_PORT_UNREACHABLE
ICMP_NET_FORBIDDEN	ICMP_HOST_FORBIDDEN	

Figure 18-3 shows how to define a rule with actions for the SMTP service, which is operated by Sendmail. This allows mail to be transferred from local users to remote hosts. However, if we wanted to block all mail being sent to and from our network, we could create a DENY action within the rule for the SMTP service. The rule could be applied selectively to specific local subnets or remote destinations. Another useful feature is the ability to apply rules only for specific time periods. For example, if you worked in a bank, you could prevent all e-mails from being sent externally after 5 P.M. at night and before 9 A.M. in the morning.

Once the new rule has been entered, it can be viewed on the Policy Rules panel, along with any other rules, as shown in Figure 18-4. The panel allows new rules to be added, and existing rules to be edited, moved, or deleted. For each packet filtering rule, the service, source address, destination address, action time frame, and name are shown.

When a new firewall configuration is activated, the configuration is verified and if successfully installed, a status message, as shown in Figure 18-5, will be displayed. Clicking the More button will provide more details of the configuration change.

SunScreen performs more than just packet filtering—it can be used to set up a virtual private network (VPN), and can perform advanced Network Address Translation (NAT) functions.

18.3 Perform Security Audits

After installing a new Solaris system, or after inheriting an old Solaris system, one of the first tasks that should be conducted is a security audit. The audit should conform to the local site security policy (there is a security policy, right?).

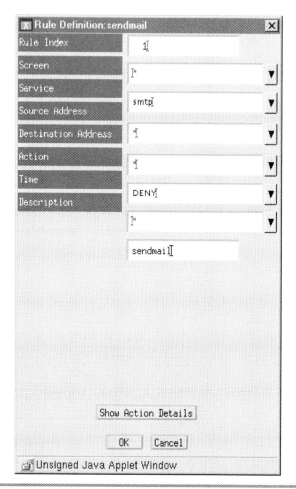

Figure 18-3   Rule definition

A typical security policy might specify the services that are allowed to run from your server, and prohibit the running of any other services. Often, the security policy will be determined by the requirements of your Internet service provider (ISP), since the security of their network ultimately depends on the security of local hosts.

A security audit should first examine what services are being offered, and determine an action plan based on services that should be disabled. In addition,

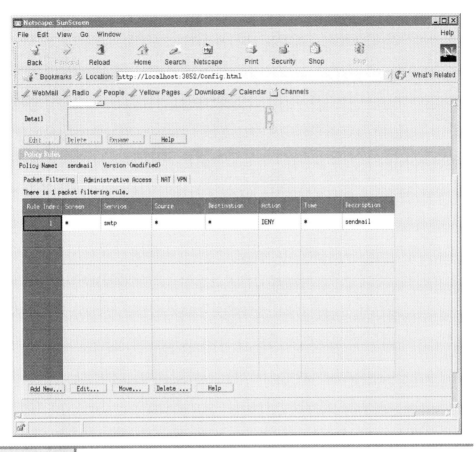

Figure 18-4   Policy Rules interface

monitoring and logging solutions should be installed for services that are sanctioned, so that it is possible at all times to determine what activity is occurring on any service. For example, a denial of service attack may involve hitting a specific port (such as port 80, the Web server port) with a large number of packets, aimed at reducing overall performance of the Web server and the host system. If you don't have logs of all this activity, it will be difficult to determine why your system performance is slow and/or where any potential attacks have originated. The final phase of a security audit involves comparing the current list of services running on the system to the security bulletins that

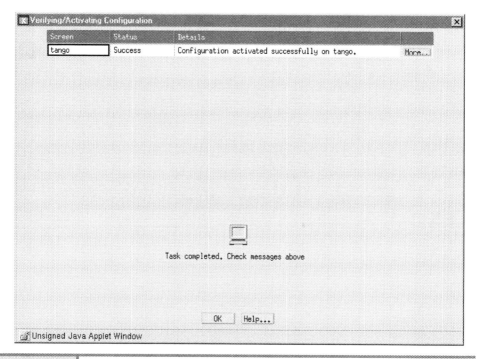

Figure 18-5 Configuration change confirmation

are released by the Computer Emergency Response Team (CERT) (**http://www
.cert.org/**), and similar computer security groups. After determining the versions
of software running on your system, you should determine which packages
require patching and/or upgrading in order to eliminate the risks from known
vulnerabilities.

Introducing SAINT

As you can guess from this "to do" list, running a security audit and implementing
solutions based on the audit can be time-consuming tasks. Fortunately, there
are a number of tools available that can significantly reduce the amount of time
required to conduct security audits, and cross-check existing applications with
known security holes. One of these programs is called SAINT, which is freely
available from World Wide Digital Security at **http://www.wwdsi.com/saint/**.

18

SAINT, currently in version 3.0, is the Security Administrator's Integrated Network Tool, and is based in part on an earlier auditing tool known as SATAN. Both SATAN and SAINT have the ability to scan all of your system services, and identify potential and/or known vulnerabilities. These are classified according to their risk: some items may be critical, requiring immediate attention, while other items may come in the form of suggestions rather than requirements. For example, while many local services are vulnerable to a buffer overflow, where the fixed boundaries on an array are deliberately overwritten by a remote client to "crash" the system, other issues, such as the use of "r" remote access commands, may be risky but acceptable in suitably protected local area networks. Thus, SAINT is not prescriptive in all cases, and suggested actions are always to be performed at the discretion of the local administrator.

Some administrators are concerned that using programs like SAINT actually contributes to cracking and system break-ins, because they provide a ready-made toolkit that can be used to identify system weaknesses in preparation for a break-in. However, if sites devote the necessary resources to monitoring system usage and identifying potential security threats, the risk posed by SAINT is minimal (particularly if its "suggestions" are acted upon). Indeed, World Wide Digital Security actually use a Web version of SAINT (called WebSAINT) as the basis for security consulting. For a fee, they will conduct a comprehensive security audit of your network from the perspective of a remote (rather than a local) user. This can be very useful when attempting to identify potential weaknesses in your frontline systems, such as routers, gateways, and Web servers.

In this section we will examine how to install and configure the SAINT program, and run an audit on a newly installed Solaris 9 system. This will reveal many of the common issues that arise when Solaris is installed out of the box. Most of these issues are covered by CERT advisories (**http://www.cert.org/**). CERT is an organization that continually monitors security issues and vulnerabilities, and raises the alarm when they are identified. Sun often releases patches very soon after a CERT vulnerability is discovered on shipped Solaris products. For example, a patch is available for a well-known vulnerability existing in the Berkeley Internet Daemon (BIND) package, which matches IP addresses with fully qualified domain names (**http://www.cert.org/advisories/CA-99-14-bind.html**). However, some CERT advisories are of a more general nature, since no specific code fix will solve the problem. One example is the identification of a distributed denial of service system known as "Stacheldraht," which combines the processing power and network resources of a group of systems (that are geographically distributed) and can prevent Web servers from serving pages to clients (**http://www.cert.org/advisories/CA-2000-01.html**). CERT releases advisories on a regular basis, so it's advisable to keep up-to-date with all current security issues by reading their news.

One of the great strengths of the SAINT system is that it has an extensive catalog of CERT advisories and in-depth explanations of what each CERT advisory means for the local system. Every SAINT vulnerability is associated with a CVE number that matches descriptions of each security issue from the Common Vulnerabilities and Exposures database (**http://cve.mitre.org/**). Each identified vulnerability contains a hyperlink back to the CVE database, so that information displayed about every issue is updated directly from the source. New patches and bug fixes are also listed.

SAINT has the ability to identify security issues for the following services:

- Domain Name Service (DNS), which is responsible for mapping the fully qualified domain name of Internet hosts to a machine-friendly IP address. In particular, some versions of the Berkeley Internet Daemon (BIND), commonly used for DNS resolution, are susceptible to vulnerabilities.

- File Transfer Program (FTP), which allows remote users to retrieve files from the local file system, has historically been associated with serious daemon buffer overflow problems.

- Internet Message Access Protocol (IMAP), which supports advanced e-mail exchange facilities between mail clients and mail servers, also has buffer overflow issues that have previously allowed remote users to execute privileged commands arbitrarily on the mail server.

- Network File System (NFS) service, which shares disk partitions to remote client systems, is often misconfigured to provide world read access to all shared volumes, when this access should only be granted to specific users.

- Network Information Service (NIS), which is a distributed network service that shares maps of users, groups, and passwords between hosts to minimize administrative overheads, can be compromised if a rogue user can detect the NIS service operating.

● Sendmail mail transport agent (MTA), which once allowed Solaris commands to be embedded within e-mails, and these commands were executed without authentication on the server side.

SAINT works by systematically scanning ports for services that have well-known weaknesses, and then reporting these weaknesses back to the user. In addition, it runs a large number of password checks for default passwords on system accounts, or accounts that often have no password. SAINT checks all of the services and weaknesses that it knows about, and the database of known exploits grows with each new release. SAINT also tests the susceptibility of your system to denial of service attacks, where a large number of large-sized packets are directed to a specific port on your system. This tactic is typically used against Web servers, and some high-profile cases in recent years have highlighted the inherent weakness of networked systems that allow traffic on specific ports without some kind of regulation. Many of the system daemons checked by SAINT will have a so-called "buffer overflow" problem, where a system may be compromised because memory is overwritten with arbitrary values outside the declared size of an array. In this context, "compromised" means that a buffer overflow may allow a rogue user to overtake the executing process and/or gain root privileges. Without appropriate bounds checking, passing a GET request to a Web server of 1,025 bytes when the array size is 1,024 would clearly result in unpredictable behavior, as the C language does not prevent a program from doing this. Since Solaris daemons are typically written in C, a number have been fixed in recent years to prevent this problem from occurring (but you may be surprised at just how often new weaknesses are exposed).

1-Minute Drill

● What is the purpose of a security audit?
● How does SAINT work?
● What is a buffer overflow attack?

● To determine an action plan based on services that should be disabled.
● Systematically scans ports for services that have well-known exploits.
● Memory is overwritten with arbitrary values outside the declared size of an array in a daemon.

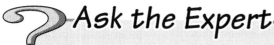

Ask the Expert

Question: What should I do if a security vulnerability, such as a buffer overflow, is identified, but a patch is not yet available from Sun?

Answer: You should disable the daemon until a patch is released. While this may inconvenience your users, it's important to prevent these attacks because they can give root access to intruders.

18.4 Install SAINT

The latest release of SAINT may be downloaded from **http://www.wwdsi.com/ saint/**. To build SAINT, you will need to install the GNU C compiler and GNU assembler. The Perl interpreter and Netscape Web browser supplied with Solaris 9 are also required. After downloading and unpacking the source, preinstallation configuration can be performed with the following command:

```
# ./configure
```

The configuration program will check that you have all of the necessary software to run SAINT on your local system, including a C compiler, socket libraries, ANSI C header files, Perl, and RPC commands:

```
loading cache ./config.cache
checking for gcc... (cached) gcc
checking whether the C compiler (gcc  ) works... yes
checking whether the C compiler (gcc  ) is a cross-compiler... no
checking whether we are using GNU C... (cached) yes
checking whether gcc accepts -g... (cached) yes
checking for a BSD compatible install... ./install-sh -c
checking whether make sets ${MAKE}... (cached) yes
checking for main in -lPW... (cached) no
checking for main in -lX11_s... (cached) no
checking for main in -lXm_s... (cached) no
checking for main in -lXt_s... (cached) no
checking for main in -lc_s... (cached) no
checking for main in -lnsl... (cached) yes
checking for main in -lresolv... (cached) yes
```

18

```
checking for main in -lrpc... (cached) no
checking for rpc socket compatibility... yes
checking for runtime linkage option... yes
checking for main in -lsocket... (cached) yes
checking for getpwnam in -lsun... (cached) no
checking for +DAportable... no
checking how to run the C preprocessor... (cached) gcc -E
checking for linux/limits.h... (cached) no
checking for /usr/src/linux... no
checking for ANSI C header files... (cached) yes
checking for uid_t in sys/types.h... (cached) yes
checking type of array argument to getgroups... (cached) gid_t
checking if sys_errlist is declared... no
checking if system netinet headers work... yes
checking for rpcgen... (cached) /usr/bin/rpcgen
creating ./config.status
creating Makefile
Reconfiguring...
Checking to make sure all the targets are here...
Trying to find Perl... /usr/local/bin/perl5.00503
Changing the source in PERL scripts...
Trying to find HTML/WWW browser...
Looking for UNIX commands...
Found /bin/remsh; using this instead of rsh
Can't find nmap
Can't find nmblookup
Can't find smbclient
Doing substitutions on the shell scripts...
Changing paths in config/paths.pl...
Changing paths in config/paths.sh...
```

Although some programs, such as the samba daemons (smbd and nmbd) and nmap are not installed, this will not prevent SAINT from running. After configuration has been completed, the scripts *config/paths.pl* and *config/paths.sh* will be updated with the new settings. The binaries may then be built by using the command

```
# make
```

The sources will then be compiled by using the C compiler and the *make* utility:

```
# make
make[1]: Entering directory `/tmp/saint-3.0'
```

```
cd src/misc; make "LIBS=-L/usr/ucblib -R/usr/ucblib
-lrpcsvc -lrpcsoc  -lnsl -lresolv -lsocket" "
XFLAGS=-g -O2   -DSTDC_HEADERS=1 -DGETGROUPS_T=
gid_t " "RPCGEN=/usr/bin/rpcgen"
make[2]: Entering directory `/tmp/saint-3.0/src/misc'
gcc -O -I. -g -O2   -DSTDC_HEADERS=1 -DGETGROUPS_T=gid_t
    -c md5.c -o md5.o
gcc -O -I. -g -O2   -DSTDC_HEADERS=1 -DGETGROUPS_T=gid_t
    -c md5c.c -o md5c.o
gcc -O -I. -g -O2   -DSTDC_HEADERS=1 -DGETGROUPS_T=
gid_t  -o ../../bin/md5 md5.o md5c.o
gcc -O -I. -g -O2   -DSTDC_HEADERS=1 -DGETGROUPS_T=
gid_t  -o ../../bin/sys_socket sys_socket.c
gcc -O -I. -g -O2   -DSTDC_HEADERS=1 -DGETGROUPS_T=
gid_t  -o ../../bin/timeout timeout.c
gcc -O -I. -g -O2   -DSTDC_HEADERS=1 -DGETGROUPS_T=
gid_t  -o ../../bin/rcmd rcmd.c -L/usr/ucblib -R/usr/ucblib
 -lrpcsvc -lrpcsoc  -lnsl -lresolv -lsocket
gcc -O -I. -g -O2   -DSTDC_HEADERS=1 -DGETGROUPS_T=
gid_t  -o ../../bin/safe_finger safe_finger.c
/usr/bin/rpcgen rex.x 2>/dev/null
gcc -O -I. -g -O2   -DSTDC_HEADERS=1 -DGETGROUPS_T=gid_t
    -c rex.c -o rex.o
gcc -O -I. -g -O2   -DSTDC_HEADERS=1 -DGETGROUPS_T=
gid_t   -c rex_xdr.c -o rex_xdr.o
. . . .
```

All of the source files will be built during this phase. If the build is successful, you should see the following lines at the end of the display:

```
$MOSAIC="/opt/netscape/netscape";
$TCP_SCAN="bin/tcp_scan";
$FTP_SCAN="bin/ftp-scan";
$UDP_SCAN="bin/udp_scan";
$FPING="bin/fping";
$NFS_CHK="bin/nfs-chk";
$YP_CHK="bin/yp-chk";
$SAFE_FINGER="bin/safe_finger";
$MD5="bin/md5";
$SYS_SOCKET="bin/sys_socket";
```

When you're building cross-platform applications like SAINT, you may well see some warnings generated by the compiler about data types and casts; however, these can usually be ignored. On the other hand, if an error is encountered, you'll need to check your environment and perhaps make a bug report to WDSI. For example, if your LD_LIBRARY_PATH is not set to include the appropriate system library directories, you'll need to update its value in your shell.

After making SAINT successfully, you may also install the man page:

18

```
# make install
mkdir -p /usr/local/man/man1
./install-sh -c -o root -g 0 -m 444 saint.1
/usr/local/man/man1/saint.1
```

At this point, you're ready to begin your SAINT security audit.

The following books are recommended reading for learning more about Solaris security:

- *Solaris Security* by Peter Gregory (published by Prentice Hall, 2000)

- *Applied Cryptography* by Bruce Schneier (published by Wiley, 1996)

Ask the Expert

Question: After performing a security audit, I'm really worried about my system's security. What should I do?

Answer: Read widely and ensure that you install the appropriate security patches as they are released by Sun. Try out some of the standard packages at the COAST archive, which is the most comprehensive security archive on the Internet (**ftp://coast.cs.purdue.edu/pub/tools/unix**). Here, you will find the sources to cryptographic software, replacements for standard daemons, firewalls, intrusion detection systems, security libraries, logging tools, network and password utilities, scanners, and various system utilities. Another good source of tools is Wietse Venema's software repository, available at: **ftp://ftp.porcupine.org/pub/security/index. html#software**. This includes tools such as the Coroner's Toolkit, used for computer forensics; a secure replacement for Sendmail called postfix; TCP wrappers, which are used to log connections to selected network daemons; and a replacement for the standard RPC portmapper.

- *Building Internet Firewalls* by Brent Chapman and Elizabeth Zwicky (published by O'Reilly, 1996)

- *Practical UNIX and Internet Security* by Simon Garfinkel and Gene Spafford (published by O'Reilly, 1996)

18.5 Run SAINT

SAINT can be started by typing the command

```
# ./saint
```

This starts up the Netscape Web browser, with the URL shown in Figure 18-6. The following message is printed in the shell window:

```
Security Administrator's Integrated Network Tool
Portions copyright (C) 2000 World Wide Digital Security, Inc.
Portions copyright (C) 1995 by Satan Developers.
SAINT is starting up...
```

SAINT has several pages, including data management, target selection, data analysis and configuration management. These pages can be visited sequentially in order to conduct your audit. The data management page, shown in Figure 18-7, allows you to create a new SAINT database in which to store the results of your current audit. Alternatively, you may open an existing SAINT database if you have created one previously, and/or merge data from other SAINT scans.

Next, you will need to use the Target Selection page to identify the host system that you wish to scan using SAINT, as shown in Figure 18-8. Here, you need to enter the fully qualified domain name of the host that you wish to scan. Alternatively, if you have a large number of hosts to scan, it may be more useful to create a file containing a list of hosts. This file could then be used by a system behind the firewall to identify locally visible weaknesses, and used by a system external to the firewall to reveal any threats visible to the outside world. You may also elect to scan all hosts in the local area network, which should only be performed after hours as it places a heavy load on network bandwidth.

You also need to select a scanning level option, which includes the following:

- Light scanning, which is difficult to detect

- Normal scanning, which is easy to detect

Figure 18-6 SAINT (Security Administrator's Integrated Network Tool)

- Heavy scanning, which won't crash Windows NT targets

- Heavy+ scanning, which may well crash Windows NT targets

There is a final option that just checks the "top ten" security flaws, as identified by the report at **http://www.sans.org/topten.htm**. These flaws include BIND weaknesses, vulnerable CGI programs, remote procedure call (RPC) weaknesses, Sendmail buffer overflow, mountd, UNIX NFS exports, user IDs (especially root/administrator with no passwords), IMAP and POP buffer overflow vulnerabilities, and SNMP community strings set to public and private.

Figure 18-7 Data Management page

Always remember that attempting to break into a computer system is a criminal offense in many jurisdictions: you should obtain written authorization from the owner of your system before embarking on a security-related exercise of this kind; otherwise, it may be misconstrued as a real attack.

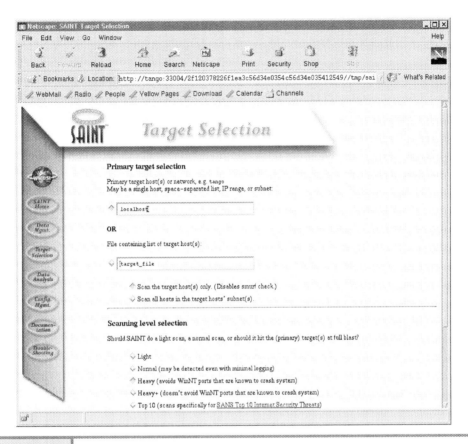

18

| **Figure 18-8** | Target Selection page |

18.6 Interpret SAINT Results

Once the target selection is complete, the data collection process begins by
executing a number of scripts on the server and reporting the results through
the Web browser. Data is collected by testing many different Solaris services,

including ping, finger, RPC, login, rsh, Sendmail, tooltalk, snmp, and rstatd. A number of status messages will appear in the browser window, as shown here:

```
Data collection in progress...
03/28/02-13:43:16 bin/timeout 60 bin/fping cassowary.targethost.com
03/28/02-13:43:16 bin/timeout 20 bin/finger.saint cassowary.targethost.com .PLUS
03/28/02-13:43:16 bin/timeout 20 bin/ostype.saint cassowary.targethost.com .PLUS
03/28/02-13:43:16 bin/timeout 60 bin/udpscan.saint
19,53,69,111,137-139,161-162,177,8999,1-18,20-52,54-68,70-
110,112-136,140-160,163-176,178-1760,1763-2050,32767-33500
cassowary.targethost.com .PLUS
03/28/02-13:43:16 bin/timeout 20 bin/dns.saint cassowary.targethost.com .PLUS
03/28/02-13:43:16 bin/timeout 20 bin/rpc.saint cassowary.targethost.com .PLUS
03/28/02-13:43:16 bin/timeout 60 bin/tcpscan.saint
12754,15104,16660,20432,27665,1-9999
cassowary.targethost.com .PLUS
03/28/02-13:43:17 bin/timeout 20 bin/ddos.saint cassowary.targethost.com .PLUS
03/28/02-13:44:16 bin/timeout 20 bin/rsh.saint cassowary.targethost.com .PLUS
03/28/02-13:44:16 bin/timeout 20 bin/login.saint -o
-u deanna -p deanna telnet cassowary.targethost.com .PLUS
03/28/02-13:44:16 bin/timeout 20 bin/rsh.saint
-u ua_inf0 cassowary.targethost.com .PLUS
03/28/02-13:44:17 bin/timeout 20 bin/login.saint -o
-u ua_de0 telnet cassowary.targethost.com .PLUS
03/28/02-13:44:17 bin/timeout 20 bin/sadmind.saint
SunOS 5.9 cassowary.targethost.com .PLUS
03/28/02-13:44:17 bin/timeout 20 bin/login.saint -o
-u ua_os8 telnet cassowary.targethost.com .PLUS
03/28/02-13:44:17 bin/timeout 20 bin/rsh.saint -u
root cassowary.targethost.com .PLUS
03/28/02-13:44:18 bin/timeout 20 bin/login.saint -o -u
ua_de4 telnet cassowary.targethost.com .PLUS
03/28/02-13:44:19 bin/timeout 20 bin/login.saint -o -u
uaprod -p uaprod telnet cassowary.targethost.com .PLUS
```

SAINT uses several different modules to probe vulnerabilities in the system, including tcpscan, udpscan, and ddos, which scan for TCP, UDP, and denial of service issues, respectively. In addition, a number of well-known username and password combinations are also attempted in order to break into an account—you would imagine that root/root would never be used as a username and password combination, but it does happen.

Once all of the data has been collected, the results of the scan are then displayed on the reporting and analysis (Data Analysis) page, as shown in Figure 18-9. It is possible to list vulnerabilities by their danger level, by the type of vulnerability, or by the number of vulnerabilities in a specific category. Most administrators will want to deal with the most dangerous vulnerabilities, so the first option should be selected. In addition, it is possible to view information about the target system by class of service, the type of system, the domain name, the subnet, and by hostname.

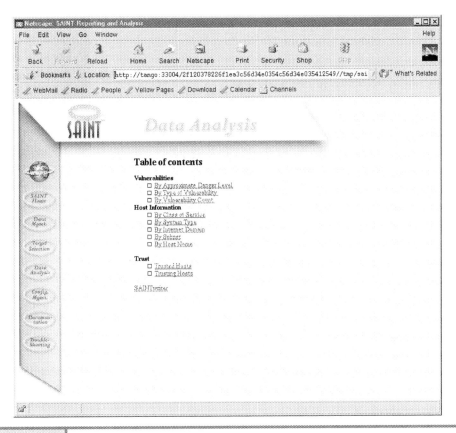

| **Figure 18-9** | Reporting and analysis |

18.7 Identify Vulnerabilities

Vulnerabilities are listed in terms of danger level: there are critical problems, areas of concern, and potential problems, as shown in Figure 18-10. For the local host cassowary, which was a standard Solaris install out of the box, two critical problems were identified—both associated with gaining root access via buffer overflow:

- The CDE-based Calendar Manager service may be vulnerable to a buffer overflow attack, as identified in CVE 1999-0320 and 1999-0696.

The Calendar Manager is used to manage appointments and other date/time based functions.

● The remote administration daemon (sadmind) may be vulnerable to a buffer overflow attack, a described in CVE 1999-0977. The remote administration daemon is used to manage system administration activities across a number of different hosts.

There were also two areas of concern identified, with information gathering vulnerabilities exposed:

● The finger daemon returned personal information about users that could be used to stage an attack. For example, the home directory, full name, and project were displayed (CVE 1999-0612).

● The remote users list daemon was active, providing a list of users on the system to any remote user (CVE 1999-0626). Like the finger daemon, information gathered from the ruserd could be used to stage an attack.

Two possible vulnerabilities were identified:

● The chargen program is vulnerable to UDP flooding used in denial of service attacks, such as Fraggle (CVE 1999-0103).

● The Sendmail server allows mail relaying, which may be used by remote users to forward mail using the server. This makes it easy for companies promoting SPAM to make it appear as if their mail originated from your server.

Six recommendations were made to limit Internet access, including stopping all of the "r" services: these make it easy for a remote user to execute commands on the local system, such as spawning a shell or obtaining information about system load, but have been used in the past to break into systems. In addition, some Sendmail commands (such as EXPN and VRFY) are allowed by the Sendmail configuration: this allows remote users to obtain a list of all users on the current system, which is often the first step to obtaining their passwords.

If you are concerned that a rogue user may be using SAINT against your network, you may download and run one of the many SAINT-detecting programs,

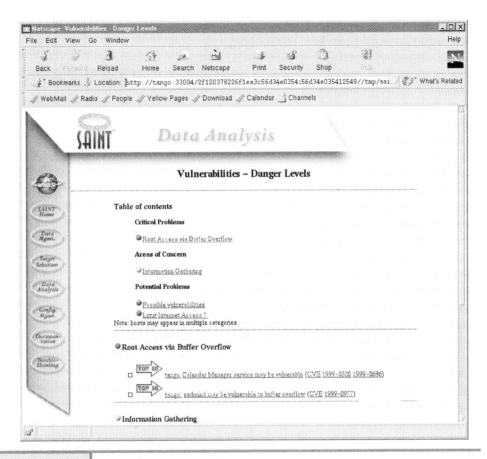

18

Figure 18-10 Identifying vulnerabilities

such as Courtney (**http://ciac.llnl.gov/ciac/ToolsUnixNetMon.html#Courtney**).
Courtney monitors TCP traffic to determine whether or not a single remote
machine is systematically scanning the ports within a specified time frame.
Obviously, this program is useful for detecting all kinds of port scanning, not
just SAINT.

☑ *Mastery Check*

1. What of the following are *not* actions associated with ALLOW rules in the SunScreen Firewall?

   A. LOG_NONE

   B. LOG_MANY

   C. SNMP_NONE

   D. LOG_SUMMARY

2. Which of the following services is *not* tested for vulnerabilities by SAINT?

   A. Network Information Service (NIS)

   B. Sendmail

   C. Network File System (NFS)

   D. Simple Object Access Protocol (SOAP)

3. What file contains the services database?

   A. */etc/services.db*

   B. */etc/services*

   C. */etc/db.services*

   D. */etc/inetd.conf*

4. What file contains the inetd configuration?

   A. */etc/services.db*

   B. */etc/services*

   C. */etc/db.services*

   D. */etc/inetd.conf*

5. What is the main purpose of a firewall?

   A. To cache Internet documents

   B. To provide proxying services

Mastery Check

     C. To filter packets

     D. To limit the number of Web connections

6. What feature does SunScreen 3.1 *not* provide?

     A. Gigabit Ethernet

     B. IPv6

     C. SNMP management

     D. Direct editing of security policy tables

7. To block FTP traffic at the firewall, which TCP port should be disabled?

     A. 21

     B. 23

     C. 514

     D. 513

8. To block Telnet traffic at the firewall, which TCP port should be disabled?

     A. 21

     B. 23

     C. 514

     D. 513

9. To block shell traffic at the firewall, which TCP port should be disabled?

     A. 21

     B. 23

     C. 514

     D. 513

☑ Mastery Check

10. To block login traffic at the firewall, which TCP port should be disabled?

    A. 21

    B. 23

    C. 514

    D. 513

11. To block exec traffic at the firewall, which TCP port should be disabled?

    A. 512

    B. 513

    C. 517

    D. 540

12. To block biff traffic at the firewall, which UDP port should be disabled?

    A. 512

    B. 513

    C. 517

    D. 540

13. To block talk traffic at the firewall, which UDP port should be disabled?

    A. 512

    B. 513

    C. 517

    D. 540

14. To block uucp traffic at the firewall, which TCP port should be disabled?

    A. 512

    B. 513

☑ *Mastery Check*

    C. 517

    D. 540

15. Which of the following is *not* required to build SAINT?

    A. C compiler

    B. Socket libraries

    C. ANSI C header files

    D. GNOME libraries

18

Part 5

Managing Intranet Services

Module 19

Samba

Critical Skills

Interoperability between Solaris and other operating systems continues to be a barrier to the more widespread adoption of UNIX services at the workgroup level. For example, while many workgroups would like to make use of the reliable and high-capacity RAID-based file systems available through Solaris servers, the file system must be viewable through Windows Explorer. In addition, users often wish to share printers between Solaris and non-Solaris systems. Although Sun provides Network File System (NFS) services to share Solaris volumes to clients, the installation of a third-party PC-NFS product on potentially thousands of clients is not an attractive proposition.

Fortunately, one product uses the native Windows file sharing protocol (the Session Message Block protocol, or SMB) to export disk volumes to Windows clients: that product is Samba. The two advantages that Samba has over competing products are its maturity (more than 10 years of continual development and refinement) and its cost (free). Until recently, Samba was not released as part of the standard Solaris distribution—administrators had to download and install Samba separately. However, beginning with the release of Solaris 9, the distribution includes Samba 2, which offers many more features than the original Samba 1 system, including the fastest SMB file serving benchmark recorded at the time of release (193 Mbps). Samba 2 also offers complete integration into the Window NT domain authentication system.

This module will examine how to configure Samba on Solaris to provide reliable file and print services for Windows clients.

19.1 Learn Samba Concepts

In the age of fat client PCs with massive amounts of storage available—sometimes in the hundreds of megabytes—why would anyone need to use centralized storage on a server? Many good reasons could be cited for eschewing local storage of important files on clients, and several competing architectures are available. For example, Sun has released a very thin client called a Sun Ray, which provides nothing more than a high-resolution terminal for a central Solaris server. Is this harking back to the days of terminal-based computing? Possibly, although with the benefits of having to maintain software and user databases on only one server system instead of hundreds of clients, the cost benefits can be enormous. In addition, client systems generally do not have a backup device attached, meaning that many key documents created by users in organizations are subject to hard-disk failure; in recognizing that individual disks do have a mean time to failure (MTTF), Solaris provides RAID support through Veritas Volume Manager, which enables a system to continue serving files even during a disk failure.

The hot-swappable disk bays of Solaris servers also allow disks to be replaced while the system is up, and disks can be brought online without a reboot. This is just not possible with a client PC. While some may argue that files can be backed up from PCs to a central server, the network bandwidth required to do this is large where a lot of PCs require networked backups— it is ultimately more efficient in terms of network capacity simply to store files centrally and ensure that they are highly available and regularly backed up.

Solaris is not alone in providing centralized file serving facilities; Windows also provides similar services. Pitched against Sun's NFS product is the Windows file serving system based on SMB. While Solaris and Windows both support TCP/IP networking, each operating system has developed its own file-sharing system. This is largely because of the differences in file system structure and user authentication between the two systems. However, the adoption of common authentication systems, such as Kerberos, may see a future integration of file-sharing technologies. For the present, however, Windows provides no support for NFS, and Solaris provides no native support for serving files using SMB. That's where Samba comes in, because it runs on Solaris and yet supports SMB file sharing and the NetBIOS name lookup protocol, which is used by Windows as a name service.

When Windows users check their Network Neighborhood, they don't see hosts that have been looked up using the Domain Name System (DNS); they see hosts that are located using NetBIOS. The fact that many of these hosts also have a DNS name that matches the NetBIOS name is coincidental. Typically, a Windows user locates file-sharing hosts using Explorer and then maps exported volumes to a local drive letter. For example, the host *DANISH* may export a drive with the name *pastry*, giving a path *DANISH\PASTRY* that a client can map to a local drive letter, such as *E*:. This allows local applications to read and write data to remote server volumes as if they were local devices. When located within a Windows NT domain, user authentication and access rights can be applied using the Security Access Manager, which provides a high level of file security. In addition to being able to mount remote volumes, printers that are attached to a remote Windows system may also be mounted locally, and print jobs can be submitted and monitored using the local Printer Control Panel.

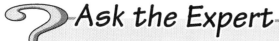
Ask the Expert

Question: I love NFS. Why should I use Samba?

Answer: If you have to support only UNIX and Linux clients, NFS is natively supported. However, if you have to support Windows clients, NFS support is a pain to maintain.

Question: But if Samba is so good, why does Sun supply NFS?

Answer: Sun also supplies Samba with the Solaris 9 distribution. NFS is still useful in a UNIX environment.

Samba Services

To provide Windows file sharing services, Samba supports two daemons: the smbd, which implements all of the file sharing operations, and nmbd, which provides support for NetBIOS naming. Since the Explorer and Network Neighborhood do not support DNS, NetBIOS support is crucial for allowing clients to find a Samba server! While smbd is spawned multiple times in response to client requests, only one instance of nmbd should be spawned on each server.

19.2 Manage nmbd

To support the NetBIOS name lookup protocol, nmbd runs on the standard port 137, responding to reqterm and issuing its own requests where necessary. It is also possible to use nmbd to support WINS (Windows Internet Name Server) services.

When running a Windows file server, reviewing NetBIOS naming status is easy from the Windows command line. The following command, executed on the NT server DELTA, displays a list of all clients that are currently using a shared volume:

```
C:\> \WINNT\SYSTEM32\nbtstat -s
                NetBIOS Connection Table

Local Name   State         In/Out   Remote Host      Input    Output
----------------------------------------------------------------------
DELTA <00>   Connected     Out      KAPPA <20>       201KB    121KB
DELTA <00>   Connected     Out      BETA  <20>       2MB      3MB
DELTA <00>   Connected     Out      ALPHA <20>       154KB    999KB
```

This printout shows three client systems accessing shares from DELTA: KAPPA, with 202KB transferred in and 121KB transferred out; BETA, with 2MB transferred in and 3MB transferred out; and ALPHA, with 154KB transferred in, and 999KB transferred out. The files that are currently opened by each client are not listed. It is also possible to check which hosts are currently responding to NetBIOS requests within the local NT domain by issuing the following command:

```
C:\> \WINNT\SYSTEM32>net view
Server Name                Remark

------------------------------------------------
\\DELTA                    Server
\\KAPPA                    Joe Bloggs
\\BETA                     Jane Doe
\\ALPHA                    Jack Russell
\\OMEGA                    Mail server
\\TANGO                    Web Server
The command completed successfully.
```

The equivalent command in Samba is the nmblookup command. By using nmblookup, different domains can be queried for the hosts that support NetBIOS. For example, to check the hosts in the BIOS workgroup, the following command could be used:

```
$ nmblookup BIOS
querying BIOS on 205.43.31.255
205.43.25.197 BIOS<00>
205.43.25.1 BIOS<00>
205.43.25.29 BIOS<00>
205.43.25.7 BIOS<00>
205.43.25.184 BIOS<00>
205.43.25.9 BIOS<00>
```

To start the nmbd server from the command line, the following command could be used:

```
# /usr/local/samba/bin/nmbd -D
```

While it is possible to run nmbd through the Internet super daemon (inetd), this is not recommended for performance reasons.

1-Minute Drill

- What is Samba?
- How is Samba different from NFS?
- What command is used to check the status of Samba?

19.3 Manage smbd

The smbd server is usually started from a script in */etc/init.d*, but it can also be started from the command line using the following command:

```
# /usr/local/samba/bin/smbd -D
```

Like nmbd, it is possible to run Samba from the inetd, but this is not recommended. The main configuration file for samba is *smb.conf*, which is usually located in the *lib* subdirectory of the samba installation directory. An entry must be made in *smb.conf* for each file system that is to be exported by the server. A typical *smb.conf* file is shown here:

```
[global]
workgroup = BIOS
netbios name = ALPHA
server string = Solaris Samba Server V2.2.0
interfaces = 205.43.31.1
security = SHARE
log file = /usr/local/samba/log/log.%m
max log size = 1024
socket options = TCP_NODELAY SO_RCVBUF=8192 SO_SNDBUF=8192
dns proxy = Yes
guest account = guest
hosts allow = localhost, 205.43.31.1/255.255.255.0

[printers]
```

- A service that enables sharing of Solaris volumes using the Microsoft SMB protocol.
- Samba allows Windows users to mount Solaris exported volumes natively. NFS requires Windows users to install and run third-party software to mount Solaris exported volumes.
- smbstatus

```
comment = Epson Laser Printer
path = /var/spool/hp
print ok = Yes
browseable = Yes

[homes]
comment = Alpha Exported Home Directories
read only = No
browseable = Yes

[temporary]
comment = Temporary Directories
read only = No
browseable = Yes
path = /tmp
```

This *smb.conf* file has four sections defined: the global section, which sets up server-wide parameters, such as TCP socket options and network interface IP addresses; the printers section, which contains an entry for a shared printer; the homes section, which enables home directories to be exported (much like the NFS automounter); and the temporary section, which defines temporary file space.

Project 19-1: Checking Client Access

This project shows you how to verify that a Samba server is available for Windows clients by running a local client. This is an important procedure to use when clients experience difficulty in connecting to a Samba server.

Step-by-Step

1. Make a connection to the server and verify that it is available:

```
smbclient -L delta
Added interface ip=205.43.31.1 bcast=205.43.31.255
nmask=255.255.255.0
Domain=[BIOS] OS=[Unix] Server=[Samba 2.2.0]
        Sharename       Type        Comment
        ---------       ----        -------
        temporary       Disk        Temporary Space
        homes           Disk        User Home Directories
        IPC$            IPC         IPC Service (Samba 2.2.0)
```

```
Server             Comment
---------          -------
DELTA              Samba 2.2.0

Workgroup          Master
---------          -------
BIOS               KAPPA
```

2. Attempt to mount a shared volume:

```
smbclient //DELTA/temporary
```

3. Use one the following commands to check that files are accessible from the volume:

- `cd <dir>`   Change working directory
- `dir <dir>`   Display directory contents
- `get <file>`   Retrieve a single file from the server
- `ls <dir>`   Display directory contents
- `mget <files>`   Retrieve multiple files from the server
- `mput <files>`   Store multiple files on the server
- `put <file>`   Store a single file on the server

Summary

The `smbclient` command can be used to verify the status of the Samba server.

19.4 Configure smbd

Many documents at **http://au1.samba.org/samba/docs/** contain all of the possible configuration parameters contained within *smb.conf*. The most commonly used options in the global section include the following:

Option	Description
abort shutdown script	Specifies the script name used for shutdown
add printer command	Allows the Add Printer Wizard to be used to connect to a Samba-shared printer

Option	Description
add share command	Specifies the command used to add a new share
add user script	Specifies the command used to add users to the domain
add machine script	Specifies the command used to add systems to the domain
allow trusted domains	Determines whether external trusted domains are supported
announce as	Allows Samba server to announce itself as a specific Windows version
bind interfaces only	Allows specific network interfaces to be used only for Samba
browse list	Permits client list browsing
change notify timeout	Changes directory scan interval
change share command	Specifies the command used to change an existing share
character set	Maps Solaris character sets to MS-DOS code pages
client code page	Specifies the code page on the client side
code page directory	Specifies directory in which code pages are stored
coding system	Defines mapping for Japanese filenames
config file	Specifies an alternative name for the configuration file
deadtime	Sets time interval that must elapse before a client connection is assumed to be expired
debug hires timestamp	Implements high resolution, millisecond timestamping
debug pid	Records smbd process IDs in the log file
debug timestamp	Allows timestamping to be disabled
default service	Specifies a service to be supplied if the requested service is not available
delete printer command	Specifies a command for deleting a printer definition
delete share command	Specifies the command used to delete an existing share
delete user script	Specifies the command used to delete users from the domain
disable spoolss	Enables Lanman-style printing
dns proxy	Enables DNS proxying
domain admin group	Lists users who belong to the domain admin group
domain guest group	Lists users who belong to the domain guest group
domain logons	Permits access to workgroup members
domain master	Allows nmbd to act as a domain master
encrypt passwords	Specifies that passwords should be encrypted, as required by most versions of Windows NT
enhanced browsing	Enables enhanced browsing of master browsers

Option	Description
getwd cache	Enables caching of working directory lookups
hide local users	Conceals server-side users from clients
hide unreadable	Conceals files that are not accessible by the client
homedir map	Specifies the path to an automount map to support centralized home directories for users
hosts equiv	Specifies the file that contains a list of hosts that are considered equivalent for authentication
interfaces	Specifies which network interfaces should be used by Samba
keepalive	Sets the number of seconds for which a connection should be kept alive; can have a large impact on performance if set too high
lanman auth	Enables Lanman-style authentication
lm announce	Enables Lanman-style broadcasting
lm interval	Sets an interval for Lanman-style broadcasting
load printers	Specifies whether printers defined in the printcap will be exposed by default to browsing
local master	Enables nmbd to assume the master browser role
lock directory	Specifies the local directory for locks to be written
log file	Specifies the path to the log file
log level	Specifies a level for logging that determines how much output is generated
max disk size	Sets a maximum logical size for a shared volume
max log size	Sets a maximum size for a log file
netbios aliases	Allows aliases for the local server to be announced through NetBIOS
netbios name	Sets the local NetBIOS name
nis homedir	Enables support for the automounter
passwd program	Sets the name of the password program on the server side
root directory	Sets the root directory for the server to something different than the installation directory
time offset	Establishes the number of hours to add to GMT to obtain the correct local time
username level	Uses a pattern matching algorithm to match uppercase Windows usernames to mixed and lowercase Solaris usernames
wins proxy	Determines whether or not the server acts as a WINS proxy

19.5 Test smbd Parameters

A useful feature of Samba is the testparm program, which can be used to check the syntax of the *smb.conf* file before trying to start Samba using a modified version. The output is verbose and should be grepped for any errors that show up:

```
$ testparm
Load smb config files from /usr/local/samba/lib/smb.conf
Processing section "[printers]"
Processing section "[homes]"
Loaded services file OK.
WARNING: You have some share names that are longer than 8 chars
These may give errors while browsing or may not be accessible
to some older clients
Press enter to see a dump of your service definitions
```

Here we can see that the definition of the "temporary" volume may cause problems for some clients. Each of the sections are then examined individually to check for errors:

```
# Global parameters
[global]
        workgroup = EASTAUS
        netbios name =
        netbios aliases =
        server string = Samba 2.0.6
        interfaces =
        bind interfaces only = No
        security = USER
        encrypt passwords = Yes
        update encrypted = No
        allow trusted domains = Yes
        hosts equiv =
        min passwd length = 5
        map to guest = Never
        null passwords = No
        password server =
        ...
```

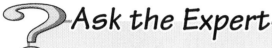

Ask the Expert

Question: How do I troubleshoot Samba?

Answer: With some difficulty. Use ping to check that the client can "see" the server on the network. Check that the nmbd and smbd processes are running on the server. Run `testparm` to check that the configuration file syntax is correct. Use `smbstatus` to check whether some clients can connect but not others. Check that the client has the correct domain or workgroup settings installed.

19.6 Check Samba Status

If the syntax of the *smb.conf* file is verified, and the Samba server is started on port 139, the `smbstatus` command can be used to list all the clients that are accessing volumes on the local server:

```
$ smbstatus
Samba version 2.2.0
Service       uid       gid       pid       machine
-------------------------------------------------
temporary     paul      paul      434       BETA
   Wed Feb 1 10:45:00 2002
homes         paul      paul      435       BETA
Wed Feb 1 10:45:30 2002
homes         john      users     554       GAMMA
Thu Feb 2 00:15:34 2002
temporary     jane      users     234       SIGMA
Wed Feb 1 10:45:30 2002
Locked files:
Pid    DenyMode    R/W         Oplock         Name
-------------------------------------------------
434    DENY_NONE   RDWR        NONE           /tmp/files.txt
      Wed Feb 1 10:51:34 2002
435    DENY_NONE   RDONLY      NONE           /home/paul/secret
      Wed Feb 1 10:56:21 2002
554    DENY_NONE   RDWR        NONE           /home/john/phone
       Thu Feb 2 00:20:34 2002
Share mode memory usage (bytes):
   2096928(99%) free + 112(0%) used + 112(0%)
    overhead = 2097152(100%) total
```

19.7 Troubleshoot smbd

The preceding output shows that the users paul and jane are accessing temporary space, and that paul and john are accessing their home directories. The user identifier (UID), group identifier (GID), and associated process identifier (PID) of each request and user is shown, along with the client hostname and date of connection. Reviewing smbstatus can be useful in troubleshooting clients that cannot connect to a server: if other clients are accessing a share successfully, the fault must lie on the client side or on the connection between client and server, rather than the server itself. In addition to user information, file locking information is also provided. This is also useful in troubleshooting server locking problems, since a Samba client may be using a file, while a user on the server cannot write the file for which a lock is in place. Finally, shared memory usage for the process is displayed, which can be useful for fine tuning the Samba configuration in terms of the number of volumes and users supported.

19

☑ Mastery Check

1. What command is used to run the samba service?

   A. samba

   B. sambad

   C. smbd

   D. sambaservice

2. What command is used to run the NetBIOS naming service?

   A. netbios

   B. nmbd

   C. netbiosd

   D. smbd

☑ *Mastery Check*

3. What command is used to validate the syntax of the Samba configuration file?

   A. `testsamba`

   B. `testnetbios`

   C. `testparm`

   D. `netbiostest`

4. What command is used to initialize client access?

   A. `smbclient`

   B. `smbstatus`

   C. `sambaclient`

   D. `netbiosclient`

5. What application provides NFS services to share Solaris volumes to clients?

   A. Samba

   B. PC-NFS

   C. Explorer

   D. Windows

6. What is the native Windows file-sharing protocol?

   A. Samba

   B. NFS

   C. Session Message Block

   D. SNA

☑ *Mastery Check*

7. What command can be used for NetBIOS lookups?

   A. `nmblookup`

   B. `nmbstatus`

   C. `nmbcheck`

   D. `netbios`

8. What command is used to run nmbd as a standalone server?

   A. `/usr/local/samba/bin/nmbd -A`

   B. `/usr/local/samba/bin/nmbd -B`

   C. `/usr/local/samba/bin/nmbd -C`

   D. `/usr/local/samba/bin/nmbd -D`

9. What does the parameter *add machine script* specify?

   A. The command used to add systems to the domain

   B. Whether external trusted domains are supported

   C. Whether the Samba server should announce itself as having a specific Windows version

   D. What network interfaces are to be used for Samba

10. What does the parameter *allow trusted domains* specify?

   A. The command used to add systems to the domain

   B. Whether external trusted domains are supported

   C. Whether the Samba server should announce itself as having a specific Windows version

   D. What network interfaces are to be used for Samba

11. What does the parameter *announce as* specify?

   A. The command used to add systems to the domain

   B. Whether external trusted domains are supported

☑ Mastery Check

    C. Whether the Samba server should announce itself as having a specific Windows version

    D. What network interfaces are to be used for Samba

12. What does the parameter *bind interfaces only* specify?

    A. The command used to add systems to the domain

    B. Whether external trusted domains are supported

    C. Whether the Samba server should announce itself as having a specific Windows version

    D. What network interfaces are to be used for Samba

13. What does the parameter *enhanced browsing* specify?

    A. Enhanced browsing of master browsers

    B. Caching of working directory lookups

    C. Concealment of server-side users from clients

    D. Concealment of files that are not accessible by the client

14. What does the parameter *getwd cache* specify?

    A. Enhanced browsing of master browsers

    B. Caching of working directory lookups

    C. Concealment of server-side users from clients

    D. Concealment of files that are not accessible by the client

15. What does the parameter *hide local users* specify?

    A. Enhanced browsing of master browsers

    B. Caching of working directory lookups

    C. Concealment of server-side users from clients

    D. Concealment of files that are not accessible by the client

Module 20

Network Information Service (NIS/NIS+)

Critical Skills

Until the release of Microsoft Windows 2000, Windows had no hierarchical domain service that could be used to manage individual group users who were located within an organizational hierarchy. Instead, a flat namespace was used to identify individual workgroups by their domain names. Of course, in large organizations with many different domains and workgroups, it was impossible to tell whether or not the SUPPORT domain belonged to the Information Technology Group from one division or another. So flat domain names were sometimes created to reflect the hierarchical nature of the organizational structures that the domains were attempting to model. Thus, the SUPPORT domain for Atlanta, Georgia, might have been named GASUPPORT, while the SUPPORT domain for Raleigh, North Carolina, may have been named NCSUPPORT. Such a system becomes unwieldy quickly, however. Fortunately, with the introduction of Active Directory, Windows 2000 users now have access to a hierarchical domain name system.

In contrast, Solaris has had a sophisticated domain name system for many years, supported by the Network Information Service (NIS), which uses a series of maps to create hierarchical namespace structures. Sometimes administrators ask why this is required, since the Domain Name Service (DNS), covered in Module 14, already provides this for Internet hosts by converting computer-friendly IP-addresses to human-friendly "names." However, NIS does not just provide naming services: a NIS server also acts as a central repository of all information about users, hosts, Ethernet addresses, mail aliases, and supported RPC services within a network. This information is physically stored in a set of maps that are intended to replace the network configuration files usually stored in a server's /etc directory, ensuring that configuration data within the local area network (LAN) is always synchronized. Many large organizations use NIS alongside DNS to manage both their Internet and LAN spaces effectively. Linux also supports NIS.

In recent years, Sun has introduced an enhanced version of NIS known as NIS+. Instead of a simple mapping system, it uses a complex series of tables to store configuration information and hierarchical naming data for all networks within an organization. Individual namespaces may contain up to 10,000 hosts, with individual NIS+ servers working together to support a completely distributed service. NIS+ also includes greater capabilities in the area of authentication, security (using DES encryption), and resource access control.

This module will examine how to install and configure the new NIS+ system. It will walk through the configuration of key NIS+ entities, such as the primary and slave servers, as well as higher level conceptual issues, such as how to plan a NIS+ network.

20.1 Plan Network Information Services

 A NIS+ namespace is most easily constructed by mirroring the domains that are created for use with DNS. This makes it easy to match internal network domain information with the external DNS information used by Internet users. However, while DNS can be used to advertise host information about an organization's servers, NIS+ hides this information from the public. Although some organizations will not have Internet connectivity, most will at least use TCP/IP networking; it makes sense to keep all DNS network mapping consistent with NIS+ host tables. Some organizations that use DNS alone have avoided NIS+ because of its reputation as a complex, time-consuming system that imposes a heavy administrative burden on system administrators, and also for security reasons. This is certainly true for small networks that have less than five hosts—configuration files can be easily copied between hosts on a regular basis to keep data consistent. However, any network of a reasonable size will soon require that up to 15 key system configuration files will need to be updated between hosts. Increasing the number of hosts by one in a network will then increase the administrative overhead well beyond the centralized maintenance of a NIS+ server. In addition, the possibility for inconsistent data being entered into the configuration files of different servers makes it impossible to ensure that correct user, group, and network data is always available. For this reason alone, NIS+ provides a solution to key data management issues for system administrators. The script-based installation and management method also makes it easier to create the necessary infrastructure to support and maintain NIS+.

This section examines the elements that go into planning and setting up a NIS+ network. The first step is usually to (optionally) register a DNS domain name, obtain a license to use a particular type of network (Class A, B, or C), and determine the range of IP addresses and subnets that will be supported within the NIS+ network. For example, the site "Paul Watters" decided to set up an internal network based on NIS+. The administrator's first task was to register the DNS domain name (**paulwatters.com**) and then set up three Class

C networks: one for the company (134.132.1.0), one for the sales division (134.132.2.1), and one for the development division (134.132.3.0). These are mapped to the DNS domains **paulwatters.com**, **sales.paulwatters.com**, and **develop.paulwatters.com**, respectively.

To support DNS, the first hosts to be set up are the DNS servers for three DNS domains: **ns.paulwatters.com** (134.132.1.16), **ns.sales.paulwatters.com** (134.132.2.16), and **ns.develop.paulwatters.com** (134.132.3.16). Each primary DNS server will be authoritative for its domain, as well as acting as a secondary for the other two domains. For example, **ns.paulwatters.com** will be the primary DNS server for the **paulwatters.com** domain, but it will also act as a secondary for the **develop.paulwatters.com** and **sales.paulwatters.com** networks. A total of 255 × 3, or 765, Class C network IP addresses are now available for the company. Figure 20-1 shows the DNS configuration for the company.

Once the DNS naming has been decided, it is then easy to create the NIS+ namespace, as the same names may be used for the network and domain names as well as the hosts. Thus, the DNS domain name **paulwatters.com** is written in NIS+ terms as "Paulwatters.Com."—notice the terminating period on the NIS+.

The NIS+ domains for Paul Watters can exactly mirror the DNS configuration, as shown in Figure 20-2. However, some differences in naming are immediately apparent: while DNS uses lowercase names by convention, which do not terminate in a period, the NIS+ convention is to name write elements in a domain beginning with capital letters and terminating with a period.

The root domain of a NIS+ network is usually equivalent to a second- or third-level DNS domain. Thus, in our **paulwatters.com** DNS example, the NIS+ root domain is **Paulwatters.Com**. Each of the DNS subdomains

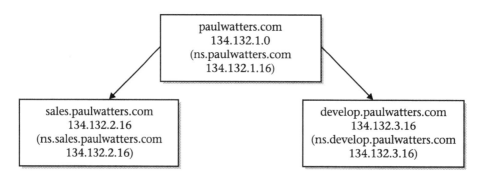

Figure 20-1   Sample network configuration for Paul Watters based on DNS

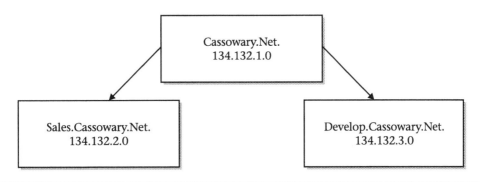

Figure 20-2   Sample network configuration for Paul Watters based on DNS and NIS+

(**develop.paulwatters.com** and **sales.paulwatters.com**) are therefore non-root domains in NIS+, even though they have their own DNS servers. However, non-root NIS+ domains can also have their own NIS+ servers. Indeed, a sensible NIS+ planning policy sees domains having at least two servers: a master server and a replica server. The master server is authoritative under normal operation. However, if the master server is not available for some reason, the replica server is able to service NIS+ clients. Figure 20-3 shows the envisaged scenario for the **Paulwatters.Com.** domain in terms of planned DNS servers and master and replica NIS+ servers.

The overall purpose of NIS+ is to provide services to clients; unsurprisingly, NIS+ client notations follow the standards set out for DNS. Thus, a DNS client like **honey.sales.paulwatters.com** has the NIS+ name **Honey.Sales.Paulwatters.Com.** This client would be serviced by the NIS+ server **Master.Sales.Paulwatters.Com**, with **Replica.Sales.Paulwatters.Com** acting as a backup. All NIS+ clients need to be manually installed and registered by using a script, during which time a directory cache is initialized, allowing for local network directory lookups for supported services. This configuration is shown in Figure 20-4.

In these examples, we've equated NIS+ namespaces with DNS namespaces, so you may be wondering why we would be bothered using NIS+, if it is so similar to DNS. In fact, the host-oriented namespace we've examined so far is only one aspect of NIS+ operation; many objects, other than hosts, can be managed within NIS+ domains, such as groups, directories and tables. Centralizing storage of these objects allows greater security than if these objects could be modified directly. In addition, authentication of client credentials uses the DES encryption algorithm,

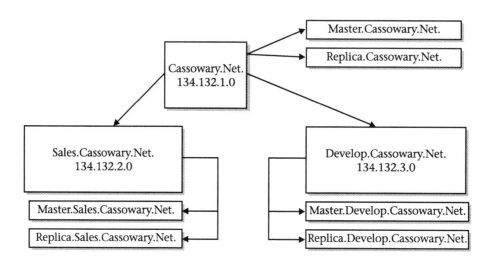

Figure 20-3 Sample NIS+ domains for Paul Watters showing required master and replica servers

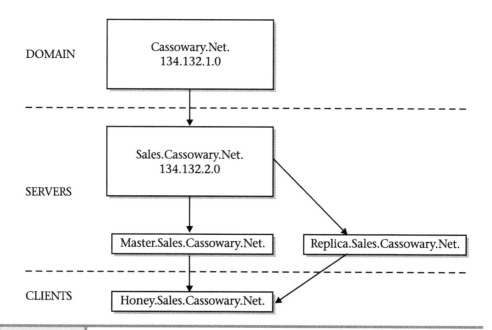

Figure 20-4 Client management for Paul Watters using NIS+

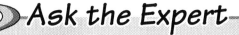

Ask the Expert

Question: I have installed DNS. Do I need to install NIS or NIS+ to connect to the Internet?

Answer: No. If you have a simple system that does not share authentication, authorization, or identification data with other hosts, DNS will give you all you need. NIS and NIS+ are most useful for building intranets.

Question: I've heard that NIS is insecure. Is that true?

Answer: Yes. That's why you should use NIS+, because it encrypts authentication tokens and generally tightens up authorization procedures at a finer level.

Question: Hasn't Sun deprecated NIS and NIS+ in favor of Lightweight Directory Access Protocol (LDAP)?

Answer: No. NIS and NIS+ are still supported, although they may eventually be deprecated in favor of directory services like LDAP. Indeed, Solaris 9 comes with the iPlanet LDAP server, so all forward-looking system administrators would be installing LDAP on new systems and planning to migrate their NIS and NIS+ based networks in the near future.

20

while DNS has little, if any, security features built in. Thus, although the similarity of NIS+ naming to DNS is useful for learning about NIS+, some important differences will be examined in the next section.

20.2 Configure NIS+

Now that we have examined how a network based around NIS+ can be created, we focus on how to configure NIS+ services on the network. Typically, a NIS+ administrator will begin by setting up the NIS+ domains, as reviewed in the previous section, followed by the configuration of master and replica servers for both root and non-root domains. Finally, clients and users are configured and added to the domain. Obviously, at least the master server must be operational before any population of NIS+ tables can take place—a replica server can wait if time is precious. A number of administrative groups should also be created prior to client configuration. Root domains must always be set up before non-root domains. The following sections review the steps required to get your NIS+ network up and running quickly.

20.3 Install and Configure the Name Service Switch

The name service switch (*/etc/nsswitch.conf*) governs how name lookups are performed under Solaris 9. We saw in Module 14 how the DNS service uses the name service switch to determine how host lookups are performed; the order in which different name resolution strategies are used can also be modified. For example, the following line specifies that IP address lookups on hostnames should be performed by firstly examining the */etc/hosts* file—if the name is not resolved, it is passed to the DNS server. If the DNS server cannot resolve the name or does not respond, NIS maps are consulted. Failing NIS, the final link in the resolution chain is a query to NIS+ tables:

```
hosts: files dns nis nisplus
```

Of course, if you didn't use NIS maps or NIS+ tables on your network, you could simply use the following entry for host lookups in */etc/nsswitch.conf*:

```
hosts: files dns
```

If your system is not connected to the Internet, and you use NIS+ as your sole network information service, you might use the following entry instead:

```
hosts: files nisplus
```

The order in which the entries are made clearly affects how the name resolution will be performed. Specifying multiple services for hostname resolutions ensures that if one of the methods attempted early in the resolution chain does not respond or provide the information required, an alternative source of information can be consulted.

The name service switch does not just dictate how hostnames are looked up: in fact, some 13 other services use *etc/nsswitch.conf* to determine how various services are resolved by the various information services available on a Solaris system. Here's a typical name service switch file that is targeted at DNS name resolution:

```
passwd:      files
group:       files
hosts:       dns [NOTFOUND=return] files
networks:    files
protocols:   files
rpc:         files
ethers:      files
netmasks:    files
bootparams:  files
publickey:   files
netgroup:    files
automount:   files
aliases:     files
services:    files
sendmailvars:   files
```

Alternatively, for a system that mainly uses NIS+, we would set up a name service switch file as follows:

```
passwd:      files nisplus
group:       files nisplus
hosts:       nisplus dns [NOTFOUND=return] files
services:    nisplus [NOTFOUND=return] files
networks:    nisplus [NOTFOUND=return] files
protocols:   nisplus [NOTFOUND=return] files
rpc:         nisplus [NOTFOUND=return] files
ethers:      nisplus [NOTFOUND=return] files
netmasks:    nisplus [NOTFOUND=return] files
bootparams:  nisplus [NOTFOUND=return] files
publickey:   nisplus
netgroup:    nisplus
automount: nisplus files
aliases: nisplus files
sendmailvars: nisplus files
```

20

This scenario favors NIS+ over files in most situations, and it doesn't even consult DNS for name resolution. The contents of your */etc/nsswitch.conf* file will depend largely on the way in which your network is configured, and whether or not DNS, NIS+, NIS, or some other naming service is operating.

20.4 Install the Root Domain

Before any other services may be installed, NIS+ requires that the master server for the root domain be created. The master server will primarily be responsible for the management of the NIS+ namespace. For example, for the **Paulwatters.Com.** domain, the DNS server (**ns.paulwatters.com**) will also be used for NIS+. This means that the nisserver script can be executed on the DNS server system (**ns.paulwatters.com**) to initialize the master server for the root domain:

```
ns.paulwatters.com# nisserver -r -d Paulwatters.Com.
```

That's all that's required for NIS+ support. However, to enable support for NIS clients within the domain, you would need to use the following command instead:

```
ns.paulwatters.com# nisserver -Y -r -d Paulwatters.Com.
```

In this example, the *–Y* flag signifies "yellow pages," which is the old name for the NIS service.

Creating Tables

As mentioned earlier, NIS+ operates by creating a centralized set of tables that act as replacements for the localized configuration files in the */etc* directory. To begin the process of creating these tables on the master server for the root domain, we need to use `nispopulate` to insert initial values into the tables:

```
ns.paulwatters.com# nispopulate -F -p /nis+files -d Paulwatters.Com.
```

The *–p* flag specifies the directory where NIS+ files are stored.

The `nispopulate` command is responsible for storing all the appropriate information in the NIS+ tables. If your master server for the root domain needs to support NIS clients, you would need to use the following command instead:

```
ns.paulwatters.com# nispopulate -Y -F -p /nis+files -d Paulwatters.Com.
```

Next, we need to determine which users on the master server for the root domain should have administrative access to the NIS+ namespace. This gives the users named as administrators the ability to modify all of the data that NIS+ clients can look up; thus, it is a role of considerable responsibility. Changes made to the NIS+ tables do not just affect the local machine—they are reflected network-wide. If we had two network administrators—honey and natashia—they could be added to the administrator's group by using the `nisgrpadm` command:

```
ns.paulwatters.com# nisgrpadm -a Paulwatters.Com.
   honey.Paulwatters.Com. natashia.Paulwatters.Com.
```

To check the configuration and create a checkpoint, you can use the `nisping` command on the domain:

```
ns.paulwatters.com# nisping -C Paulwatters.Com.
```

This concludes the configuration required to install the root domain. In the next section, we examine how to set up master and replica servers for the two non-root domains that lie underneath the **Paulwatters.Com.** domain: **Develop.Paulwatters.Com.** and **Sales.Paulwatters.Com.**

20.5 Install the Non-root Domains

The first step in installing the non-root domains **Develop.Paulwatters.Com.** and **Sales.Paulwatters.Com.** is to configure a master server for each non-root domain by using the `nisclient` command. These master servers are effectively clients of the **Paulwatters.Com.** root domain, which is why the `nisclient` command is used to initialize their settings. In this case, the server **houston.paulwatters.com** is assigned be the root server of the non-root domain **Sales.Paulwatters.Com.**, while the host **denver.paulwatters.com** is assigned to be the root server of the non-root domain **Develop.Paulwatters.Com**. As a first step in creating the master servers, we would execute the following commands on each of these hosts, respectively:

```
houston.paulwatters.com# nisclient -i -d Paulwatters.Com.
   -h Ns.Paulwatters.Com
denver.paulwatters.com# nisclient -i -d Paulwatters.Com.
    -h Ns.Paulwatters.Com
```

After the master servers have been initialized, clients for that domain can actually set up from individual user accounts. For example, for the user maya in the domain **Sales.Paulwatters.Com**, the following command would be used to allow client access to the local namespace:

```
houston.paulwatters.com$ nisclient -u
```

Alternatively, for the user natashia in the domain **Develop.Paulwatters.Com**, we would use the following to initialize client access:

```
denver.paulwatters.com$ nisclient -u
```

Now that the servers that will act as master servers for the non-root domains have been set up as clients of the server that manages the root domain, these systems must themselves be set up as master servers for their own domains. In addition, additional replica servers may be installed at this time. In the previous example, we allocated **houston.paulwatters.com** the role of being master server for the non-root domain **Sales.Paulwatters.Com**. Imagine that we now allocated **richmond.paulwatters.com** the role of replica server for the non-root domain **Sales.Paulwatters.Com**. The first step is to ensure that the NIS+ service is running via Remote Procedure Call (RPC):

```
houston.paulwatters.com# rpc.nisd
```

Next, we use a command similar to that used for setting up the master server for the root domain:

```
ns.paulwatters.com# nisserver -R -d Paulwatters.Com. \
    -h houston.paulwatters.com
```

Authority to begin serving is then set by using the following command:

```
ns.paulwatters.com# nisserver -M -d Sales.Paulwatters.Com.\
    -h houston.paulwatters.com
```

The tables for the domain **Sales.Paulwatters.Com.** must then be populated by using the same procedure as for the master server:

```
houston.paulwatters.com# nispopulate -F -p /nis+files \
    -d Sales.Paulwatters.Com.
```

The final step is assigning the role of replica server to the host **richmond.paulwatters.com** by using the `nisclient` command:

```
richmond.paulwatters.com# nisclient -R \
    -d Sales.Paulwatters.Com. -h houston.paulwatters.com
```

We now repeat these commands for the non-root domain **Develop.Paulwatters.Com.**, which has been assigned the server **layton.paulwatters.com** as a replica server:

```
denver.paulwatters.com# rpc.nisd
layton.paulwatters.com# rpc.nisd
ns.paulwatters.com# nisserver -R -d Paulwatters.Com. \
    -h denver.paulwatters.com
ns.paulwatters.com# nisserver -M -d Develop.Paulwatters.Com. -h \
denver.paulwatters.com
denver.paulwatters.com# nispopulate -F -p /nis+files \
    -d Develop.Paulwatters.Com.
layton.paulwatters.com# nisclient -R -d Develop.Paulwatters.Com. \
    -h richmond.paulwatters.com
```

20.6 Manage NIS+ Tables

All data within NIS+ is stored in tables that are loosely based on several configuration files located in the */etc* directory on a standard host. The major difference between file-centric and NIS+ administration is security and centralization of administration: on a network with 100 hosts, around 1500 individual configuration files need to be managed using a files approach, while an NIS+ approach requires maintenance of only 15 files. Any modifications to the NIS+ tables are automatically distributed to clients requesting namespace data—this applies equally to hostname resolution as it does to accessing authorization credentials, such as usernames and passwords. Trying to update a user's password file on 100 hosts takes a long time, if that user needs access to any particular host on the network. For example, students may work on any workstation within a computer lab, or stock traders may be rotated regularly throughout an office for security reasons. Access to any workstation at any time using a single set of credentials is required. NIS+ is particularly suited to this environment. If you are worried about redundancy and backups, the master/replica server model used by NIS+ ensures that even if the master server for a root or non-root domain goes down, its replica server will be able to server authoritative data until normal service is resumed.

Project 20-1: Granting Access Rights to a NIS+ Table

This project shows you how to grant complex rights on a NIS+ table such as *ethers.org_dir* by using the `nischmod` command. This procedure is necessary whenever access permissions must be changed.

Step-by-Step

1. Determine the permissions string for the file owner (for example, read and modify):

```
o=rm
```

2. Determine the permissions string for the file owner's group (for example, read only):

```
g=r
```

3. Determine the permissions string for the world (for example, create and delete):

```
o=cd
```

4. Apply the new permissions using the `nischmod` command:

```
# nischmod o=rm,g=r,w=cd ethers.org_dir
```

Summary
The `nischmod` command can be used to change table permissions much like `chmod` can be used to change file permissions.

Auto_Home

The *Auto_Home* table enables all users within a domain to access a single home directory, irrespective of which system they log into. The ability to support this kind of distributed file system centrally is one of the best features of NIS+. One of the main issues that arises when using the automounter is that local partitions called */home* cannot be mounted by the local system—this mount point is reserved for the automounter. This can cause some consternation for administrators who are unfamiliar with the automounter.

The *Auto_Home* table contains two columns: a username, which identifies the user on a network, and the hostname and path to the home directory for that user's home directory. Once an entry is created in the *Auto_Home* table, the home directory for that user will be available for mounting on any host within the network that is part of the NIS+ domain. Let's look at an example:

```
julian    sandiego:/users/export/julian
```

Here, the user julian's home directory is always mounted from the host *sandiego*, with the mount point */users/export/julian*.

Auto_Master

The *Auto_Master* is used in conjunction with the Network File System (NFS) to create maps that relate specific mount points to use the automounter. For example, if we wanted to map home directories from */staff* and */students* using *Auto_Home*, we'd need to insert the following entries into the *Auto_Master* table:

```
/staff      auto_home
/students   auto_home
```

20

Bootparams

Solaris supports the booting of diskless clients, such as X-terminals, by using the *Bootparams* table. Every diskless client within the domain will have an entry in the *Bootparams* table, which defines the root directory, swap, and dump partitions for the client. For example, the diskless client *chicago* has its root directory on the server *newyork*, but it actually accesses its swap and dump partitions from the server *newark*. The following entry would need to be inserted into the *Bootparams* table to support this functionality:

```
chicago      root=newyork:/export/root/chicago \
             swap=newark:/export/swap/chicago \
             dump=newark:/export/dump/chicago
```

Ethers

All network interface cards have a low-level hardware address associated with them called an Ethernet (MAC) address. NIS+ associates each host's Ethernet address with a specific hostname within the domain. For example, if the host *orlando* had a single network interface with the Ethernet address 01:ab:b1:c3:d2:c3, then the following entry would be inserted into the *Ethers* table:

```
01:ab:b1:c3:d2:c3    orlando
```

All entries in the *Ethers* table are statically stored as *arp* entries and are typically used by diskless X-terminals for jumpstart configurations.

Group

The *Group* table stores information about user groups that have been defined within the domain. We cover the definition and planning of groups within Solaris in Module 9. The NIS+ *Group* table stores details of the group name, a group password (if applicable), the group ID (GID), and a list of all users who are members of the group. For example, the group *staff* may have the members paul, maya, honey, and natashia, as shown in the following entry:

```
staff::10:paul,maya,honey,natashia
```

Hosts

The *Hosts* table associates an IP address with a specific hostname and/or a number of optional hostname aliases. For example, if the host *boston* had an IP address of 10.36.12.54 and an alias of *portland*, the following entry would be inserted into the *Hosts* table:

```
192.34.54.3  boston    portland
```

Mail Aliases

Mail Transport Agents (MTAs) under Solaris typically make use of the mail aliases database (*/etc/aliases*) to define mailing lists or aliases for specific users. In a NIS+ domain, the */etc/aliases* file is replaced by the *Mail Aliases* table, which can map a specific username to an alias name or a single alias to a list of valid usernames (such as a mailing list). For example, the alias *postmaster* is typically used to identify the mail administrator within a domain. To associate this alias with a specific user account (such as maya), we would insert the following alias into the *Mail Aliases* table:

```
postmaster:maya
```

Aliases can also be matched with other aliases that have already been defined. For example, many sites forward all e-mail to the root user to the alias postmaster. In combination with our existing rule that forwards all e-mail for postmaster to maya, the following entry would have the net result of forwarding all e-mail to root to the user maya:

```
root:postmaster
```

Finally, imagine that a restaurant chain had an e-mail distribution list to managers at all local restaurants. A mail alias called managers could be set up so that the managers at the different restaurants would all receive a copy of e-mails sent to the user managers. In this example, the accounts oakton, tysons, quantico, and salem would all receive a copy of any messages sent to the alias managers:

```
managers: oakton,tysons,quantico,salem
```

Netgroups

Netgroups are authorization lists that can be used to govern access to resources within a network and to determine which groups of users can perform specific operations. For example, a group called admins within the **Paulwatters.Com.** domain might be authorized to add or delete clients to the domain. A netgroups entry that defines the admins Netgroup would look like this:

```
admins    paulwatters.com
```

Netmasks

The *Netmasks* table defines all of the netmasks required for the local network. For a Class A network, the netmask is 255.0.0.0, while the netmask for a Class B network is 255.255.0.0. The most common netmask is 255.255.255.0, which is for a Class C network (for example, 204.128.64.0), as shown in the following example:

```
204.128.64.0    255.255.255.0
```

Networks

Individual networks can be defined within a NIS+ domain by inserting entries into the *Networks* table. In addition, aliases for entire networks can also be entered into the *Networks* table. For example, if the network *broadmeadow* (203.48.16.0) acted as a backup network for a primary network, it may have the alias *backup*:

```
broadmeadow    203.48.16.0    backup
```

Passwd

The *Passwd* table replaces the */etc/passwd* file that is typically used by non-NIS+ systems for user identification and authentication. The *Passwd* table contains one row for each user, containing a number of fields. These fields include the username, an encrypted password, a user ID, the primary group ID, the user's real name, and the user's home directory default login shell. In addition, some extra fields are shown, including the number of days before which a password must be changed and/or how often a password must be changed. A sample row inserted into the *Passwd* table for the user pwatters would look like this:

```
pwatters:x:1024:20:Paul Watters:/home/pwatters:/bin/csh:
10923:-1:-1:-1:-1::0
```

Protocols

The *Protocols* table lists all protocols that are supported on the network. For example, to support the TCP and UDP transport layers, the Internet Protocol (IP) must be supported, which is typically listed as protocol zero:

```
ip   0
```

RPC

The *RPC* table lists all the available RPC services on the local network. The first program that must be supported is the *rpcbind* program, which is also known as the *portmap* program, which runs on port 100000:

```
rpcbind   100000   portmap
```

   In addition, to support services like NFS, the *rquotad* and *mountd* services will also need to be supported:

```
rquotad 100011  quotad
mountd 100005
```

   For more information, see Module 21.

Services

The *Services* table contains entries that define all of the services that are available on the NIS+ network under both UDP and TCP. For example, the *sendmail* service typically runs on TCP port 25; thus, the following entry would have to be inserted into the *Services* table to be supported in the network:

```
sendmail   25/tcp
```

Timezone

The *Timezone* table sets the appropriate time zone for hosts within the NIS+ domain. For example, the following entry sets the time zone for the host *sydney* to be *Australia/NSW*:

```
sydney Australia/NSW
```

However, the server *brisbane* might well be located in a different time zone, particularly if the NIS+ extends beyond the local area:

```
brisbane Australia/QLD
```

The *Timezone* entries affect all applications that need to process dates and times, such as mail transport agents and the `cron` process scheduling application.

20.7 Manage NIS+

Having reviewed the configuration of NIS+ and the main tables that are used to define a NIS+ domain, we now examine how to use NIS+ effectively to manage hosts and resources within a domain. As we have seen, many different objects can be managed and identified within a NIS+ domain, and several commands are used to access them. In this section, we examine commands such as `nisdefault`, which displays the NIS+ settings for the local client system, as well as `nischmod`, which is used to set access rights on NIS+ objects. In addition, the `nisls` command is reviewed, which can be used for object lookups and queries. Finally, we will examine the `niscat` command, which displays the contents of table entries and can be used to examine NIS+ objects in detail.

Displaying Default Settings

The current settings for a local client system and the active user can be displayed by using the `nisdefaults` command. The `nisdefaults` command is commonly used when attempting to troubleshoot an error, such as a user's credentials not being correctly authenticated from the *Passwd* table. As an example, let's examine the `nisdefaults` for the host *ozamiz* when executed by the user honey:

```
ozamiz$ nisdefaults
Principal Name : honey.develop.paulwatters.com.
Domain Name    : develop.paulwatters.com.
Host Name      : ozamiz.develop.paulwatters.com.
Group Name     : develop
Access Rights  : ----rmcdr---r---
Time to live   : 11:00:00
Search Path    : develop.paulwatters.com. paulwatters.com.
```

The output of the `nisdefaults` command can be interpreted in the following way:

- The principal user is honey, who belongs to the NIS+ domain **develop.paulwatters.com**.

- The primary domain name is **develop.paulwatters.com**.

- The hostname of the local system is **ozamiz.develop.paulwatters.com**.

- The user honey's primary group is *develop*.

- The time-to-live settings is 11 hours.

- The client's access rights within the domain are stated.

- The search path starts with the current non-root domain (**develop.paulwatters.com**), followed by the root domain (**paulwatters.com**).

The access rights stated for the user in this example are outlined in more detail in the next section.

Understanding Object Permissions

Every user has a set of access rights for accessing objects within the network. The notation for setting and accessing object permissions is similar to that used for Solaris file systems (see Module 6 for more details). The following permissions may be set on any object or may be defined as the default settings for a particular client:

c: Set create permission
d: Set delete permission

m:	Set modify permission
r :	Set read permission

This `nischmod` command is used to set permissions on objects within the domain. The following operands are used to specify access rights for specific classes of users:

a:	All (all authenticated and unauthenticated users)
g:	Group
n :	Nobody (all unauthenticated users)
o:	Object owner
w:	World (all authenticated users)

Two operators can be used to set and remove permissions:

+:	Sets a permission.
-:	Removes a permission.

Some examples of how permissions strings are constructed will clarify how these operators and operands are combined for use with the `nichmod` command. The following command removes all modify (*m*) and create (*c*) access rights on the password table for all unauthenticated (*n*) users:

```
houston# nischmod n-cm passwd.org_dir
```

Even unauthenticated users require read (*r*) access to the password table for authentication, which can be granted with the following command:

```
houston# nischmod n+r passwd.org_dir
```

To grant modify and create access rights to the current user (in this case root) and his/her primary group on the same table, we would use the command:

```
houston# nischmod og+cm passwd.org_dir
```

NIS+ permission strings are easy to remember, but they're hard to combine into single commands where some permissions are granted while others are removed, unlike the octal codes used to specify absolute permissions on Solaris file systems. However, it is possible to combine permissions strings by using a comma to separate individual strings. The following complex string is an example of how it is possible to set permissions within a single string, but it equally shows how challenging it is to interpret:

```
houston# nischmod o=rmcd,g=rmc,w=rm,n=r hosts.org_dir
```

This command grants the following permissions to four different categories of users:

owner: Read, modify, create and delete
group: Read, modify and create
world: Read and modify
nobody: Read only

Listing Objects

The `nisls` command is used as a lookup and query command that can provide views on NIS+ directories and tables. For example, to view all of the NIS+ directories that have been populated within the local namespace, we can use the `nisls` command:

```
houston# nisls
develop.paulwatters.com.:
org_dir
groups_dir
```

Two directory object types are listed here: the *org_dir*, which lists all of the tables that have been set up within the namespace, while the *groups_dir* stores details of all NIS+ groups. We can view a list of tables by using the `nisls` command once again on the *org_dir* directory:

```
houston# nisls org_dir
org_dir.sales.paulwatters.com.:
auto_home
auto_master
bootparams
client_info
cred
ethers
group
hosts
```

```
mail_aliases
netgroup
netmasks
networks
passwd
protocols
rpc
sendmailvars
services
timezone
```

A large number of tables have been populated for this domain. The groups directory contains the admin group we created earlier, which lists all the administrators as well as several other groups that are based on distinct organizational units within the current domain:

```
houston# nisls groups_dir
groups_dir.sales.paulwatters.com.:
admin
adverts
legal
media
```

Displaying Objects

The niscat command is used to retrieve the contents of objects within the domain, primarily the data contained within NIS+ tables. For example, all hosts listed within the domain can be listed by using the following command:

```
houston$ niscat -h hosts.org_dir
houston.paulwatters.com houston 10.58.64.16
denver.paulwatters.com denver 10.58.64.17
richmond.paulwatters.com richmond 10.58.64.18
layton.paulwatters.com layton 10.58.64.19
```

Alternatively, we can use the niscat command to examine the contents of the Password table:

```
houston$ niscat passwd.org_dir
honey:*LK*:1001:1:honey:/staff/honey:/bin/tcsh:10910:-1:-1:-1:-1::0
natashia:*LK*:1002:1:natashia:/staff/natashia:/bin/bash:10920
    :-1:-1:-1:-1::0
```

```
maya:*LK*:1003:1:maya:/staff/maya:/bin/sh:10930:-1:-1:-1:-1::0
paul:*LK*:1004:1:paul:/staff/paul:/bin/csh:10940:-1:-1:-1:-1::0
```

Next, we can examine to which groups these users belong by using the `niscat` command once again:

```
houston$ niscat group.org_dir
root::0:root
staff::1:honey,natashia,maya,paul
bin::2:root,bin,daemon
sys:*:3:root,bin,sys,adm
adm::4:root,adm,daemon
uucp::5:root,uucp
mail::6:root
```

20

All of the hosts that form part of the local domain can be examined based on their Ethernet address, which is extracted from the *Ethers* table, as shown in the following example:

```
houston$ niscat ethers.org_dir
1:4a:16:2f:13:b2 houston.paulwatters.com.
1:02:1e:f4:61:2e denver.paulwatters.com.
f4:61:2e:1:4a:16 richmond.paulwatters.com.
2f:13:b2:1:02:1e layton.paulwatters.com.
```

To determine which services are offered within the local domain, we can also examine the services table:

```
houston$ niscat services.org_dir
tcpmux tcpmux tcp 1
echo echo tcp 7
echo echo udp 7
discard discard tcp 9
discard sink tcp 9
discard null tcp 9
discard discard udp 9
discard sink udp 9
discard null udp 9
systat systat tcp 11
systat users tcp 11
daytime daytime tcp 13
daytime daytime udp 13
```

Every other table that is defined within the domain may be viewed by using the `niscat` command in this way.

1-Minute Drill

- What is NIS?
- How is NIS different from DNS?
- What command is used to retrieve the contents of objects within a NIS+ domain?

- The Network Information Service
- DNS only manages hostname to IP address mapping; NIS manages many different types of information about resources such as users, groups, and passwords.
- `niscat`

☑ *Mastery Check*

1. What command is used to list all of the tables in a namespace?

  A. `namelist`

  B. `listname`

  C. `nisdir`

  D. `nisls`

2. Which entry in */etc/nsswitch.conf* ensures that NIS is selected last for naming?

  A. *hosts: files dns nis nisplus*

  B. *hosts: files dns nisplus nis*

  C. *hosts: files dns*

  D. *hosts: nis nisplus files dns*

3. What command inserts initial values into tables?

☑ Mastery Check

      A. `nispopulate`

      B. `nisinsert`

      C. `niscat`

      D. `nisinitial`

4. What command is used to initialize client access?

      A. `nisclient -u`

      B. `nisclient -x`

      C. `nissetup -u`

      D. `nissetup -x`

5. What encryption standard does NIS+ support?

      A. ElGamal

      B. DES

      C. Diffie-Hellman

      D. DSA

6. When are NIS+ names mapped to DNS names?

      A. Never

      B. For hostnames only

      C. For usernames only

      D. For hostnames and usernames

7. What is the peak namespace capacity for NIS+?

      A. 1000

      B. 5000

      C. 10,000

      D. 100,000

20

☑ *Mastery Check*

8. Which entry in */etc/nsswitch.conf* ensures that NIS+ is selected last for naming?

A. *hosts: files dns nis nisplus*

B. *hosts: files dns nisplus nis*

C. *hosts: files dns*

D. *hosts: nis nisplus files dns*

9. Which entry in */etc/nsswitch.conf* ensures that DNS is selected last for naming?

A. *hosts: files dns nis nisplus*

B. *hosts: files dns nisplus nis*

C. *hosts: files dns nisplus*

D. *hosts: nis nisplus files dns*

10. Which entry in */etc/nsswitch.conf* ensures that DNS is selected first for naming?

A. *hosts: dns files nis nisplus*

B. *hosts: files dns nisplus nis*

C. *hosts: files dns nisplus*

D. *hosts: nis nisplus files dns*

11. Which entry in */etc/nsswitch.conf* ensures that NIS+ is selected second for naming?

A. *hosts: dns files nis nisplus*

B. *hosts: files dns nisplus nis*

C. *hosts: files dns nisplus*

D. *hosts: nis nisplus files dns*

☑ *Mastery Check*

12. What command is used to initialize root domain support?

    A. `nisserver -r -d` *domain*

    B. `nisserver -i -d` *domain*

    C. `nisserver -x -d` *domain*

    D. `nisserver -z -d` *domain*

13. What command initializes NIS+ tables?

    A. `nispopulate -J -p /nis+files -d` *domain*

    B. `nispopulate -G -p /nis+files -d` *domain*

    C. `nispopulate -H -p /nis+files -d` *domain*

    D. `nispopulate -F -p /nis+files -d` *domain*

14. What command would add the administrator natalie to the administrator's group?

    A. `nisgrpadm -a Paulwatters.Com.`
       `natalie.Paulwatters.Com.`

    B. `nisgrpadm -A Paulwatters.Com.`
       `natalie.Paulwatters.Com.`

    C. `nisgrpadm -add Paulwatters.Com.`
       `natalie.Paulwatters.Com.`

    D. `nisgrpadm -new Paulwatters.Com. -a`
       `natalie.Paulwatters.Com.`

15. What command creates a domain checkpoint?

    A. `nispoint -C` *domain*

    B. `nisping -C` *domain*

    C. `checkpoint -C` *domain*

    D. `nischeck-C` *domain*

20

Module 21

Network File System

Critical Skills

The Network File System (NFS) is a client-server file serving system that allows a centralized NFS server to provide read and write access to volumes that are exported versions of local file systems. Depending on the authentication method implemented, remote clients can mount NFS exported volumes as if they were local drives. Thus, users of client systems are able to read and write data seamlessly to existing files/disks that are effectively mounted from a remote server. In addition, new files can be created, and all normal file operations can be applied.

NFS provides many important features for local networks, including the ability to centralize the provision of single home directories and mail facilities through the automounter, regardless of the client system a user is logged into. Combined with high-bandwidth local area network (LAN) topologies, using NFS allows disk space to be rationalized according to server requirements and minimizes the administration associated with maintaining users across multiple systems.

NFS was once thought to be too unreliable to support many concurrent users: stale file handles and other problems caused by the User Datagram Protocol (UDP) implementation of NFS 2 in previous versions of Solaris have been largely eradicated with the shift to the service guaranteed Transmission Control Protocol (TCP). Combined with large increases in disk speed and network throughput, and support within the Solaris kernel, NFS is considered by many to be the file sharing system of choice for Solaris.

However, with the increasing popularity of Samba and SMB file sharing, as described in Module 19, is there any future for NFS? Certainly for the primary purpose of providing a drop-in replacement for Windows-based file servers, Samba running on Solaris provides an efficient and reliable alternative to PC systems. However, NFS has a number of advantages over Samba, including UNIX-based authentication, advanced performance-tuning tools, server-side caching of client requests, and the provision of WebNFS, which provides access to file systems through the Internet. Since NFS is based on the Remote Procedure Call (RPC) technology, like many other services, it provides improved integration into the Solaris service environment. Linux administrators will also be familiar with Linux, since it now supports both NFS 2 and NFS 3. Windows administrators may have previously used the PC-NFS client software that allows Windows clients to mount NFS exported volumes from Solaris servers.

This module examines how to configure support for NFS and RPC for both NFS clients and server systems. In addition, it examines how to share home and mail directories using the automounter and shows you how to tune NFS for optimal performance.

21.1 Build Client/Server File Serving Architectures

An NFS server is responsible for providing volumes to clients so that they can be remotely mounted. Two daemons are required to support NFS operations on the server: the NFS daemon (*/usr/lib/nfs/nfsd*) and the volume mounting daemon (*/usr/lib/nfs/mountd*). The nfsd listens on a TCP port for incoming requests and services them appropriately, while the mountd returns details concerning file system access and volumes that have been mounted.

Initialization

Typically, both of these daemons are started from the */etc/init.d/nfs.server* script. Thus, if you ever need to start NFS manually, the following command can be used:

```
# /etc/init.d/nfs.server stop
```

Conversely, if you need to restart NFS services, the following command can be used:

```
# /etc/init.d/nfs.server start
```

Troubleshooting

If your NFS clients are experiencing problems, the first thing to check is whether or not the nfsd and/or mountd processes are running. To check whether or not the nfsd process is running, the following command can be used:

```
$ ps -eaf | grep nfsd
```

If no process entries are returned, the /etc/init.d/nfs.server stop and /etc/init.d/nfs.server start commands should be issued. Alternatively, if the nfsd process is running, it should be returned from the process list:

```
    root 20854      1  0   Jan 30 ?       10:54 /usr/lib/nfs/nfsd -a 32
```

21

Ask the Expert

Question: To how many clients should I cater?

Answer: How many users do you expect NFS to be serving concurrently at peak times? If you expect to be supporting a workgroup of 200 users, you'll need to modify the */etc/init.d/nfs.server* script accordingly.

Here, we can see that the nfsd process has started with two parameters: *−a*, which listens for both UDP and TCP connection requests (that is, NFS 2 and NFS 3 clients, respectively), and 32, which specifies that 32 concurrent requests can be handled by the daemon. For NFS servers with many clients, this number should be increased appropriately.

To check whether or not the mountd process is running, the following command can be used:

```
$ ps -eaf | grep mountd
```

If no process entries are returned, the `/etc/init.d/nfs.server stop` and `/etc/init.d/nfs.server start` commands should be issued. Alternatively, if the mountd process is running, it should be returned from the process list:

```
root 20855     1  0   Jan 30 ?     10:54 /usr/lib/nfs/mountd
```

Note that mountd is not generally started with any options. However, if you are trying to debug service failures, it can be useful to start mountd with the *−v* option to observe requests as they are processed.

Some additional services are optionally started from the */etc/init.d/server.nfs* script, including the Reverse Address Resolution Protocol (RARP) daemon, */usr/sbin/in.rarpd*, which is used by diskless clients to obtain an IP address. The RARP daemon matches the Ethernet address from a client request to an entry in the *ethers* database (*/etc/ethers*) which returns a hostname. This hostname is then resolved according to the name service specified by the name service switch (*/etc/nsswitch.conf*), which is typically set to the *hosts* database (*/etc/hosts*) for RARP requests. This lookup returns an IP address to the client, which may then boot successfully. If RARP is not required for your network, or any of the other services (such as the Network Booting Remote Program Load service), their entries should be commented out in the */etc/init.d/nfs.server* file.

1-Minute Drill

● What command is used to start an NFS server?

● What command is used to stop an NFS server?

● What command is used to check whether an NFS server is running?

● What command is used to check whether an NFS mount daemon is running?

21.2 Install RPC Services

Both of the NFS daemons (nfsd and mountd) use Remote Procedure Call (RPC) services to provide services to clients. RPC is a common method programming client/server applications that allows server applications to make use of a number of common services. The most commonly used service is the rpcbind service, otherwise known as the portmapper. rpcbind must be running on both the client and server to support NFS, since it is responsible for mapping program names to addresses. When a client makes an NFS request, it does so via the portmapper, so that it can locate the appropriate address for the server. A common cause of NFS failures is the absence of the rpcbind process running on the system. To check what RPC services are currently available on a server, the `rpcinfo` command can be used:

```
# rpcinfo -p
   program vers proto    port  service
    100000    4   tcp     111  rpcbind
    100000    3   tcp     111  rpcbind
    100000    2   tcp     111  rpcbind
    100000    4   udp     111  rpcbind
    100000    3   udp     111  rpcbind
    100000    2   udp     111  rpcbind
    100007    3   udp   32774  ypbind
    100007    2   udp   32774  ypbind
    100007    1   udp   32774  ypbind
    100007    3   tcp   32771  ypbind
    100007    2   tcp   32771  ypbind
```

● `/etc/init.d/nfs.server start`
● `/etc/init.d/nfs.server stop`
● `ps -eaf | grep nfsd`
● `ps -eaf | grep mountd`

21

```
100007    1    tcp    32771    ypbind
100005    1    udp    32859    mountd
100005    2    udp    32859    mountd
100005    3    udp    32859    mountd
100005    1    tcp    32813    mountd
100005    2    tcp    32813    mountd
100005    3    tcp    32813    mountd
100026    1    udp    32866    bootparam
100026    1    tcp    32815    bootparam
```

This output shows that several different RPC services are currently active on the server:

- rpcbind versions 2, 3, and 4 listening on both TCP and UDP port 111

- ypbind versions 1, 2, and 3 listening on both TCP and UDP ports 32771 and 32774, respectively (listens for NIS requests)

- mountd versions 1, 2, and 3 listening on both TCP and UDP ports 32813 and 32859, respectively

- rpc.bootparamd version 1 listening on both TCP and UDP ports 32815 and 32866, respectively (provides boot information for diskless clients)

If rpcinfo shows no rpcbind services, the portmapper may need to be restarted by using this command:

```
# /usr/sbin/rpcbind -w
```

21.3 Build NFS Services

NFS services can be deployed by using two guiding principles: centralization of services and high availability through server failover procedures. It's important to centralize services such as mail and home directories in a heterogeneous LAN; otherwise, valuable resources such as disk space are wasted. In addition, making a user's mail and home directory available on any client system reduces a user's dependence on any specific client. Thus, if client systems are taken away for repair or upgrading, a user is never inconvenienced, because all of the user's data is centrally stored. The centralization concept is taken to its logical extreme with the deployment of Sun Ray thin-client systems, which do not have a local hard disk and rely solely on a central server for file storage and access. A user is identified by a smart card that can be used to start a session on one client and switched to a separate client midway through the session to resume the session suspended from the first client. This kind of versatility demonstrates the attractiveness of service centralization.

Devising Client/Server Relationships

Centralization comes at a cost—imagine if you had designed your network around a single NFS server to provide mail and home directories to all clients. If that server was unavailable due to hardware maintenance, or if it crashed because of power failure, users on client systems would be unable to access files in their home directories, nor would they be able to retrieve their mail. Clearly this is unacceptable, so strategies must be devised to ensure continuity of service.

At the server level, this involves using a volume manager, like DiskSuite or Veritas Volume Manager, to create mirrored disks, protecting against a single point of failure. Similarly, most SPARC architecture servers offer dual power supplies and other failover technologies. Servers can also be allocated discrete NFS serving tasks, so that even if one server went down, others would not be affected. Thus, one NFS server might serve only mail directories, while another might serve only home directories. Finally, it is possible for read-only shared file systems to have backup servers defined that can take over from a server that has failed. Figure 21-1 shows how high availability strategies can be devised to provide maximum NFS uptime.

Every Solaris system that runs the nfsd and mountd services can act as an NFS server, and every Solaris system can act as an NFS client. In addition, systems that are NFS servers in one context can act as NFS clients in other contexts. For example, a mail server that exports mail directories to all clients in a local network may mount its user's home directories from a separate home directory NFS server. The system design is client/server, but the implementation can be effectively peer-to-peer between servers that serve different types of content.

When a client mounts a volume exported by an NFS server, it must be attached to a local mount point. By convention, these should be located under the */mnt* directory, with some exceptions—the automounter, for example, usually mounts home directories under */home*, much to the chagrin of administrators who attempt to create local home directories under */home* while the automounter is running.

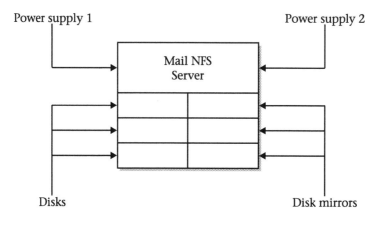

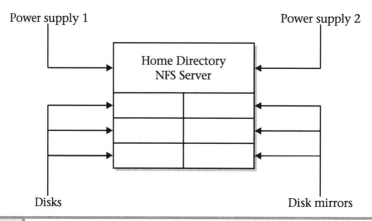

Figure 21-1 Devising high availability strategies for NFS

Ask the Expert

Question: Should I create user home directories under */home*?

Answer: Yes, but only if you don't use the automounter.

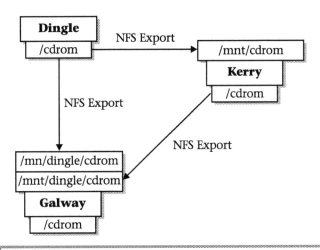

Figure 21-2 | Sharing file systems using NFS

Let's look at a concrete example of an NFS server and client relationship. Imagine that the NFS server *dingle* has a CD-ROM drive mounted locally on */cdrom*. Two clients, *kerry* and *galway*, must mount the *dingle:/cdrom* volume using NFS onto a local mount point. In the case of *kerry*, the volume is mounted in *kerry:/mnt/cdrom*, while in the case of *galway*, the volume is mounted on *galway:/mnt/dingle/cdrom*. The choice of mount points is unique to each client and is not mandated by the server. Thus, *kerry* would also be able to export its own */cdrom* volume as *kerry:/cdrom* using NFS, and *galway*, as a client, would mount it locally on *galway:/mnt/kerry/cdrom*. Thus, *galway* can have access to three CD-ROM devices: its own local CD-ROM drive mounted under */cdrom*; *kerry*'s CD-ROM drive mounted on */mnt/kerry/cdrom*; and *dingle*'s CD-ROM mounted on */mnt/dingle/cdrom*. This arrangement is shown in Figure 21-2.

21.4 Share NFS Volumes

Sharing a volume can be achieved by using the share command. For example, to share the */cdrom* directory read-only from *dingle*, the following command could be used:

```
# share -F nfs -o ro /cdrom
```

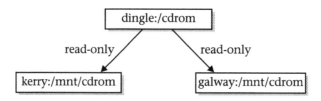

Figure 21-3   Sharing read-only volumes

This shares the */cdrom* file system to anyone on the local subnet. To restrict read-only access to *kerry*, the following command would be used:

```
# share -F nfs -o ro=kerry /cdrom
```

To provide read-only access to both *kerry* and *galway*, the following command would be used:

```
# share -F nfs -o ro=kerry,galway /cdrom
```

This configuration is shown in Figure 21-3.

Because all NFS permissions must be granted explicitly, no other clients would be able to mount *dingle:/cdrom* other than *kerry* or *galway*. In addition, no clients would be able to mount *dingle:/cdrom* read-write, even if it were physically possible. However, for a shared directory like */var/mail*, clients would obviously need to be able to mount it read-write if users were going to be able to modify their own mailboxes. Thus, if the server *kerry* exported */var/mail* read-write to *dingle* and *galway*, the following command would be used:

```
# share -F nfs -o rw=dingle,galway /var/mail
```

This configuration is shown in Figure 21-4.

1-Minute Drill

- What command is used to share NFS volumes read-only?
- What command is used to share NFS volumes read-write?

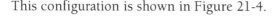

- share -F nfs -o ro
- share -F nfs -o rw

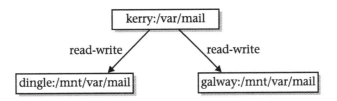

Figure 21-4   Sharing read-write volumes

Security Issues

NFS maps the usernames on one host to another and preserves the file permissions accordingly. Thus, the user pwatters on *dingle* has the same read-write permissions on a volume when it is exported to *galway* or *kerry*. A security problem immediately arises if the user pwatters on *dingle* is Paul Watters, but the pwatters user on *kerry* and *galway* is Patricia Watters. Patricia Watters would be able to read and write data stored on *dingle,* which is owned by Paul Watters, since NFS does not export volumes on a user-by-user basis: all users on an NFS client system have equal access to NFS-mounted volumes according to the privileges that their local usernames confer. There is no way to circumvent this identification mismatch, other than to ensure uniformity in naming across hosts, which is best achieved by using NIS, NIS+, or Lightweight Directory Access Protocol (LDAP).

Status and Operations

To display which volumes have been exported from an NFS server, the `share` command may be invoked without arguments. Thus, for the server *kerry*, after exporting */cdrom* read-only to *dingle* and *galway*, the following output would be displayed:

```
# share -f NFS
- /cdrom rw=dingle,galway  "/cdrom"
```

To permanently export a file system share, even after rebooting, the */etc/dfs/dfstab* must be modified to include an entry for the share in question. For every entry that you wish to share automatically after boot, the `share` command used on the command line can simply be inserted into the file. To share all volumes defined as exports in the */etc/dfs/dfstab* file at any time, and which have not already been exported, the following command can be used:

```
# shareall
```

Table 21-1 shows the most common options used with the share command.

When a volume no longer needs to be shared permanently, the entry for the volume in question should be removed from */etc/dfs/dfstab*, and the unshare command used. For example, to unshare the volume */cdrom* from *galway*, the following command would be used:

```
# unshare -F nfs /cdrom
```

Alternatively, if the volume only needed to be temporarily unshared, the entry for */etc/dfs/dfstab* should be retained, and the unshare command is used as above. The shareall command could be used to share the volume again when it's once again required. Before unsharing disk volumes from a NFS server, it's wise (and polite) to verify that the volume in question is not currently mounted by a client. The dfmounts command can be used for this purpose:

```
# dfmounts
RESOURCE   SERVER PATHNAME                 CLIENTS
    -          galway /cdrom               dingle,kerry
```

In this example, the clients *dingle* and *kerry* have mounted the volume *galway:/cdrom*, so administrators of these machines would need to be notified (by e-mail, rwall, or talk) so that they could unmount the volume before it was unshared from *galway*.

Parameter	Description
ro	Allows reading but disallows writing to an exported file system for all local clients
rw	Allows reading and writing to an exported file system for all local clients
ro=client1,client2,client3...	Allows reading but disallows writing to an exported file system only for clients client1, client2, client3, etc.
rw=client1,client2,client3...	Allows reading and writing to an exported file system only for clients client1, client2, client3, etc.

Table 21-1 Options for the **share** Command

Project 21-1: Sharing a Volume Read-Write and Read-Only

This project shows you how to share a volume (*/data*) to one host (*bunyip*) read-write, and another host read-only (*brolga*). This procedure must be followed whenever a read-only file system is to be shared from client to server.

Step-by-Step

1. Check that the volume is not being shared and mounted by a remote client:

```
# dfmounts | grep /data
```

2. Unshare the volume if it's currently shared:

```
# unshare /data
```

3. Share the volume with the read-write and read-only options:

```
# share -f NFS - /data \
  rw=bunyip \
  ro=brolga \
  "/data"
```

Summary

The `share` command can be used to share a file system read-only.

21.5 Run NFS Clients

All Solaris systems can act as an NFS client. However, like NFS servers, some daemons must be running before remote volumes can be mounted. These daemons include the status monitor (*/usr/lib/nfs/statd*) and lock daemon (*/usr/lib/nfs/lockd*) for the network. The *lockd* is responsible for performing file locking operations on files that have been opened from a remote server, which it does in consultation with the NFS server. This is important since the file could be in use by a user on the server as well as on the client, and locking

21

needs to be consistent with respect to the original file on the server file system. The *statd*, in contrast, handles the status of open and/or locked files, ensuring that if a network or system error occurs, data is not lost between client and server.

Initialization

If NFS client services do not appear to be working, the first remedial step is to check that both lockd and statd are running. This can be performed by checking the process list:

```
# ps -eaf | grep statd
  daemon   312     1  0   Jan 26 ?        0:12 /usr/lib/nfs/statd
# ps -eaf | grep lockd
    root   313     1  0   Jan 26 ?        0:09 /usr/lib/nfs/lockd
```

If one or more of these processes is not displayed, the NFS client will need to be restarted. The statd and lockd processes are normally started by the */etc/init.d/nfs.client* script during run level 3. To shut down the NFS client processes manually, the following command should be used:

```
# /etc/init.d/nfs.client stop
```

To restart the NFS client, the following command should be used:

```
# /etc/init.d/nfs.client start
```

Mounting

To mount a volume locally that has been exported from a server, the mount command is used. The first step, however, is to create an appropriate mount point on the client file system. For example, imagine that the server *auburn* has exported the volume */var/mail* to the client *lidcombe*. The super-user on *lidcombe* then intends to mount *auburn:/var/mail* on the local mount point */mnt/var/mail*. The mount point can be created by using the following command:

```
# mount -F nfs -o rw=auburn:/var/mail /mnt/var/mail
```

Alternatively, if *lidcombe* exported a CD-ROM volume (*/cdrom*) to *auburn*, and *auburn* mounted it on */mnt/cdrom*, the following command could be used on *auburn* to mount *lidcombe:/cdrom* read-only:

```
# mount -F nfs -o ro=lidcombe:/cdrom /mnt/cdrom
```

Users on Windows systems can also mount NFS volumes, because these systems can also act as NFS clients by using the Reflection NFS client (**http://www.wrq.com/products/reflection/rnfs/Welcome.html**). The Reflection NFS client has now officially replaced the Solstice NFS client that was originally supported and supplied by Sun.

Modifying /etc/vfstab

The `mount` command as shown mounts the exported volume only until it is unmounted (by using the `umount` command on the client) or if the system is rebooted. To ensure that the remote volume is mounted locally again after a reboot, an entry needs to be made in the */etc/vfstab* file, which lists all the local and remote file systems to be mounted after booting. For example, to add an entry in *lidcombe:/etc/vfstab* to mount *auburn:/var/mail* automatically after booting, the following line would need to be inserted into */etc/vfstab* on *lidcombe*:

```
auburn:/var/mail  -  /mnt/var/mail   nfs   -   yes   sys
```

This line indicates that the volume to mount is *auburn:/var/mail*, which doesn't require fsck file consistency checking; that the local mount point is */mnt/var/mail*; that the file system is NFS; that no fsck pass is required; and that the volume be mounted at boot time. In addition, the security mode is set to *sys*, which maps user IDs (UIDs) and group IDs (GIDs) from the server to the client system with respect to file permissions. For read-only devices like CD-ROMs, it may not be necessary to set a security mode in this way; in this case, no authentication is necessary. For example, to mount *lidcombe:/cdrom* on *auburn* at boot time, the following entry would be inserted into */etc/vfstab* on *auburn*:

```
lidcombe:/cdrom  -  /mnt/cdrom   nfs   -   yes   none
```

21

In this case, no authentication is performed. Other authentication modes that may be used are always listed in */etc/nfssec.conf*, including Kerberos.

After an entry has been created in */etc/vfstab*, it can be mounted at any time by using the mount command. For example, to mount *lidcombe:/cdrom* on *auburn* after the line above has been entered into */etc/vfstab*, the following command can be used:

```
# mount /mnt/cdrom
```

Alternatively, to mount all volumes defined in */etc/vfstab* that have not already been mounted, the following command can be used:

```
# mountall
```

Unmounting

If you need to unmount a volume because the NFS server sharing it is going to stop doing so, perhaps for maintenance, the umount command should be used on the client before the volume is unshared on the server. For example, to unmount *lidcombe:/cdrom* from */mnt/cdrom* on *auburn*, the following command would be used:

```
# umount /cdrom
```

Alternatively, a client can unmount all the NFS volumes it has currently mounted by using the umountall command:

```
# umountall -F nfs
```

1-Minute Drill

- What command is used to share all volumes defined as exports in the */etc/dfs/dfstab* file?
- What command is used to unmount all NFS mounted volumes?

- shareall
- umountall

21.6 Improve NFS Performance

NFS 2 had a reputation as a slow, error-prone system for exchanging data. For example, many database vendors recommend against storing database files on NFS mounted volumes, because data integrity could be severely affected if rollback logs, for example, were suddenly unavailable to the server. While this is still good advice for databases, NFS 3 is intended for high-performance file serving applications. In conjunction with the automounter and NIS+, NFS is often used to centralize home directories on a single server that has RAID mirroring and striping enabled (using DiskSuite) to maximize redundancy of data storage, as well as to increase the total amount of virtual addressable disk space. If your entire user base relies on good NFS performance, it's critical that you monitor the performance of the NFS server at all times, especially during periods of peak load. The parameters that affect NFS performance are available network bandwidth, the amount of free virtual and physical RAM, and the system load. In this section, we will examine how to combine data from several different Solaris commands to continuously monitor the performance of NFS servers.

21

NFS Statistics

The `nfsstat` command can be used to examine the characteristics of all NFS shares, as well as their overall performance. For example, if two volumes were mounted by the client *frinton* from the server *london* (*/staff* and */cdrom*), using NFS 3, the default characteristics as reported by `nfsstat -m` would look like this:

```
# nfsstat -m
/cdrom from auburn:/cdrom
 Flags:   vers=3,proto=tcp,sec=sys,hard,intr,link,symlink,acl,rsize=32768,
    wsize=32768,retrans=5
/var/mail from lidcombe:/var/mail
 Flags:   vers=3,proto=tcp,sec=sys,hard,intr,link,symlink,acl,rsize=32768,
    wsize=32768,retrans=5
```

The two volumes have been mounted using the same NFS mount options, including the read and write packet sizes, as well as a packet retransmission count of 5. To obtain the performance characteristics of the shared volumes, we

would use the `nfsstat` command with the –s option, which reports both
connection-oriented and connectionless statistics:

```
# nfsstat -s
Server rpc:
Connection oriented:
calls         badcalls      nullrecv      badlen        xdrcall
418029153     0             0             0             0
dupchecks     dupreqs
2291698       0
```

This output indicates that, for connection-oriented statistics, 418,029,153
RPC calls have been registered by the server since it was last started, and 2,291,698
duplicated RPC caching checks (dupchecks) carried out. The dupcheck to RPC
calls ratio is approximately 0.5 percent, which is quite acceptable. No other
RPC call types, such as badcalls (where the RPC call was not accepted), were
recorded; no RPC calls with an impossible size (badlen); and no duplicate
requests (dupreqs) or calls that were impossible to interpret (xdrcall).

```
Connectionless:
calls         badcalls      nullrecv      badlen        xdrcall
6385714       0             0             0             0
dupchecks     dupreqs
0             0
```

The connectionless statistics are even more encouraging: although 6,385,714
RPC calls were recorded, no badcall, nullrecv, badlen, xdrcall, dupchecks, or
dupreqs were recorded. These figures suggest that the network bandwidth is
currently sufficient for the processing of RPC calls; however, should a large
number of badcalls or xdrcalls be noted, a network analyzer may be required
to determine where the bottleneck is occurring.

```
Server nfs:
calls         badcalls
424410642     0
Version 2: (6149413 calls)
null          getattr       setattr       root          lookup
49 0%         789279 12%    0 0%          0 0%          2283432 37%
readlink      read          wrcache       write         create
2050 0%       2333064 37%   0 0%          0 0%          2152 0%
remove        rename        link          symlink       mkdir
42 0%         13 0%         0 0%          0 0%          0 0%
rmdir         readdir       statfs
```

```
0 0%           737956 12%    1376 0%
Version 3: (416101332 calls)
null           getattr       setattr         lookup            access
347397 0%      295158834 70% 22595 0%        44046984 10%      67088057 16%
readlink       read          write           create            mkdir
638029 0%      5287349 1%    105316 0%       191586 0%         1480 0%
symlink        mknod         remove          rmdir             rename
178 0%         0 0%          4703 0%         991 0%            441 0%
link           readdir       readdirplus     fsstat            fsinfo
124 0%         1210283 0%    1962077 0%      3466 0%           4635 0%
pathconf       commit
25789 0%       1018 0%
```

Specific to NFS, we can examine the functions of the various RPC calls that were recorded, for both NFS 2 and NFS 3. For NFS 2, the highest number of calls related to actual file reads (37 percent) and lookups (37 percent), with the remainder associated with retrieving client attributes through the cache (12 percent) and reading directories (12 percent). For NFS 3, the picture is a little more troubling, with some 70 percent of the calls being associated with retrieving client attributes through the cache, and only 1 percent of calls being related to actual file reads. This suggests that the NFS server is performing poorly, and the size of the Directory Name Lookup Cache (DNLC) should be expanded to improve performance. This can be set by modifying the *ncsize* parameter in */etc/system* to a higher value.

However, since this value directly modifies the behavior of the kernel, caution should be taken in modifying any entries in */etc/system*.

21.7 Use the Automounter

The automounter is an advanced daemon that works with NFS to make distributed file systems more efficient. This is because file systems are mounted only when requested by a user, and they are automatically unmounted when they're no longer being used (within a 5 minute timeout window). This saves valuable network bandwidth and CPU time, and it reduces the chance of a client or server crash resulting in a stale file handle or a lock file without a "live" owner. In addition, automount reduces the amount of client configuration required to mount NFS volumes, since special maps (stored in files on the server) are provided that notify clients of the shares that the server has available at any point in time. A map contains details of the NFS server and its exported volumes, including mount options and full pathname on the server.

21

Although it's possible for the root user to mount and unmount remote volumes at will, normal users don't have this power. Thus, when they use a mounted volume occasionally, the connection is maintained statefully, which can be quite inefficient. In addition, if the server is ever rebooted, clients may inadvertently attempt to access files on exported volumes that were previously mounted and that are no longer available. The automounter works to reduce the chance of errors occurring and also to make more efficient use of network resources. The volumes that are most commonly used with the automounter are user home directories (*/home*) and user mail directories (*/var/mail*). Since a user may log into any one of a number of client file systems, the user's mail and home directories can be made instantly available upon request.

Initialization

The automounter is generally started during multi-user startup, through the */etc/init.d/autofs* script. To verify that the automounter is running, the process list can be checked:

```
# ps -ef | grep automountd
root 374     1  0 12:58:02 ?          0:56 /usr/lib/autofs/automountd
```

If nothing is returned from the process list, the automounter will need to be restarted. If the automounter needs to be stopped, the following command can be used:

```
# /etc/init.d/autofs stop
```

To restart the automounter, the following command may be used:

```
# /etc/init.d/autofs start
```

In addition, if the automounter maps are modified, the automounter will need to be stopped and restarted using these same commands.

When the automounter starts on a client system, no volumes are mounted: instead, each autofs mount point is associated with a map. The volumes mounted by the automounter can be verified by using the `automount` command:

```
# automount
automount: no mounts
automount: no unmounts
```

In this example, no volumes have yet been mounted or unmounted. However, as volumes are mounted, the `automount` command will return their details. On the server side, volumes are not exported until requested by the first client. Once a connection request is made from a client, the volume is exported. However, once the timeout period has passed and no requests have been received, the volume is unshared until the next client request.

1-Minute Drill

● What command is used to start the automounter?

● What command is used to stop the automounter?

● What command used to display automounted volumes?

Maps

The map that is responsible for configuring other maps is called the *master* map and is stored in */etc/auto_master*. When started, the automounter reads in the master map, which defines other maps to be used for exporting volumes. These other automounter maps come in two main flavors: direct maps, where a direct mapping is made between the directories exported from the server and their mount points, and indirect maps, where a common root directory is shared between all mount points in the map, but where each individual subdirectory may be derived from multiple servers. Indirect maps are used to share home directories from a server that can be mounted by clients under */home*, where these directories are exported from different servers for different users. Because all users have their home directories located under */home*, an indirect map is appropriate. Direct maps are not associated with specific directories; thus more flexibility in naming is allowed. We'll examine the master map, indirect maps, and direct maps in the following sections.

Master Map

The master map contains entries consisting of a directory path followed by a map name. A direct map has the directory path entered as /-, since it is not restricted to a single directory, while an indirect map has the directory path in

---

● `/etc/init.d/autofs start`
● `/etc/init.d/autofs stop`
● `automount`

absolute terms as it exists in the server's file system. If the first entry in the master map on a server is +*auto_master*, the NIS+ *auto_master* table is used instead of the local definitions.

A typical master map contains entries like the following:

```
/home     auto_home
```

This is an indirect map that permits home directories to be shared. Alternatively, entries like the following designate a direct map:

```
/-        auto_direct
```

In both cases, the map name shown adjacent to the directory corresponds to the file in */etc* that defines the map. Thus, the indirect map *auto_home* is defined in */etc/auto_home* and the direct map *auto_direct* is defined in */etc/auto_direct*.

Indirect Maps

The most commonly used indirect map is the *auto_home* map, since it allows a client to mount home directories exported from different servers based on user needs. This benefits organizations like colleges where large numbers of users log into a different client system each time they use the system.

The */etc/auto_home* file defines the *auto_home* map and the corresponding mappings for individual users. The following example shows how the home directories for the users gwyn, ralph, and tony can all be mounted from different servers on the same client system:

```
gwyn      finance:/home/gwyn
ralph     admin:/home/ralph
tony      sales:/staff/tony
```

Alternatively, all three users may access their home directories from a single central server:

```
gwyn      sun1:/home/gwyn
ralph     sun1:/home/ralph
tony      sun1:/home/tony
```

Since the *home* directory is consistently matched with all entries in
/etc/auto_home, there is no need to prefix the user directories on the client
(gwyn, ralph, and tony) with the full */home* path.

Direct Maps

Direct maps allow more flexibility than indirect maps, since mount points and
directories can be mixed and matched as required without exported directories
having to share the same root. For a directory like */home*, which is mapped by
an indirect map, the automounter does not allow any secondary uses of the
directory. For direct maps, no such restrictions are enforced.

A good example involves drawing data from two different volumes and
integrating them together. Imagine that two servers each had a CD-ROM of
genome data that needed to be processed concurrently by a client; a map could
be created to allow the two disks to be mounted under separate directories:

```
/mnt/dataset1    svr1:/cdrom
/mnt/dataset2    svr2:/cdrom
```

21

In this case, data from two different sources is mounted on two different
directories on the client. Other mount points, such as */mnt/cdrom*, may be used
to mount a local CD-ROM drive, for example.

☑ *Mastery Check*

1. What command is used to check the RPC services that are currently
   available on a server?

   A. checkrpc

   B. rpcinfo

   C. rpccheck

   D. inforpc

2. What command is used to start RPC services on a server?

   A. rpcbind

   B. rpcstart

☑ Mastery Check

    C. `/etc/init.d/rpc.server`

    D. `startrpc`

3. What command is used to export NFS volumes?

    A. `export`

    B. `export_nfs`

    C. `share`

    D. `share_nfs`

4. What command is used to share all volumes defined in dfstab?

    A. `allshare`

    B. `share_nfs_all`

    C. `share -F nfs all`

    D. `shareall`

5. What command is used to stop exporting a volume?

    A. `unshare`

    B. `unexport`

    C. `share -U`

    D. `export_nfs -U`

6. How can you verify that an exported volume is not currently mounted by a client?

    A. `dfcheck`

    B. `dfmounts`

    C. `nfs_client check`

    D. `dfshares`

☑ *Mastery Check*

7. How can you start an NFS server?

   A. `/etc/init.d/nfs.server start`

   B. `/usr/local/bin/nfs`

   C. `/opt/SUNWnfs/nfs.server start`

   D. `/sbin/nfs_server`

8. How can you start an NFS client?

   A. `/etc/init.d/nfs.client start`

   B. `/usr/local/bin/nfs_client`

   C. `/opt/SUNWnfs/nfs.client start`

   D. `/sbin/nfs_client`

9. How can you mount all volumes (local and shared) defined in */etc/vfstab*?

   A. `mount`

   B. `/usr/local/bin/nfs.mount`

   C. `mountall`

   D. `mount_vfstab`

10. What command is used to check the status of shared volumes?

   A. `nfsstat -f`

   B. `nfsstat -c`

   C. `nfsstat -r`

   D. `nfsstat -m`

11. How can you check the connection-oriented statistics for NFS?

   A. `nfsstat -s`

   B. `nfsstat -r`

21

☑ *Mastery Check*

    C. `nfsstat -m`

    D. `nfsstat -con`

12. What command is used to check the volumes mounted by the automounter?

    A. `automount check`

    B. `automount -f`

    C. `automount -c`

    D. `automount`

13. What does the master map contain?

    A. Entries consisting of a map name

    B. Entries consisting of a filename followed by a map name

    C. Entries consisting of a directory path followed by a map name

    D. Entries consisting of a username followed by a map name

14. What does the */etc/auto_home* file define?

    A. The *auto_home* map

    B. User's export quotas

    C. Home directory size

    D. The master map

15. To increase the size of the DNLC, what parameter should be modified in */etc/system*?

    A. *ncsize*

    B. *dnlc_size*

    C. *cache*

    D. *shmem:max*

Module 22

Using LDAP

Critical Skills

A white pages telephone directory is a useful source of information that allows users to perform queries for names, based on surnames, and retrieve a record or set of records that matches a criteria. Originally, many networks implemented "white pages" services based on the X.500 standard, which defined a full Directory Access Protocol (DAP) for storing organizational directory information. This database included address and telephone numbers, just like a standard white pages for searching phone entries. However, X.500 was a "heavyweight" protocol, since it did not fit neatly within the layered TCP/IP suite. More recently, the "Lightweight" DAP (LDAP) has become a much more popular alternative for managing organizational data, providing simplified client access by using standard TCP/IP tools. In addition to improving upon X.500's accessibility, LDAP also provides for the storage of a number of different data types, including text, pictures, and audio for users and groups, extending the capabilities of LDAP beyond a traditional "white pages" service.

Solaris 9 provides a complete client/server LDAP solution through the iPlanet Directory Server (iDS). Although originally developed as part of the Sun-Netscape alliance, iPlanet products are now developed exclusively by Sun. Although Solaris 8 provided client support for LDAP, it lacked a full-featured LDAP server. Solaris 9 provides the iDS, allowing integration of other applications within the Sun Open Network Environment (ONE), including commerce, portal, communications, and integration services. Since iDS provides a central resource for storing user and group data, individual applications can make use of LDAP's user profile services without having to develop separate user management software. This ultimately reduces time to market for applications written in Java or C, since iDS is supplied with developer toolkits and APIs that support easy simple LDAP integration into these development environments. iDS can be integrated with the Meta Directory service to allow user and group data from various sources to be queried from a single interface. This allows complex internal data sources to be integrated for a consistent presentation to user applications, providing a crucial piece of middleware for supporting enterprise applications.

In terms of security, iDS supports the Secure Socket Layer (SSL), meaning that queries can be protected from direct interception by packet sniffing. Certificate- and password-based authentication are both supported by iDS. Directories can also be backed up to an offline medium, such as a tape, or to an online medium, such as a standby server. Clustering of servers permits a further level of high availability, in addition to rapid, online updates between servers.

If you're currently using Network Information Service (NIS/NIS+), you may be wondering what benefits LDAP will bring to your organization. One benefit is high availability, conferred by the distributed nature of LDAP storage. While NIS/NIS+ is dependent on a number of key servers, such as primary and slave servers, LDAP replication allows directory services to be maintained if one or more servers is unavailable. In addition, LDAP is supported industry-wide, rather than being Solaris-specific, as is NIS/NIS+. This is both a blessing and a limitation for Solaris-only shops: because NIS/NIS+ provides far more Solaris-specific functionality, allowing operations on maps and tables that are associated with specific system databases, these sites may not replace NIS/NIS+ with LDAP. However, LDAP may be supported for specific types of applications, such as those associated with e-commerce, where customer data is stored in a LDAP directory. Indeed, some third-party e-commerce applications require LDAP support to be available before they can operate. Although LDAP may not replace NIS/NIS+ at many sites, it will almost certainly be running alongside NIS/NIS+.

One of the key benefits of iDS, in a heterogeneous network environment, is that Solaris iDS servers can serve other operation system clients, such as Microsoft Windows or Linux, and vice versa. This increases the opportunities for interoperability with systems that implement Windows on the front end, Linux on the back end, and Solaris running all enterprise applications. Using iDS in this way allows investment in existing systems to be achieved, especially when systems other than those running Solaris are involved.

LDAP is not without some significant limitations that should be kept in mind when planning an iDS deployment. The major issue is that LDAP is not a substitute for a relational database, since it does not allow the same queries permitted on a relational database such as Oracle. This is a significant limitation, as many applications require data to be stored, or complex queries and joins to be performed, that are beyond the scope of LDAP (no SQL equivalent exists in LDAP, for instance). The bottom line is that if LDAP is being used to manage reference data with fixed query types, it is suitable. However, if you need to extend the data structures supported by LDAP in a significant way, you will need to either interface iDS lookups with queries on an external database's tables or simply use an external database and ignore LDAP. In many cases, using the former option can be simplified by developing applications in Java, using the class libraries and API supplied with iDS, since ResultSet objects retrieved from a database, and defined through the Java Database Classes (JDBC), can be

22

mapped to entries retrieved using LDAP. In addition, LDAP supports many predefined object types and schema elements associated with users, groups, and organizations, allowing some additional elements to be introduced where permitted.

In this module, we review some key LDAP concepts and the configuration of the iDS server. In addition, we examine how to use iDS in conjunction with a sister product, the iPlanet Web Proxy Server (iWPS), to authorize Internet resource access based on LDAP directory lookups. This demonstrates the tight integration between the iPlanet products and highlights how iDS supports higher level ONE applications by providing highly available access to user and group data.

22.1 Design LDAP Systems

Because LDAP is a directory service, its basic data element is known as an *entry*. Like a phone book entry, a number of attributes are associated with the LDAP entry when its regarded as an object. For example, a phone directory object has a surname, first name, address, and phone number, which together comprise a single entry when instantiated. The overall organization of entries in an LDAP directory is defined by a schema, which consists of a rule set that determines what attributes can be associated with different object types. Although it is possible to define your own schema and data models, all LDAP servers support a standard schema that promotes interoperability and is the basis for the LDAP standard, as proposed in RFC 2307. Alternatively, your application can extend the standard schema with some additional object attributes, although these may not be accessible by other servers.

LDAP is used in Solaris 9 as a naming service that is compatible with existing NIS and NIS+ services. This allows integration at the present time, but it also suggests future deprecation of the NIS and NIS+ services. iDS contains a set of objects and their attributes that are able to store all the data contained within NIS/NIS+ maps and tables. Additional schema data must also be stored within the LDAP directory to support client operations.

The directory structure for LDAP is arranged hierarchically, from a single top node within the Directory Information Tree (DIT) to as many levels of abstraction as are required to support an organization's directory requirements. The tree structure might, for example, be based on purely geographical information with the top node representing a country, or on organizational lines with the top node corresponding to a company name. All entries within the tree can be identified by their Distinguished Name (DN), and each attribute of the entry can be described as a Relative Distinguished Name (RDN).

Let's consider an example DIT, for an U.S.-based company called Puzito, with all of the common elements found therein. At the first level, the country *c* would be defined as US, so the DN would simply be *c=US*. At the second level, the organization *o* would be defined as *puzito.com*, so the DN is defined as *dc=puzito, dc=com, c=US*, where *dc* represents the Domain Component (DC). On the third level, the organizational unit *ou* would be defined as *Sales*, so the DN is defined as *ou=Sales, dc=puzito, dc=com, c=US*. On the fourth level, an individual user is identified by a Common Name (CN) of *Joe Bloggs* and a corresponding UID of *jbloggs*. Thus, the DN is *uid=jbloggs, ou=Sales, dc=puzito, dc=com, c=US*. Thus, it is possible to distinguish individuals belonging to organizations and departments in specific countries, by simply using a DN, if the DIT is defined at a fine-grained level, and assuming that no two users in the same department have exactly the same name.

iDS stores all data in LDIF files. This standard is used by all LDAP directory servers and many messaging systems to store user and group data. Thus, it is possible to export a LDIF file with an organization's data from a previous version of iDS, and import it here. Alternatively, third-party products may be able to export LDIF files that can also be read into iDS, to initialize the directory structure. Let's look at an example entry in a LDIF file for the directory entry we've defined above:

```
dn: cn=Joe Bloggs, o=puzito.com, c=US
cn: Joe Bloggs
sn: Bloggs
mail: jbloggs@puzito.com
objectClass: people
```

As you can see, the LDIF file structure simply reflects the attributes that are defined within the directory, written sequentially to the file immediately following the DN.

22.2 Set Up iPlanet Directory Server (iDS)

Configuring iDS is a two-stage process: the first stage involves installing and configuring the server to run iDS, and the second stage involves setting up iDS to support LDAP clients (as described in the next section). To begin the process of configuring the server to run iDS, the *directoryserver* program must be executed:

```
# /usr/sbin/directoryserver setup
```

You can either install the iPlanet Directory Server (iDS) or the standalone iPlanet Console. After selecting iDS, you are presented with three different installation options: express, which presents few opportunities for customization but is very fast; typical, which offers some configuration before installation; and custom, which offers maximum flexibility but is the slowest installation method.

Three packages comprise the iDS installation:

● Server Core Components, comprising all of the common objects used by iDS

● iPlanet Directory Suite, which contains the management console and the iDS software

● Administration Server, which contains packages for system administration and directory management

After selecting the appropriate packages to install, you need to indicate whether the current installation will store configuration information or whether this will be stored in another server. If data will be stored in another server, the hostname, port number, username, and password must all be entered so that the correct target iDS installation for configuration can be identified.

Following the selection of the configuration iDS target, you need to indicate whether the current installation will store user and group information or whether this will be stored in another server. Again, if data will be stored in another server, the hostname, port number, DN, password, and suffix must all be entered so that the correct target iDS installation for user and group data can be identified.

Next, the new iDS server must be set up, with a unique server identifier, a port number that is not used by any other application, and the appropriate suffix for the local installation. The default port number for LDAP is 389, while LDAP over SSL typically runs on port 636.

The administrator ID and password for the local iDS installation must be selected and entered next. This ID and password are also used for managing the local LDAP server using the management console. Since the administrator ID and password can be used to gain access to the iDS server and to modify user and group data without restriction, it's important that these credentials are chosen carefully to avoid easy guessing by rogue users.

The Administration domain must be entered next. Since iDS can manage multiple domains simultaneously from a single server, it's important that their data is kept functionally and physically separate. Typically, the Administration domain matches the Internet domain name. However, each server needs to have a separate Administration domain if it is located under a top-level domain. For example, if two separate iDS servers are running in the **cassowary.net** domain— one for Engineering and one for Sales—the Administration domains could be **engineering.cassowary.net** and **sales.cassowary.net**, respectively.

The directory manager's password for the local iDS installation must be selected and entered next. Since the directory manager ID and password can be used to gain access to the iDS server and modify user and group data with few restrictions, it's important that these credentials are chosen carefully so as to avoid dictionary-based cracking.

The administration server for iDS is used to manage all aspects of the LDAP service. The administration server runs as a Web server, meaning that any HTML browser can be used to view and configure all current settings for the iDS server. A port must be chosen to access the iDS administration server. The URL for the administration server is then given by appending the port number with a

22

Ask the Expert

Question: Should I ditch NIS+ and go with LDAP?

Answer: Only if you don't need any of the key features of NIS+, such as Solaris-specific support for centralizing much of the administrative data that is shared between systems on the same network.

Question: Is LDAP reliable?

Answer: Yes, because it has in-built high availability features.

Question: Does LDAP have complete functionality?

Answer: Yes, as far as LDAP goes—but you will often find yourself asking why LDAP doesn't support some fairly obvious operations!

colon to the hostname. For example, the URL *http://ldap.cassowary.net:38575/* suggests a LDAP server running on port 38575 of the host **ldap.cassowary.net**.

22.3 Configure iDS

To configure iDS to provide services to clients, the idsconfig command is used. The service configuration can be manually entered on the command line or it can be supplied from an external file when the *–i* option is passed. Alternatively, a configuration file from one system (generated by passing the *–o* option) can also be read in from an external file. If multiple iDS instances are installed, configuration information from the first installation can be used by subsequent installations. idsconfig can be started with the following command:

```
# /usr/lib/ldap/idsconfig
```

The following output shows a sample idsconfig session for **sales .cassowary.net**. In the first section, you are required to review the basic configuration of the directory service, including the port number, directory manager DN, and its password:

```
Enter the port number for iDS (h=help): [389]
Enter the directory manager DN: [cn=Directory Manager]
Enter passwd for cn=Directory Manager :
Enter the domainname to be served (h=help): [sales.cassowary.net]
```

Next, you need to review the directory and server details, including the base DN, profile name, and list of servers:

```
Enter LDAP BaseDN (h=help): [dc=sales,dc=cassowary,dc=net]
Enter the profile name (h=help): [default]
Are you sure you want to overwrite profile cn=default? y
Default server list (h=help): [192.64.18.1]
Preferred server list (h=help):
Choose desired search scope (one, sub, h=help): [one]
```

Security choices must be made next, including the credential level and authentication method:

```
The following are the supported credential levels:
1 anonymous
2 proxy
3 proxy anonymous
Choose Credential level [h=help]: [1] 1
The following are the supported Authentication Methods:
1 none
2 simple
3 sasl/DIGEST-MD5
4 tls:simple
5 tls:sals/DIGEST-MD5
Choose Authentication Method (h=help): [1] 2
Current authenticationMethod: simple
Do you want to add another Authentication Method? N
```

After reviewing the server configuration, you now need to configure client access. This includes setting timeouts for profile and directory access, password formats, and time and size limits:

```
Do you want the clients to follow referrals (y/n/h)? [n] n
Do you want to modify the server timelimit value (y/n/h)? [n] n
Do you want to modify the server sizelimit value (y/n/h)? [n] n
Do you want to store passwd's in "crypt" format (y/n/h)? [n] y
Do you want to setup a Service Authentication Methods (y/n/h)? [n] n
Search time limit in seconds (h=help): [60]
Profile Time To Live in seconds (h=help): [3600]
Bind time limit in seconds (h=help): [10] 2
Do you wish to setup Service Search Descriptors (y/n/h)? [n] n
```

Finally, you are presented with a configuration summary, before any actions are performed by idsconfig:

```
Summary of Configuration
1 Domain to serve : sales.cassowary.net
2 BaseDN to setup : dc=sales,dc=cassowary,dc=net
3 Profile name to create : default
4 Default Server List : 192.64.18.1
5 Preferred Server List :
6 Default Search Scope : one
7 Credential Level : anonymous
8 Authenication Method : simple
9 Enable Follow Referrals : FALSE
10 iDS Time Limit :
```

```
11 iDS Size Limit :
12 Enable crypt passwd storage : 1
13 Service Auth Method pam_ldap :
14 Service Auth Method keyserv :
15 Service Auth Method passwd-cmd:
16 Search Time Limit : 30
17 Profile Time to Live : 43200
18 Bind Limit : 2
19 Service Search Descriptors Menu
```

22.4 Create Directory Entries

The ldapaddent command is used to create entries in the LDAP container for all the standard system databases stored in files under the /etc directory. All of the following Solaris databases (with the corresponding *ou*) can be transferred into LDAP by this method:

- *aliases (ou=Aliases)*

- *bootparams (ou=Ethers)*

- *ethers* (requires bootparams database to be installed first) *(ou=Ethers)*

- *group (ou=Group)*

- *hosts (ou=Hosts)*

- *netgroup (ou=Netgroup)*

- *netmasks* (requires networks database to be installed first) *(ou=Networks)*

- *networks (ou=Networks)*

- *passwd (ou=People)*

- *shadow* (requires passwd database to be installed first) *(ou=People)*

- *protocols (ou=Protocols)*

- *publickey (ou=Hosts)*

- *rpc (ou=Rpc)*

- *services (ou=Services)*

A simple script can be created to automate the process of adding each of these databases to LDAP, when the *bindDN* password is supplied on the command line:

```
#!/bin/sh
ldapaddent -D "cn=directory manager" -w $1 -f /etc/aliases aliases
ldapaddent -D "cn=directory manager" -w $1 -f /etc/bootparams bootparams
ldapaddent -D "cn=directory manager" -w $1 -f /etc/ethers ethers
ldapaddent -D "cn=directory manager" -w $1 -f /etc/group group
ldapaddent -D "cn=directory manager" -w $1 -f /etc/hosts hosts
ldapaddent -D "cn=directory manager" -w $1 -f /etc/netgroup netgroup
ldapaddent -D "cn=directory manager" -w $1 -f /etc/networks networks
ldapaddent -D "cn=directory manager" -w $1 -f /etc/netmasks netmasks
ldapaddent -D "cn=directory manager" -w $1 -f /etc/passwd passwd
ldapaddent -D "cn=directory manager" -w $1 -f /etc/shadow shadow
ldapaddent -D "cn=directory manager" -w $1 -f /etc/protocols protocols
ldapaddent -D "cn=directory manager" -w $1 -f /etc/publickey publickey
ldapaddent -D "cn=directory manager" -w $1 -f /etc/rpc rpc
ldapaddent -D "cn=directory manager" -w $1 -f /etc/services services
```

This script can be used on all client systems that will use LDAP.

22

22.5 Configure LDAP Clients

The ldapclient program can be used for several purposes, including starting LDAP client services on client systems and reviewing the LDAP cache. To initialize a client, the address of the LDAP server where its profile is stored must be supplied on the command line. The LDAP cache manager (*ldap_cachemgr*) is responsible for ensuring that the correct configuration data is returned to a client upon initialization, especially if changes have been made to the profile. One of the following subcommands must be supplied on the command line to specify the behavior of ldapclient:

Command	Description
genprofile	Creates a LDIF (LDAP Data Interchange Format) configuration file that can be exported to another system or imported at some future time
init	Initializes a LDAP client from a LDAP server using a profile
list	Prints a list of entries stored in the client cache to standard output
manual	Initializes a LDAP client from a LDAP server using parameters specified on the command line

Command	Description
mod	Permits the modification of parameter values after initialization has been completed
uninit	Uninitializes a LDAP client from a LDAP server

The following parameters can be modified by using the `ldapclient mod` command, or passed directly for manual initialization using the `ldapclient manual` command:

Parameter	Description
attributeMap	Used to modify the default schema for a specific service.
authenticationMethod	Stipulates the authentication method to be used (none, simple, sasl/CRAM-MD5, sasl/DIGEST-MD5, tls:simple, tls:sasl/CRAM-MD5, or tls:sasl/DIGEST-MD5). *None* means no security at all, while *simple* means that a password is sent in the clear and is vulnerable to interception. The other methods use a message digest algorithm to enhance security.
bindTimeLimit	The maximum number of seconds allowed for a bind operation to be performed.
certificatePath	The full path to the certificate database.
credentialLevel	Specifies the type of credential required for authentication (either anonymous or proxy).
defaultSearchBase	Specifies the baseDN for searching.
defaultSearchScope	Determines the scope for searching on the client side.
domainName	Fully qualified domain name.
followReferrals	Determines whether the referral setting is used.
objectclassMap	Used to designate a different schema.
preferredServerList	Lists a set of alternative LDAP servers to be contacted prior to the default.
profileName	Determines the name of the client profile.
profileTTL	Refresh epoch for the client cache to obtain new information from the server.
proxyDN	Specifies the DN for the proxy server.
proxyPassword	States the password for the proxy server.
searchTimeLimit	Restricts the amount of time for each LDAP search.
serviceAuthenticationMethod	Determines the authentication method for the *passwd-cmd*, *keyserv*, and *pam_ldap* services.

Parameter	Description
serviceCredentialLevel	Specifies the type of credential required for service authentication (either anonymous or proxy). Proxy access for clients can occur only if a proxy account has previously been created in the directory, and the *proxyDN* and *proxyPassword* attributes have been defined. Anonymous is not recommended, since it provides no security at all.
serviceSearchDescriptor	Allows a different baseDN to be specified on a per-service basis.

Let's look at some different examples of how LDAP clients can be initialized by using `ldapclient`. In the first example, the LDAP server 192.64.18.1 will be used to initialize the local client by using the `init` subcommand:

```
# ldapclient init 192.64.18.1
```

No additional parameters are necessary. However, a manual installation is much more complex, as all non-default parameters must be specified. Sometimes, only a single parameter will differ from the default: for example, if simple authentication was required, instead of no authentication (the default), the following command would be used:

```
# ldapclient manual -a authenticationMethod=simple \
-a defaultServerList=192.64.18.1
```

Alternatively, if a higher level search base needed to be specified, the following command could be used:

```
# ldapclient manual -a authenticationMethod=simple \
-a defaultSearchBase=dc=cassowary,dc=net        \
-a defaultServerList=192.64.18.1
```

To generate a LDIF format configuration file, we would use the `genprofile` subcommand and redirect the output to a file (*/tmp/default.ldif*):

```
# ldapclient genprofile -a profileName=default \
-a defaultSearchBase=dc=cassowary,dc=net        \
-a defaultServerList=192.64.18.1 \
> /tmp/default.ldif
```

22

22.6 Query the Directory

The `ldapsearch` command is used to query the directory for a specific entry and to display the attributes of an entry once located. A query string composed of a logical condition is passed on the command line along with a set of attributes that are to be displayed. For example, to search for the common name *Paul Watters* and display the results, the following command would be used:

```
$ ldapsearch -u "cn=Paul Watters" cn
cn=Paul A Watters, ou=Engineering, o=cassowary.net, c=US
cn=Paul Watters
```

Alternatively, if the UID of the user you were searching for was known, and you wanted to look up the common name, the following command could be used:

```
$ ldapsearch -u -t "uid=paul" cn
cn=Paul A Watters, ou=Engineering, o=cassowary.net, c=US
cn=Paul Watters
```

It's possible to perform a wider area search than just looking for a single individual. For example, to print a description of all organizations lying below the country US in the DIT, the following command would be used:

```
$ ldapsearch -L -b "c=US" description
dn: o=cassowary.net, c=US
description: Cassowary Computing Pty Ltd
```

22.7 Modify Directory Entries

The `ldapmodify` command is used to create, read, update, or delete entries in the directory. In addition, a `ldapadd` command is used to create new directory entries. However, this command is equivalent to invoking `ldapmodify` with the *–a* (add) option. In addition, while it is possible to enter data using standard input, most users will perform actions based on data stored in a file (after all, if you make a mistake when typing and you have to cancel the data entry, all of the input will be lost).

If we want to create a new entry for *Moppet Watters* in the directory, the following data should be inserted into a file called *newdata.txt*:

```
dn: cn=Moppet Watters, o=cassowary.net, c=US
objectClass: person
cn: Mopster Watters
sn: Watters
title: Mascot
mail: moppet@cassowary.net
uid: moppet
```

To insert this data into the directory, the following command would be used:

```
# ldapmodify -a -f newdata.txt
```

To delete this entry from the directory, we would first insert the following data into *delentry.txt*:

```
dn: cn=Moppet Watters, o=cassowary.net, c=US
changetype=delete
```

22

We could then delete the entry from the directory by using the following command:

```
# ldapmodify -f delentry.txt
```

1-Minute Drill

● What is a LDIF file?

● What is the Directory Information Tree (DIT)?

● What command is used to configure iDS?

● A LDAP Data Interchange Format file
● The LDAP directory structure
● */usr/lib/ldap/idsconfig*

Applications

One of the key benefits of using iDS is its ability to integrate other ONE applications, such as the iPlanet Web Proxy Server (iWPS). The iWPS is a full-featured proxy/cache system that surpasses its competitors in functionality, performance, and scale. iWPS provides access to a wide range of features, including user- and group-based authentication for selective access to sites, services, and protocols, which can be based on a local database or integrated with a LDAP server (such as the iPlanet Directory Server). iWPS has the advantage of being able to be remotely administered via a SSL connection from a remote browser. Thus, it is possible for a single administrator to manage geographically distant sites from a single client. In addition, multiple servers can be clustered together to form a fault-tolerant, highly available proxying service, which is essential for large organizations.

While not directly involved in conducting e-commerce transactions, iWPS forms a key part of e-commerce infrastructure, because it can be used to secure access to specific systems and improve the overall performance of data throughput by making use of local content caching. Many freeware products are available and are commonly used to perform proxy/caching functions—such as Squid, available from **http://www.squid-cache.org/**. Squid features a large number of commercial-grade features, such as HTTPS proxying, in addition to standard HTTP and FTP proxying. In addition, Squid supports SNMP monitoring and DNS caching, which are also included with iWPS. So why would you use iWPS in preference to a freeware product? Simply put, Squid is useful for sites that do not use other iPlanet products and for sites with low volumes. This is because iWPS uses the standard administration server to manage cache and proxying services, and because it features high availability and clustering features that are simply not provided by Squid. Thus, iWPS can scale at the same pace as your iPlanet infrastructure, depending on the volume of requests handled by your site. New iWPS servers can be easily added into the pool of available services to provide proxy/cache services to local clients.

These advantages extend to other commercial products, although it is certainly possible to use a third-party proxy/cache system with other iPlanet products. However, you will not be able to reap the integration benefits of using a complete iPlanet solution. One area in which this becomes critical is LDAP integration with the iPlanet Directory Server (iDS): because access control lists (ACLs) can be specified on a user and group basis, it makes sense to integrate iWPS with iDS rather than a third-party product. Using iDS for user authentication and authorization can also improve performance. However, a significant limitation of iWPS compared to its rivals is that it does not perform any kind of virus scanning of data stored in the cache, leaving local clients open to attack if they retrieve stored material that is infected. If the local network and all clients have appropriate anti-virus measures installed, this issue is not significant.

When configuring iWPS, the port number of the proxy server must be specified. This is the port that clients must specify in their browser setup as their HTTP, HTTPS, and FTP proxy port. For example, in Windows Internet Explorer, users must select Tools | Internet Options | Connections | LAN Settings, and then check the Use A Proxy Server checkbox to set this up. The hostname of the proxy server and the port must be specified here for all services. Alternatively, if different proxy servers are to be used for different services, the user must first click the Advanced button, which brings up a window that allows different port numbers and hostnames to be used for specifying proxy servers that provide different services. While iWPS provides all proxying services through one port, different servers might be used for providing proxying for unique services (such as **www-proxy** might proxy HTTP, while **ftp-proxy** might proxy for HTTPS). Typically, the proxy port is set to 8080, to mirror the default HTTP port of 80, but this can be customized for local networks if a port conflict exists with another TCP service on the proxy host. This port number must be different than the port number for the administration server, as using the same port number would also create a port conflict.

Once installed for use with iDS, the iWPS management console has a pane that interacts with iDS (Users & Groups). Users & Groups is the main operations screen for managing users and groups that require access to the proxy. It is possible to allow/deny access to specific sites or protocols based on a user's identity and/or the user's group membership. For example, members of the group Children may not be able to access **someadultsite.com**, while members of the group Adults may well be given access to it.

The New User option allows you access to a new user to the directory service. You can specify the following fields:

- Given Name (First Name)

- Surname (Last Name)

- Full Name

- User ID

- Password

- E-Mail Address

22

The Manage Users option allows you to modify the data fields for existing users. A simple search interface is provided: you simply type the name of the user you wish to find in the Find User field of the User & Groups console. The search term can be any of the full name, last name, user ID, phone number, or e-mail address options. In addition, a term that it is fully or partially contained within a record can also be searched.

The License Tracking option allows you to view the installed licenses for the various iPlanet/Netscape servers running on the system, including Collabra, Directory, Enterprise, and Compass. The New Group option allows you to add a new group to the database. You can enter both a group name and a group description.

The Manage Groups option allows you to modify the data fields for existing groups. A simple search interface is provided: you simply type the name of the user you wish to find in the Find Group field. The search term can be either the group name or group description. In addition, a term that is fully or partially contained within a record can also be searched. Once a record is located, group members and certificates can be added and the group owner can be set.

The New Organizational Unit option allows you to create organizational unit definitions, whose data can be populated in the Manage Organizational Units section. At this point, you can enter the new unit name into the Unit Name field, and enter an optional description into the Description field. In addition, it's possible to locate the new unit within an existing organizational hierarchy by selecting a superordinate organizational unit from the Add Organizational Unit To drop-down list.

The Manage Organizational Units option allows you to modify the data fields for existing organizational units. A simple search interface is provided: you simply type the name of the user you wish to find in the Find Organizational Unit field. The search term can be either the unit name or unit description. In addition, a term that is fully or partially contained within a record can be searched. Once a record is located, the unit name can be modified as well as the description. In addition, a phone, fax, and mailing address can be supplied for the unit.

The Import option allows you to import directory information from an existing LDAP Data Interchange Format (LDIF) file. This standard is used by all LDAP directory servers and many messaging systems to store user and group data. Thus, it is possible to export a LDIF file with an organization's data from a previous version of iWPS, and import it here. Alternatively, a non-iPlanet product may be able to export a LDIF file, which can also read into iWPS to initialize the directory structure.

Project 22-1: Creating a Directory Entry

This project shows you how to create a directory entry by using the `ldapmodify` command for the user *Paul Watters*. This procedure is necessary whenever a new user or entity is entered into the directory.

Step-by-Step

1. Create a file called *paulwatters.txt*.

```
# vi paulwatters.txt
```

2. Insert the appropriate fields that are to be stored in the record:

```
dn: cn=Paul Watters, o=paulwatters.com, c=US
objectClass: person
title: Dr
mail: doctor@paulwatters.com
uid: pwatters
```

3. Insert the data into the directory:

```
# ldapmodify -a -f newdata.txt
```

Summary

The `ldapmodify` command can be used to modify LDAP directory entries.

22

☑ *Mastery Check*

1. Which of the following is the correct BaseDN for **engineer .paulwatters.com**?

A. *dc=engineer,dc=paulwatters,dc=com*

B. *dc=com,dc=paulwatters,dc=engineer*

C. *dc=com,paulwatters,engineer*

D. *dc= engineer, paulwatters,com*

☑ Mastery Check

2. What is the default port for LDAP services?

A. 80

B. 1024

C. 389

D. 264

3. Which of the following organizational units is not supported by Solaris?

A. *group (ou=Group)*

B. *hosts (ou=Hosts)*

C. *netgroup (ou=Netgroup)*

D. *db (ou=metadb)*

4. Which of the following cannot be used with the `ldapclient mod` command?

A. *certificatePath*

B. *credentialLevel*

C. *certificateKey*

D. *defaultSearchBase*

5. What sort of protocol is DAP?

A. Lightweight

B. Heavyweight

C. Middleweight

D. Bantam

6. What sort of protocol is LDAP?

A. Lightweight

B. Heavyweight

☑ Mastery Check

    C. Middleweight

    D. Bantam

7. What extensions does LDAP provide?

    A. Text

    B. Pictures

    C. Audio

    D. All of the above

8. What improvement does the Solaris 9 LDAP implementation provide over the Solaris 8 LDAP implementation?

    A. 10,000-user limit

    B. 5000 images

    C. Indexable properties

    D. Server and client support

9. What transport-layer security does iDS provide?

    A. Passwords

    B. Replication

    C. E-commerce

    D. Secure Socket Layer

10. What Sun-specific technology will LDAP eventually replace?

    A. NFS

    B. NIS

    C. Oracle

    D. Linux

22

☑ Mastery Check

11. What is the key definition for organizational entries in LDAP?

   A. User

   B. Group

   C. Schema

   D. Table

12. What is the standard port for LDAP over SSL?

   A. 323

   B. 636

   C. 789

   D. 922

13. What command is used for configuring iDS?

   A. `idsconfig`

   B. `iDSconfig`

   C. `configiDS`

   D. `DSconf`

14. What system databases can be stored in a LDAP container?

   A. *aliases*

   B. *bootparams*

   C. *ethers*

   D. All of the above

15. What system databases can be stored in a LDAP container?

   A. *hosts*

   B. *netgroups*

   C. *passwds*

   D. All of the above

Appendix

Answers to Mastery Checks

In Table A-1, on the following page, you'll find the answer key to the Mastery Check questions found at the end of every module.

Module \ Question	1	2	3	4	5	6	7	8	9	10	11	12	13	14	15	16
1	D	D	C	A	A	C	A	A	B	C	D	A	A	B	C	D
2	A	D	D	B	B	A	C	A	C	A	B	A	D	B	A	
3	B	C	A or C	A	B	D	C	A	A	A	D	A	B	C	D	
4	D	C	B	D	C	C	B	C	A	D	A	D	D	C	B	
5	A	B	C	D	A	B	C	D	B	C	D	A	B	D	A	
6	A	B	C	D	A	B	C	D	A	B	C	D	A	B	C	
7	D	C	B	A	D	C	B	A	A	B	C	D	A	B	C	
8	B	C	A	D	A	B	A	B	C	D	A	C	A	D	B	
9	B	A	D	C	D	C	B	A	A	B	C	D	D	B	D	
10	B	A	C	D	A	B	C	D	D	C	B	A	B	C	D	
11	B	C	C	A	A	B	C	D	A	B	C	D	C	B	C	
12	A	A	C	A	A	C	B	B	D	D	B	B	C	A	D	
13	A	B	C	D	A	B	C	D	B	C	D	D	B	C	D	
14	A	B	D	C	A	A	B	D	C	C	D	A	A	B	C	D
15	A	D	B	D	A	B	C	D	D	C	A	C	A			
16	A	B	C	D	A	B	C	D	B	C	D	A	B	C	D	
17	A	B	C	D	A	B	C	D	A	B	C	D	B	C	D	
18	B	D	C	D	C	B	A	B	C	D	A	A	C	D	D	
19	C	B	C	A	B	C	A	D	A	B	C	D	A	B	C	
20	D	B	A	A	B	B	C	A	D	A	D	A	D	A	B	
21	B	A	C	D	A	B	A	A	C	D	A	D	C	A	A	
22	A	C	D	C	B	A	D	D	D	B	C	B	A	D	A	

Table A-1   Answer Key to the Mastery Check Questions

Index

INTERNATIONAL CONTACT INFORMATION

AUSTRALIA
McGraw-Hill Book Company Australia Pty. Ltd.
TEL +61-2-9415-9899
FAX +61-2-9415-5687
http://www.mcgraw-hill.com.au
books-it_sydney@mcgraw-hill.com

CANADA
McGraw-Hill Ryerson Ltd.
TEL +905-430-5000
FAX +905-430-5020
http://www.mcgrawhill.ca

GREECE, MIDDLE EAST,
NORTHERN AFRICA
McGraw-Hill Hellas
TEL +30-1-656-0990-3-4
FAX +30-1-654-5525

MEXICO (Also serving Latin America)
McGraw-Hill Interamericana Editores S.A. de C.V.
TEL +525-117-1583
FAX +525-117-1589
http://www.mcgraw-hill.com.mx
fernando_castellanos@mcgraw-hill.com

SINGAPORE (Serving Asia)
McGraw-Hill Book Company
TEL +65-863-1580
FAX +65-862-3354
http://www.mcgraw-hill.com.sg
mghasia@mcgraw-hill.com

SOUTH AFRICA
McGraw-Hill South Africa
TEL +27-11-622-7512
FAX +27-11-622-9045
robyn_swanepoel@mcgraw-hill.com

UNITED KINGDOM & EUROPE
(Excluding Southern Europe)
McGraw-Hill Education Europe
TEL +44-1-628-502500
FAX +44-1-628-770224
http://www.mcgraw-hill.co.uk
computing_neurope@mcgraw-hill.com

ALL OTHER INQUIRIES Contact:
Osborne/McGraw-Hill
TEL +1-510-549-6600
FAX +1-510-883-7600
http://www.osborne.com
omg_international@mcgraw-hill.com

CPSIA information can be obtained
at www.ICGtesting.com
Printed in the USA
BVHW090941290921
617743BV00012B/243

9 780072 223170